尾田栄一郎

I've heard it's possible for people to live 140 years, but their lives are shortened by the amount of work and stress they have to endure. I'm working day and night as a manga author, so I'll probably only live to be 135. (SULK) Life is too short. Time to start volume 54!

-Eiichiro Oda, 2009

iichiro Oda began his manga career at the age of 17, when his one-shot cowboy manga **Wanted!** won second place in the coveted Tezuka manga awards. Oda went on to work as an assistant to some of the biggest manga artists in the industry, including Nobuhiro Watsuki, before winning the Hop Step Award for new artists. His pirate adventure **One Piece**, which debuted in **Weekly Shonen Jump** in 1997, quickly became one of the most popular manga in Japan.

ONE PIECE VOL. 54
IMPEL DOWN PART 1

SHONEN JUMP Manga Edition

This graphic novel contains material that was originally published in English in SHONEN JUMP #85–86. Artwork in the magazine may have been slightly altered from that presented here.

STORY AND ART BY EIICHIRO ODA

English Adaptation/Lance Caselman
Translation/Laabaman, HC Language Solutions, Inc.
Touch-up Art & Lettering/Vanessa Satone
Design/Sean Lee
Editors/Yuki Murashige, Alexis Kirsch, John Bae

Published by VIZ Media, LLC
P.O. Box 77010
San Francisco, CA 94107

10 9 8 7 6
First printing, July 2010
Sixth printing, December 2016

PARENTAL ADVISORY
ONE PIECE is rated T for Teen and is recommended for ages 13 and up. This volume contains fantasy violence and tobacco usage.
ratings.viz.com

www.viz.com

THE WORLD'S MOST POPULAR MANGA
www.shonenjump.com

SHONEN JUMP MANGA

ONE PIECE

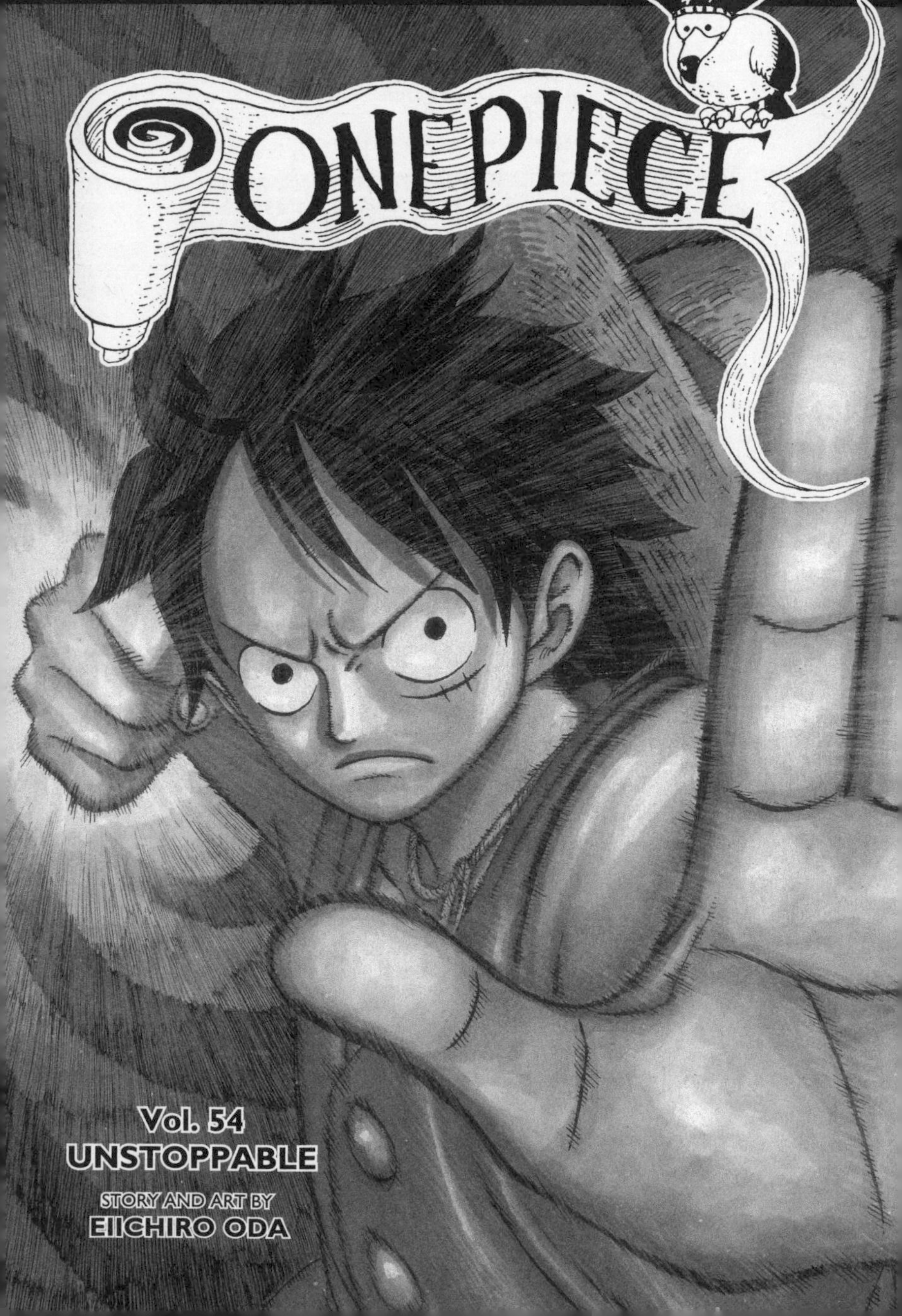

Vol. 54
UNSTOPPABLE

STORY AND ART BY
EIICHIRO ODA

Warriors of Kuja

The empress of Amazon Lily, captain of the Kuja Pirates and one of the Seven Warlords of the Sea.

Boa Hancock

Second of the Gorgon Sisters

Boa Sandersonia

Youngest of the Gorgon Sisters

Boa Marigold

Former empress of Amazon Lily

Gloriosa (Grandma Nyon)

Boundlessly optimistic and able to stretch like rubber, he is determined to become King of the Pirates.
Bounty: 300 million berries

Monkey D. Luffy

A former bounty hunter and master of the "three-sword" style. He aspires to be the world's greatest swordsman.
Bounty: 120 million berries

Roronoa Zolo

A thief who specializes in robbing pirates. Nami hates pirates, but Luffy convinced her to be his navigator.
Bounty: 16 million berries

Nami

A village boy with a talent for telling tall tales. His father, Yasopp, is a member of Shanks's crew.
Bounty: 30 million berries (Sniper King)

Usopp

The bighearted cook (and ladies' man) whose dream is to find the legendary sea, the "All Blue."
Bounty: 77 million berries

Sanji

A blue-nosed man-reindeer and the ship's doctor.
Bounty: 50 berries

Tony Tony Chopper

A mysterious woman in search of the Ponegliff on which true history is recorded.
Bounty: 80 million berries

Nico Robin

A softhearted cyborg and talented shipwright.
Bounty: 44 million berries

Franky

A skeleton warrior with an afro. He dreams of being reunited with Laboon, the tame whale he parted with fifty years ago.
Bounty: 33 million berries

Brook

The Straw Hats Total bounty: 700,000,050 berries

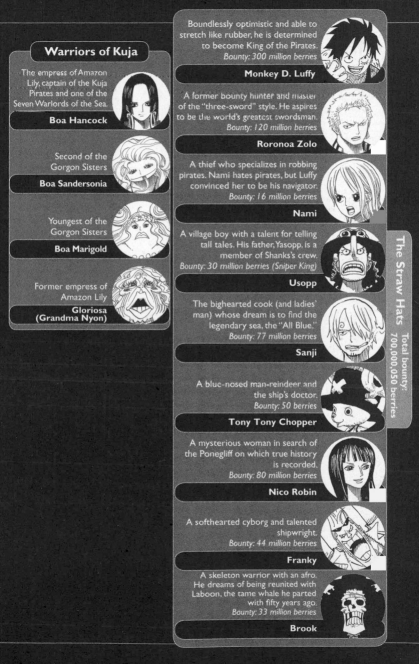

THE STORY OF ONE PIECE

Volume 54

Monkey D. Luffy started out as just a kid with a dream—to become the greatest pirate in history! Stirred by the tales of pirate "Red-Haired" Shanks, Luffy vowed to become a pirate himself. That was before the enchanted Devil Fruit gave Luffy the power to stretch like rubber, at the cost of being unable to swim—a serious handicap for an aspiring sea dog. Undeterred, Luffy set out to sea and recruited some crewmates—master swordsman Zolo; treasure-hunting thief Nami; lying sharpshooter Usopp; the high-kicking chef Sanji; Chopper, the walkin' talkin' reindeer doctor; mysterious archaeologist Robin; cyborg shipwright Franky; and Brook, a musical skeleton!

Having entered the Grand Line, Luffy and crew get a new ship, the *Thousand Sunny*, to replace the *Merry Go*. They head for Fish-Man Island, but they soon find themselves encountering a number of strange and formidable characters on Saobody Archipelago, including the Celestial Dragons, Admiral Kizaru, and Kuma, who uses a mysterious power to scatter the crew far and wide.

Luffy ends up on Amazon Lily, an island of women forbidden to men, which is ruled by Boa Hancock, one of the Seven Warlords of the Sea. There he is nearly put to death when he discovers Hancock's secret. But Luffy wins her over, and empress and pirate decide to set forth together to rescue Luffy's brother Ace, who is to be executed in six days. But can they make it in time? And will the crew ever be reunited?

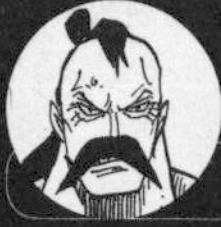

Navy Vice Admiral

Momonga

The Second Division Commander of the Whitebeard Pirates and Luffy's older brother. He was defeated by Blackbeard Teech and is currently imprisoned in Impel Down.

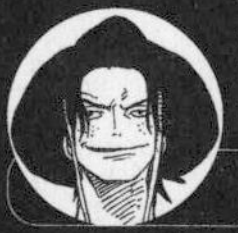

Portgaz D. Ace

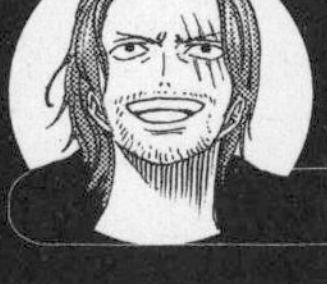

A pirate that Luffy idolizes. Shanks gave Luffy his trademark straw hat.

"Red-Haired" Shanks

Vol. 54
Unstoppable

CONTENTS

Chapter 523:
HELL

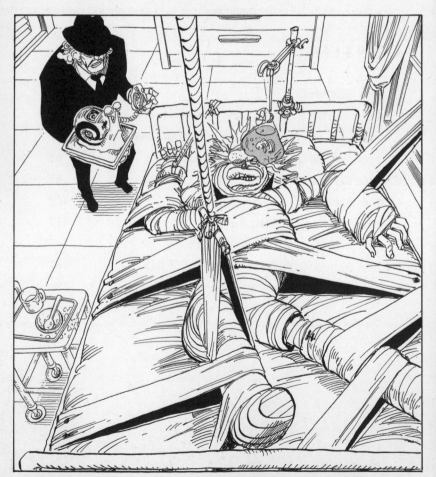

CP9'S INDEPENDENT REPORT, VOL. 29: "TRANSPONDER
SNAIL FOR SPANDAM IN THE INTENSIVE CARE UNIT"

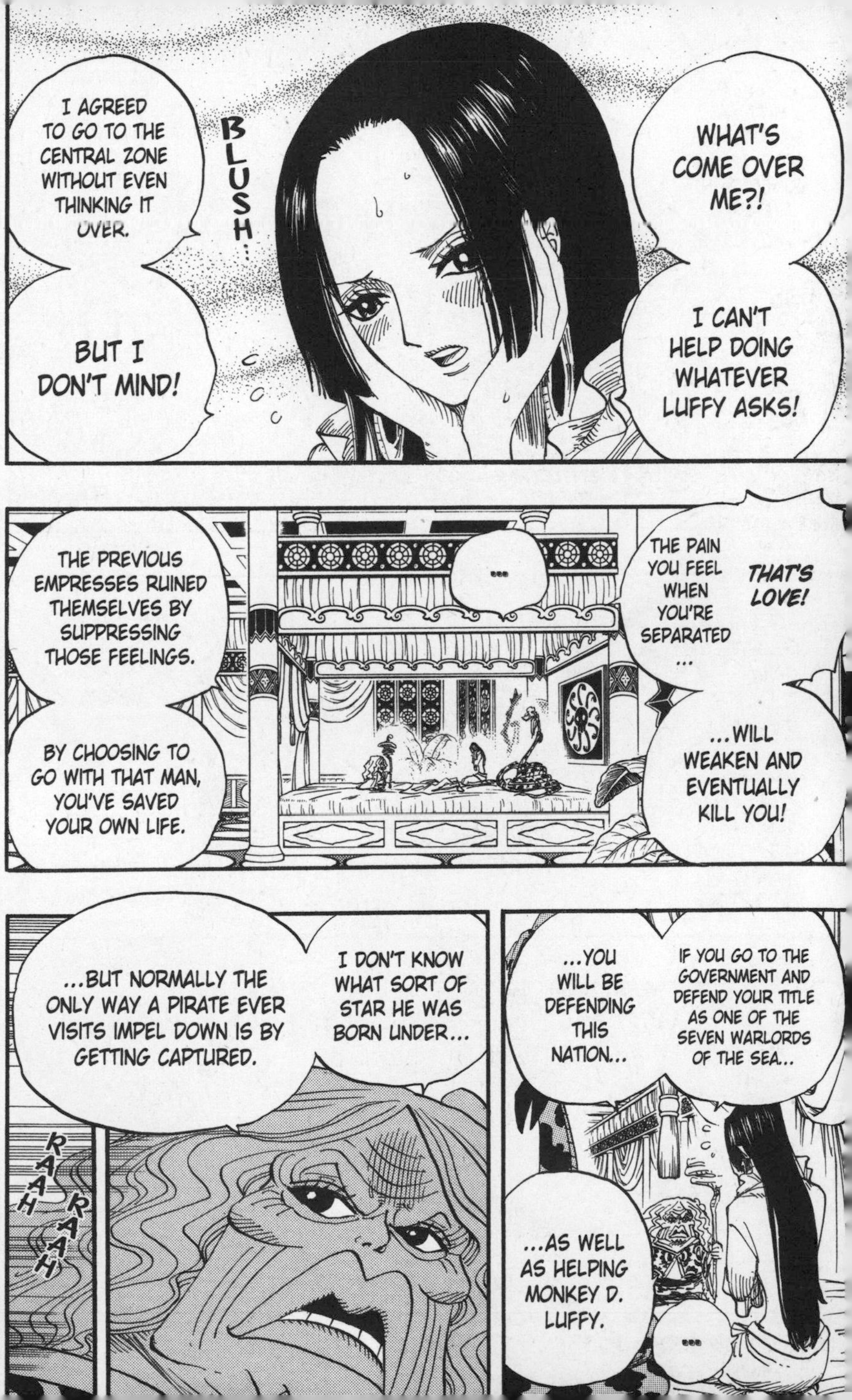
WHAT'S COME OVER ME?!
I CAN'T HELP DOING WHATEVER LUFFY ASKS!
BLUSH...
I AGREED TO GO TO THE CENTRAL ZONE WITHOUT EVEN THINKING IT OVER.
BUT I DON'T MIND!
THE PAIN YOU FEEL WHEN YOU'RE SEPARATED ...
THAT'S LOVE!
...WILL WEAKEN AND EVENTUALLY KILL YOU!
...
THE PREVIOUS EMPRESSES RUINED THEMSELVES BY SUPPRESSING THOSE FEELINGS.
BY CHOOSING TO GO WITH THAT MAN, YOU'VE SAVED YOUR OWN LIFE.
IF YOU GO TO THE GOVERNMENT AND DEFEND YOUR TITLE AS ONE OF THE SEVEN WARLORDS OF THE SEA...
...YOU WILL BE DEFENDING THIS NATION...
...AS WELL AS HELPING MONKEY D. LUFFY.
...
I DON'T KNOW WHAT SORT OF STAR HE WAS BORN UNDER...
...BUT NORMALLY THE ONLY WAY A PIRATE EVER VISITS IMPEL DOWN IS BY GETTING CAPTURED.
RAAAH
RAAAH

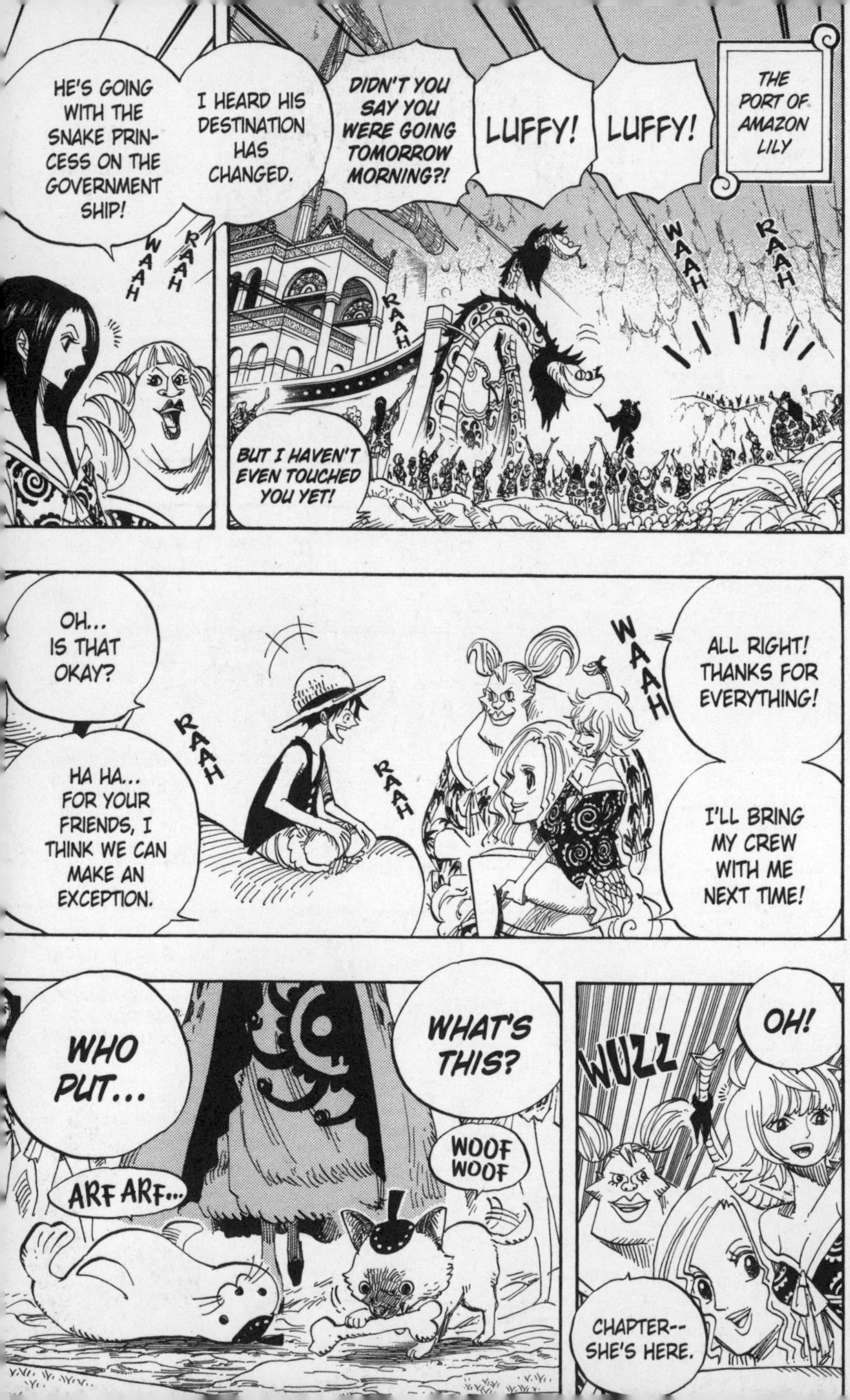
THE PORT OF AMAZON LILY
LUFFY!
LUFFY!
DIDN'T YOU SAY YOU WERE GOING TOMORROW MORNING?!
WAAH
RAAH
RAAH
BUT I HAVEN'T EVEN TOUCHED YOU YET!
I HEARD HIS DESTINATION HAS CHANGED.
HE'S GOING WITH THE SNAKE PRIN-CESS ON THE GOVERNMENT SHIP!
RAAH
WAAH
ALL RIGHT! THANKS FOR EVERYTHING!
I'LL BRING MY CREW WITH ME NEXT TIME!
WAAH
RAAH
RAAH
OH... IS THAT OKAY?
HA HA... FOR YOUR FRIENDS, I THINK WE CAN MAKE AN EXCEPTION.
OH!
WUZZ
CHAPTER-- SHE'S HERE.
WHAT'S THIS?
WOOF WOOF
WHO PUT...
ARF ARF...

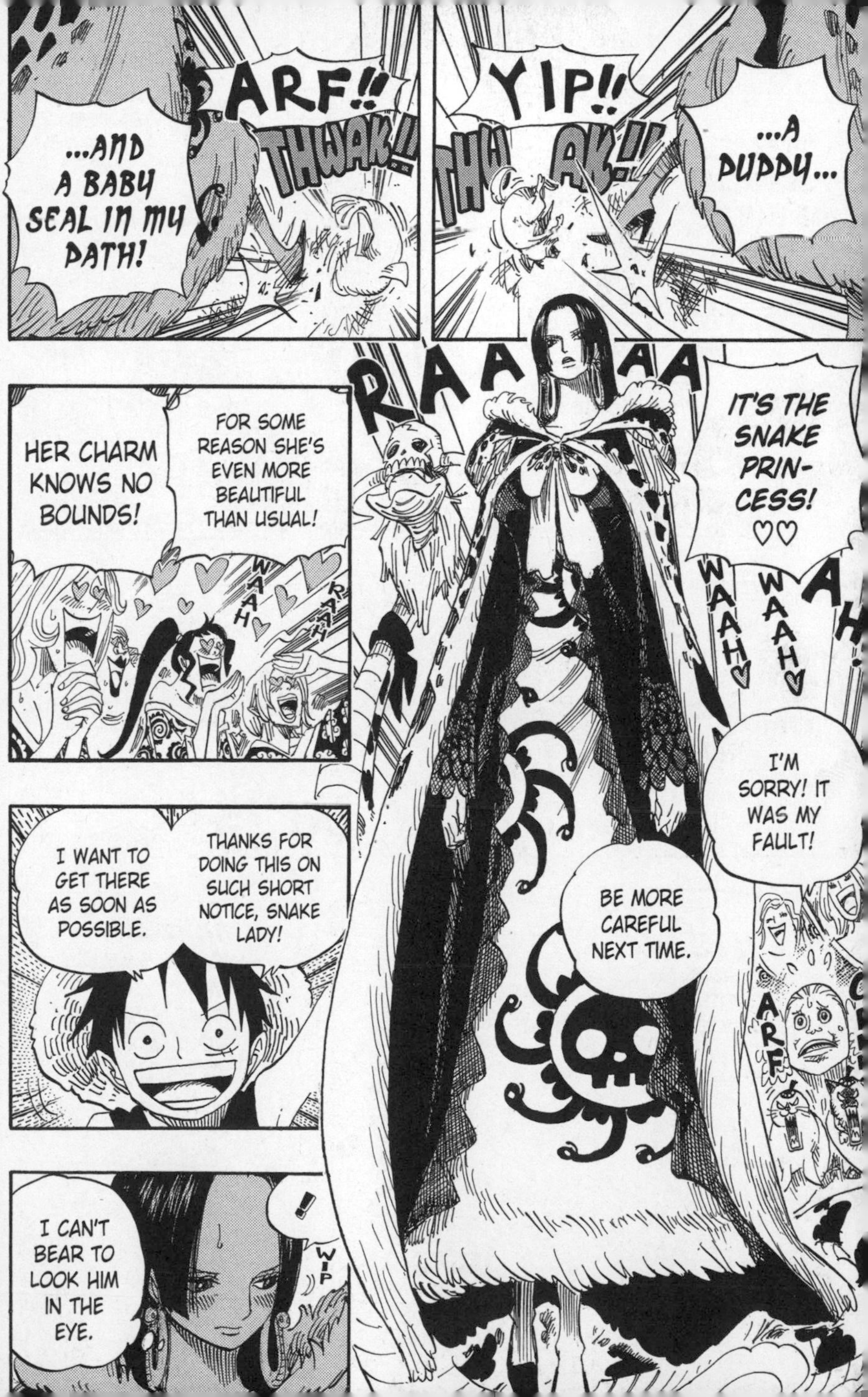
YIP!!
THWAK!!
...A PUPPY...
ARF!!
THWAK!!
...AND A BABY SEAL IN MY PATH!
RAAAAA
IT'S THE SNAKE PRINCESS! ♡♡
WAAAH♡
WAAAH♡
AH
I'M SORRY! IT WAS MY FAULT!
BE MORE CAREFUL NEXT TIME.
ARF
FOR SOME REASON SHE'S EVEN MORE BEAUTIFUL THAN USUAL!
HER CHARM KNOWS NO BOUNDS!
WAAAH
RAAAH
THANKS FOR DOING THIS ON SUCH SHORT NOTICE, SNAKE LADY!
I WANT TO GET THERE AS SOON AS POSSIBLE.
!
WIP
I CAN'T BEAR TO LOOK HIM IN THE EYE.

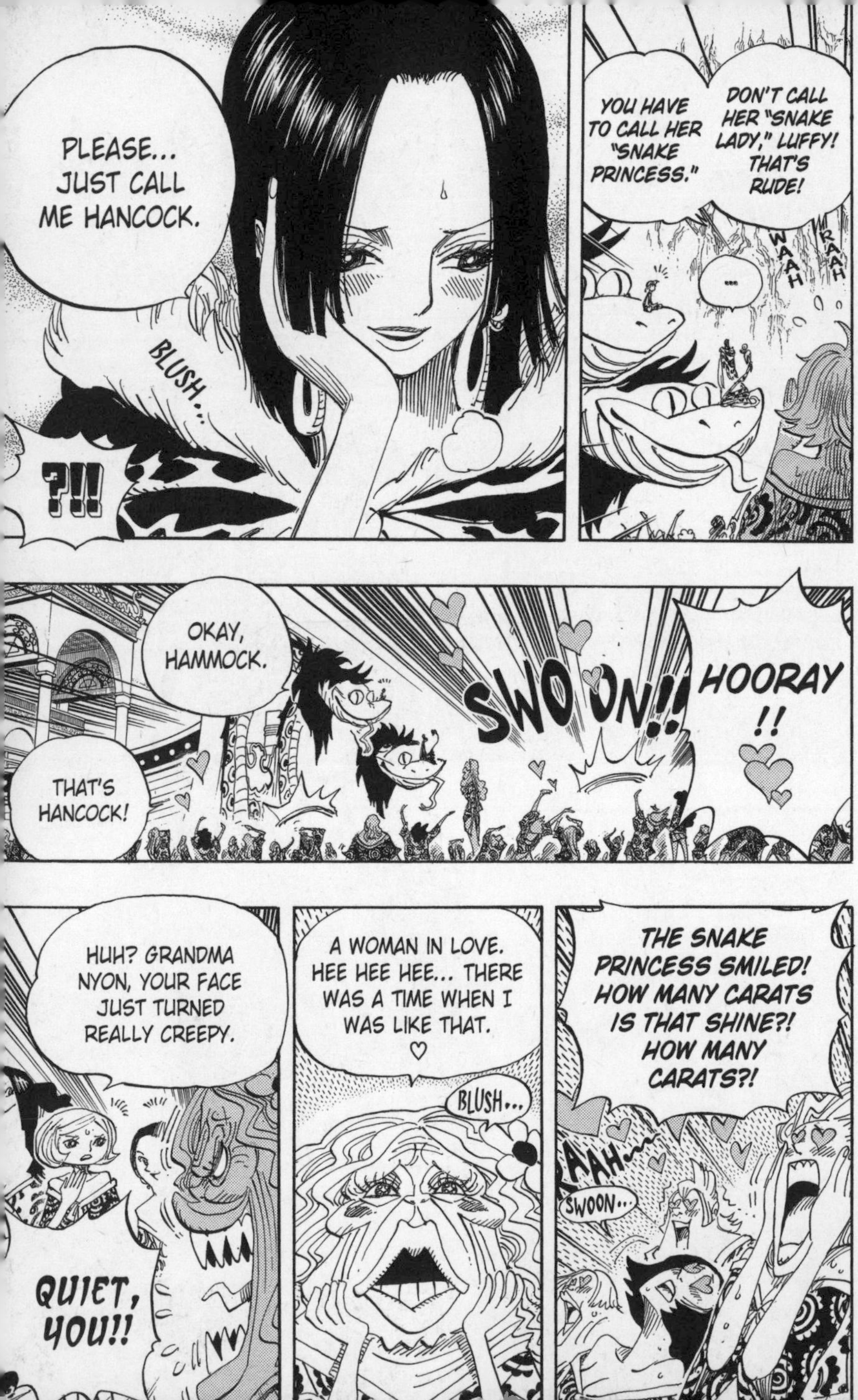
DON'T CALL HER "SNAKE LADY," LUFFY! THAT'S RUDE!
YOU HAVE TO CALL HER "SNAKE PRINCESS."
RAAH
WAAH
...
PLEASE... JUST CALL ME HANCOCK.
BLUSH...
?!!
HOORAY!!
SWOON!!
OKAY, HAMMOCK.
THAT'S HANCOCK!
THE SNAKE PRINCESS SMILED! HOW MANY CARATS IS THAT SHINE?! HOW MANY CARATS?!
SWOON...
A WOMAN IN LOVE. HEE HEE HEE... THERE WAS A TIME WHEN I WAS LIKE THAT. ♡
BLUSH...
HUH? GRANDMA NYON, YOUR FACE JUST TURNED REALLY CREEPY.
QUIET, YOU!!

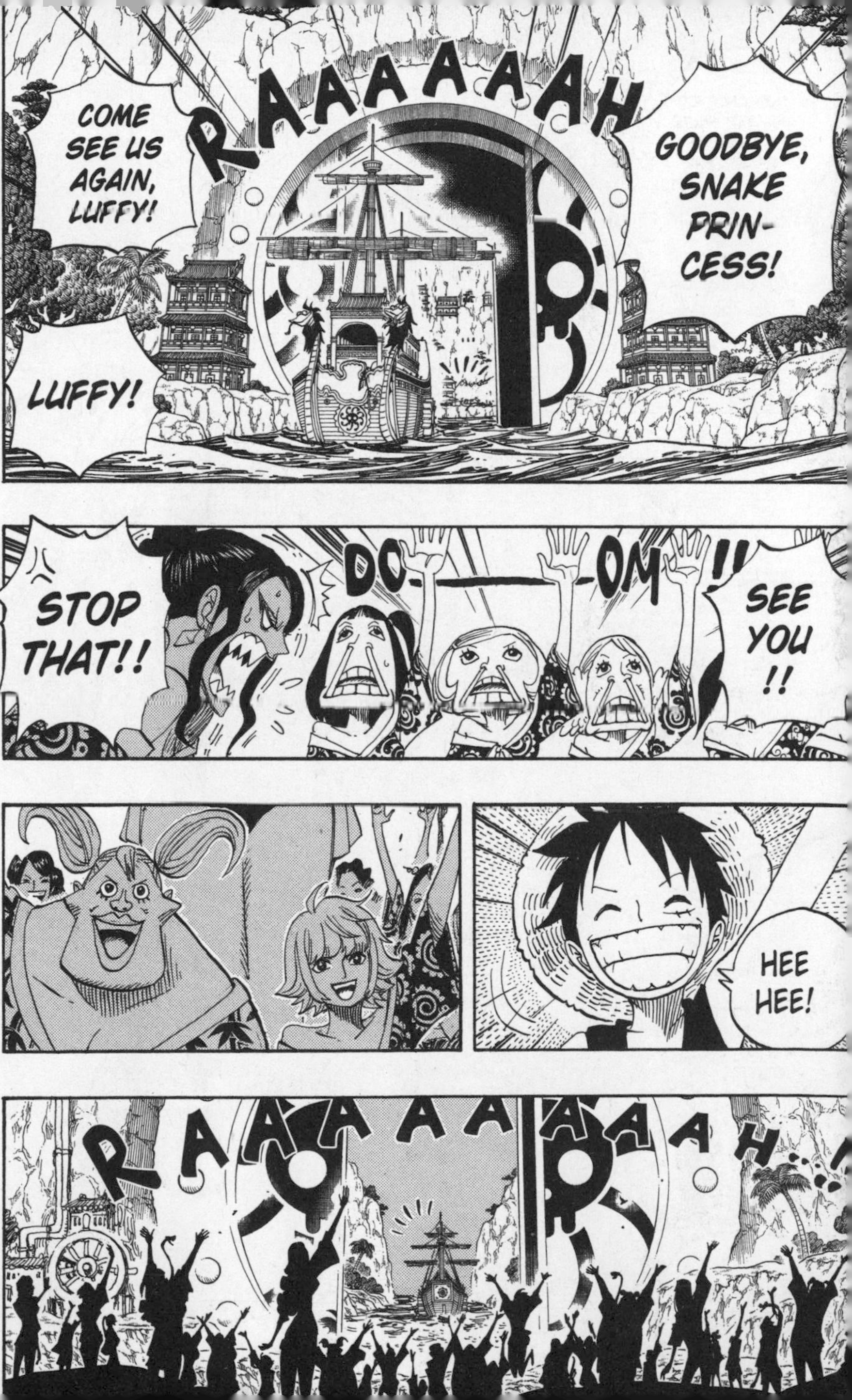
GOODBYE, SNAKE PRINCESS!
RAAAAAAH
COME SEE US AGAIN, LUFFY!
LUFFY!
SEE YOU!!
DO————OM!!
STOP THAT!!
HEE HEE!
RAAAAAAAAH...!!

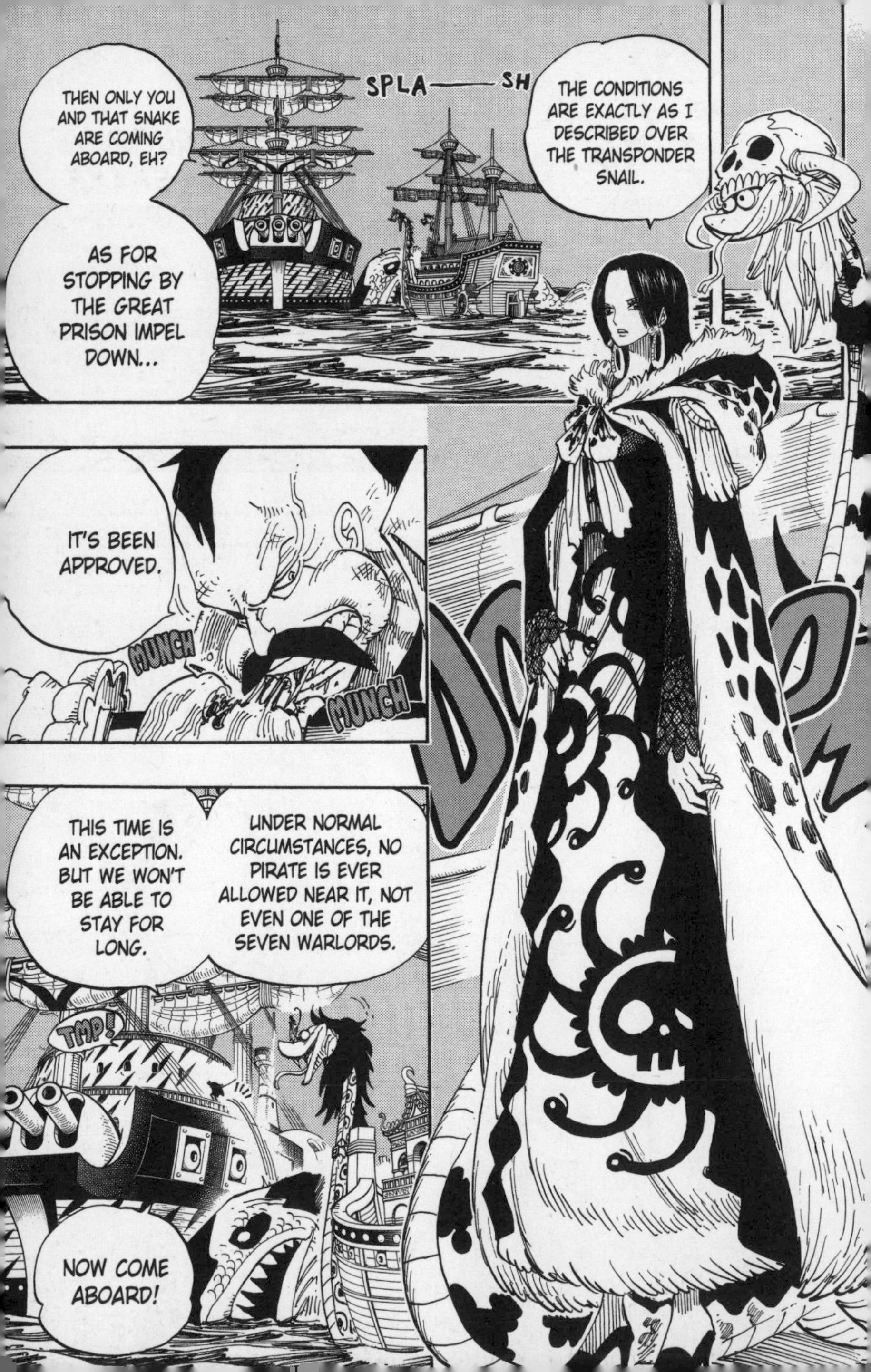
THE CONDITIONS ARE EXACTLY AS I DESCRIBED OVER THE TRANSPONDER SNAIL.
SPLA——SH
THEN ONLY YOU AND THAT SNAKE ARE COMING ABOARD, EH?
AS FOR STOPPING BY THE GREAT PRISON IMPEL DOWN...
IT'S BEEN APPROVED.
MUNCH
MUNCH
UNDER NORMAL CIRCUMSTANCES, NO PIRATE IS EVER ALLOWED NEAR IT, NOT EVEN ONE OF THE SEVEN WARLORDS.
THIS TIME IS AN EXCEPTION. BUT WE WON'T BE ABLE TO STAY FOR LONG.
TMP!
NOW COME ABOARD!

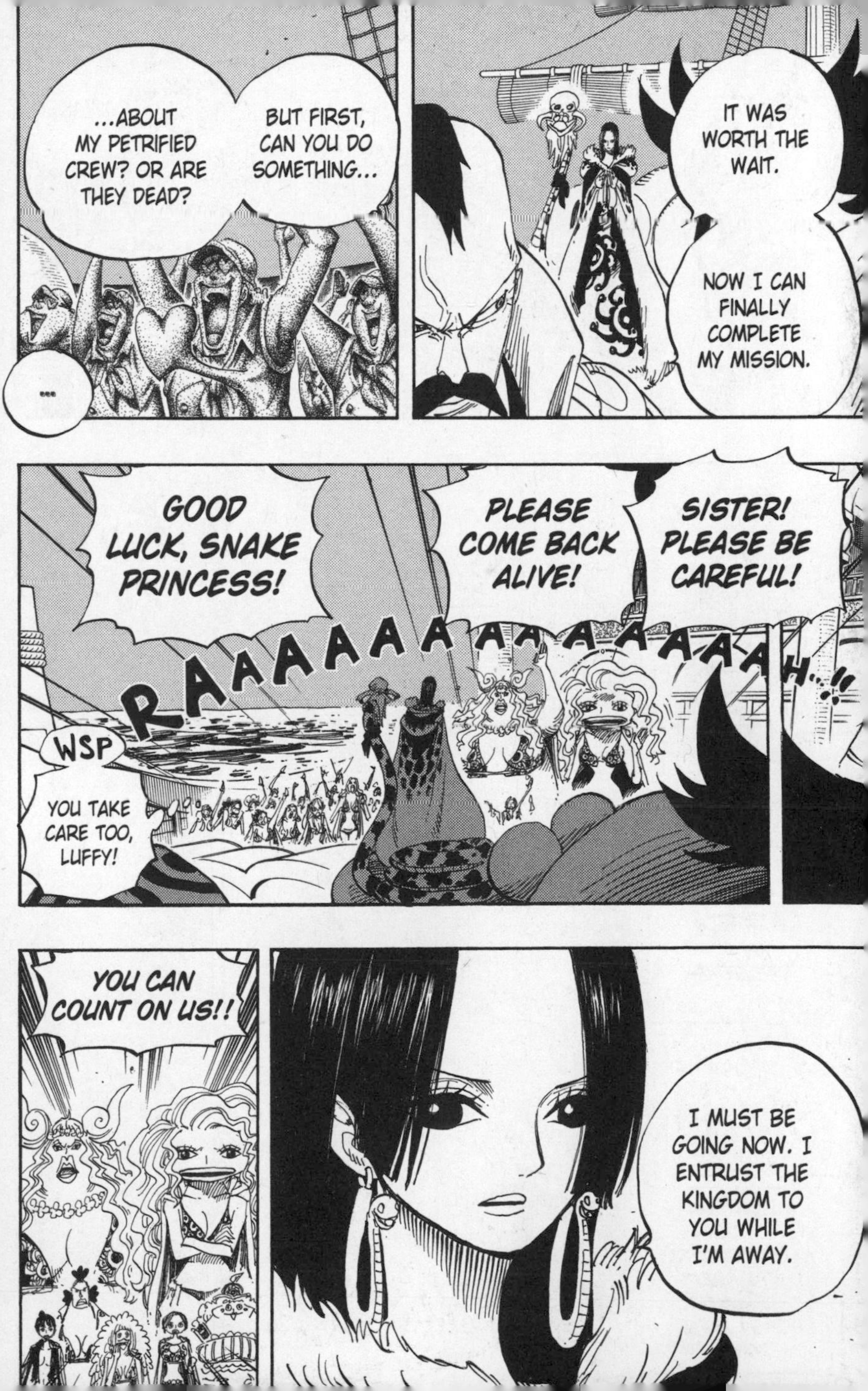
IT WAS WORTH THE WAIT.
NOW I CAN FINALLY COMPLETE MY MISSION.
BUT FIRST, CAN YOU DO SOMETHING...
...ABOUT MY PETRIFIED CREW? OR ARE THEY DEAD?
...
SISTER! PLEASE BE CAREFUL!
PLEASE COME BACK ALIVE!
GOOD LUCK, SNAKE PRINCESS!
RAAAAAAAAAAAAAH...!!
WSP
YOU TAKE CARE TOO, LUFFY!
I MUST BE GOING NOW. I ENTRUST THE KINGDOM TO YOU WHILE I'M AWAY.
YOU CAN COUNT ON US!!

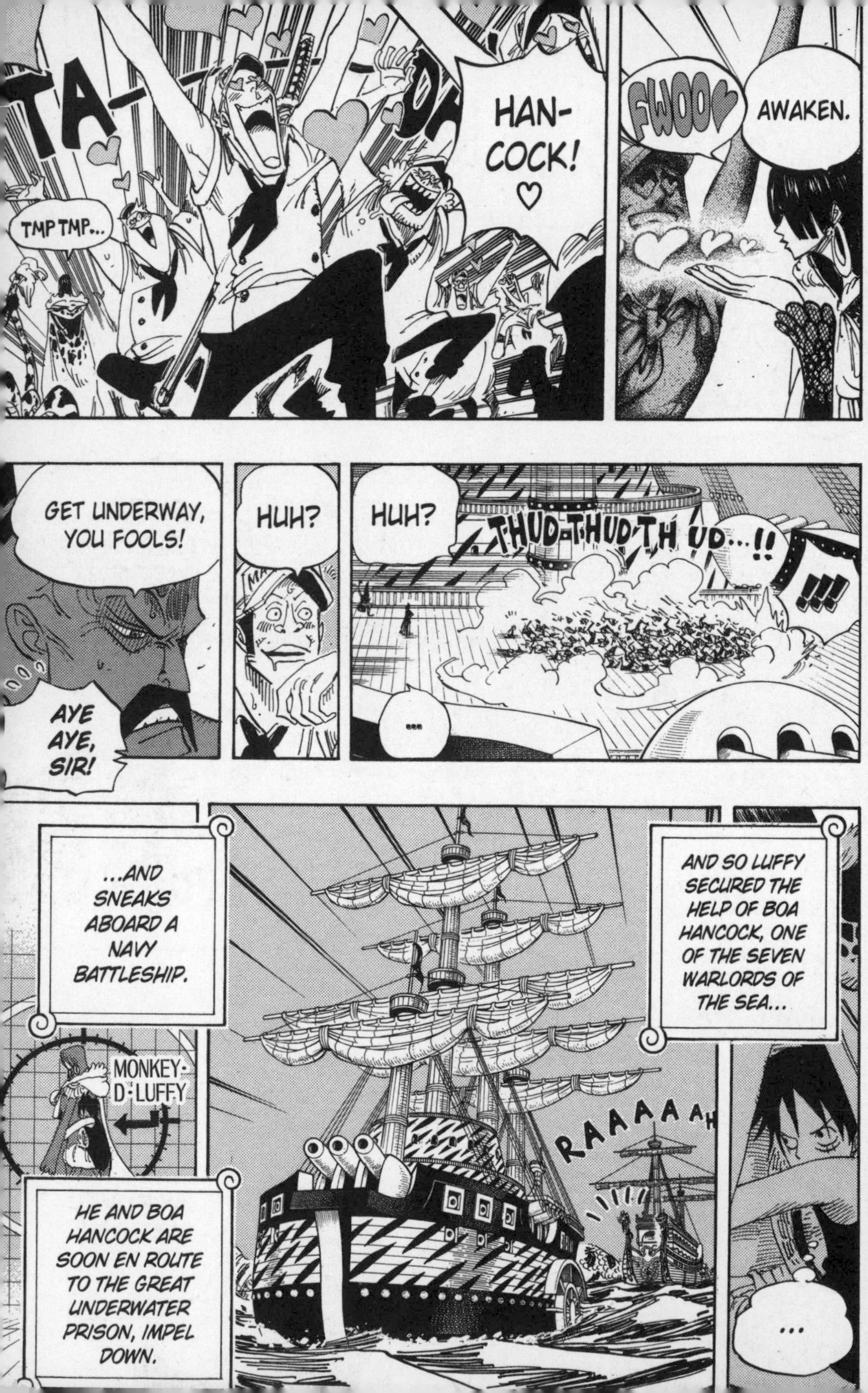
FWOO♥
AWAKEN.
HAN-COCK! ♡
TA–
TMP TMP...
HUH?
THUD THUD THUD...!!
!!!
...
HUH?
GET UNDERWAY, YOU FOOLS!
AYE AYE, SIR!
AND SO LUFFY SECURED THE HELP OF BOA HANCOCK, ONE OF THE SEVEN WARLORDS OF THE SEA...
...
RAAAAAH
...AND SNEAKS ABOARD A NAVY BATTLESHIP.
MONKEY-D-LUFFY
HE AND BOA HANCOCK ARE SOON EN ROUTE TO THE GREAT UNDERWATER PRISON, IMPEL DOWN.

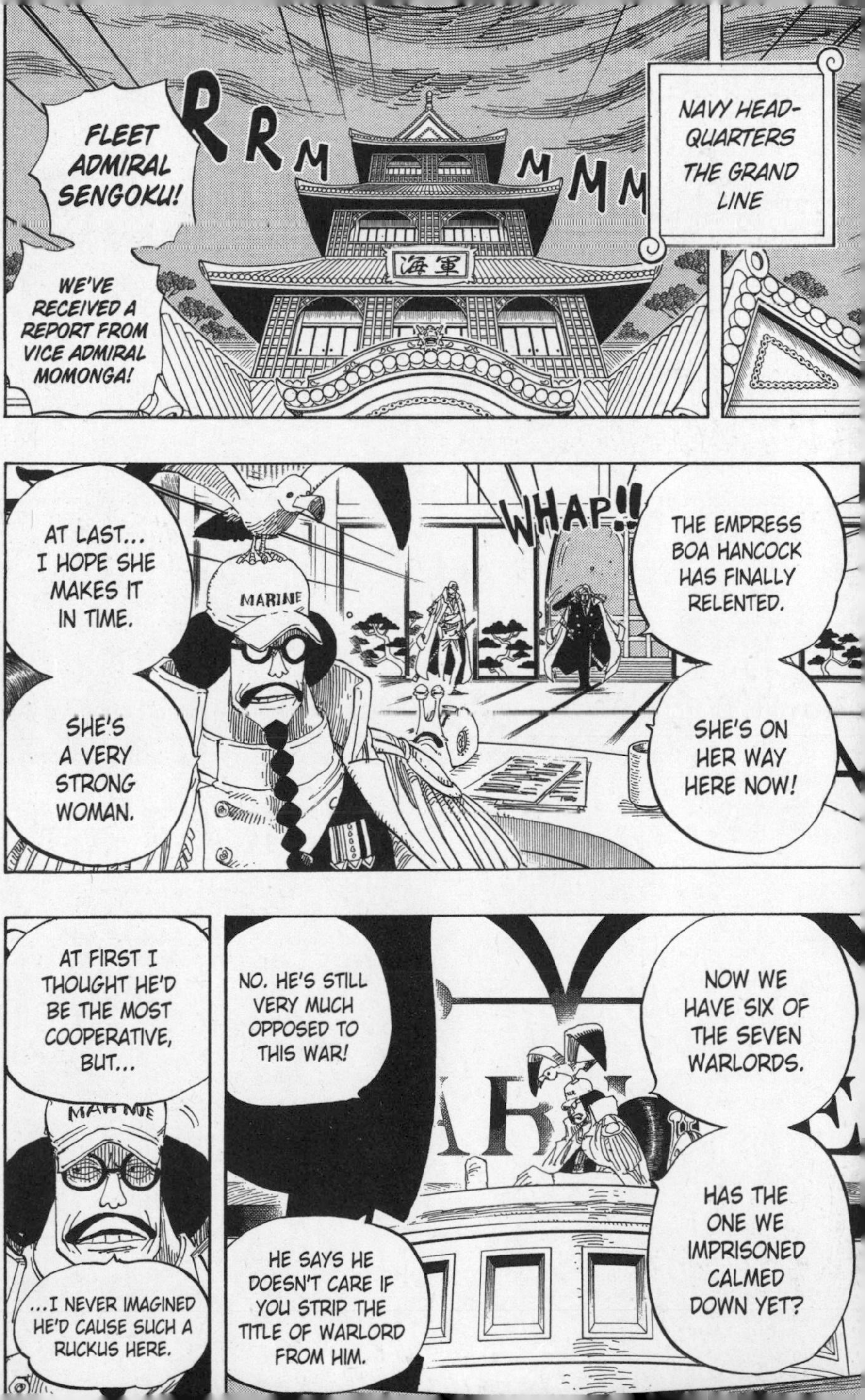
NAVY HEAD-QUARTERS THE GRAND LINE
RRMMMM
海軍
FLEET ADMIRAL SENGOKU!
WE'VE RECEIVED A REPORT FROM VICE ADMIRAL MOMONGA!
THE EMPRESS BOA HANCOCK HAS FINALLY RELENTED.
SHE'S ON HER WAY HERE NOW!
WHAP!!
AT LAST... I HOPE SHE MAKES IT IN TIME.
MARINE
SHE'S A VERY STRONG WOMAN.
NOW WE HAVE SIX OF THE SEVEN WARLORDS.
HAS THE ONE WE IMPRISONED CALMED DOWN YET?
NO. HE'S STILL VERY MUCH OPPOSED TO THIS WAR!
HE SAYS HE DOESN'T CARE IF YOU STRIP THE TITLE OF WARLORD FROM HIM.
AT FIRST I THOUGHT HE'D BE THE MOST COOPERATIVE, BUT...
...I NEVER IMAGINED HE'D CAUSE SUCH A RUCKUS HERE.

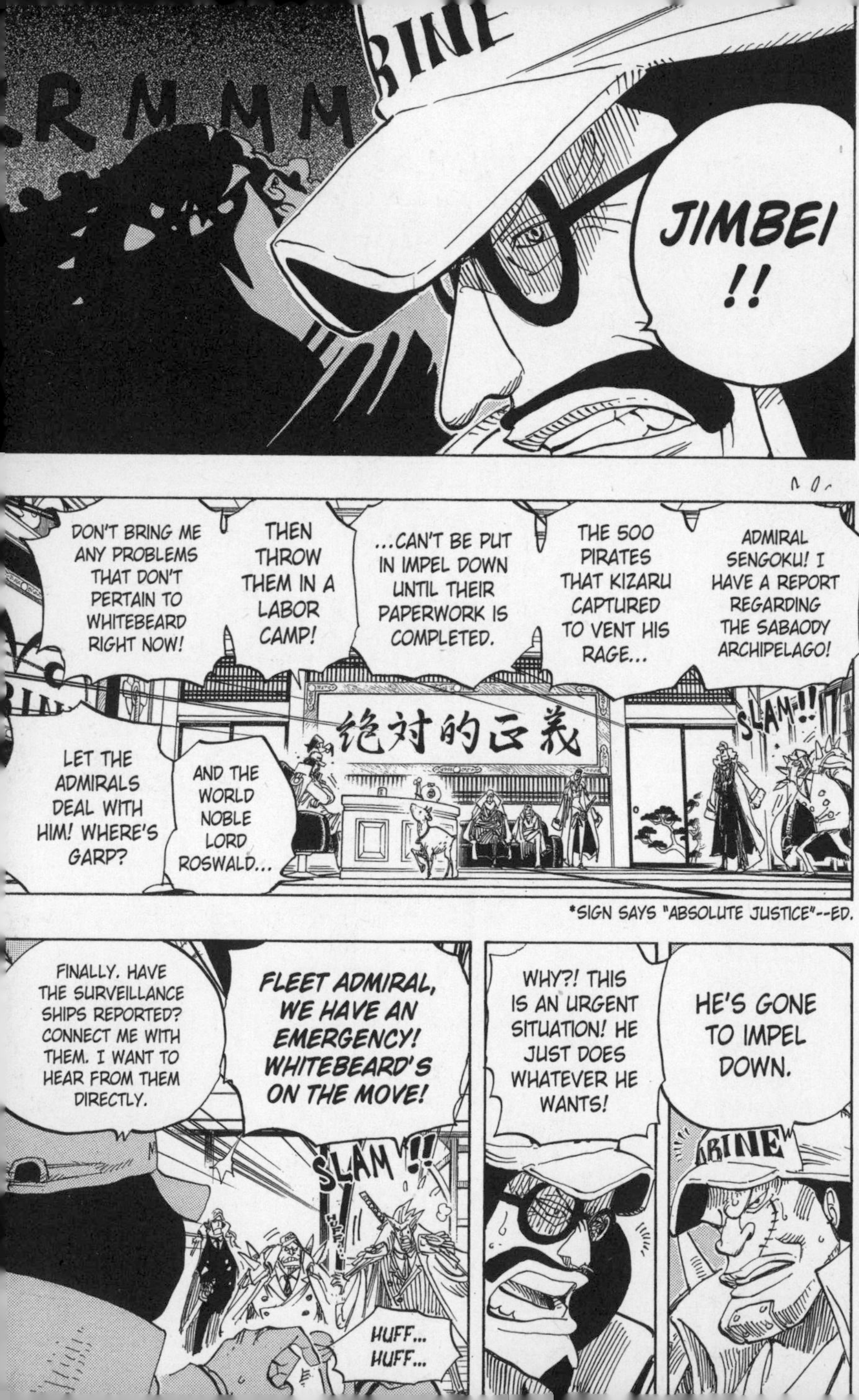
JIMBEI !!
RMMM
ADMIRAL SENGOKU! I HAVE A REPORT REGARDING THE SABAODY ARCHIPELAGO!
THE 500 PIRATES THAT KIZARU CAPTURED TO VENT HIS RAGE...
...CAN'T BE PUT IN IMPEL DOWN UNTIL THEIR PAPERWORK IS COMPLETED.
THEN THROW THEM IN A LABOR CAMP!
DON'T BRING ME ANY PROBLEMS THAT DON'T PERTAIN TO WHITEBEARD RIGHT NOW!
SLAM!!
絶対的正義
AND THE WORLD NOBLE LORD ROSWALD...
LET THE ADMIRALS DEAL WITH HIM! WHERE'S GARP?
HE'S GONE TO IMPEL DOWN.
WHY?! THIS IS AN URGENT SITUATION! HE JUST DOES WHATEVER HE WANTS!
FLEET ADMIRAL, WE HAVE AN EMERGENCY! WHITEBEARD'S ON THE MOVE!
FINALLY. HAVE THE SURVEILLANCE SHIPS REPORTED? CONNECT ME WITH THEM. I WANT TO HEAR FROM THEM DIRECTLY.
SLAM!!
HUFF... HUFF...

*SIGN SAYS "ABSOLUTE JUSTICE"--ED.

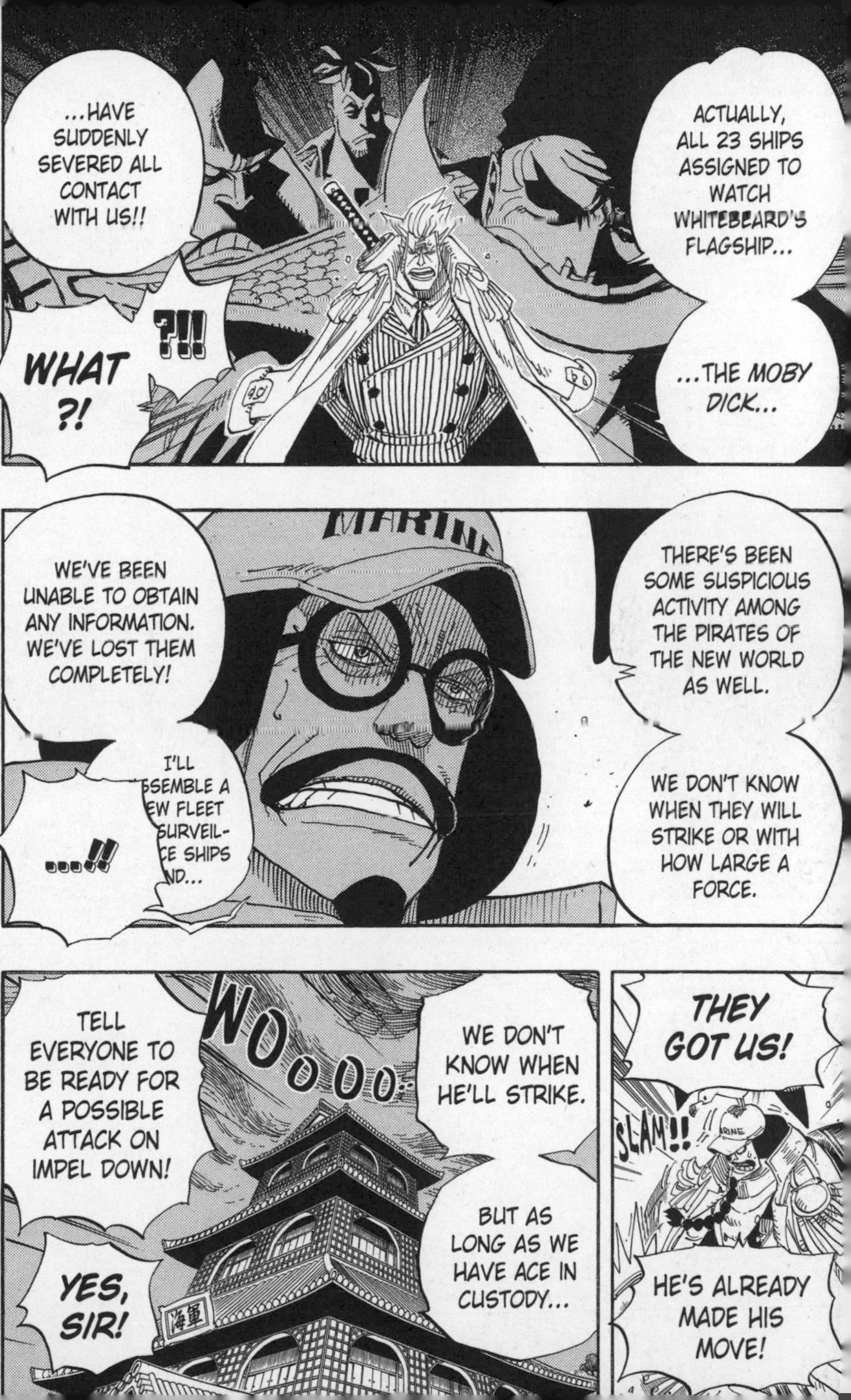
ACTUALLY, ALL 23 SHIPS ASSIGNED TO WATCH WHITEBEARD'S FLAGSHIP...
...THE *MOBY DICK*...
...HAVE SUDDENLY SEVERED ALL CONTACT WITH US!!
?!!
WHAT ?!
THERE'S BEEN SOME SUSPICIOUS ACTIVITY AMONG THE PIRATES OF THE NEW WORLD AS WELL.
WE DON'T KNOW WHEN THEY WILL STRIKE OR WITH HOW LARGE A FORCE.
WE'VE BEEN UNABLE TO OBTAIN ANY INFORMATION. WE'VE LOST THEM COMPLETELY!
I'LL SSEMBLE A EW FLEET SURVEIL- CE SHIPS ND...
...!!
THEY GOT US!
SLAM!!
HE'S ALREADY MADE HIS MOVE!
WE DON'T KNOW WHEN HE'LL STRIKE.
BUT AS LONG AS WE HAVE ACE IN CUSTODY...
WOOOOO
TELL EVERYONE TO BE READY FOR A POSSIBLE ATTACK ON IMPEL DOWN!
YES, SIR!
海軍

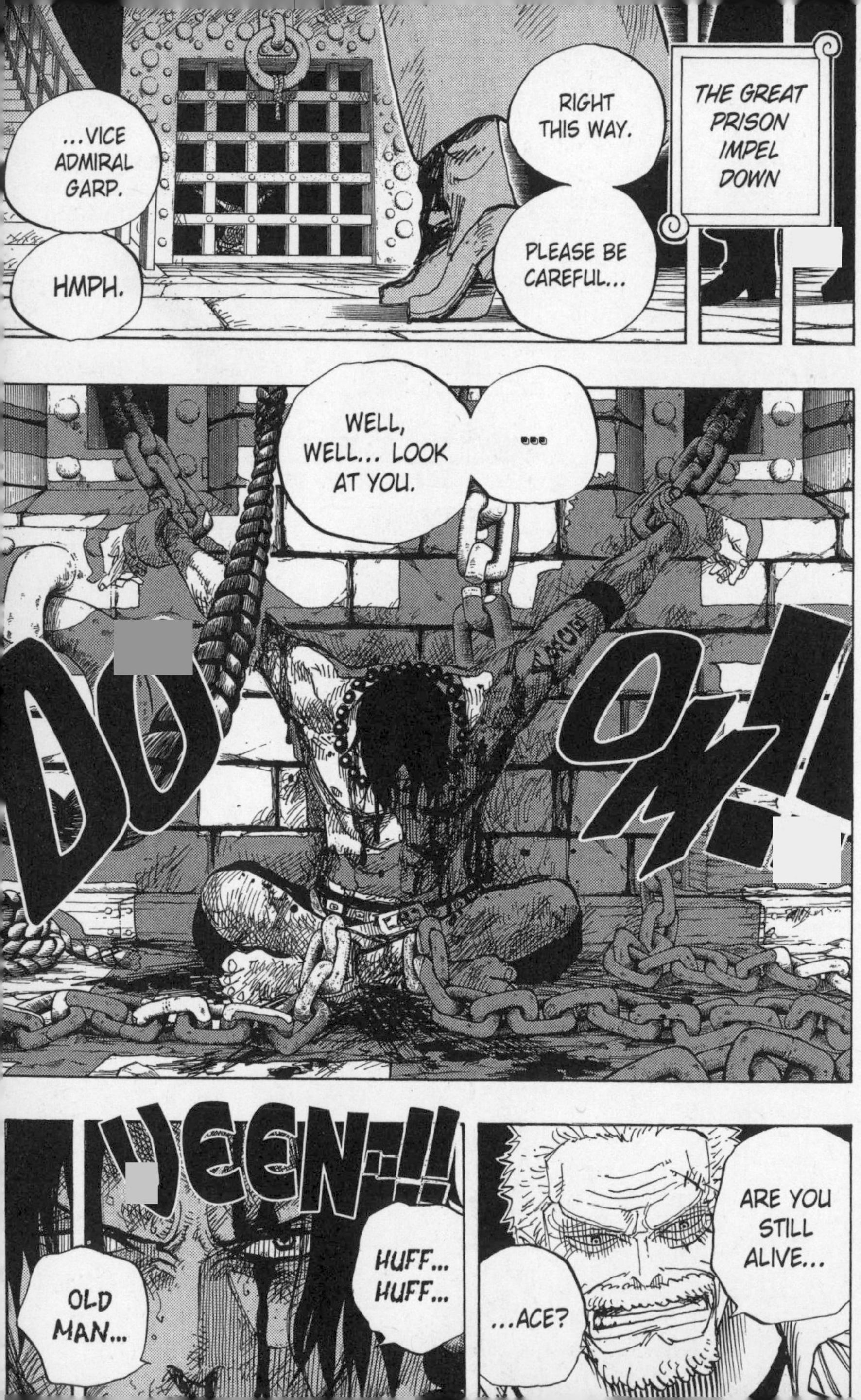
THE GREAT PRISON IMPEL DOWN
RIGHT THIS WAY.
PLEASE BE CAREFUL...
...VICE ADMIRAL GARP.
HMPH.
...
WELL, WELL... LOOK AT YOU.
DO
OH!
ARE YOU STILL ALIVE...
...ACE?
UEEN--!!
HUFF... HUFF...
OLD MAN...

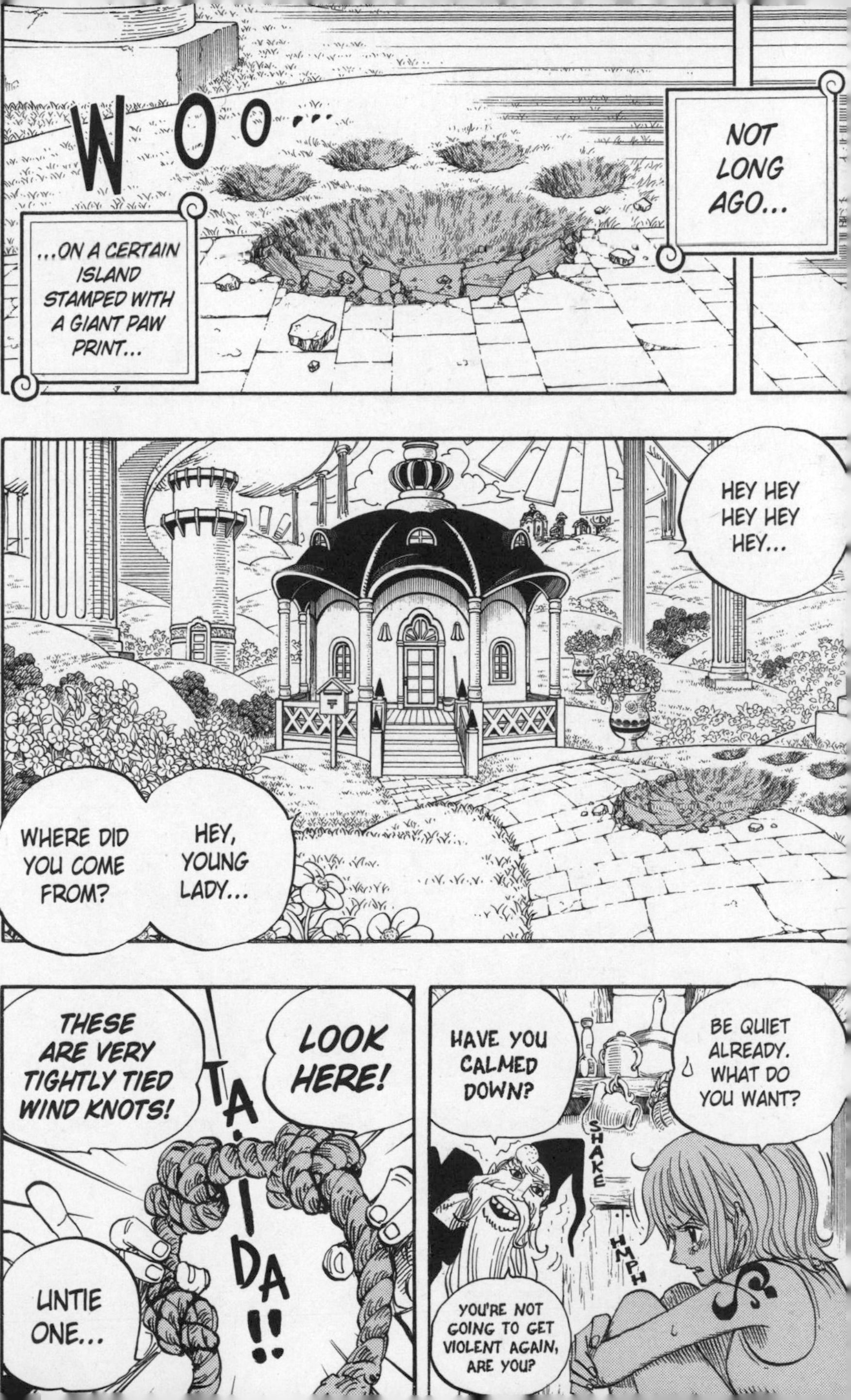
NOT LONG AGO...
WOO...
...ON A CERTAIN ISLAND STAMPED WITH A GIANT PAW PRINT...
HEY HEY HEY HEY HEY...
HEY, YOUNG LADY...
WHERE DID YOU COME FROM?
BE QUIET ALREADY. WHAT DO YOU WANT?
HAVE YOU CALMED DOWN?
SHAKE
HMPH
YOU'RE NOT GOING TO GET VIOLENT AGAIN, ARE YOU?
LOOK HERE!
THESE ARE VERY TIGHTLY TIED WIND KNOTS!
TA-DA!!
UNTIE ONE...

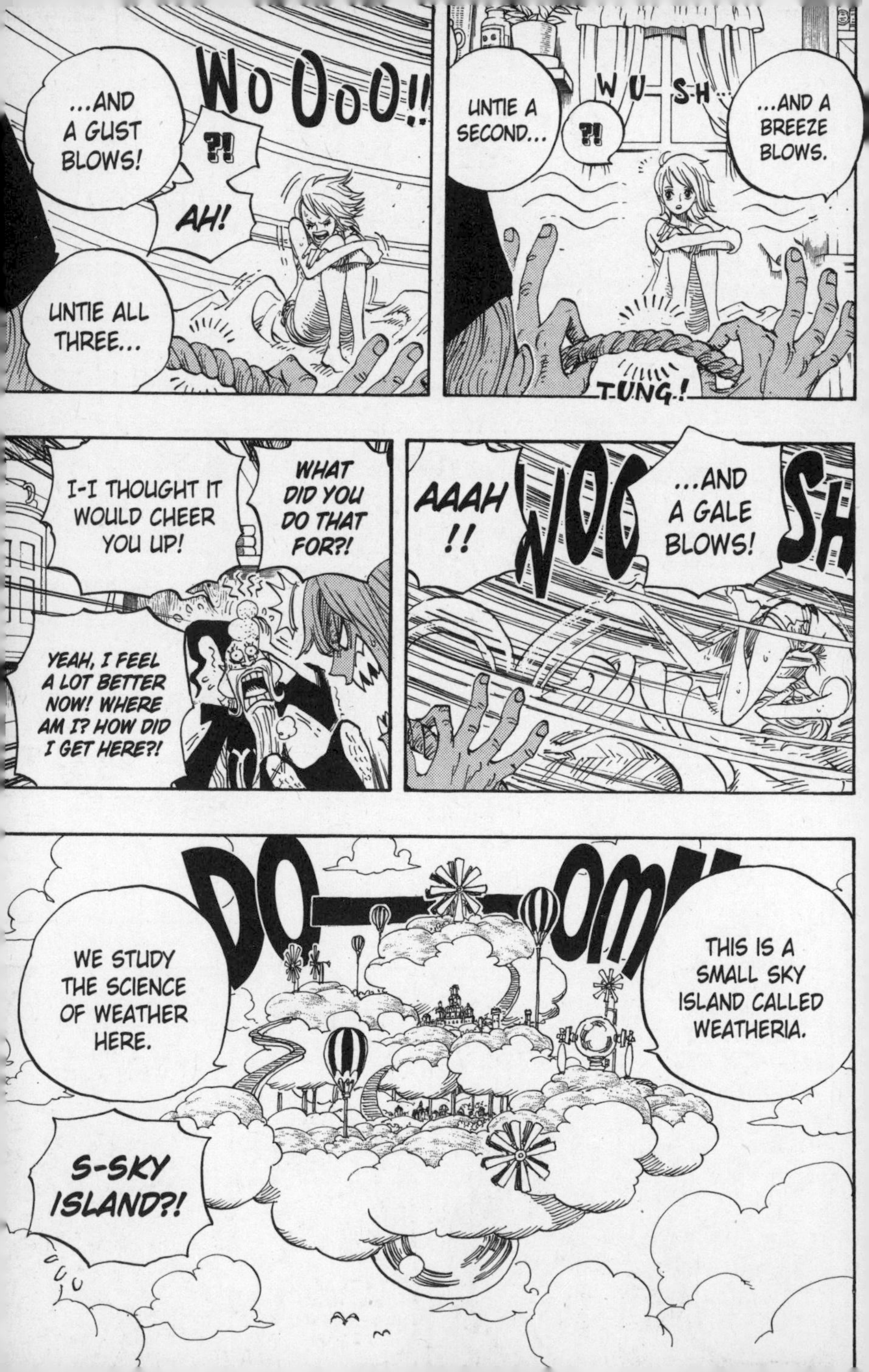
...AND A BREEZE BLOWS.
W U S H...
?!
UNTIE A SECOND...
TUNG!
WOOOOO!!
...AND A GUST BLOWS!
?!
AH!
UNTIE ALL THREE...
SH
...AND A GALE BLOWS!
WOO
AAAH!!
WHAT DID YOU DO THAT FOR?!
I-I THOUGHT IT WOULD CHEER YOU UP!
YEAH, I FEEL A LOT BETTER NOW! WHERE AM I? HOW DID I GET HERE?!
THIS IS A SMALL SKY ISLAND CALLED WEATHERIA.
DO—OM
WE STUDY THE SCIENCE OF WEATHER HERE.
S-SKY ISLAND?!

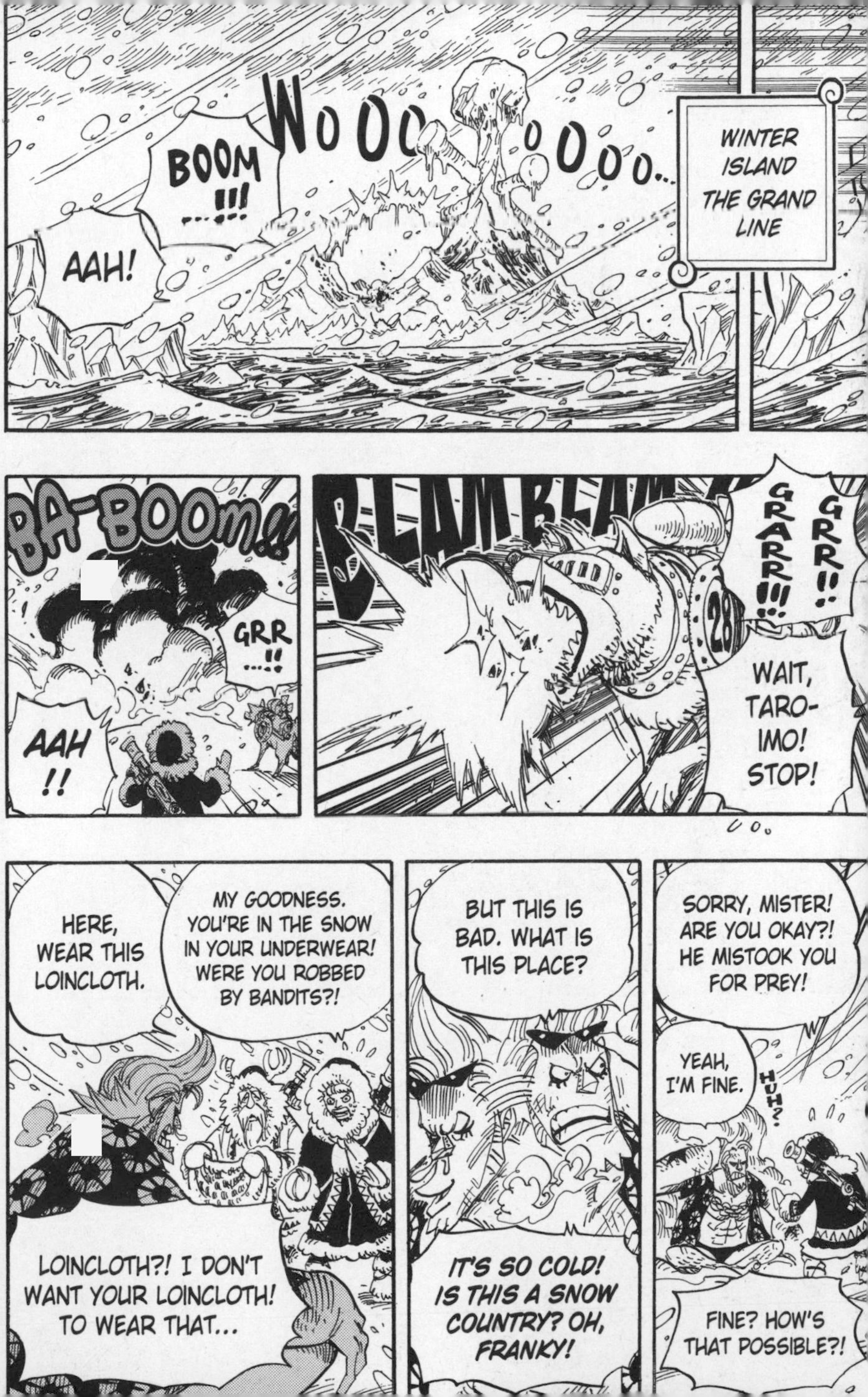
WINTER ISLAND THE GRAND LINE
WOOOOOOO...
BOOM!!!
AAH!
BLAM BLAM
GRR!!
GRARR!!!
WAIT, TARO-IMO! STOP!
BA-BOOM!!
GRR...!!
AAH!!
SORRY, MISTER! ARE YOU OKAY?! HE MISTOOK YOU FOR PREY!
YEAH, I'M FINE.
HUH?
FINE? HOW'S THAT POSSIBLE?!
BUT THIS IS BAD. WHAT IS THIS PLACE?
IT'S SO COLD! IS THIS A SNOW COUNTRY? OH, FRANKY!
MY GOODNESS. YOU'RE IN THE SNOW IN YOUR UNDERWEAR! WERE YOU ROBBED BY BANDITS?!
HERE, WEAR THIS LOINCLOTH.
LOINCLOTH?! I DON'T WANT YOUR LOINCLOTH! TO WEAR THAT...

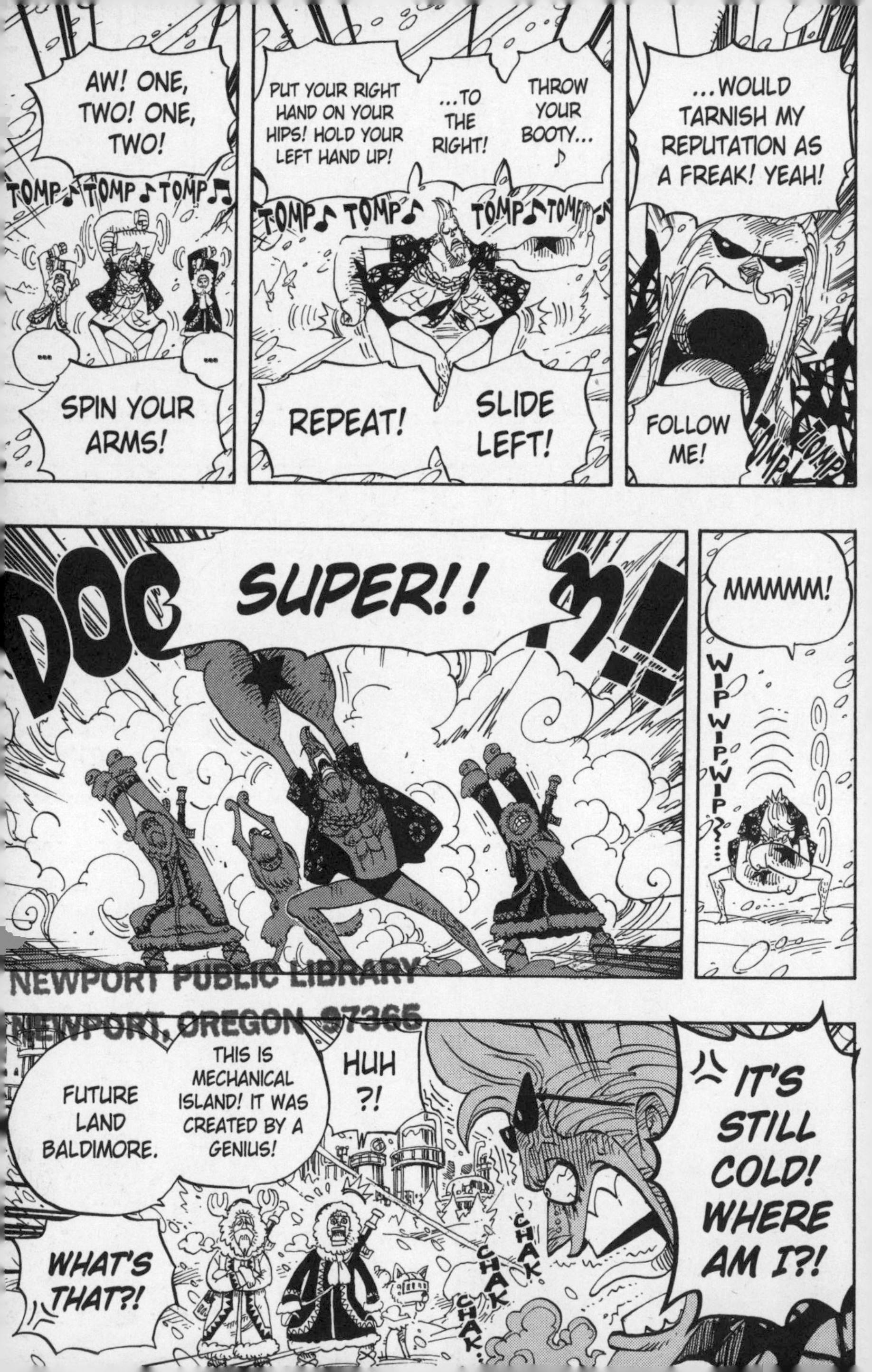
...WOULD TARNISH MY REPUTATION AS A FREAK! YEAH!
FOLLOW ME!
TOMP! TOMP!
THROW YOUR BOOTY... ♪
...TO THE RIGHT!
PUT YOUR RIGHT HAND ON YOUR HIPS! HOLD YOUR LEFT HAND UP!
TOMP ♪ TOMP ♪ TOMP ♪ TOMP ♪
SLIDE LEFT!
REPEAT!
AW! ONE, TWO! ONE, TWO!
TOMP ♪ TOMP ♪ TOMP ♫
...
...
SPIN YOUR ARMS!
MMMMMM!
WIP WIP WIP WIP ?...
DOO
SUPER!!
M!!
IT'S STILL COLD! WHERE AM I?!
CHAK CHAK CHAK CHAK
HUH ?!
THIS IS MECHANICAL ISLAND! IT WAS CREATED BY A GENIUS!
FUTURE LAND BALDIMORE.
WHAT'S THAT?!

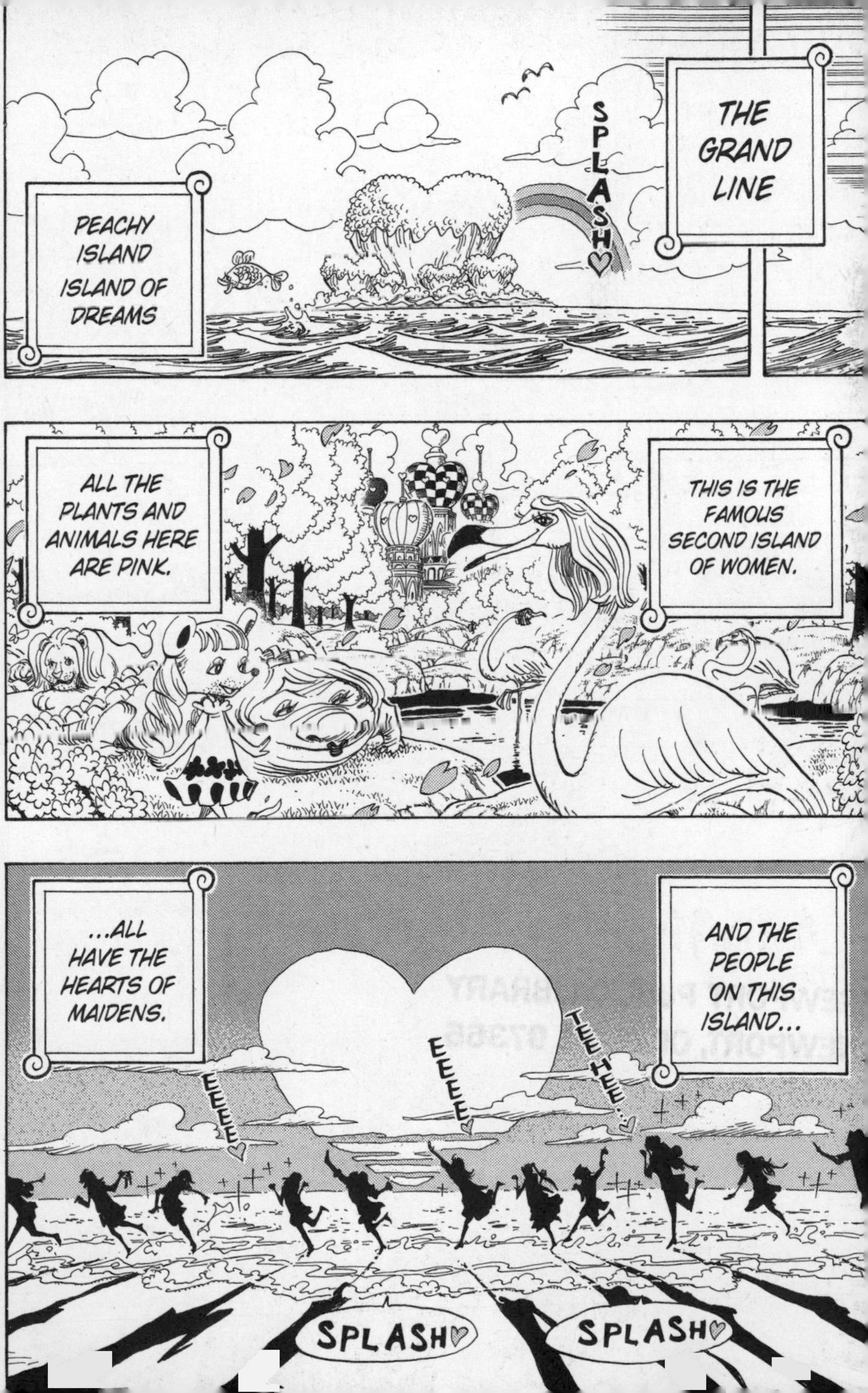
THE GRAND LINE
SPLASH♥
PEACHY ISLAND
ISLAND OF DREAMS
THIS IS THE FAMOUS SECOND ISLAND OF WOMEN.
ALL THE PLANTS AND ANIMALS HERE ARE PINK.
AND THE PEOPLE ON THIS ISLAND...
TEE HEE...
EEEE♥
EEEE♥
...ALL HAVE THE HEARTS OF MAIDENS.
SPLASH♥
SPLASH♥

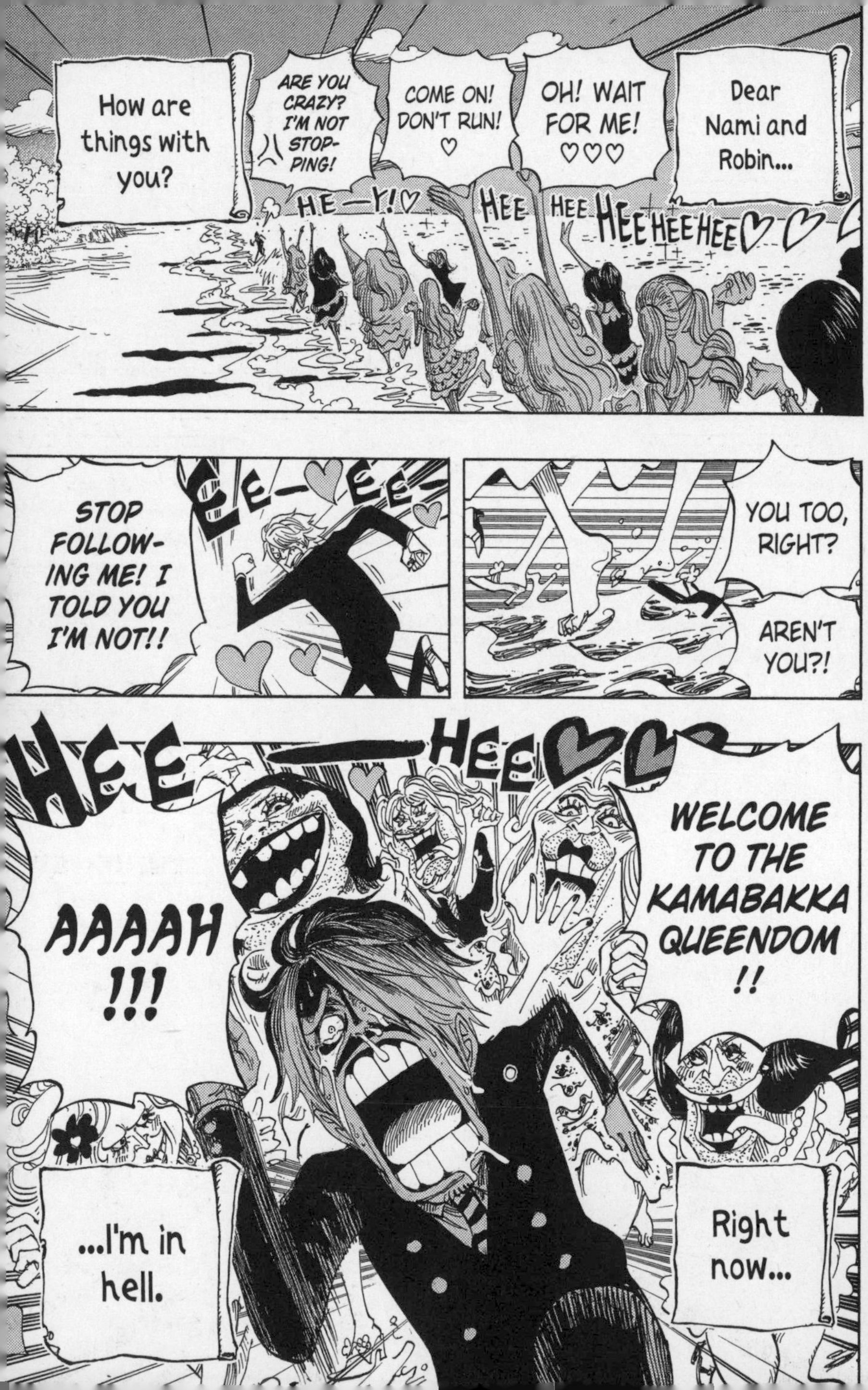
Dear Nami and Robin...
HEE HEE HEEHEEHEE♡♡
OH! WAIT FOR ME! ♡♡♡
COME ON! DON'T RUN! ♡
HE—Y!♡
ARE YOU CRAZY? I'M NOT STOPPING!
How are things with you?
YOU TOO, RIGHT?
AREN'T YOU?!
EE—EE
STOP FOLLOWING ME! I TOLD YOU I'M NOT!!
HEE—HEE♡♡
WELCOME TO THE KAMABAKKA QUEENDOM!!
AAAAH!!!
Right now...
...I'm in hell.

SBS Question Corner

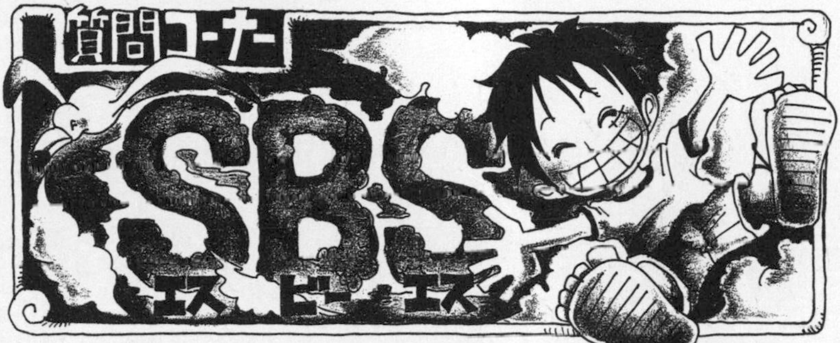
質問コーナー
SBS
エス ビー エス
(Tomomi Surimachi, Saitama)

Reader(Q): I don't know who you are, but there's something I have to tell you. Gack! The Question Corner is starting! (Drops dead.)

--Horsemeat Man

Oda(A): Hey, Horsemeat Man! Horsemeat Man! Get ahold of yourself! You told me you'd give this engagement ring to her! Horsemeat Man! Shut up! Okay, the Question Corner is starting now.

Q: I want to see Killer unmasked.

--Choco

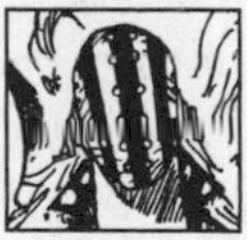

A: Yeah me too

Q: Hello, Mr. Oda. In volume 53, chapter 518, Luffy was unaffected by Boa Hancock's Love-Love Mellow, but he did react to Nami's "Happiness Punch" in chapter 213 of volume 23. Why was Nami's body effective against him but not the Snake Princess's? Is Nami that much better?

--Kazu

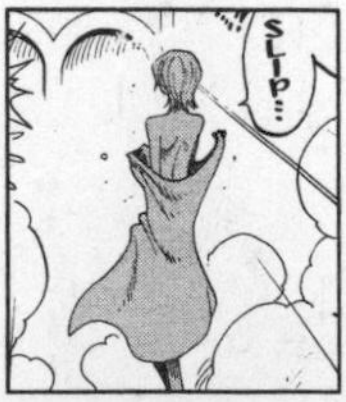
SLIP...

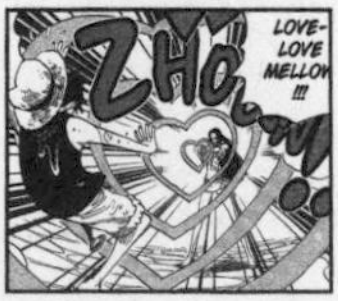
LOVE-LOVE MELLOW!!!

A: I get this question a lot. I'm surprised how many of you guys noticed it! Maybe you should stop reading manga and study harder for school! But then I'm the one drawing this stuff. Anyway, I noticed this when I was drawing it, but I thought everybody would be confused if Luffy got a nosebleed when he saw Hancock's form. As for Luffy reacting to Nami, I think it happened twice: once in volume 18 and again in volume 23. And Usopp was present both times! So he's the culprit here! In other words, Luffy reacted to Hancock as he normally would when he's alone. But Usopp's the same age as Luffy, so when he's around, Luffy behaves like a schoolboy on a field trip! So you see there's no contradiction here! The problem is Usopp!

Chapter 524:
UNSTOPPABLE

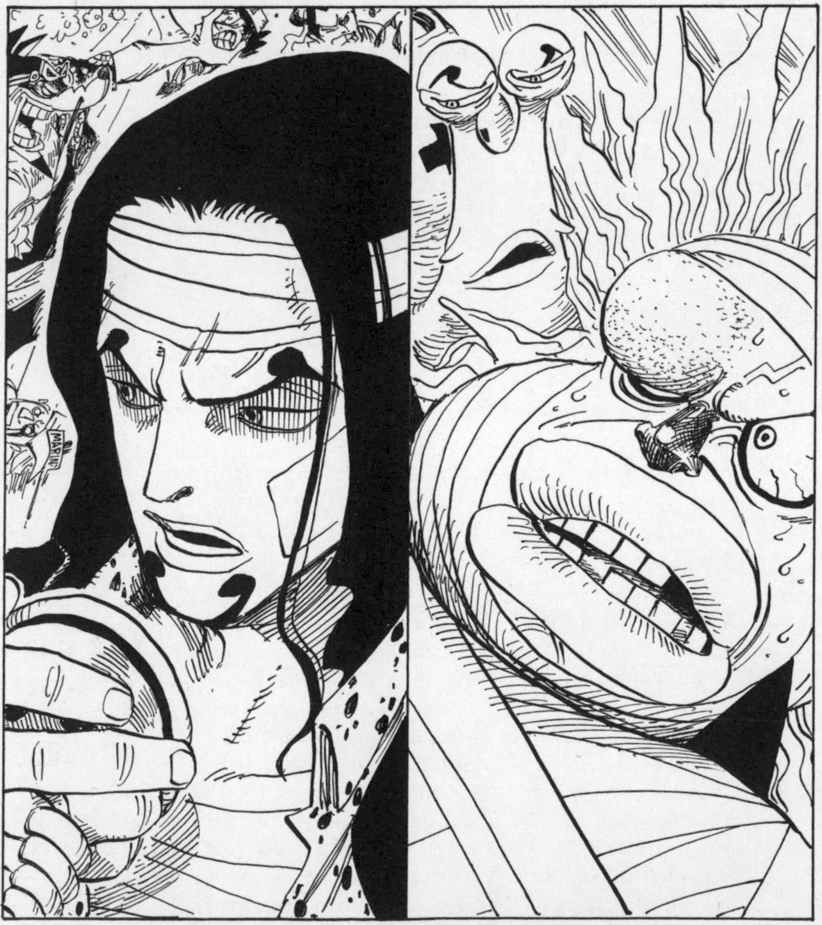

CP9 INDEPENDENT REPORT, VOL. 30:
"THIS IS YOUR FORMER SUBORDINATE, ROB LUCCI."

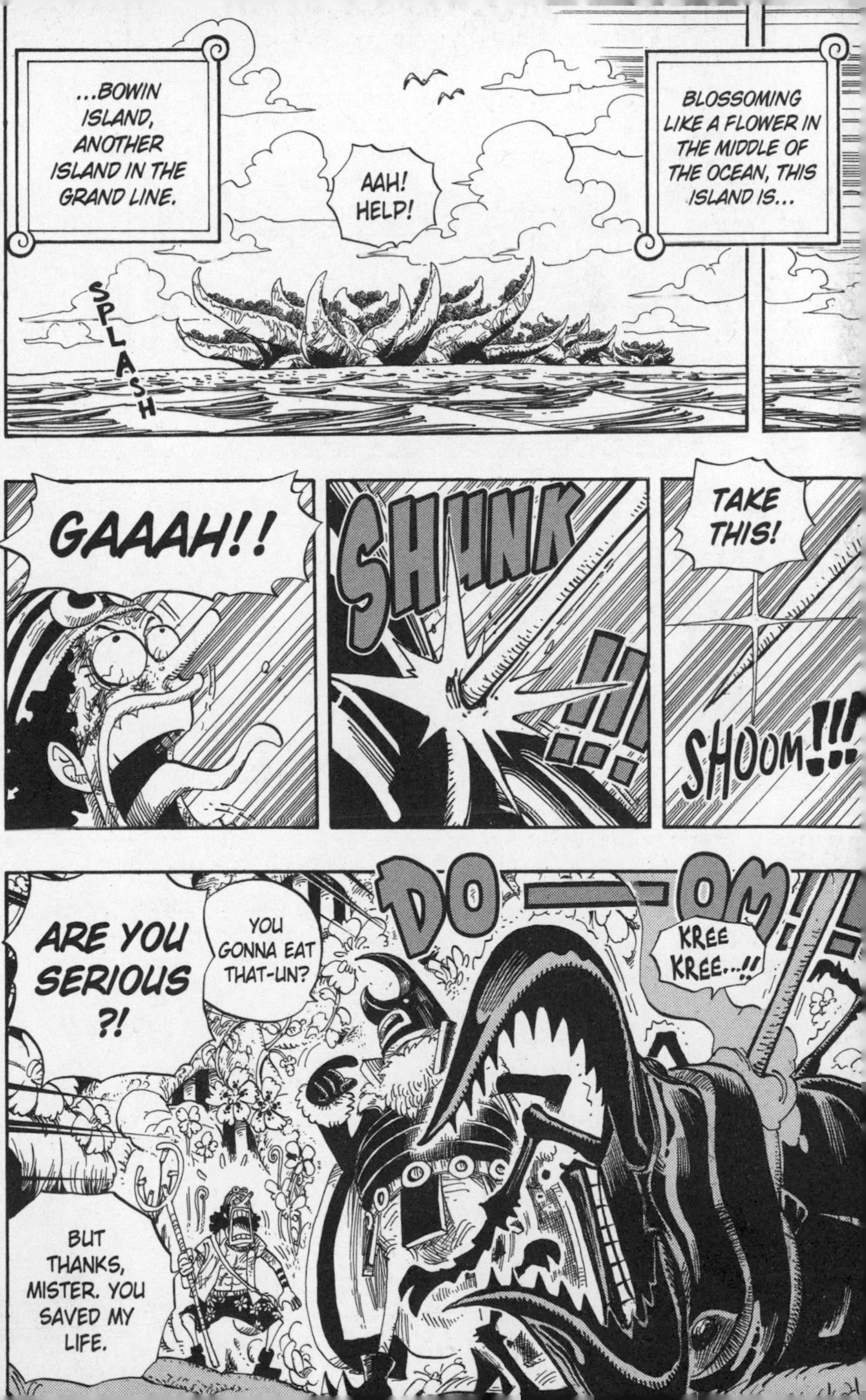
BLOSSOMING LIKE A FLOWER IN THE MIDDLE OF THE OCEAN, THIS ISLAND IS...
AAH! HELP!
...BOWIN ISLAND, ANOTHER ISLAND IN THE GRAND LINE.
SPLASH
TAKE THIS!
SHOOM!!!
SHUNK!!
GAAAH!!
DO-OM!!
KREE KREE...!!
YOU GONNA EAT THAT-UN?
ARE YOU SERIOUS?!
BUT THANKS, MISTER. YOU SAVED MY LIFE.

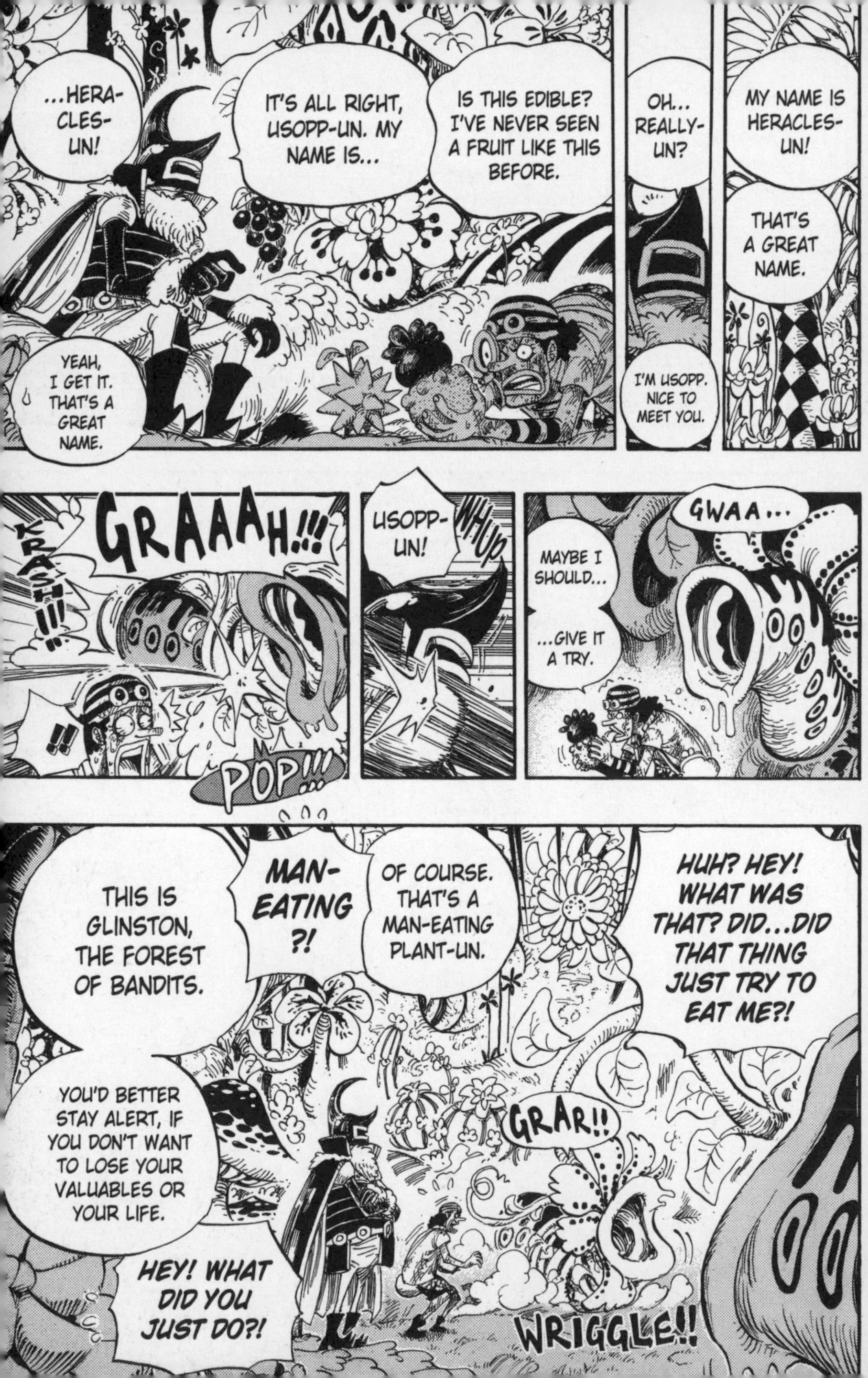
MY NAME IS HERACLES-UN!
THAT'S A GREAT NAME.
OH... REALLY-UN?
I'M USOPP. NICE TO MEET YOU.
IS THIS EDIBLE? I'VE NEVER SEEN A FRUIT LIKE THIS BEFORE.
IT'S ALL RIGHT, USOPP-UN. MY NAME IS...
...HERA-CLES-UN!
YEAH, I GET IT. THAT'S A GREAT NAME.
GWAA...
MAYBE I SHOULD...
...GIVE IT A TRY.
WHUP
USOPP-UN!
GRAAAH!!!
KRASH!!!
!!
POP!!!
HUH? HEY! WHAT WAS THAT? DID...DID THAT THING JUST TRY TO EAT ME?!
OF COURSE. THAT'S A MAN-EATING PLANT-UN.
MAN-EATING?!
THIS IS GLINSTON, THE FOREST OF BANDITS.
GRAR!!
YOU'D BETTER STAY ALERT, IF YOU DON'T WANT TO LOSE YOUR VALUABLES OR YOUR LIFE.
WRIGGLE!!
HEY! WHAT DID YOU JUST DO?!

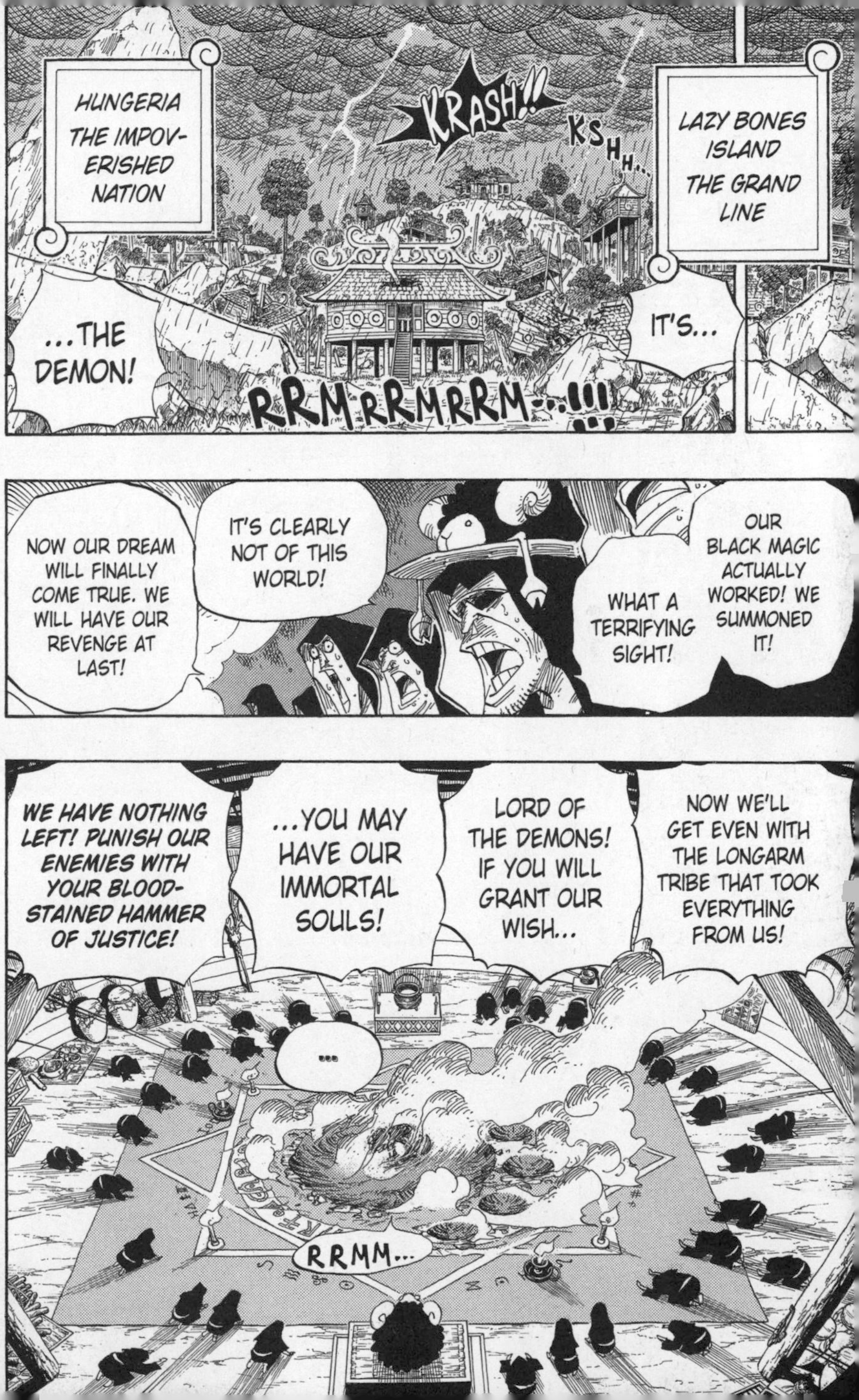
LAZY BONES ISLAND THE GRAND LINE
HUNGERIA THE IMPOVERISHED NATION
KRASH!!
KSHH...
IT'S...
...THE DEMON!
RRMRRMRRM...!!!
OUR BLACK MAGIC ACTUALLY WORKED! WE SUMMONED IT!
WHAT A TERRIFYING SIGHT!
IT'S CLEARLY NOT OF THIS WORLD!
NOW OUR DREAM WILL FINALLY COME TRUE. WE WILL HAVE OUR REVENGE AT LAST!
NOW WE'LL GET EVEN WITH THE LONGARM TRIBE THAT TOOK EVERYTHING FROM US!
LORD OF THE DEMONS! IF YOU WILL GRANT OUR WISH...
...YOU MAY HAVE OUR IMMORTAL SOULS!
WE HAVE NOTHING LEFT! PUNISH OUR ENEMIES WITH YOUR BLOOD-STAINED HAMMER OF JUSTICE!
...
RRMM...

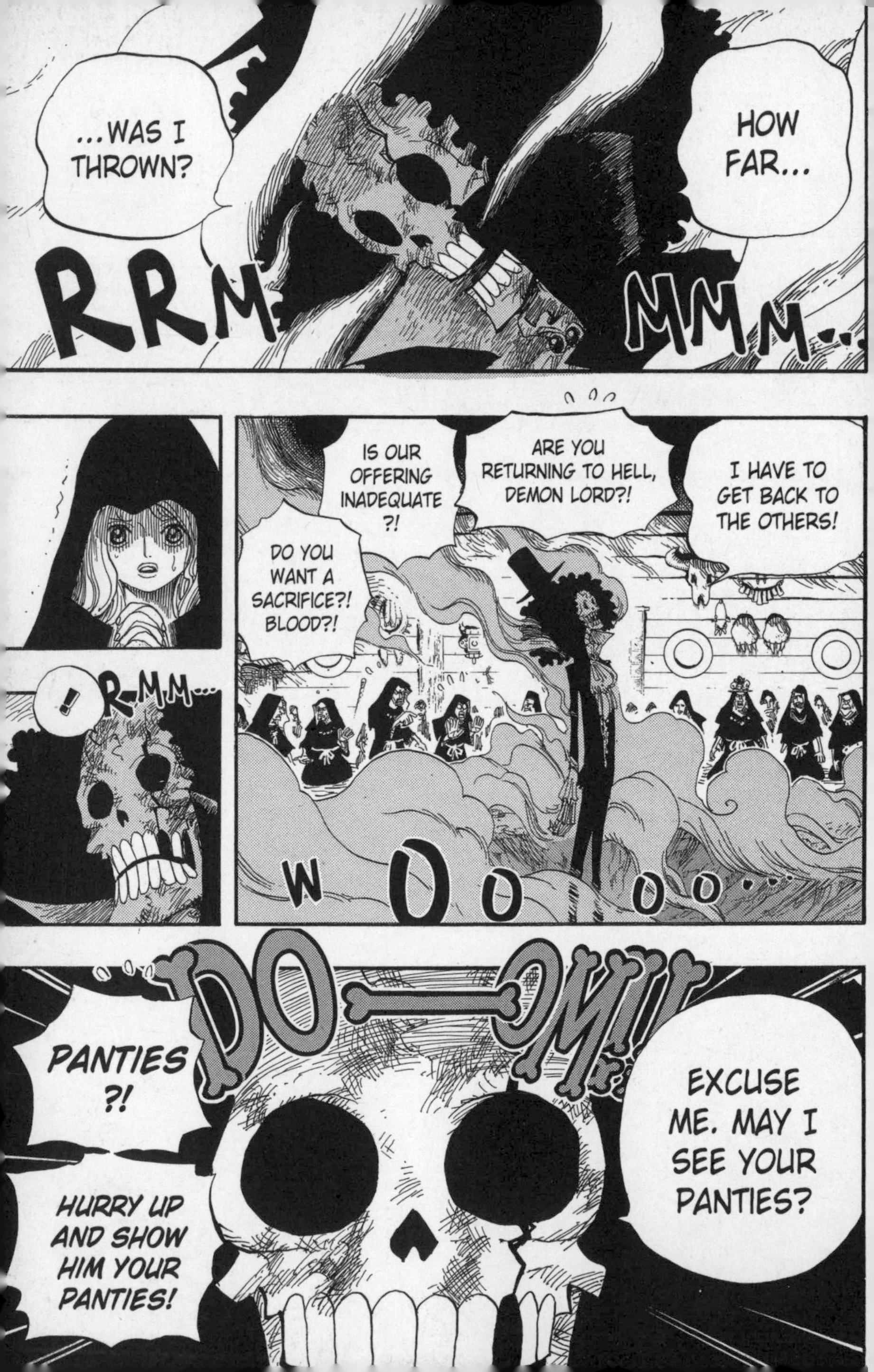
HOW FAR...
...WAS I THROWN?
RRM MMM...
I HAVE TO GET BACK TO THE OTHERS!
ARE YOU RETURNING TO HELL, DEMON LORD?!
IS OUR OFFERING INADEQUATE ?!
DO YOU WANT A SACRIFICE?! BLOOD?!
WOOOO...
!
RMM...
EXCUSE ME. MAY I SEE YOUR PANTIES?
DO—OM!!
PANTIES ?!
HURRY UP AND SHOW HIM YOUR PANTIES!

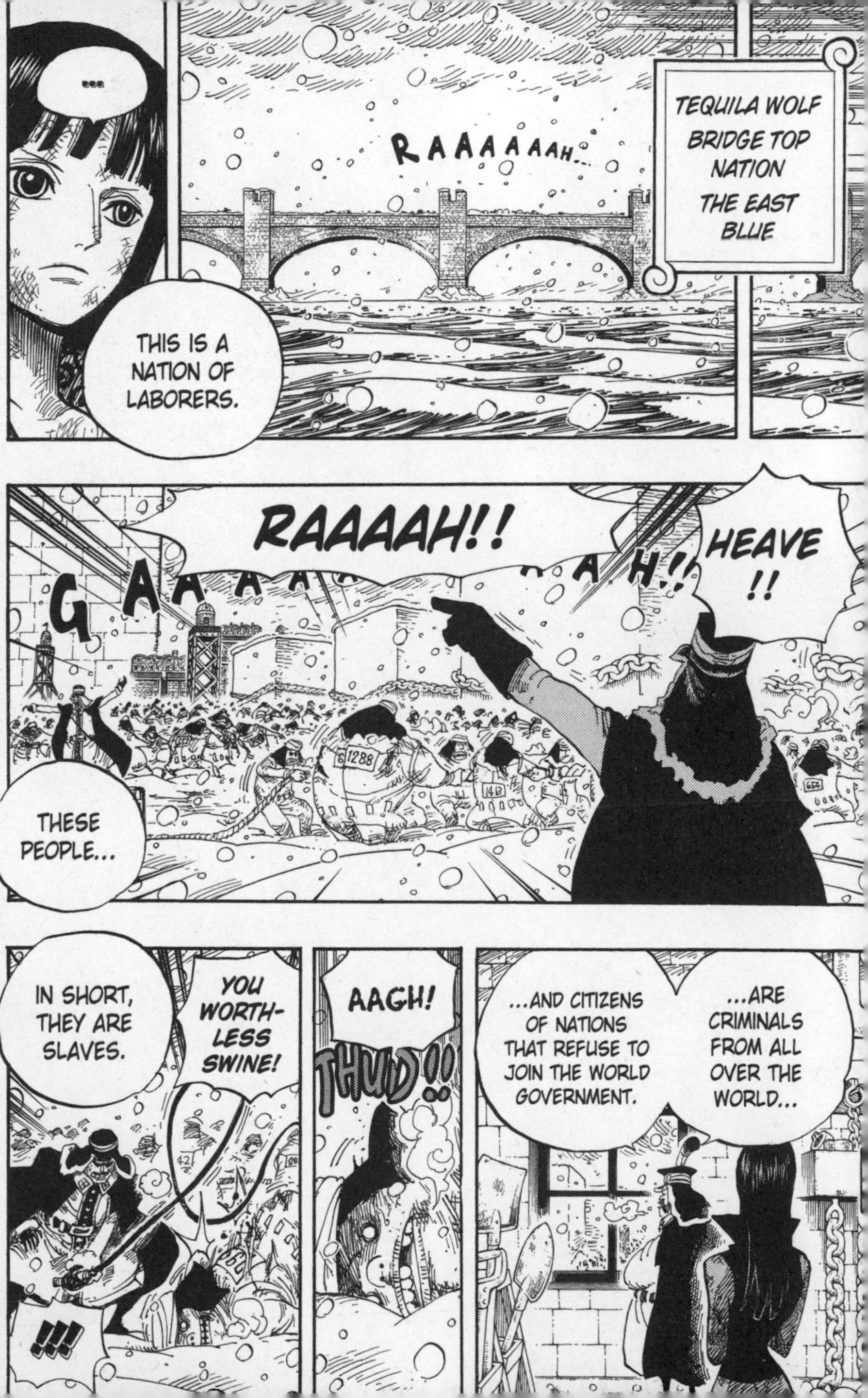
TEQUILA WOLF
BRIDGE TOP NATION
THE EAST BLUE
RAAAAAAH...
...
THIS IS A NATION OF LABORERS.
HEAVE !!
RAAAAH!!
THESE PEOPLE...
...ARE CRIMINALS FROM ALL OVER THE WORLD...
...AND CITIZENS OF NATIONS THAT REFUSE TO JOIN THE WORLD GOVERNMENT.
AAGH!
THUD!!
YOU WORTH-LESS SWINE!
IN SHORT, THEY ARE SLAVES.
!!!

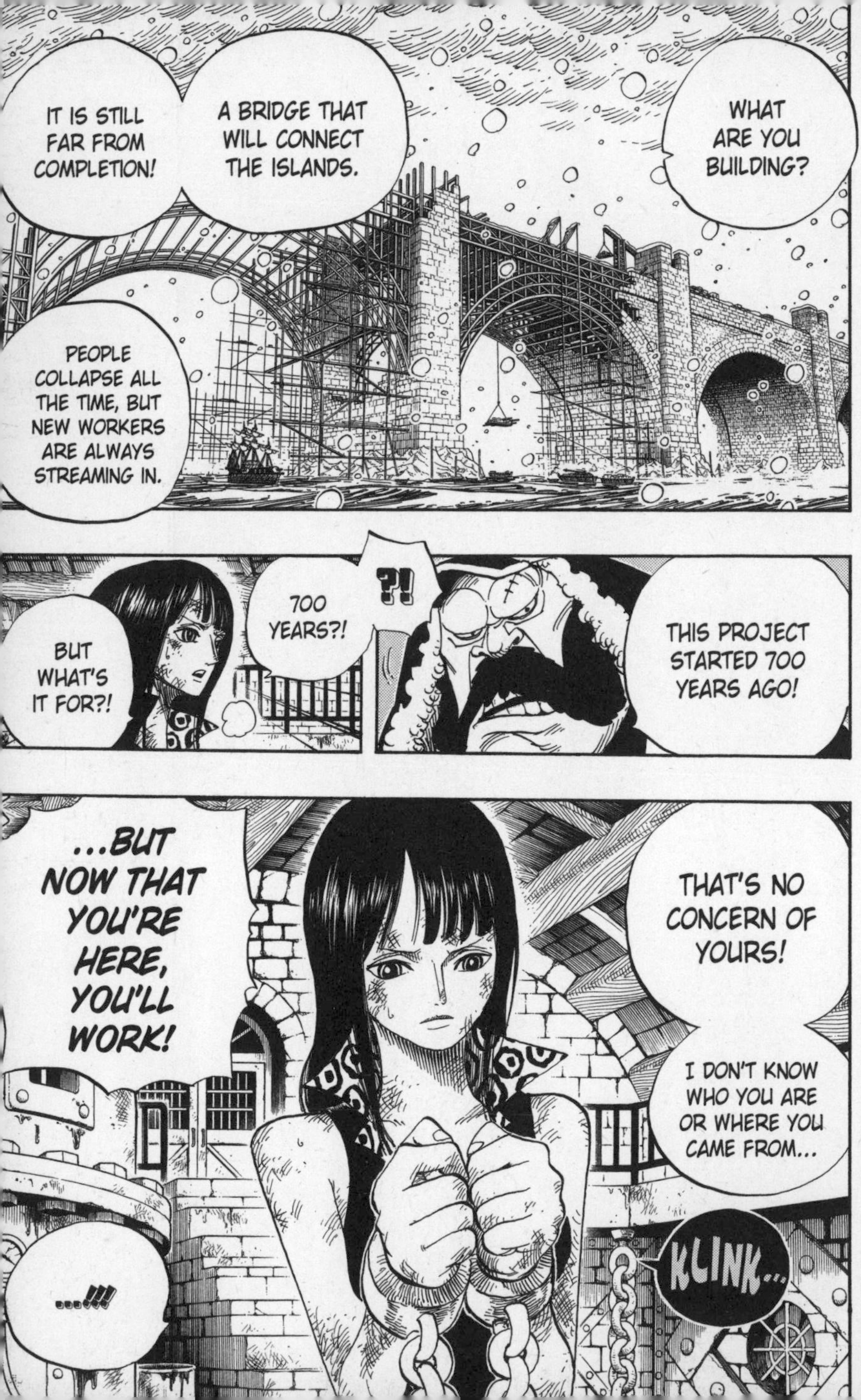
WHAT ARE YOU BUILDING?
A BRIDGE THAT WILL CONNECT THE ISLANDS.
IT IS STILL FAR FROM COMPLETION!
PEOPLE COLLAPSE ALL THE TIME, BUT NEW WORKERS ARE ALWAYS STREAMING IN.
THIS PROJECT STARTED 700 YEARS AGO!
?!
700 YEARS?!
BUT WHAT'S IT FOR?!
THAT'S NO CONCERN OF YOURS!
I DON'T KNOW WHO YOU ARE OR WHERE YOU CAME FROM...
...BUT NOW THAT YOU'RE HERE, YOU'LL WORK!
KLINK...
...!!!

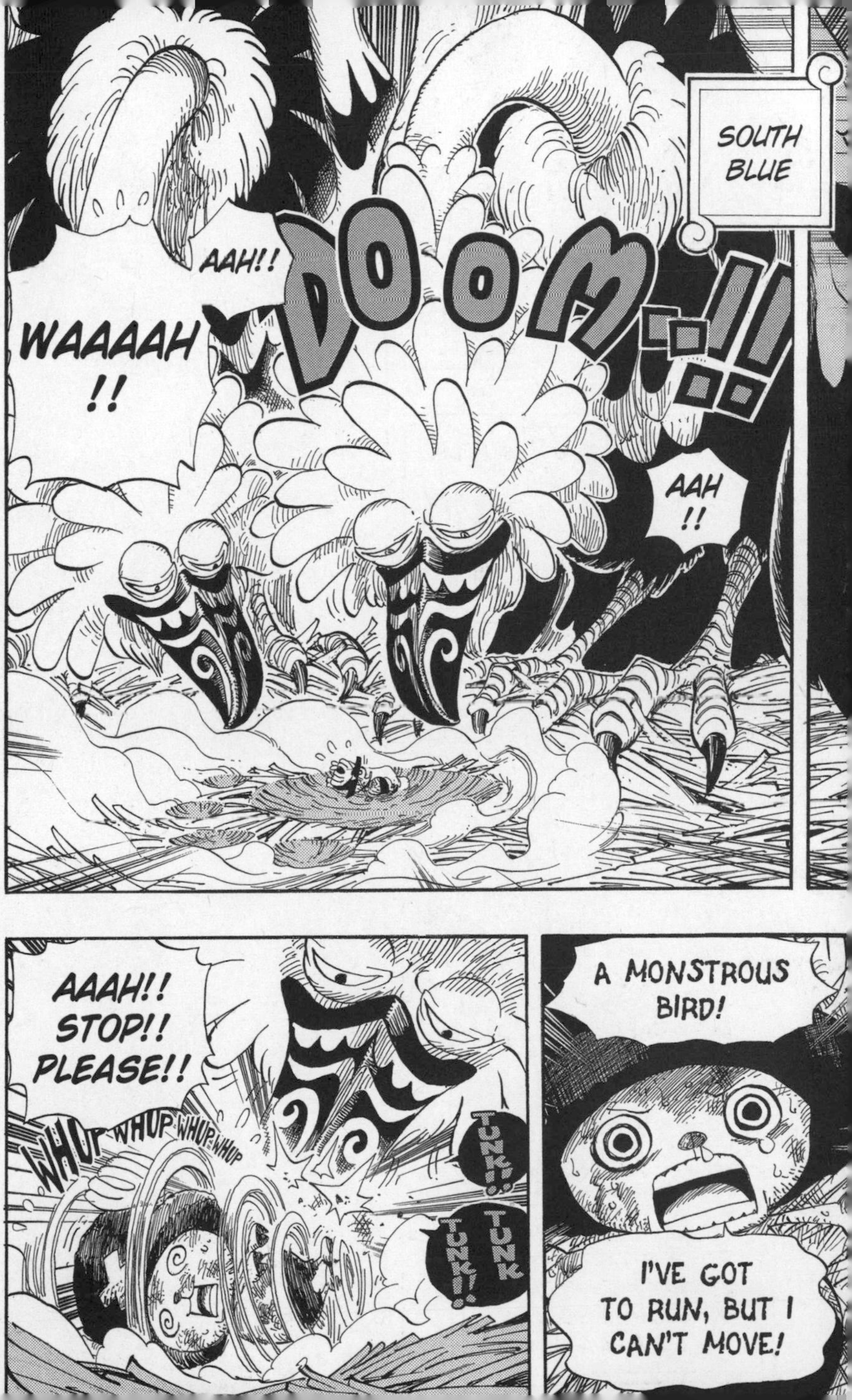
SOUTH BLUE
DOOM..!!
AAH!!
WAAAAH !!
AAH !!
A MONSTROUS BIRD!
I'VE GOT TO RUN, BUT I CAN'T MOVE!
AAAH!! STOP!! PLEASE!!
TUNK!!
TUNK
TUNK!!
WHUP WHUP WHUP WHUP

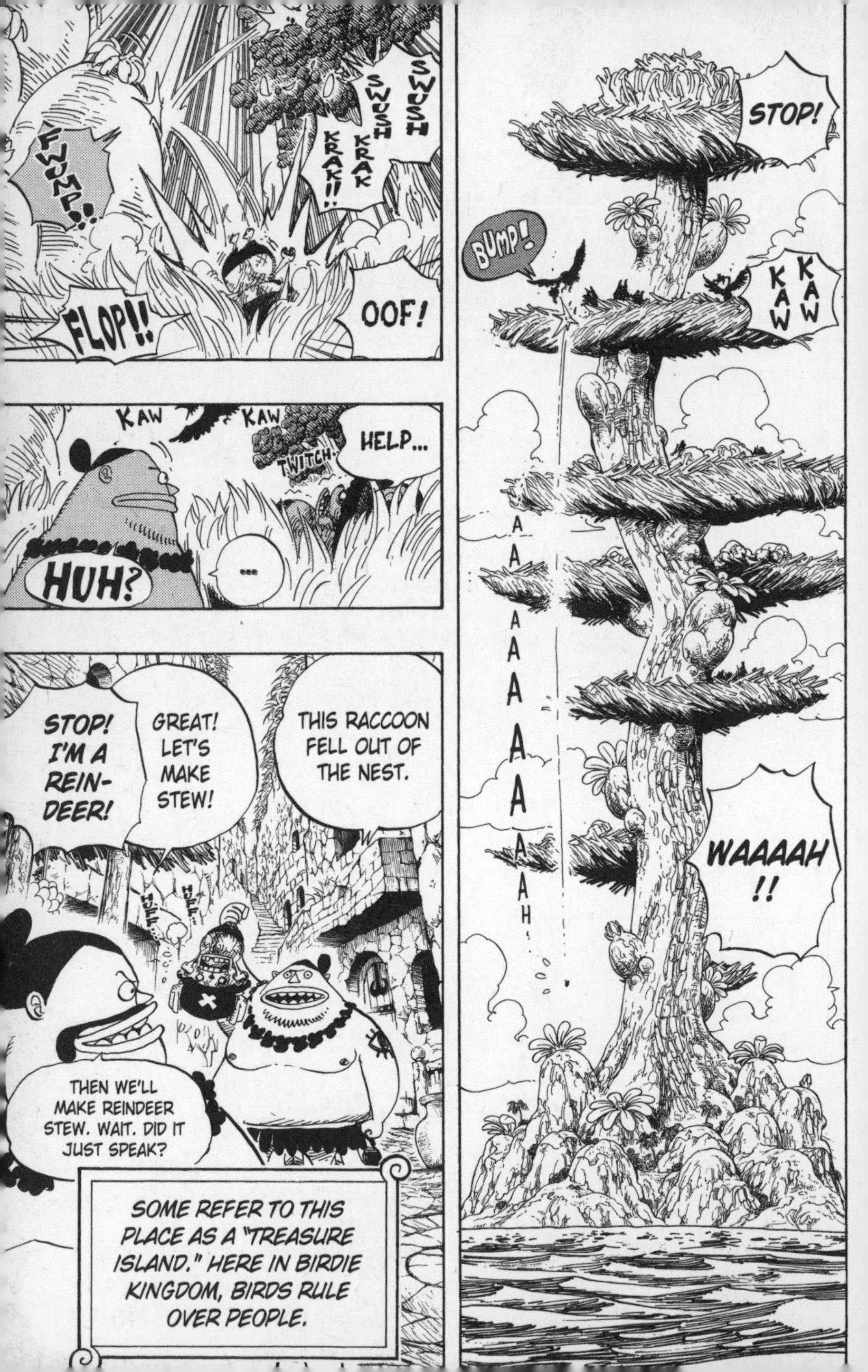
STOP!
KAW KAW
BUMP!
WAAAAH!!
AAAAAAAAAAH
SWUSH SWUSH
KRAK KRAK!!
FWUMP!!
OOF!
FLOP!!
HELP...
KAW KAW
TWITCH
HUH?
...
THIS RACCOON FELL OUT OF THE NEST.
GREAT! LET'S MAKE STEW!
STOP! I'M A REIN-DEER!
HUFF... HUFF...
THEN WE'LL MAKE REINDEER STEW. WAIT. DID IT JUST SPEAK?
SOME REFER TO THIS PLACE AS A "TREASURE ISLAND." HERE IN BIRDIE KINGDOM, BIRDS RULE OVER PEOPLE.

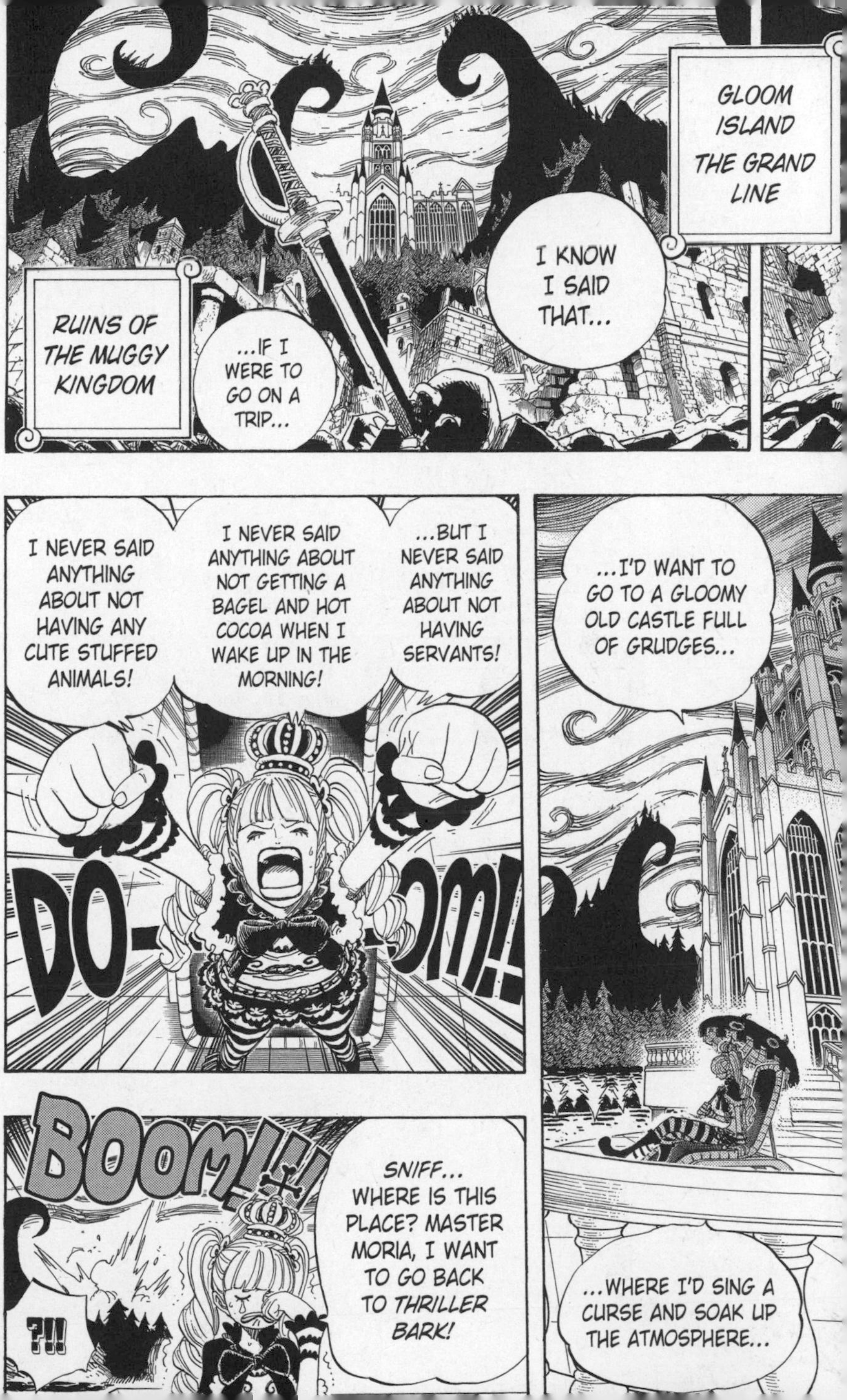
GLOOM ISLAND THE GRAND LINE
I KNOW I SAID THAT...
...IF I WERE TO GO ON A TRIP...
RUINS OF THE MUGGY KINGDOM
...I'D WANT TO GO TO A GLOOMY OLD CASTLE FULL OF GRUDGES...
...WHERE I'D SING A CURSE AND SOAK UP THE ATMOSPHERE...
...BUT I NEVER SAID ANYTHING ABOUT NOT HAVING SERVANTS!
I NEVER SAID ANYTHING ABOUT NOT GETTING A BAGEL AND HOT COCOA WHEN I WAKE UP IN THE MORNING!
I NEVER SAID ANYTHING ABOUT NOT HAVING ANY CUTE STUFFED ANIMALS!
DO-OM!!
SNIFF... WHERE IS THIS PLACE? MASTER MORIA, I WANT TO GO BACK TO THRILLER BARK!
BOOM!!!
?!!

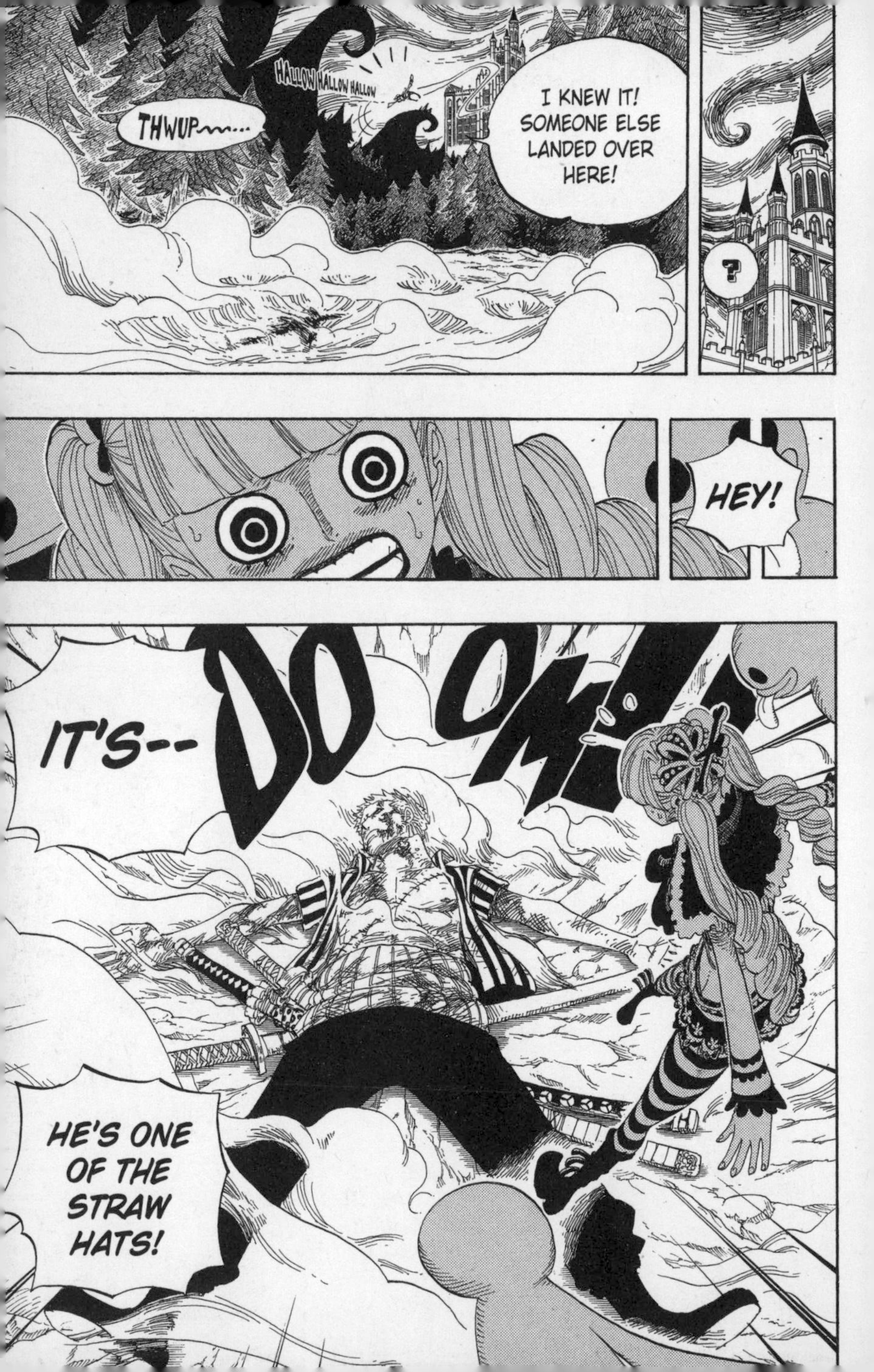
?
I KNEW IT! SOMEONE ELSE LANDED OVER HERE!
HALLOW HALLOW HALLOW
THWUP~~...
HEY!
DOOM!!
IT'S--
HE'S ONE OF THE STRAW HATS!

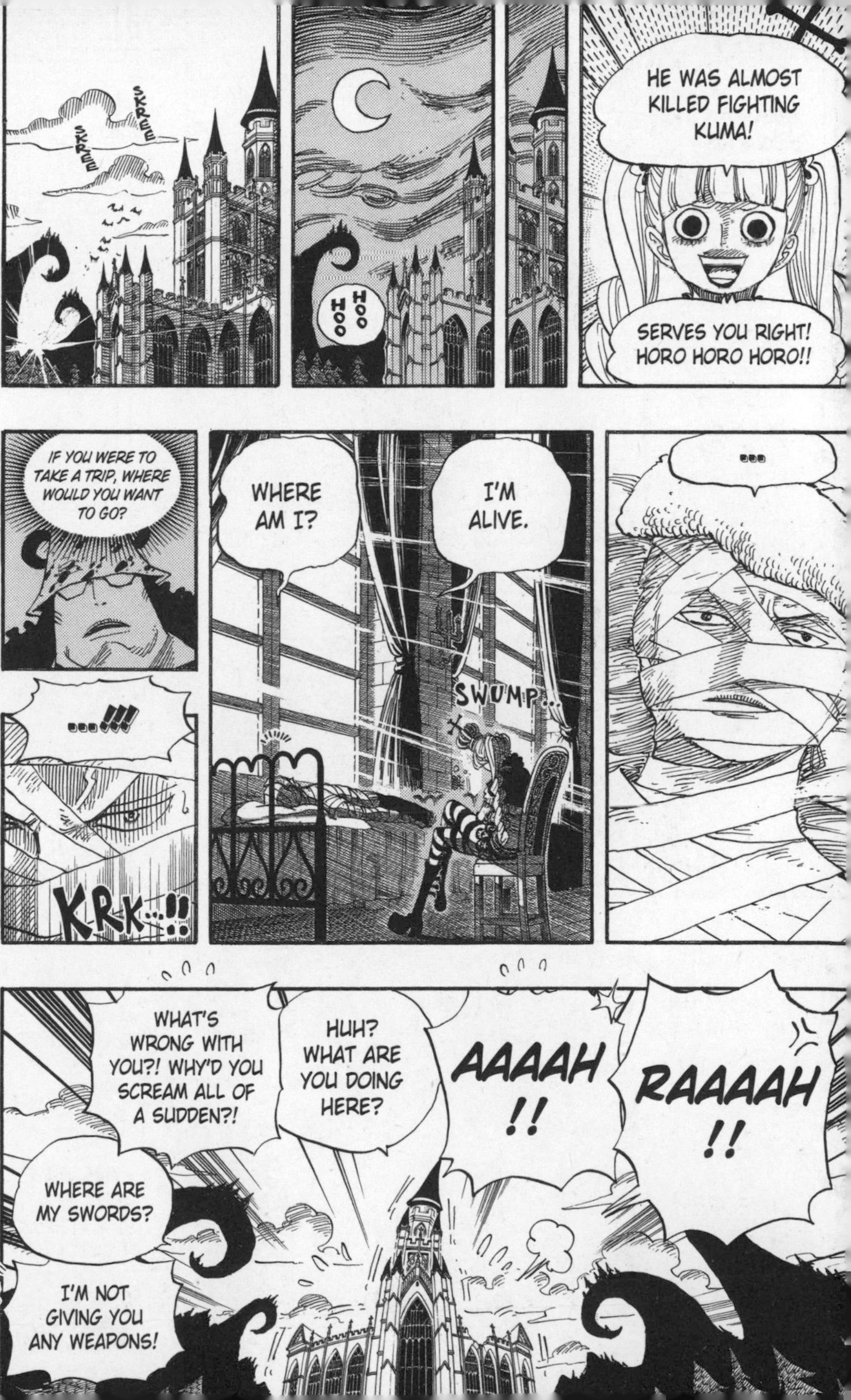
HE WAS ALMOST KILLED FIGHTING KUMA!
SERVES YOU RIGHT! HORO HORO HORO!!
HOO HOO
SKREE
SKREE
...
I'M ALIVE.
WHERE AM I?
SWUMP...
IF YOU WERE TO TAKE A TRIP, WHERE WOULD YOU WANT TO GO?
...!!!
KRK...!!
RAAAAH!!
AAAAH!!
HUH? WHAT ARE YOU DOING HERE?
WHAT'S WRONG WITH YOU?! WHY'D YOU SCREAM ALL OF A SUDDEN?!
WHERE ARE MY SWORDS?
I'M NOT GIVING YOU ANY WEAPONS!

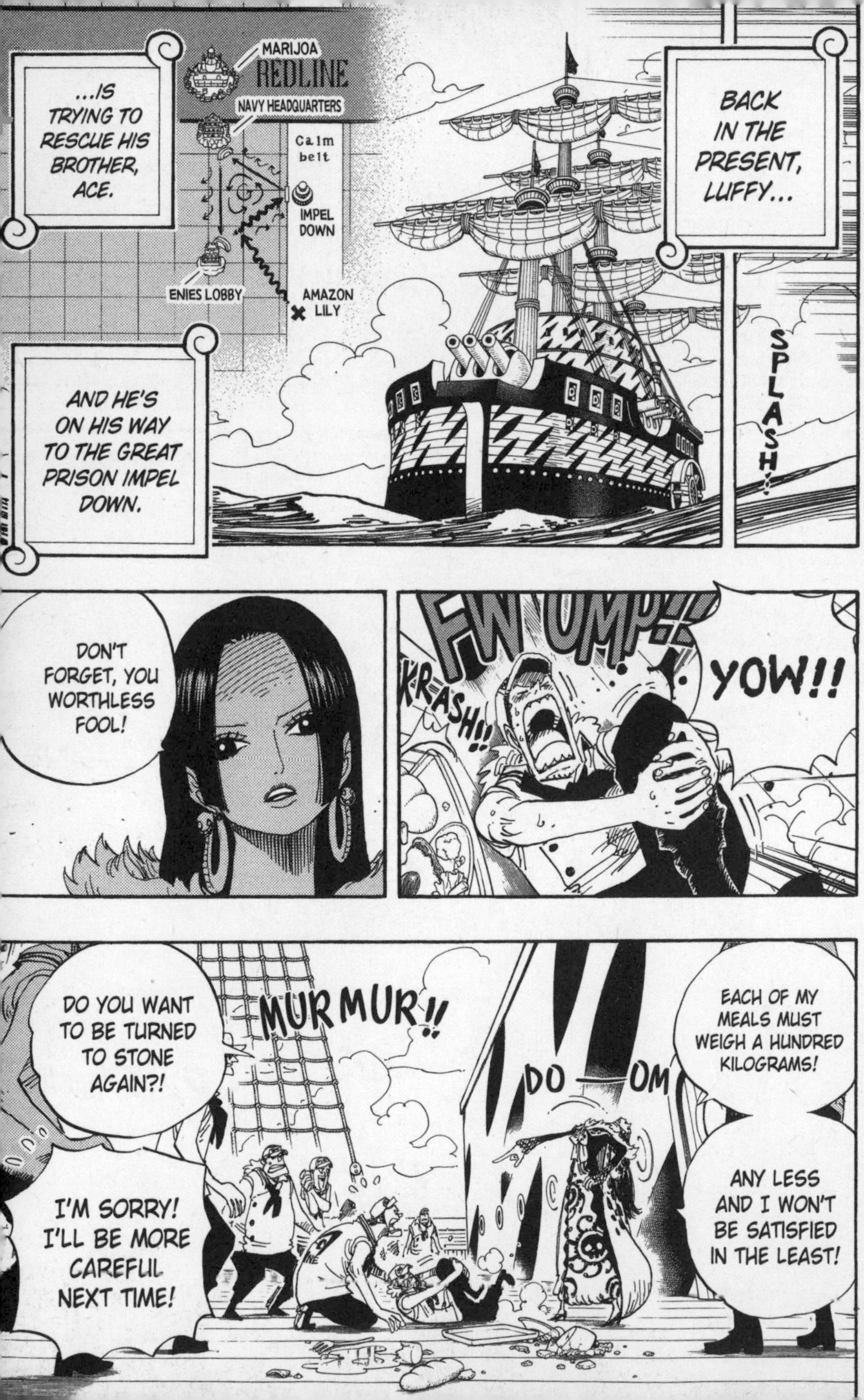
BACK IN THE PRESENT, LUFFY...
SPLASH!!
...IS TRYING TO RESCUE HIS BROTHER, ACE.
MARIJOA
REDLINE
NAVY HEADQUARTERS
Calm belt
IMPEL DOWN
ENIES LOBBY
AMAZON LILY
AND HE'S ON HIS WAY TO THE GREAT PRISON IMPEL DOWN.
FWUMP!!
KRASH!!
YOW!!
DON'T FORGET, YOU WORTHLESS FOOL!
EACH OF MY MEALS MUST WEIGH A HUNDRED KILOGRAMS!
ANY LESS AND I WON'T BE SATISFIED IN THE LEAST!
DO—OM
MURMUR!!
DO YOU WANT TO BE TURNED TO STONE AGAIN?!
I'M SORRY! I'LL BE MORE CAREFUL NEXT TIME!

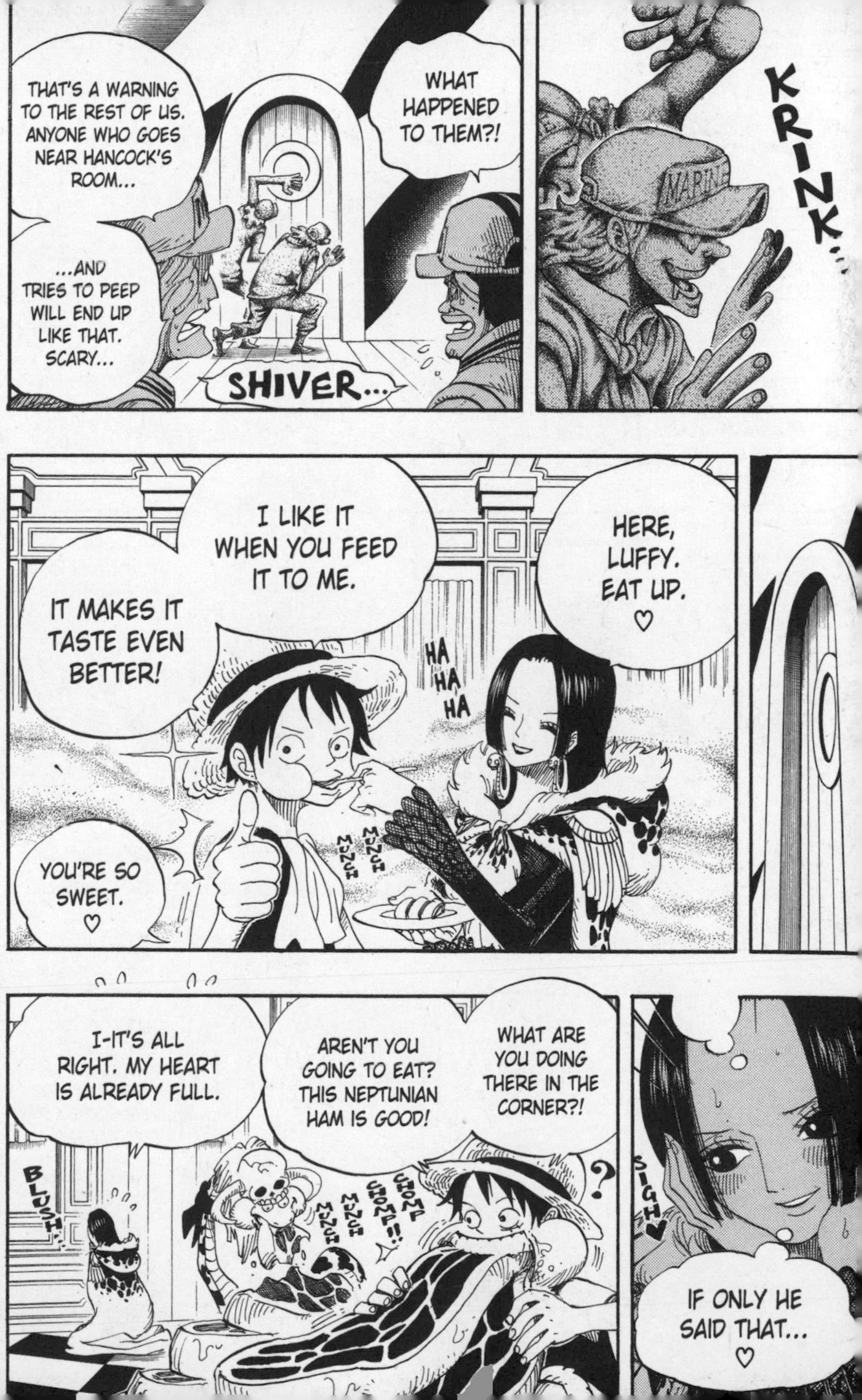
KRINK...
WHAT HAPPENED TO THEM?!
THAT'S A WARNING TO THE REST OF US. ANYONE WHO GOES NEAR HANCOCK'S ROOM...
...AND TRIES TO PEEP WILL END UP LIKE THAT. SCARY...
SHIVER...
HERE, LUFFY. EAT UP. ♡
HA HA HA
I LIKE IT WHEN YOU FEED IT TO ME.
IT MAKES IT TASTE EVEN BETTER!
MUNCH MUNCH
YOU'RE SO SWEET. ♡
SIGH♥
IF ONLY HE SAID THAT... ♡
WHAT ARE YOU DOING THERE IN THE CORNER?!
AREN'T YOU GOING TO EAT? THIS NEPTUNIAN HAM IS GOOD!
CHOMP CHOMP!!
?
MUNCH MUNCH
I-IT'S ALL RIGHT. MY HEART IS ALREADY FULL.
BLUSH...

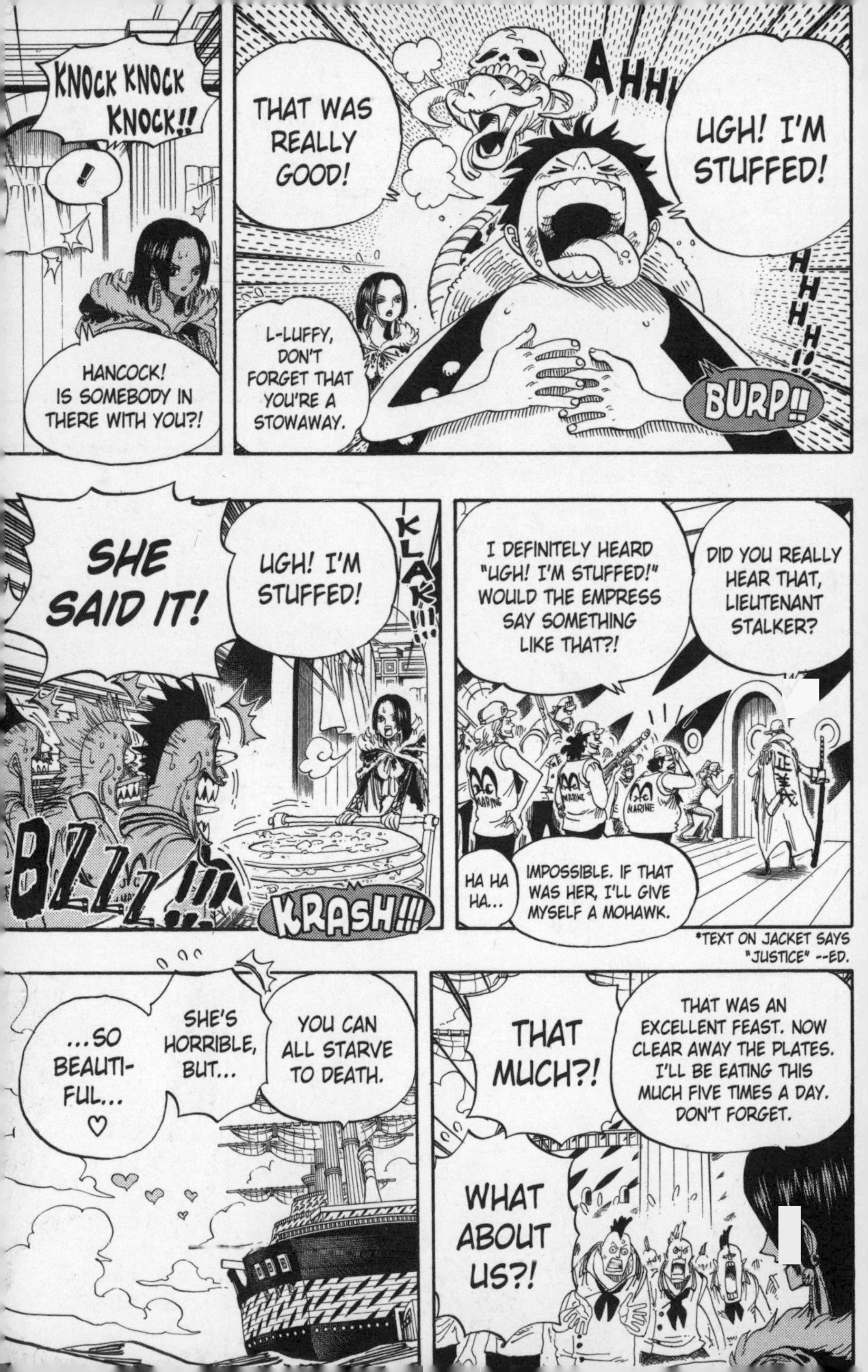
UGH! I'M STUFFED!
AHHHHHHH!!
THAT WAS REALLY GOOD!
BURP!!
L-LUFFY, DON'T FORGET THAT YOU'RE A STOWAWAY.
KNOCK KNOCK KNOCK!!
!
HANCOCK! IS SOMEBODY IN THERE WITH YOU?!
DID YOU REALLY HEAR THAT, LIEUTENANT STALKER?
I DEFINITELY HEARD "UGH! I'M STUFFED!" WOULD THE EMPRESS SAY SOMETHING LIKE THAT?!
IMPOSSIBLE. IF THAT WAS HER, I'LL GIVE MYSELF A MOHAWK.
HA HA HA...
*TEXT ON JACKET SAYS "JUSTICE" --ED.
KLAK!!!
UGH! I'M STUFFED!
SHE SAID IT!
KRASH!!!
BZZZZ!!!
THAT WAS AN EXCELLENT FEAST. NOW CLEAR AWAY THE PLATES. I'LL BE EATING THIS MUCH FIVE TIMES A DAY. DON'T FORGET.
THAT MUCH?!
WHAT ABOUT US?!
YOU CAN ALL STARVE TO DEATH.
SHE'S HORRIBLE, BUT...
...SO BEAUTIFUL... ♡

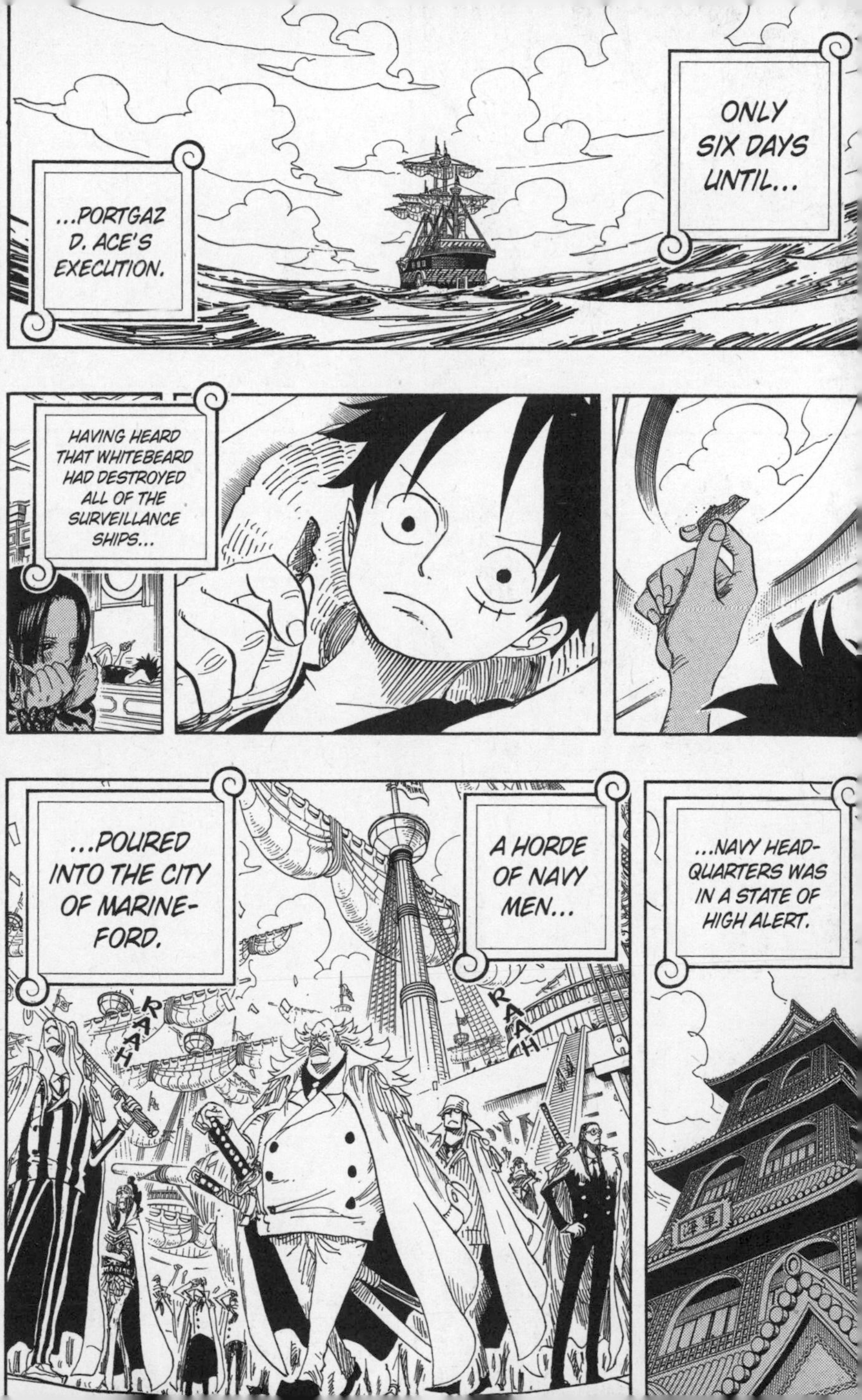
ONLY SIX DAYS UNTIL...
...PORTGAZ D. ACE'S EXECUTION.
HAVING HEARD THAT WHITEBEARD HAD DESTROYED ALL OF THE SURVEILLANCE SHIPS...
...NAVY HEAD-QUARTERS WAS IN A STATE OF HIGH ALERT.
A HORDE OF NAVY MEN...
...POURED INTO THE CITY OF MARINE-FORD.
RAAH
RAAH

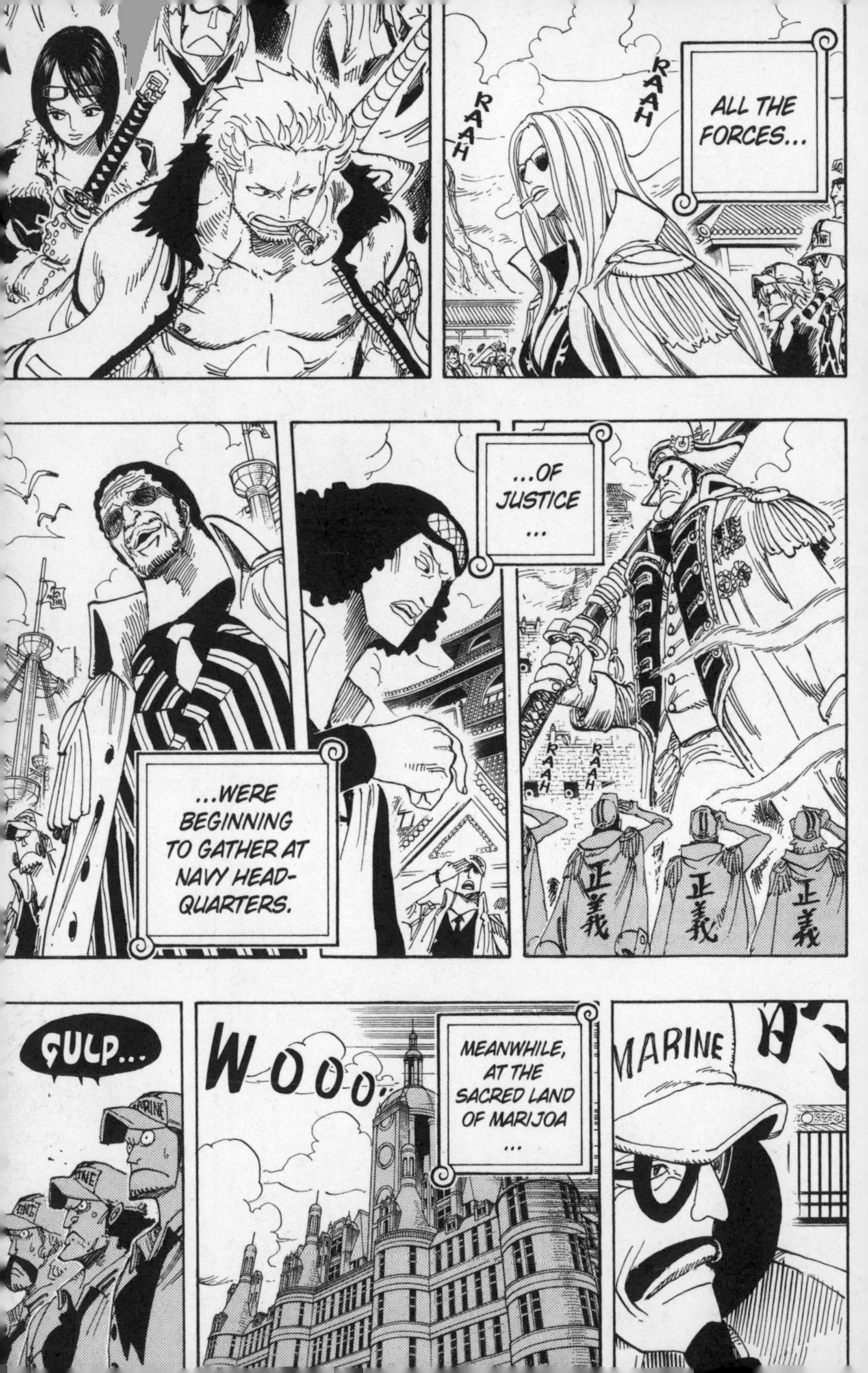
ALL THE FORCES...
RAAH
RAAH
...OF JUSTICE ...
RAAH
RAAH
...WERE BEGINNING TO GATHER AT NAVY HEAD-QUARTERS.
MARINE
MEANWHILE, AT THE SACRED LAND OF MARIJOA ...
WOOO...
GULP...

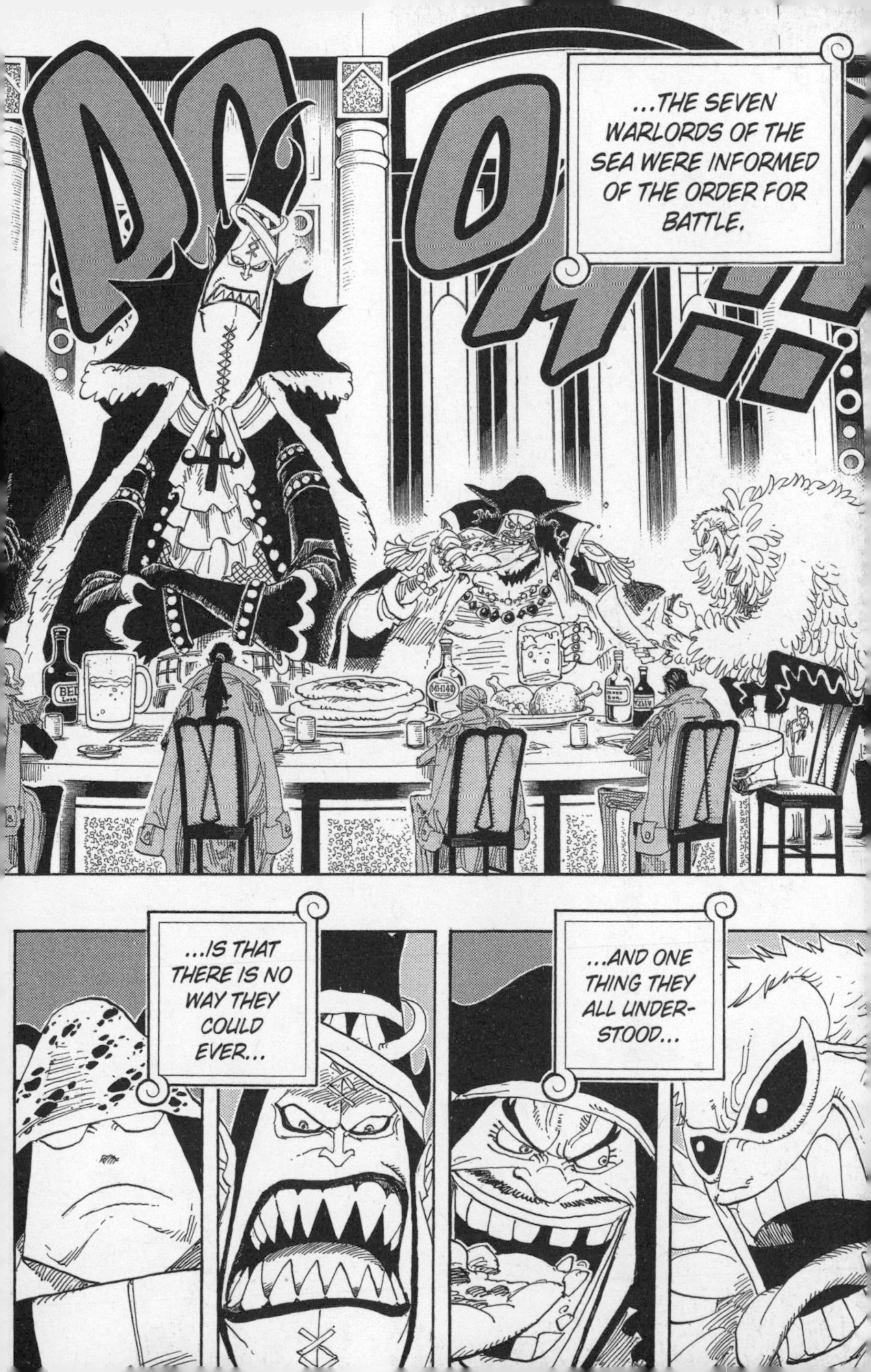
...THE SEVEN WARLORDS OF THE SEA WERE INFORMED OF THE ORDER FOR BATTLE.
...AND ONE THING THEY ALL UNDER-STOOD...
...IS THAT THERE IS NO WAY THEY COULD EVER...

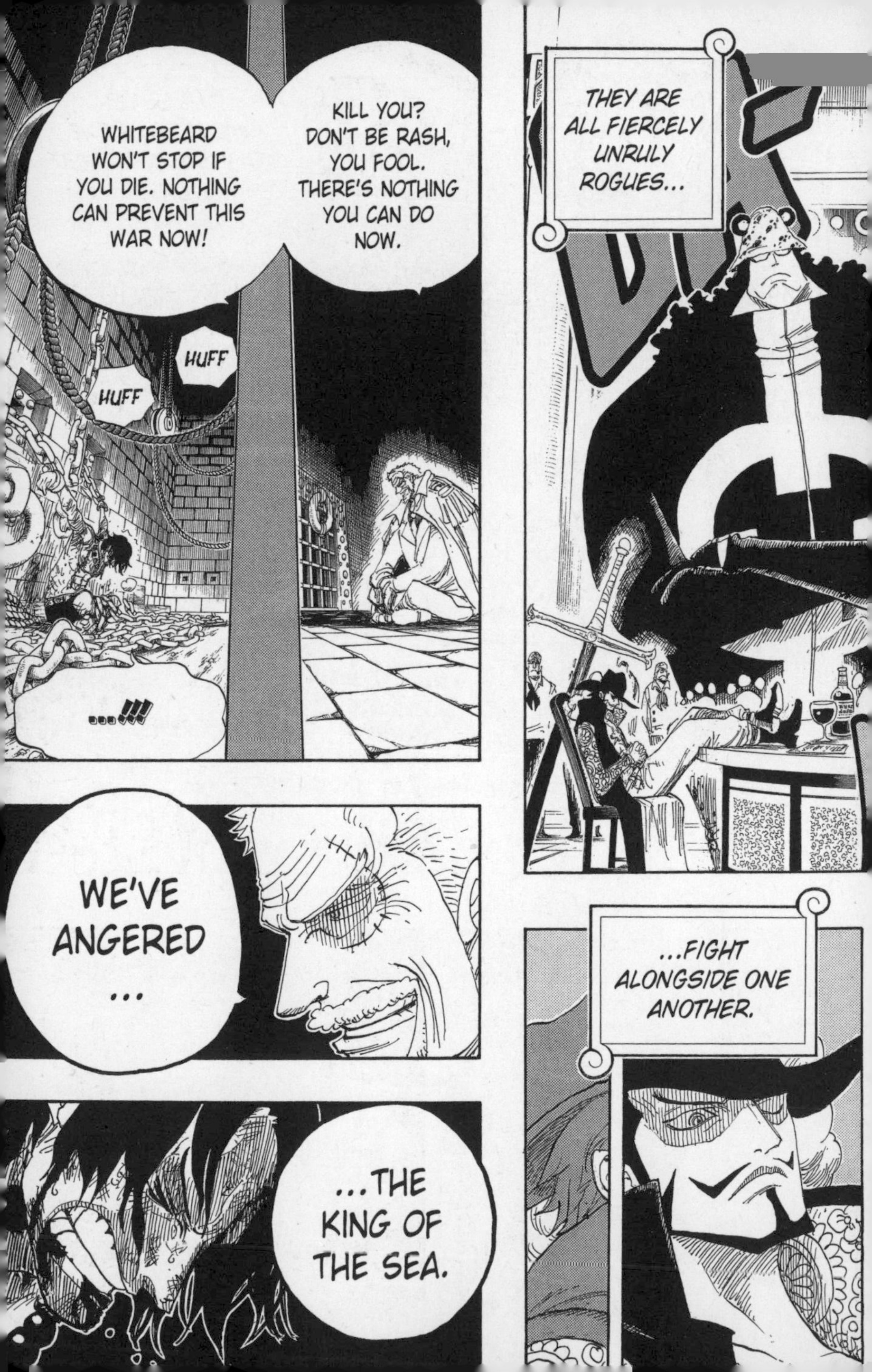
THEY ARE ALL FIERCELY UNRULY ROGUES...
...FIGHT ALONGSIDE ONE ANOTHER.
KILL YOU? DON'T BE RASH, YOU FOOL. THERE'S NOTHING YOU CAN DO NOW.
WHITEBEARD WON'T STOP IF YOU DIE. NOTHING CAN PREVENT THIS WAR NOW!
HUFF
HUFF
...!!!
WE'VE ANGERED ...
...THE KING OF THE SEA.

SBS Question Corner

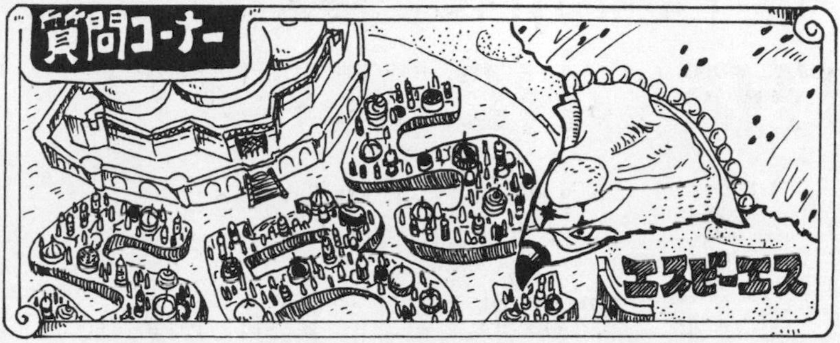

質問コーナー
エスビーエス

(Mari Chiba, Iwate)

Q: Hello, I am an avid reader of *One Piece*. Here's my question. I reread the whole series from volume 1, and I noticed that Luffy almost never has any sort of internal dialogue. Why is that?

--Aqua Ribbon

A: And you didn't see this until volume 54? It's my policy to depict things in a certain way. It's just one of those things I decided to do from the beginning. In Luffy's case:

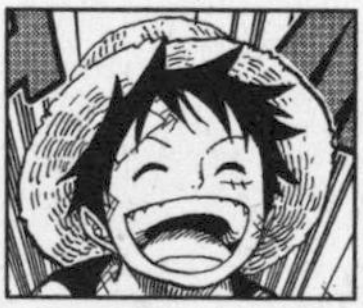

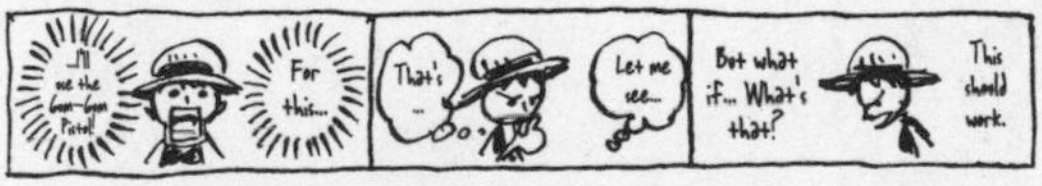

This should work.
But what if... What's that?
Let me see...
That's...
For this...
...I'll use the Gum-Gum Pistol!

I make a conscious effort not to do anything like this. I want the readers to see Luffy as a man of action, so he always thinks out loud or just does something. During the Sky Island arc, I used internal dialogue with Montblanc Cricket, but that hardly counted. Luffy will always act before he thinks.

Q: Mr. Oda, I can't close my zipper! Oh, wait, forget I said that. Anyway, here's my question. Is Wanze one of the Four Emperors? All my friends think that's the case.

--Slacking Pirates

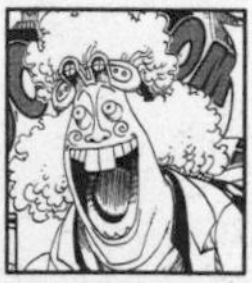

A: How's your zipper?! I'm really worried now.

Q: I have a question. On page 183, in chapter 521, Marigold is so thin! And she looks really pretty too! What happened to her?! Please tell me! ♡

--Chopper Lover ♡

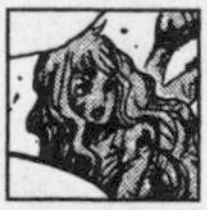

A: She didn't get fat! It's all muscle! She gained weight to get stronger! That's why she worked out and got all those muscles! She had to eat a lot too!

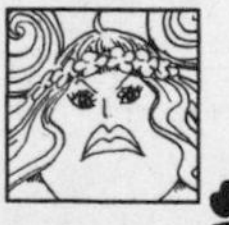

Chapter 525:
THE UNDERWATER PRISON IMPEL DOWN

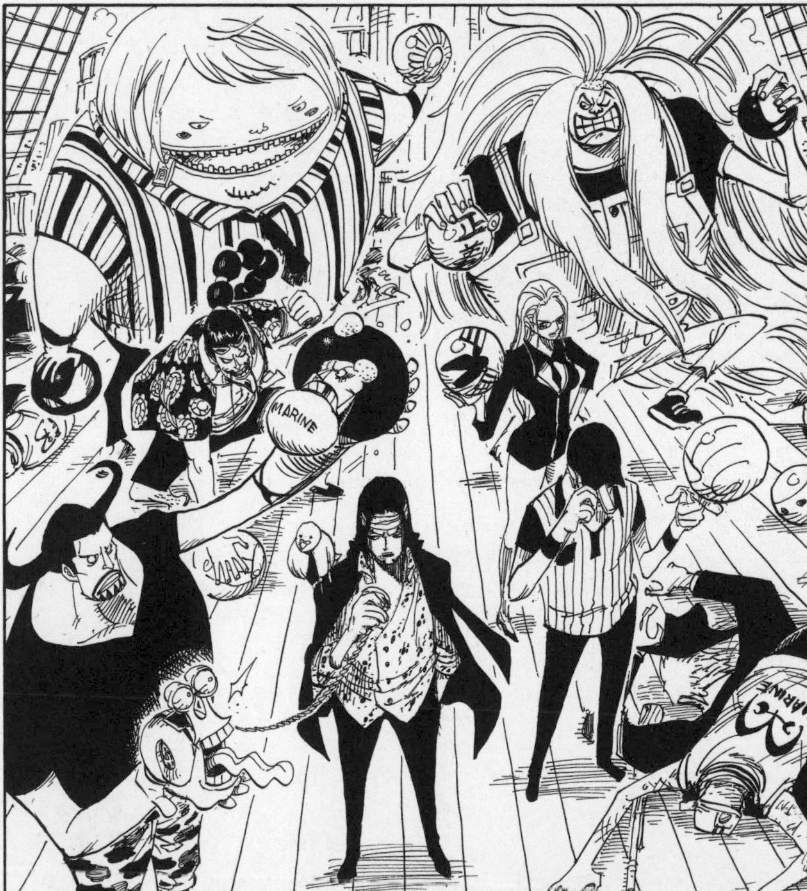

MARINE
MARINE

CP9 INDEPENDENT REPORT, VOL. 31:
"WE WILL RETURN ONE DAY"

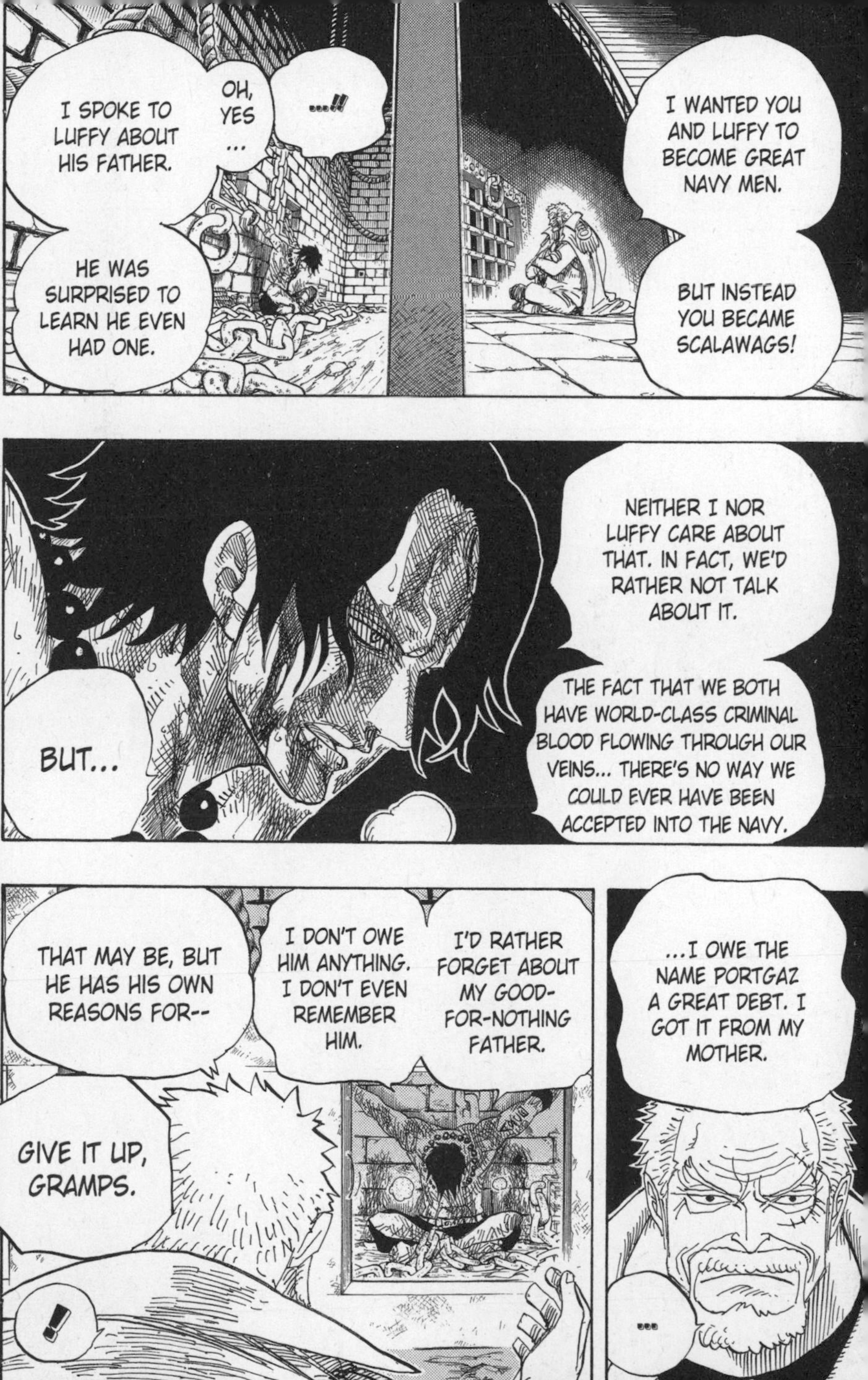
I WANTED YOU AND LUFFY TO BECOME GREAT NAVY MEN.
BUT INSTEAD YOU BECAME SCALAWAGS!
...!!
OH, YES ...
I SPOKE TO LUFFY ABOUT HIS FATHER.
HE WAS SURPRISED TO LEARN HE EVEN HAD ONE.
NEITHER I NOR LUFFY CARE ABOUT THAT. IN FACT, WE'D RATHER NOT TALK ABOUT IT.
THE FACT THAT WE BOTH HAVE WORLD-CLASS CRIMINAL BLOOD FLOWING THROUGH OUR VEINS... THERE'S NO WAY WE COULD EVER HAVE BEEN ACCEPTED INTO THE NAVY.
BUT...
...I OWE THE NAME PORTGAZ A GREAT DEBT. I GOT IT FROM MY MOTHER.
...
I'D RATHER FORGET ABOUT MY GOOD-FOR-NOTHING FATHER.
I DON'T OWE HIM ANYTHING. I DON'T EVEN REMEMBER HIM.
THAT MAY BE, BUT HE HAS HIS OWN REASONS FOR--
GIVE IT UP, GRAMPS.
!

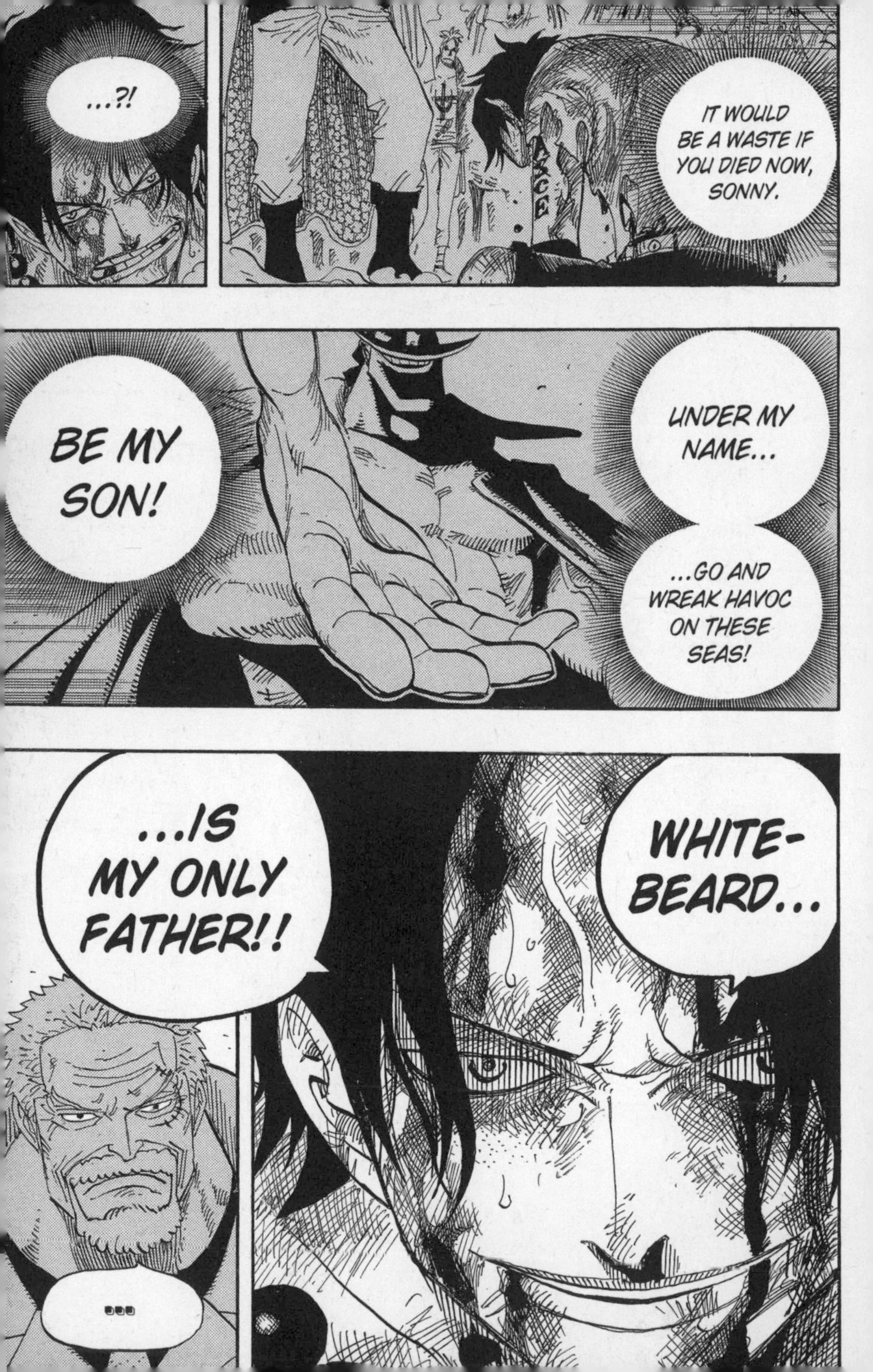
IT WOULD BE A WASTE IF YOU DIED NOW, SONNY.
...?!
UNDER MY NAME...
...GO AND WREAK HAVOC ON THESE SEAS!
BE MY SON!
WHITE-BEARD...
...IS MY ONLY FATHER!!
...

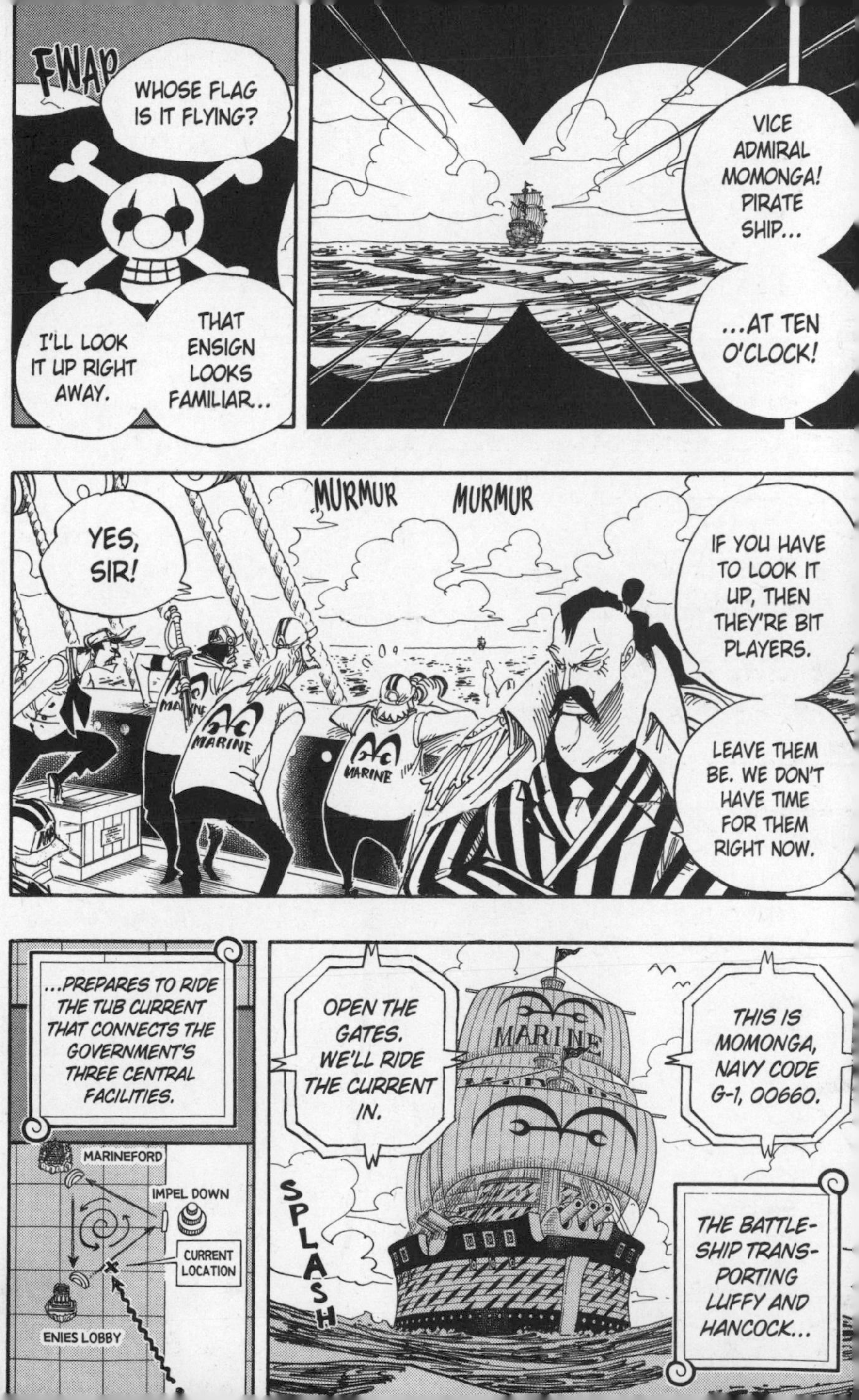
VICE ADMIRAL MOMONGA! PIRATE SHIP...
...AT TEN O'CLOCK!
FWAP
WHOSE FLAG IS IT FLYING?
THAT ENSIGN LOOKS FAMILIAR...
I'LL LOOK IT UP RIGHT AWAY.
IF YOU HAVE TO LOOK IT UP, THEN THEY'RE BIT PLAYERS.
LEAVE THEM BE. WE DON'T HAVE TIME FOR THEM RIGHT NOW.
MURMUR
MURMUR
YES, SIR!
MARINE
MARINE
MARINE
THIS IS MOMONGA, NAVY CODE G-1, 00660.
OPEN THE GATES. WE'LL RIDE THE CURRENT IN.
MARINE
THE BATTLE-SHIP TRANS-PORTING LUFFY AND HANCOCK...
SPLASH
...PREPARES TO RIDE THE TUB CURRENT THAT CONNECTS THE GOVERNMENT'S THREE CENTRAL FACILITIES.
MARINEFORD
IMPEL DOWN
CURRENT LOCATION
ENIES LOBBY

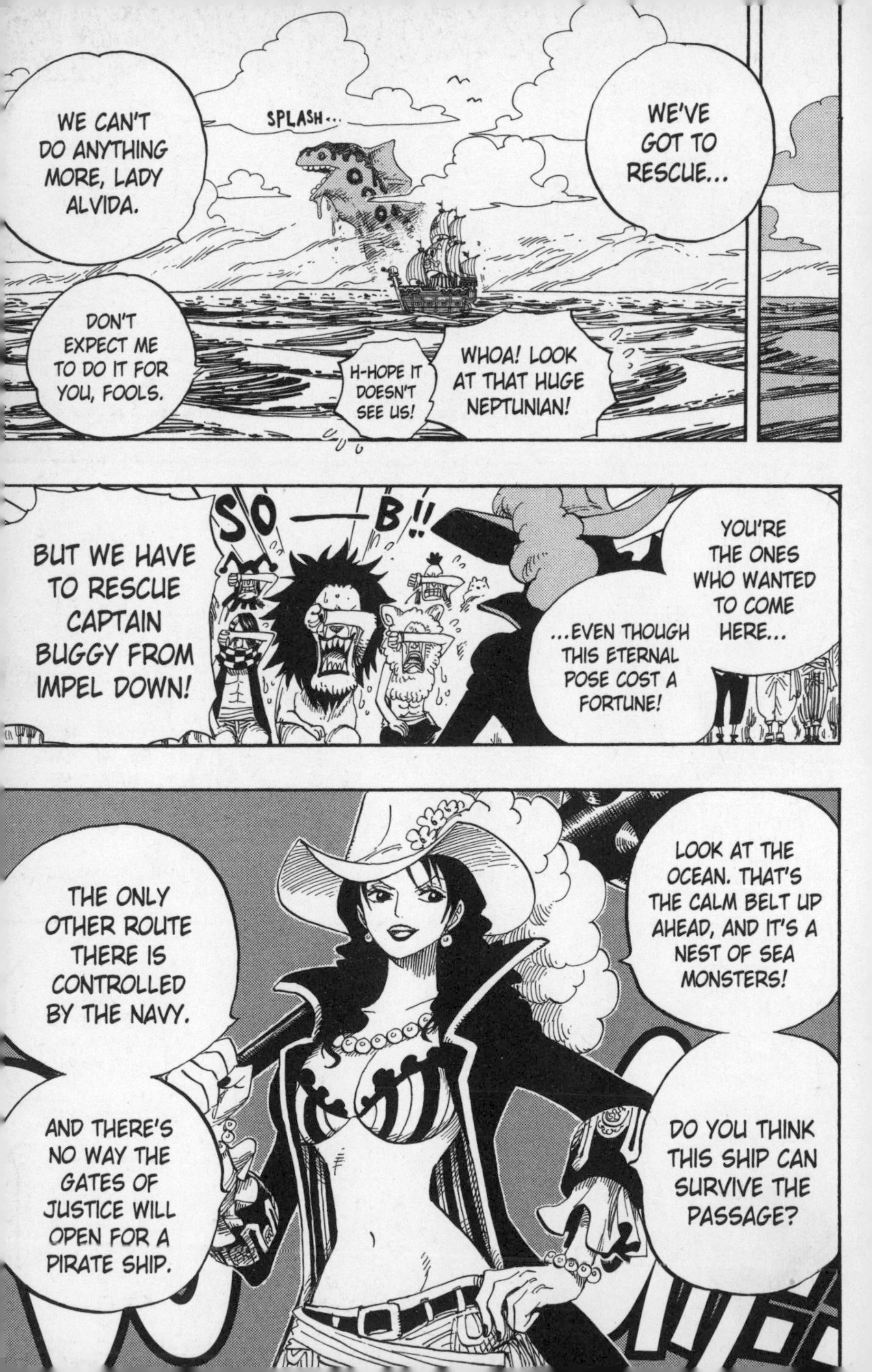
WE'VE GOT TO RESCUE...
WE CAN'T DO ANYTHING MORE, LADY ALVIDA.
SPLASH...
WHOA! LOOK AT THAT HUGE NEPTUNIAN!
H-HOPE IT DOESN'T SEE US!
DON'T EXPECT ME TO DO IT FOR YOU, FOOLS.
YOU'RE THE ONES WHO WANTED TO COME HERE...
...EVEN THOUGH THIS ETERNAL POSE COST A FORTUNE!
SO——B!!
BUT WE HAVE TO RESCUE CAPTAIN BUGGY FROM IMPEL DOWN!
LOOK AT THE OCEAN. THAT'S THE CALM BELT UP AHEAD, AND IT'S A NEST OF SEA MONSTERS!
THE ONLY OTHER ROUTE THERE IS CONTROLLED BY THE NAVY.
DO YOU THINK THIS SHIP CAN SURVIVE THE PASSAGE?
AND THERE'S NO WAY THE GATES OF JUSTICE WILL OPEN FOR A PIRATE SHIP.

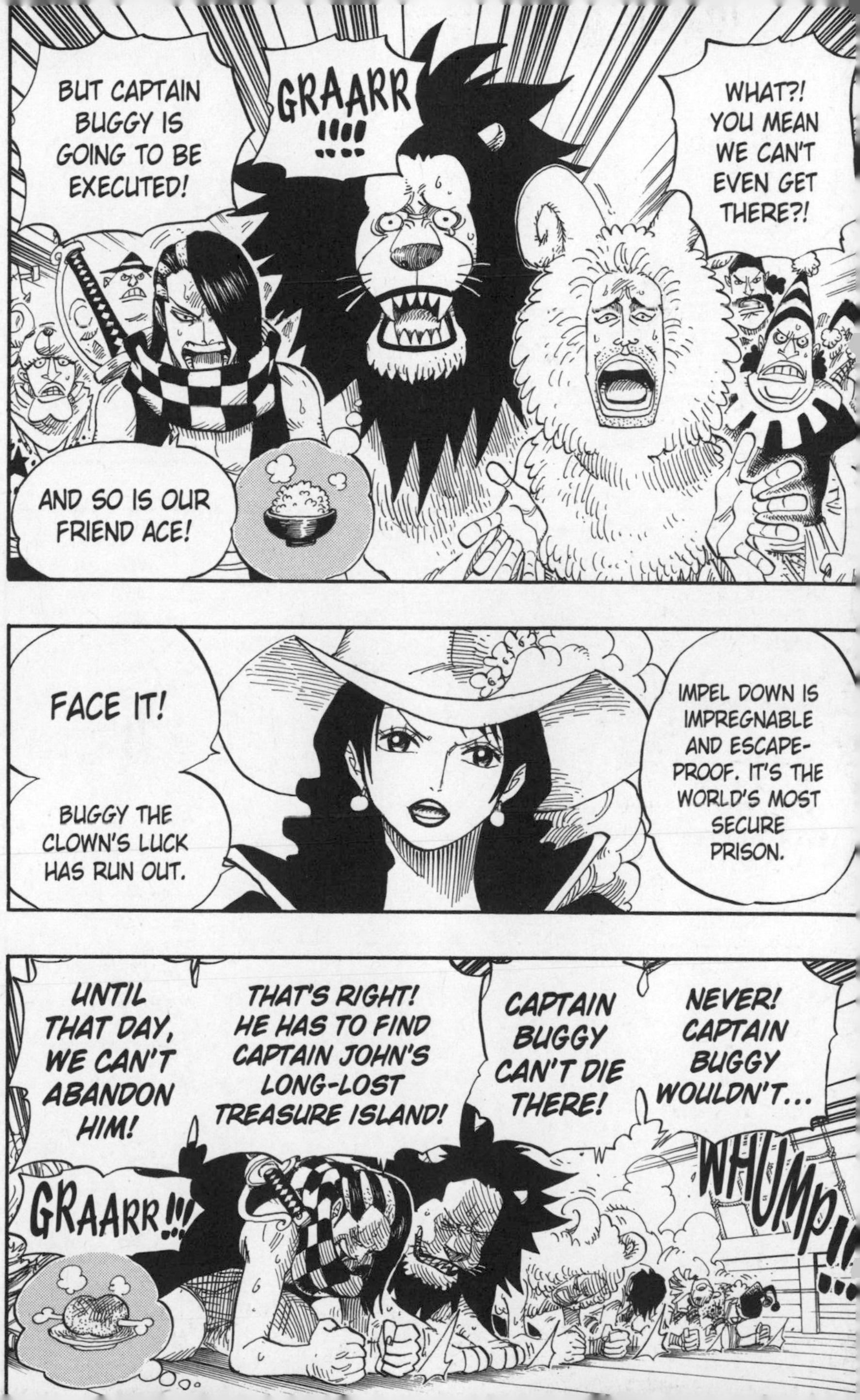
WHAT?! YOU MEAN WE CAN'T EVEN GET THERE?!
GRAARR !!!!
BUT CAPTAIN BUGGY IS GOING TO BE EXECUTED!
AND SO IS OUR FRIEND ACE!
IMPEL DOWN IS IMPREGNABLE AND ESCAPE-PROOF. IT'S THE WORLD'S MOST SECURE PRISON.
FACE IT!
BUGGY THE CLOWN'S LUCK HAS RUN OUT.
NEVER! CAPTAIN BUGGY WOULDN'T...
CAPTAIN BUGGY CAN'T DIE THERE!
THAT'S RIGHT! HE HAS TO FIND CAPTAIN JOHN'S LONG-LOST TREASURE ISLAND!
UNTIL THAT DAY, WE CAN'T ABANDON HIM!
WHUMP!!!
GRAARR!!!

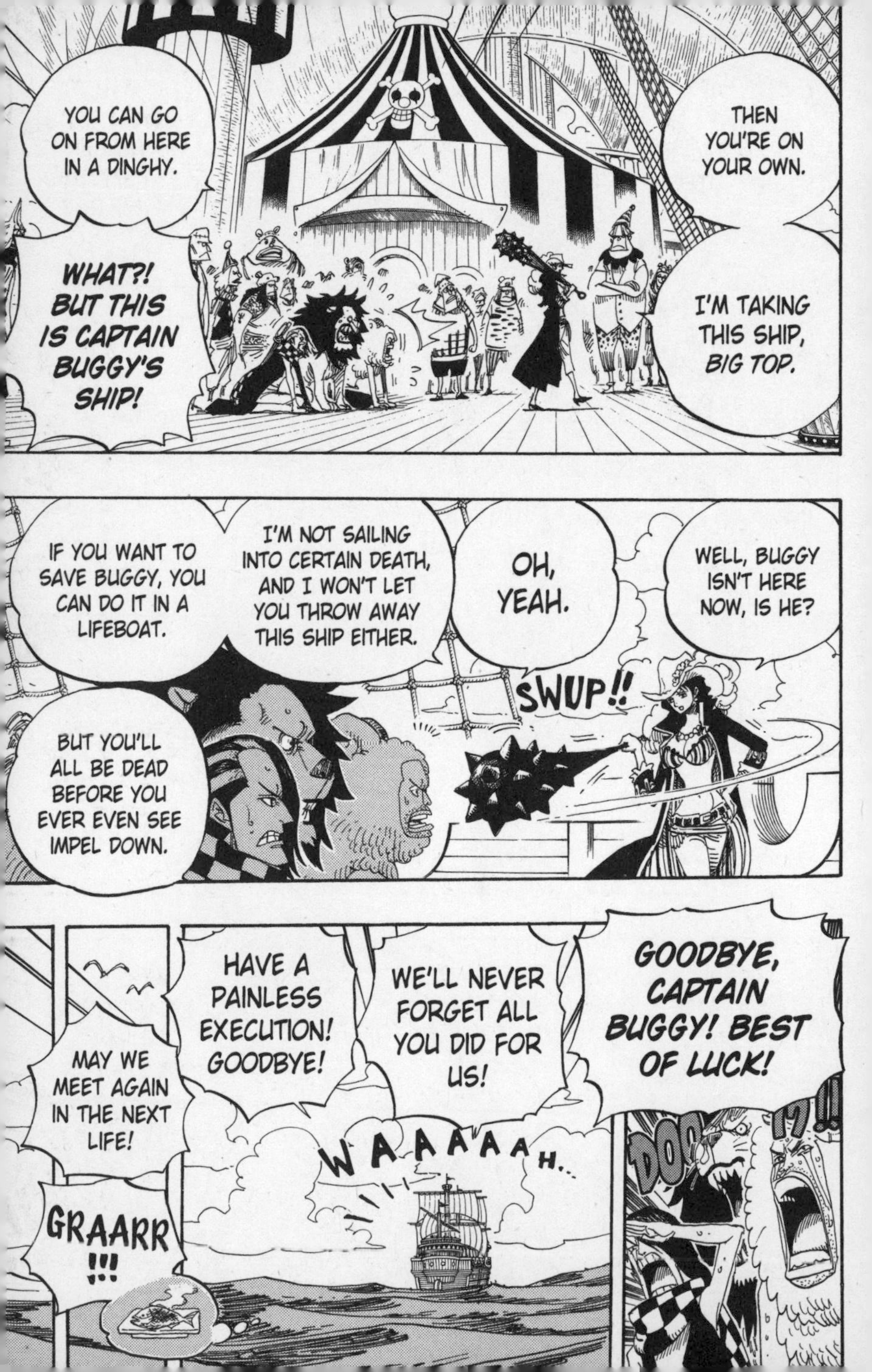
THEN YOU'RE ON YOUR OWN.
I'M TAKING THIS SHIP, BIG TOP.
YOU CAN GO ON FROM HERE IN A DINGHY.
WHAT?! BUT THIS IS CAPTAIN BUGGY'S SHIP!
WELL, BUGGY ISN'T HERE NOW, IS HE?
OH, YEAH.
I'M NOT SAILING INTO CERTAIN DEATH, AND I WON'T LET YOU THROW AWAY THIS SHIP EITHER.
IF YOU WANT TO SAVE BUGGY, YOU CAN DO IT IN A LIFEBOAT.
SWUP!!
BUT YOU'LL ALL BE DEAD BEFORE YOU EVER EVEN SEE IMPEL DOWN.
GOODBYE, CAPTAIN BUGGY! BEST OF LUCK!
DOOM!!
WE'LL NEVER FORGET ALL YOU DID FOR US!
HAVE A PAINLESS EXECUTION! GOODBYE!
MAY WE MEET AGAIN IN THE NEXT LIFE!
WAAAAAAH...
GRAARR!!!

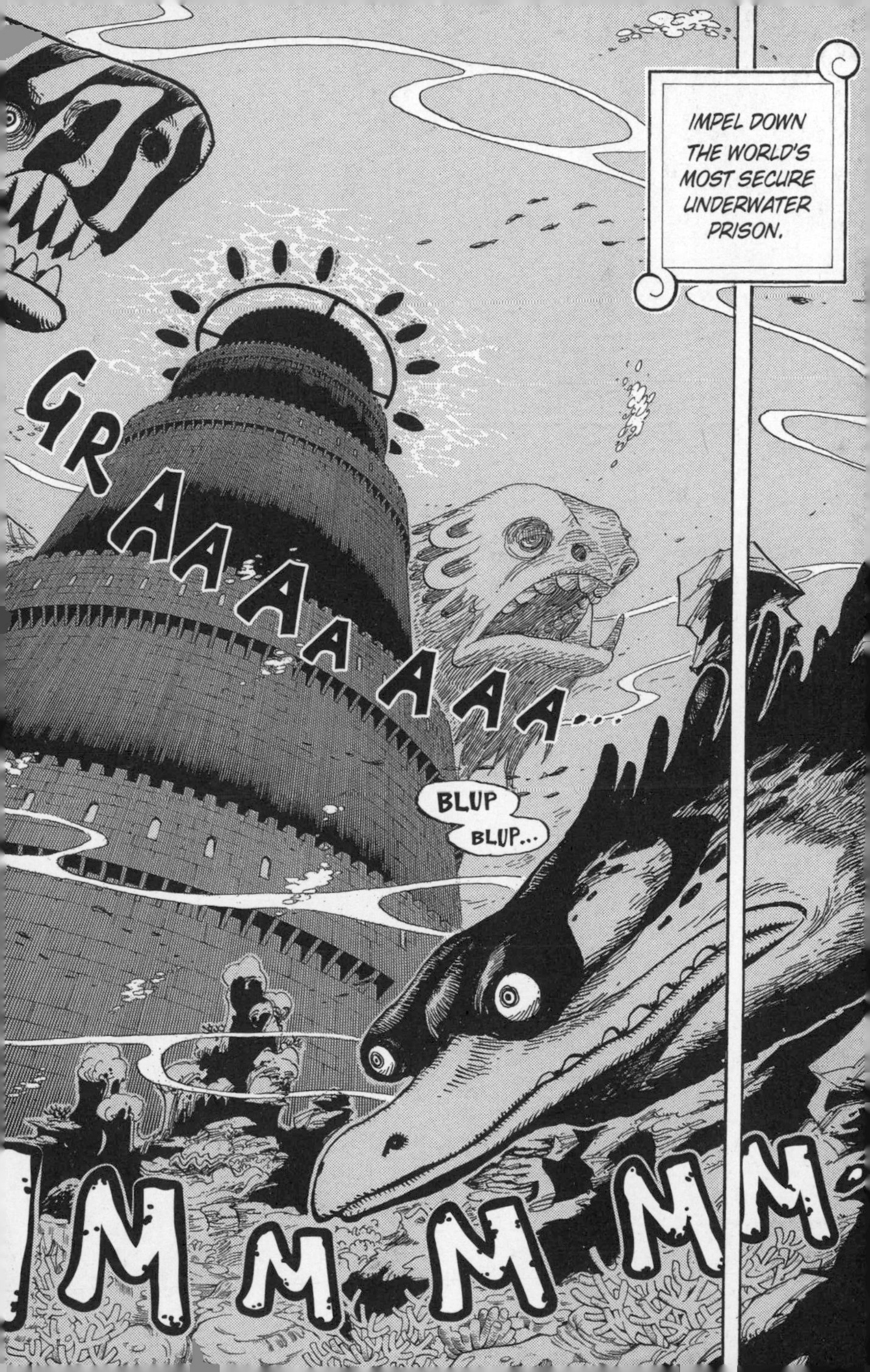
IMPEL DOWN
THE WORLD'S MOST SECURE UNDERWATER PRISON.
GRAAAAAAAA...
BLUP BLUP...
MMMMM

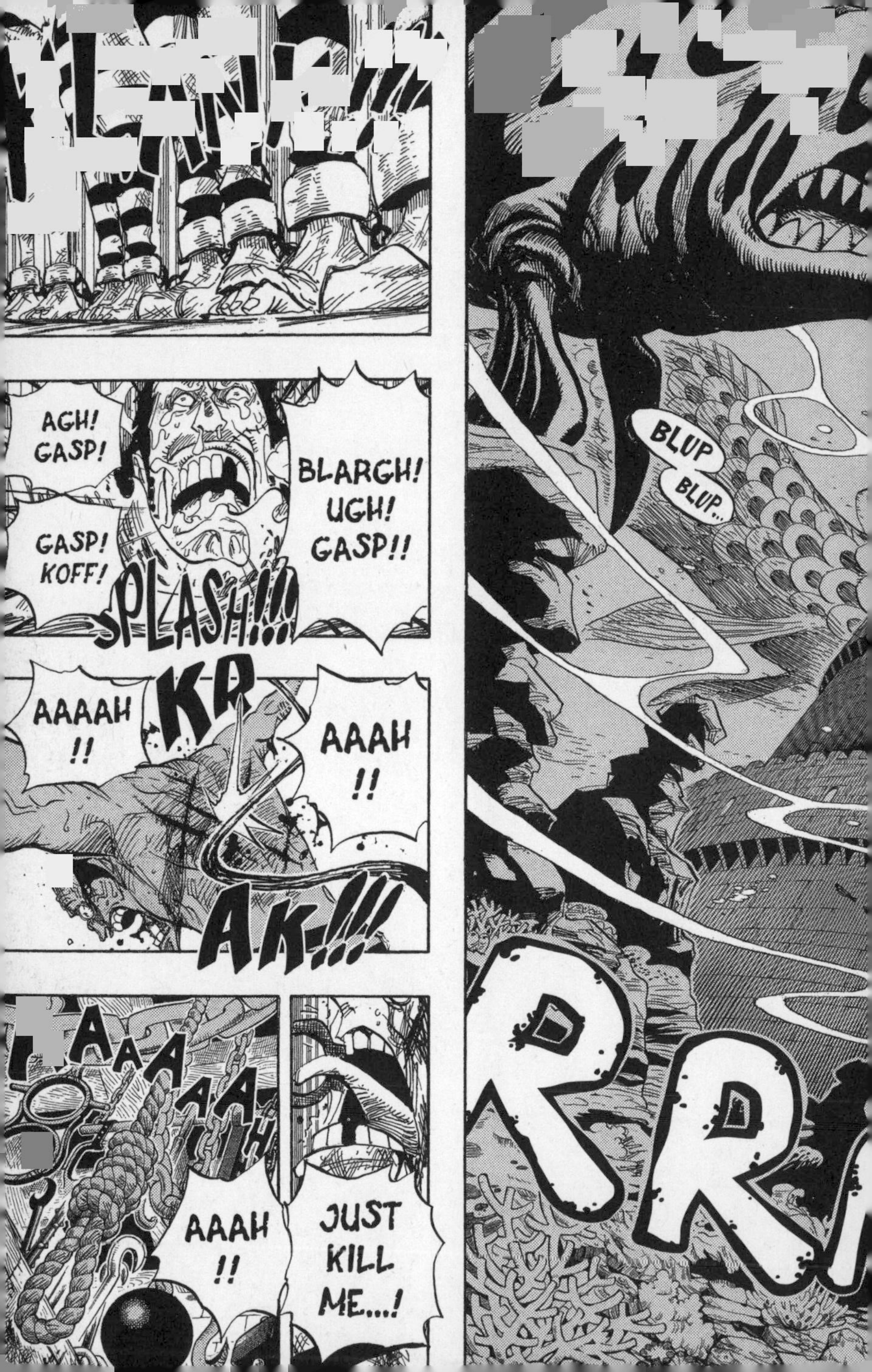
BLUP
BLUP...
RR
BLARGH! UGH! GASP!!
AGH! GASP!
GASP! KOFF!
SPLASH!!!
AAAH!!
KR
AK!!!
AAAAH!!
JUST KILL ME...!
AAAAAA
AAAH!!

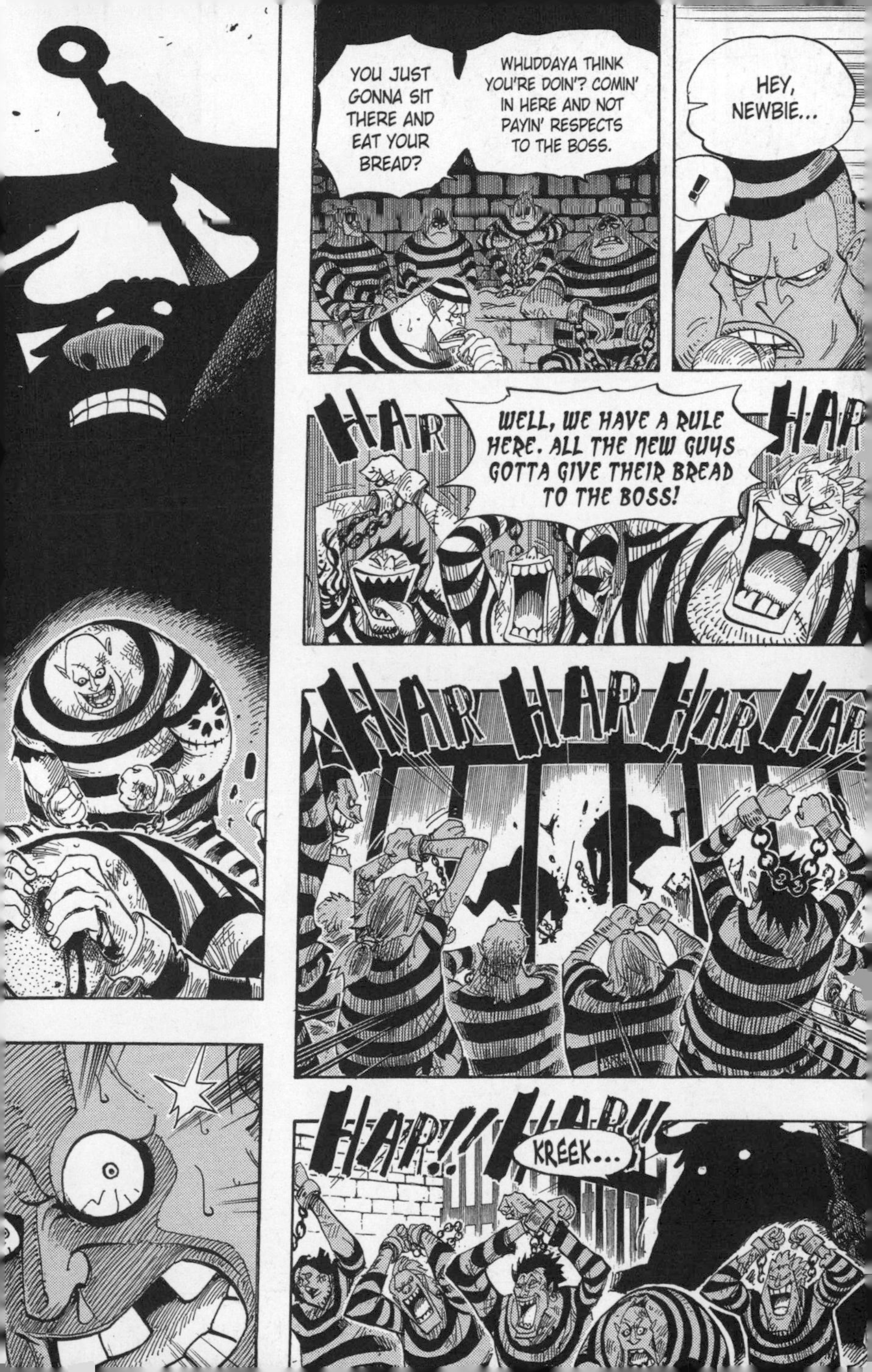
HEY, NEWBIE...
!
WHUDDAYA THINK YOU'RE DOIN'? COMIN' IN HERE AND NOT PAYIN' RESPECTS TO THE BOSS.
YOU JUST GONNA SIT THERE AND EAT YOUR BREAD?
HAR
WELL, WE HAVE A RULE HERE. ALL THE NEW GUYS GOTTA GIVE THEIR BREAD TO THE BOSS!
HAR
HAR HAR HAR HAR
HAR!! HAR!!
KREEK...

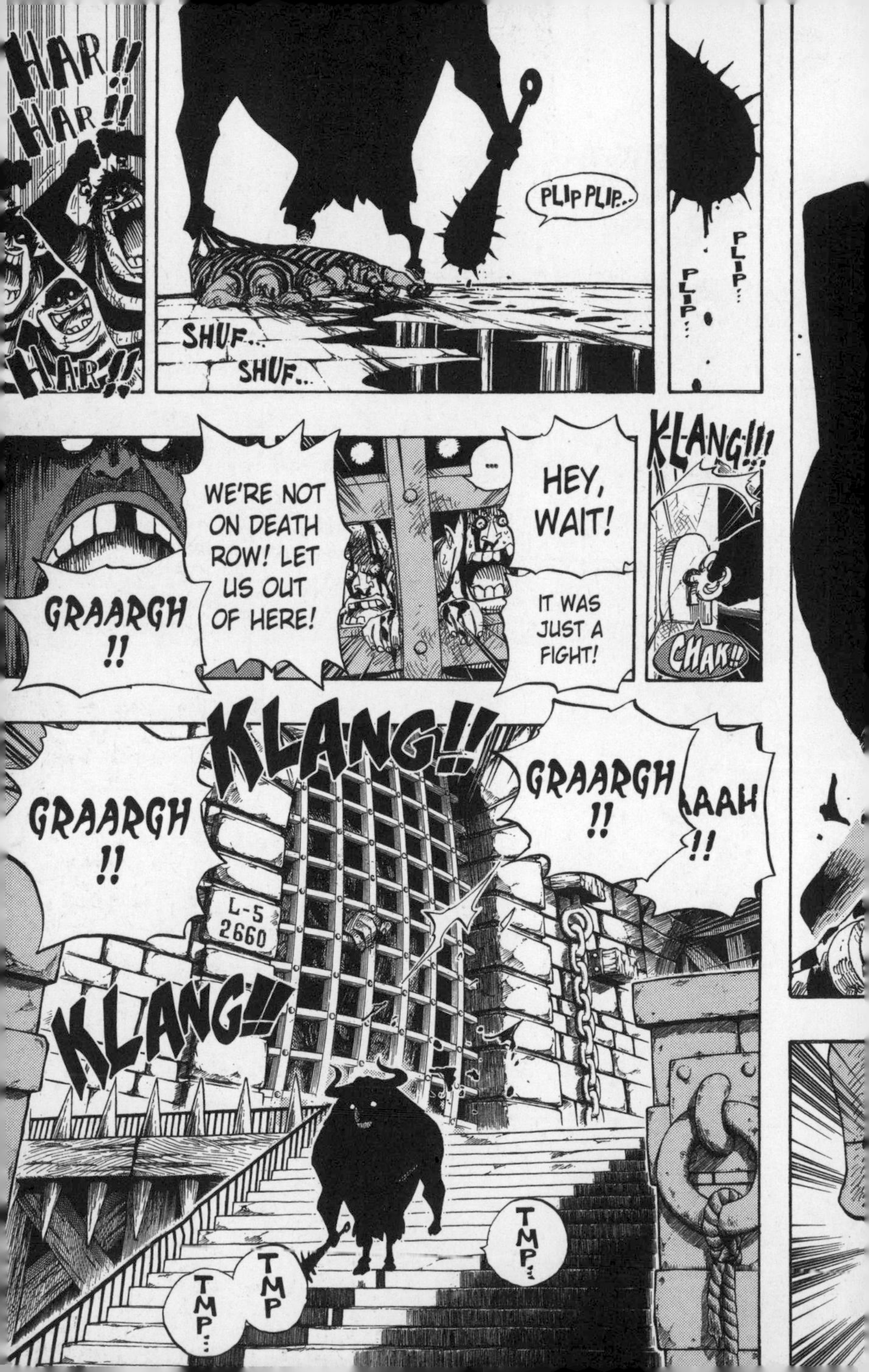
PLIP
PLIP...
PLIP PLIP...
SHUF...
SHUF...
HAR!!
HAR!!
HAR!!
K-LANG!!!
CHAK!!
...
HEY, WAIT!
IT WAS JUST A FIGHT!
WE'RE NOT ON DEATH ROW! LET US OUT OF HERE!
GRAARGH!!
AAH!!
GRAARGH!!
KLANG!!
GRAARGH!!
L-5
2660
KLANG!!
TMP...
TMP
TMP...

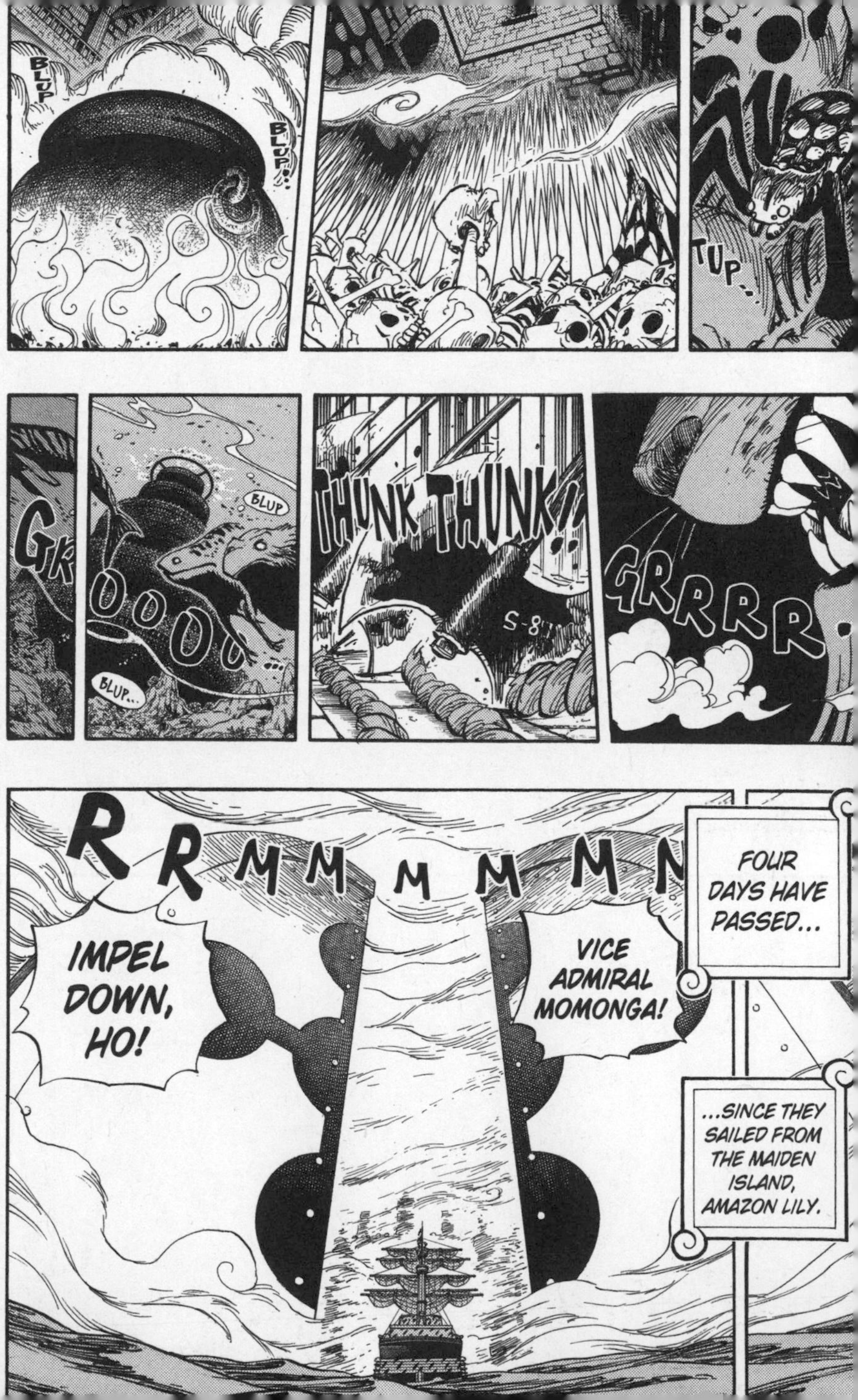
TUP...
BLUP
BLUP...
GRRRR
THUNK THUNK!!
GROOOO
BLUP
BLUP...
FOUR DAYS HAVE PASSED...
...SINCE THEY SAILED FROM THE MAIDEN ISLAND, AMAZON LILY.
RRMMMMMMN
VICE ADMIRAL MOMONGA!
IMPEL DOWN, HO!

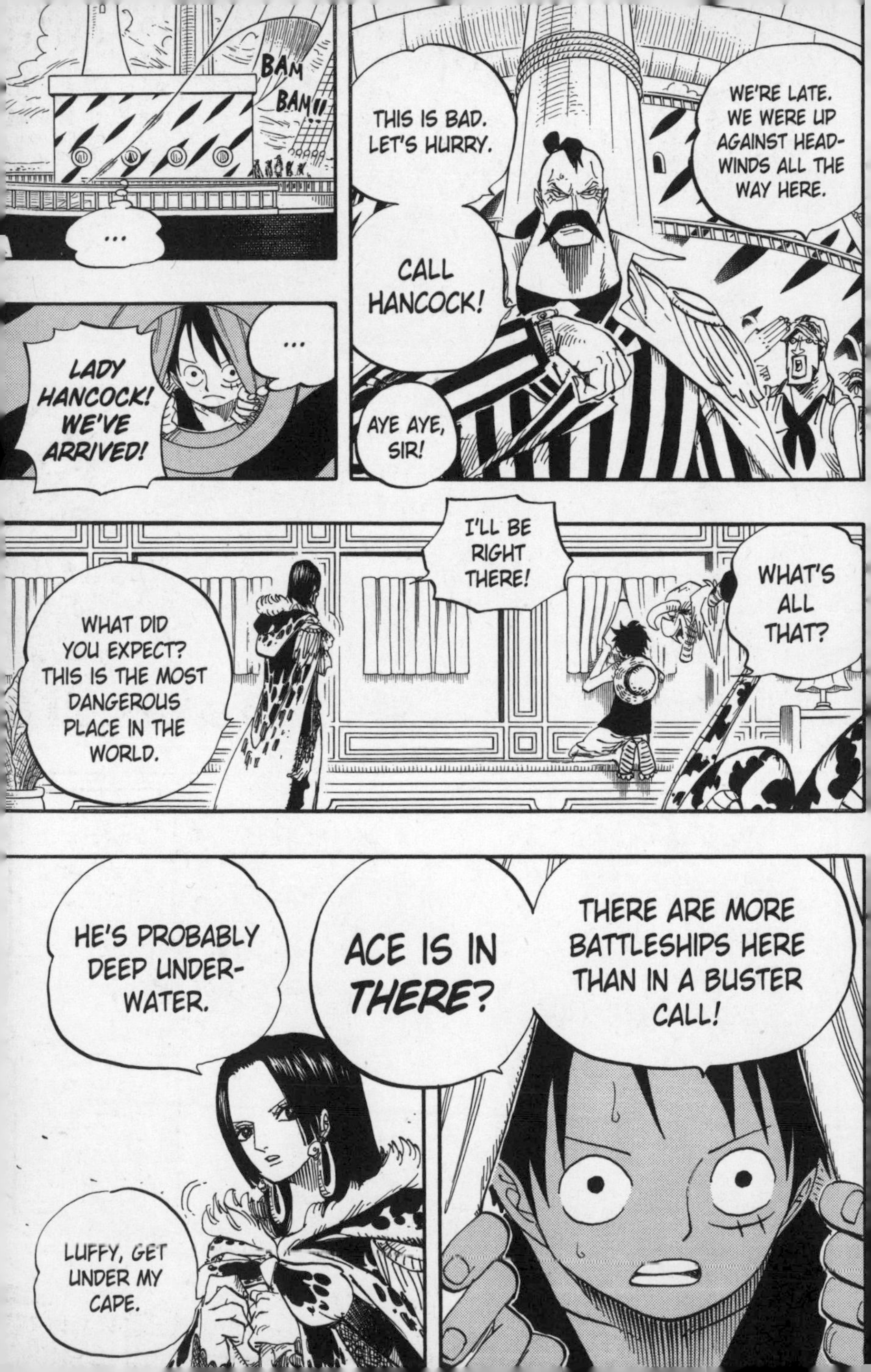
WE'RE LATE. WE WERE UP AGAINST HEADWINDS ALL THE WAY HERE.
THIS IS BAD. LET'S HURRY.
CALL HANCOCK!
AYE AYE, SIR!
BAM
BAM!!
...
...
LADY HANCOCK! WE'VE ARRIVED!
WHAT'S ALL THAT?
I'LL BE RIGHT THERE!
WHAT DID YOU EXPECT? THIS IS THE MOST DANGEROUS PLACE IN THE WORLD.
THERE ARE MORE BATTLESHIPS HERE THAN IN A BUSTER CALL!
ACE IS IN THERE?
HE'S PROBABLY DEEP UNDERWATER.
LUFFY, GET UNDER MY CAPE.

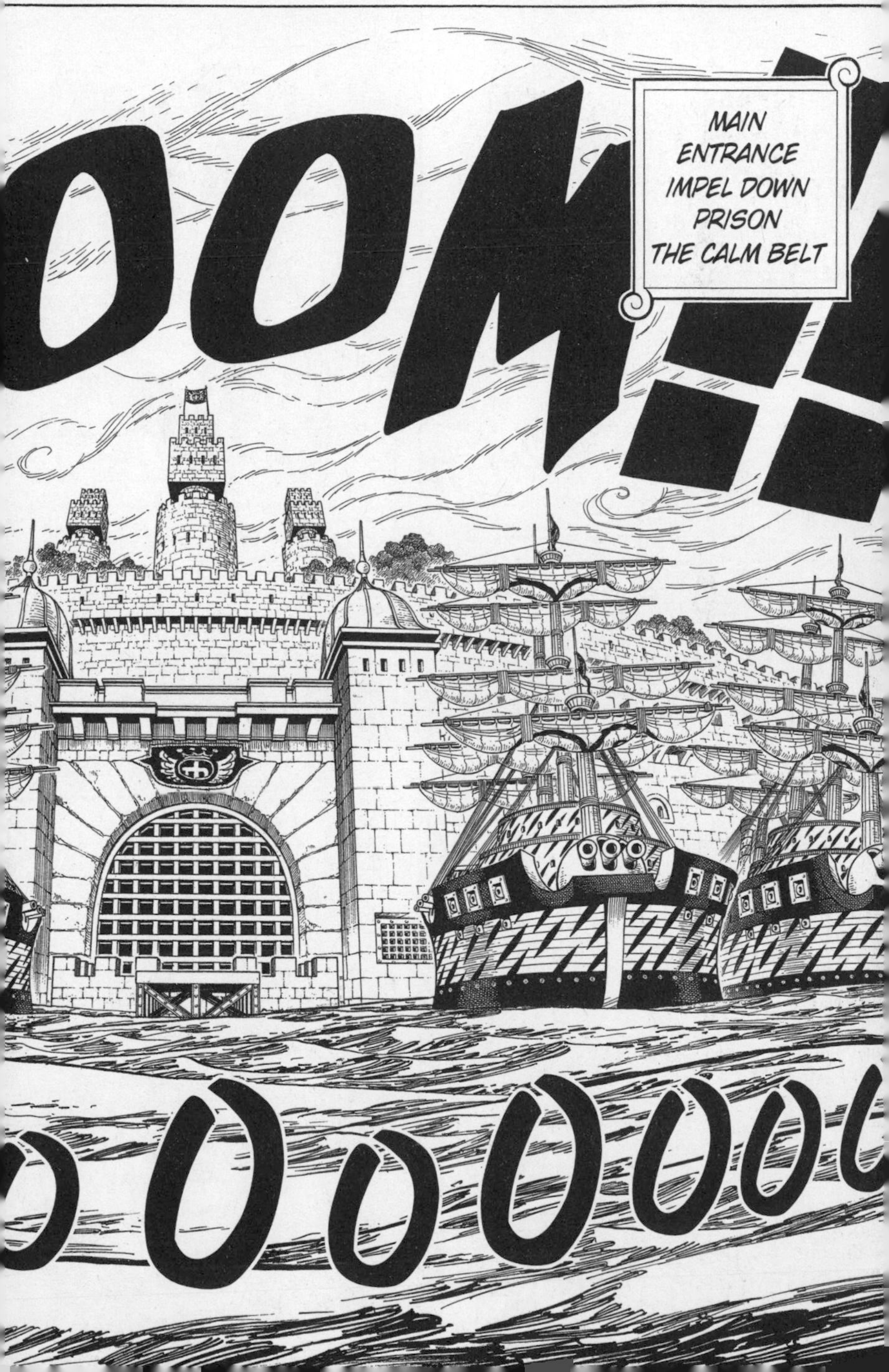
OOM!!
MAIN ENTRANCE
IMPEL DOWN
PRISON
THE CALM BELT
OOOOOOOO

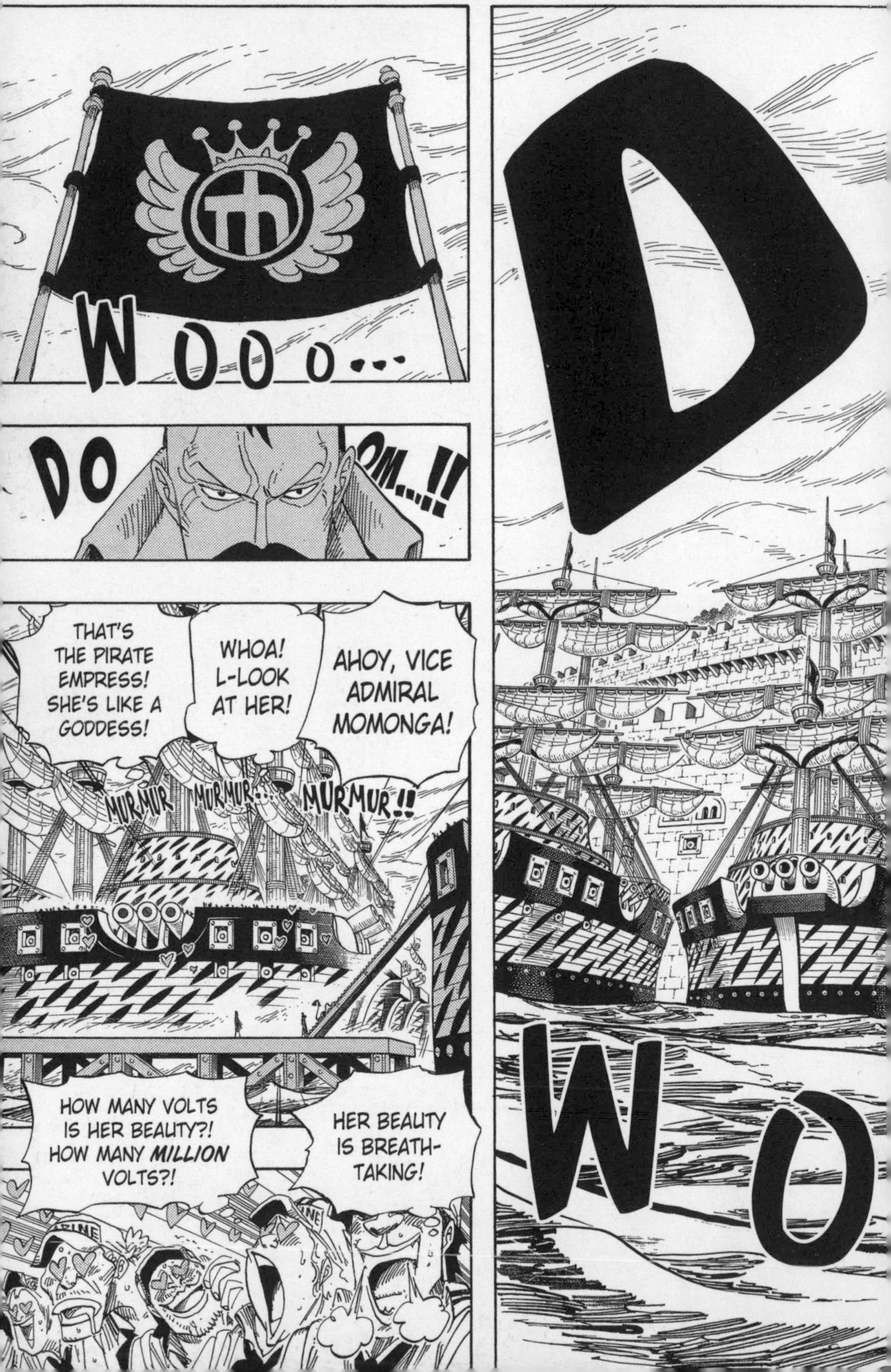
D
WO
WOOO...
DO
OM...!!
AHOY, VICE ADMIRAL MOMONGA!
WHOA! L-LOOK AT HER!
THAT'S THE PIRATE EMPRESS! SHE'S LIKE A GODDESS!
MURMUR!!
MURMUR...
MURMUR
HER BEAUTY IS BREATH-TAKING!
HOW MANY VOLTS IS HER BEAUTY?! HOW MANY *MILLION* VOLTS?!

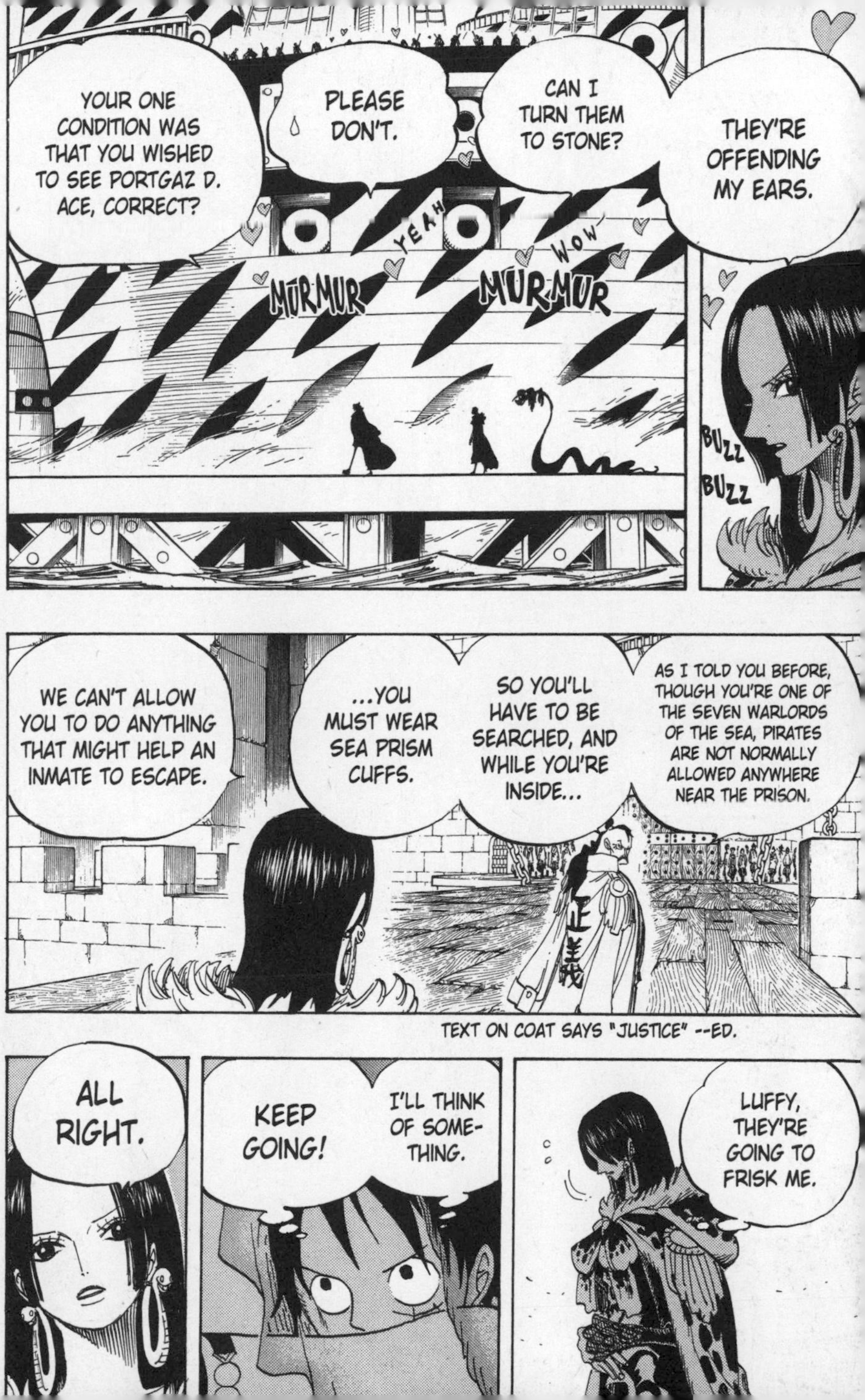
THEY'RE OFFENDING MY EARS.
BUZZ
BUZZ
CAN I TURN THEM TO STONE?
WOW
MURMUR
PLEASE DON'T.
YEAH
MURMUR
YOUR ONE CONDITION WAS THAT YOU WISHED TO SEE PORTGAZ D. ACE, CORRECT?
AS I TOLD YOU BEFORE, THOUGH YOU'RE ONE OF THE SEVEN WARLORDS OF THE SEA, PIRATES ARE NOT NORMALLY ALLOWED ANYWHERE NEAR THE PRISON.
SO YOU'LL HAVE TO BE SEARCHED, AND WHILE YOU'RE INSIDE...
...YOU MUST WEAR SEA PRISM CUFFS.
WE CAN'T ALLOW YOU TO DO ANYTHING THAT MIGHT HELP AN INMATE TO ESCAPE.
TEXT ON COAT SAYS "JUSTICE" --ED.
LUFFY, THEY'RE GOING TO FRISK ME.
I'LL THINK OF SOME-THING.
KEEP GOING!
ALL RIGHT.

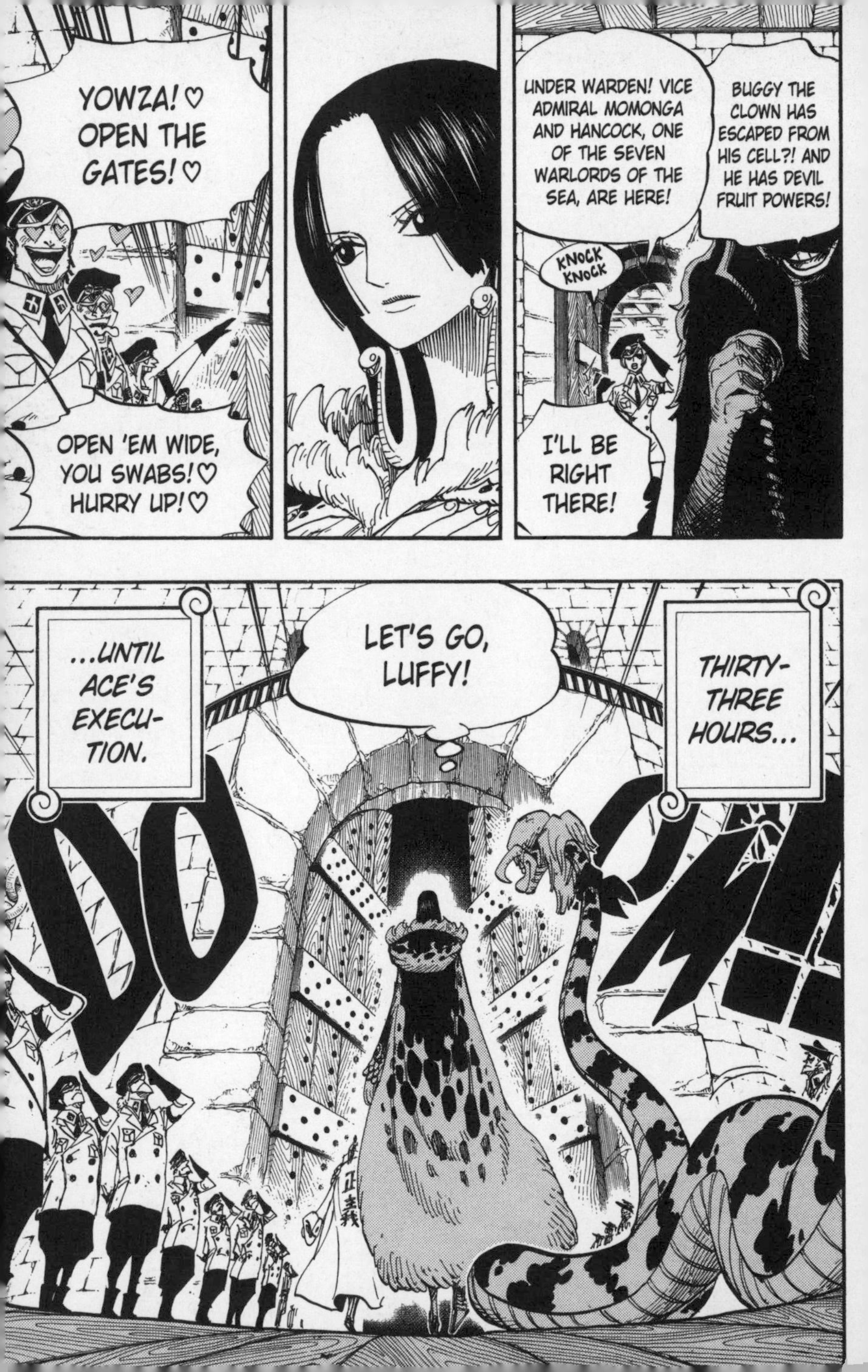
UNDER WARDEN! VICE ADMIRAL MOMONGA AND HANCOCK, ONE OF THE SEVEN WARLORDS OF THE SEA, ARE HERE!
BUGGY THE CLOWN HAS ESCAPED FROM HIS CELL?! AND HE HAS DEVIL FRUIT POWERS!
KNOCK KNOCK
I'LL BE RIGHT THERE!
YOWZA! ♡ OPEN THE GATES! ♡
OPEN 'EM WIDE, YOU SWABS! ♡ HURRY UP! ♡
THIRTY-THREE HOURS...
LET'S GO, LUFFY!
...UNTIL ACE'S EXECUTION.
DOOM

IN THE GREAT PRISON

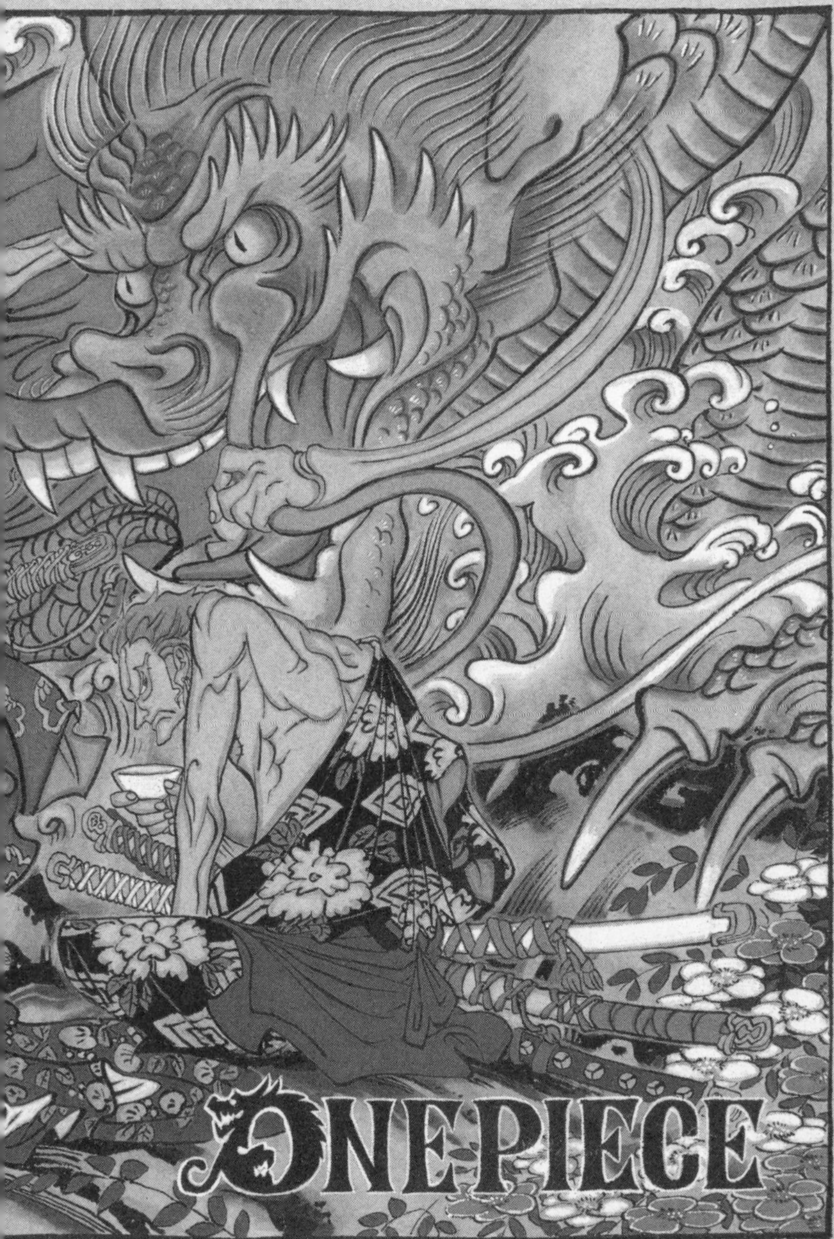
ONE PIECE

Chapter 526: ADVENTURE

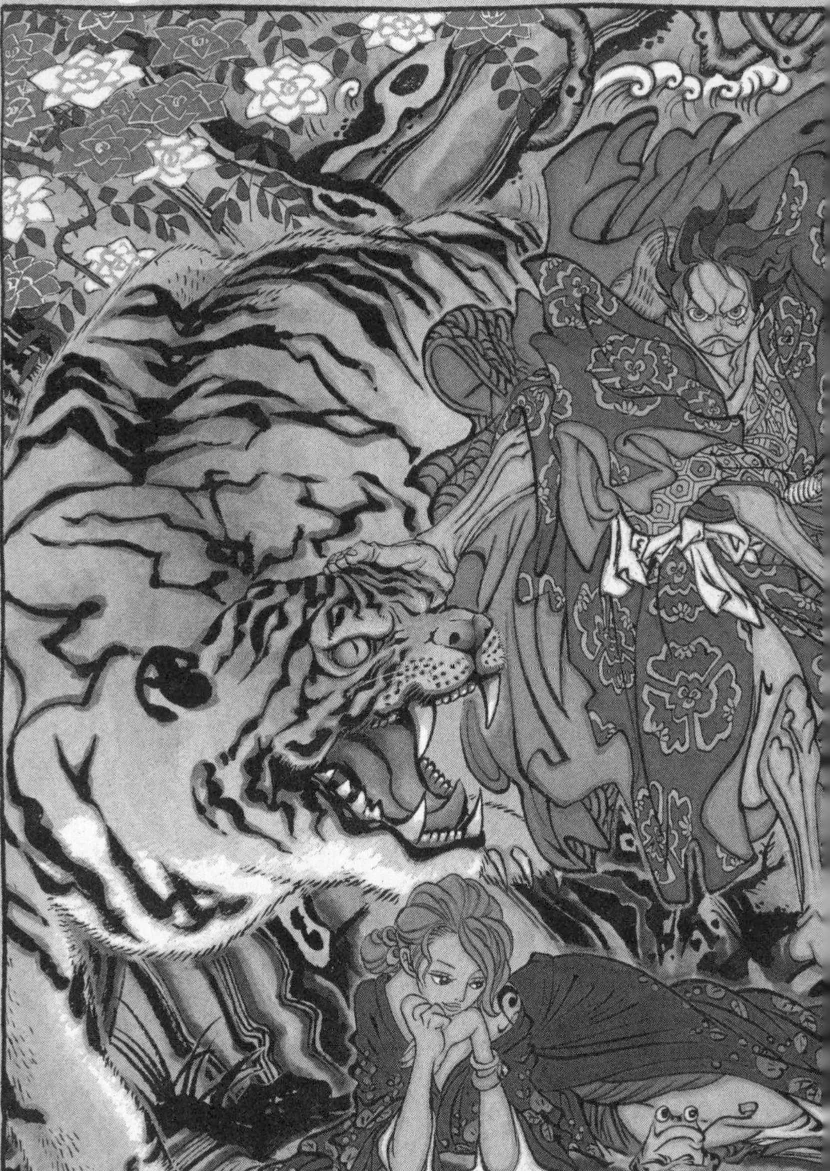

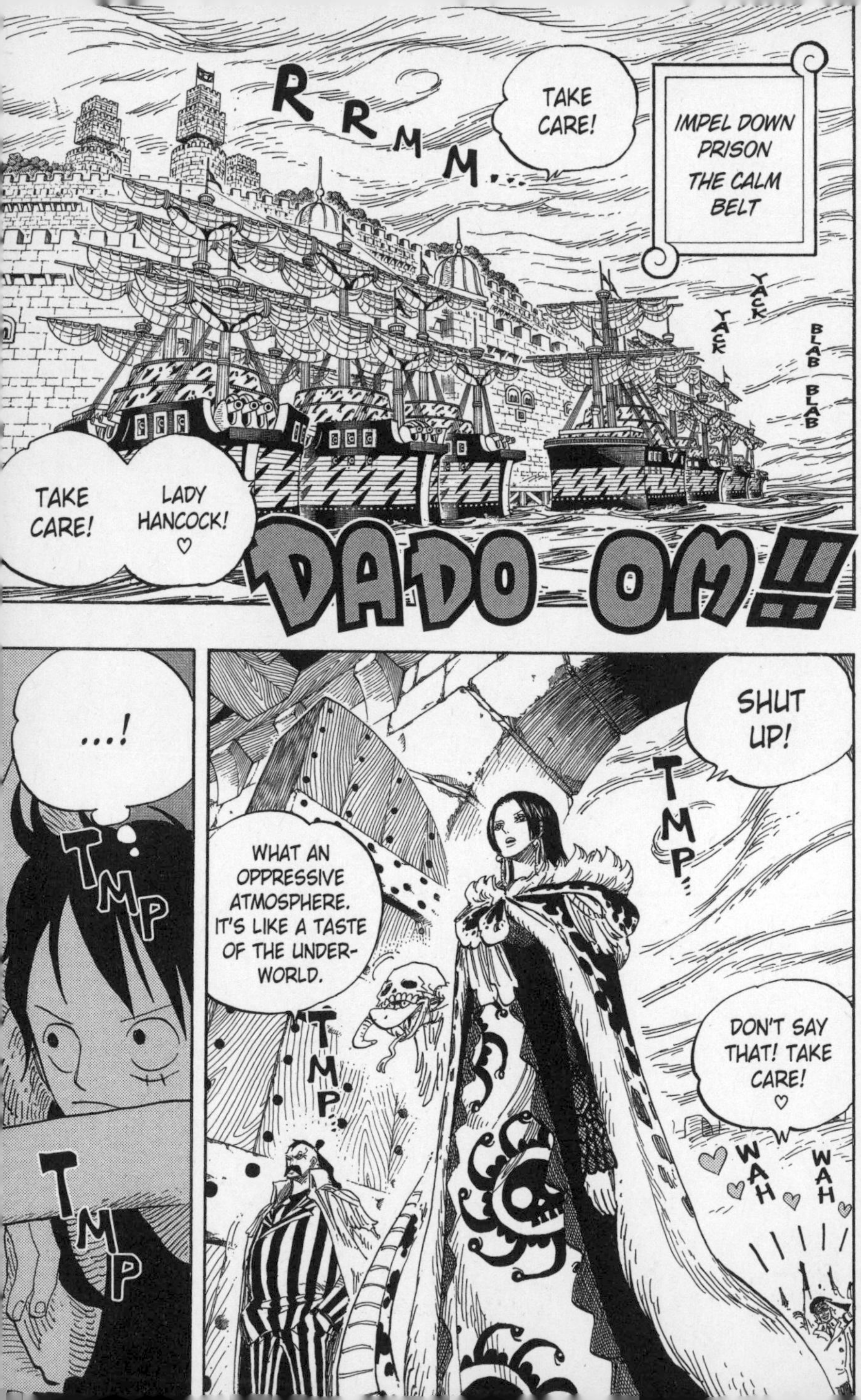
IMPEL DOWN PRISON THE CALM BELT
TAKE CARE!
RRMM...
YACK YACK
BLAB BLAB
TAKE CARE! LADY HANCOCK! ♡
DADO OM!!
SHUT UP!
TMP...
WHAT AN OPPRESSIVE ATMOSPHERE. IT'S LIKE A TASTE OF THE UNDER-WORLD.
TMP...
DON'T SAY THAT! TAKE CARE! ♡
WAH WAH
...!
TMP
TMP

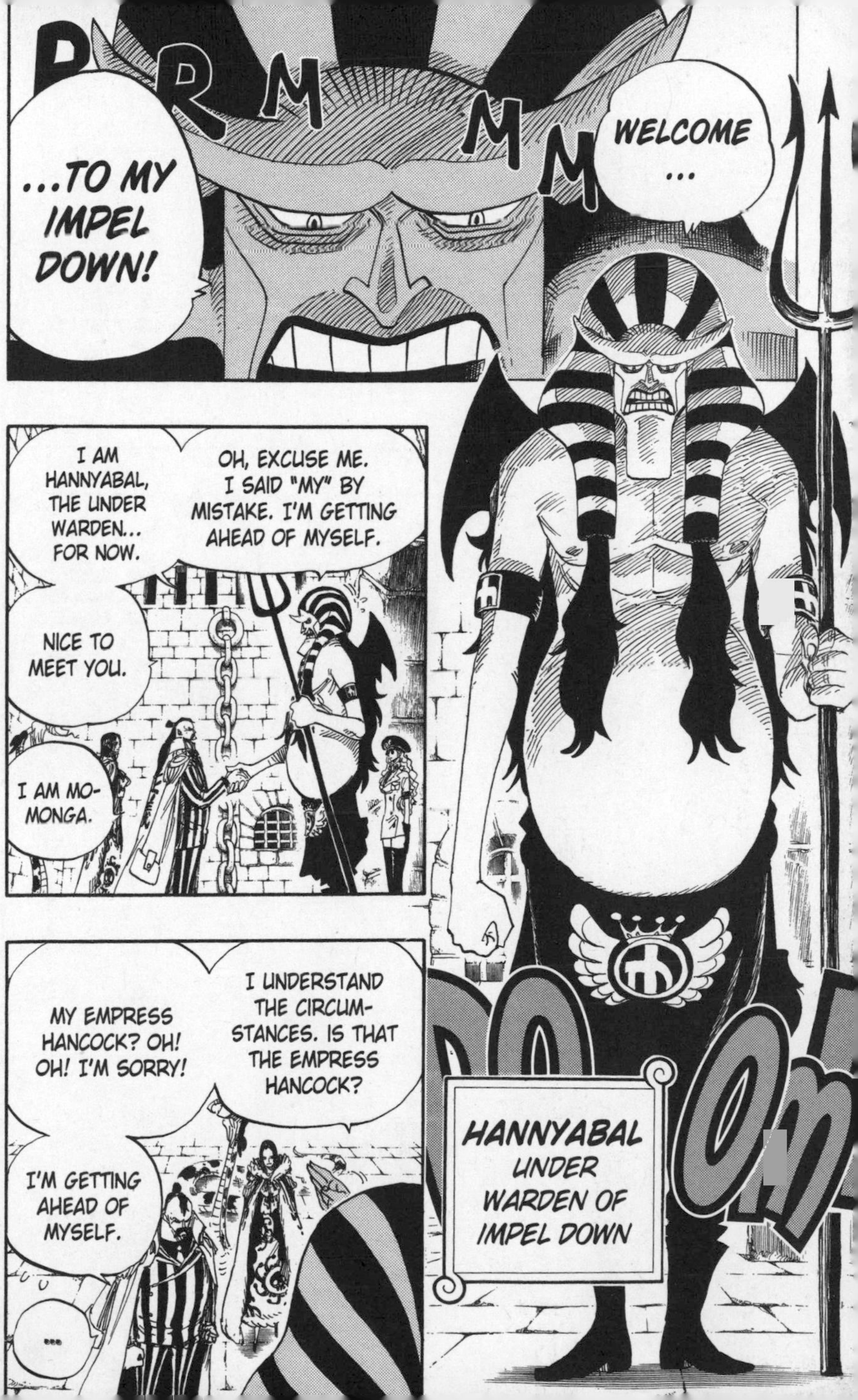
DRMMM
WELCOME ...
...TO MY IMPEL DOWN!
HANNYABAL
UNDER WARDEN OF IMPEL DOWN
OH, EXCUSE ME. I SAID "MY" BY MISTAKE. I'M GETTING AHEAD OF MYSELF.
I AM HANNYABAL, THE UNDER WARDEN... FOR NOW.
NICE TO MEET YOU.
I AM MO-MONGA.
I UNDERSTAND THE CIRCUM-STANCES. IS THAT THE EMPRESS HANCOCK?
MY EMPRESS HANCOCK? OH! OH! I'M SORRY!
I'M GETTING AHEAD OF MYSELF.
...

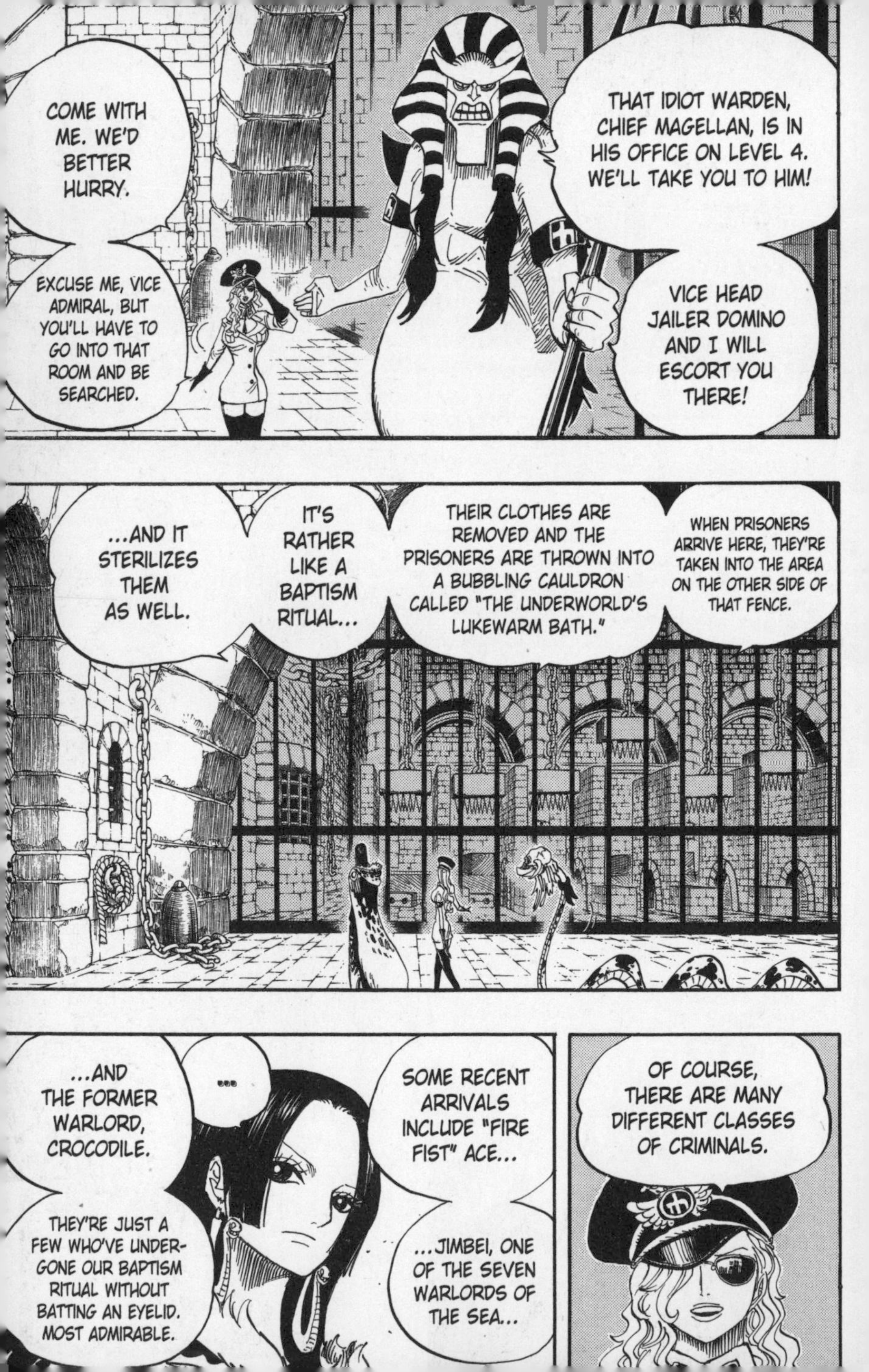
THAT IDIOT WARDEN, CHIEF MAGELLAN, IS IN HIS OFFICE ON LEVEL 4. WE'LL TAKE YOU TO HIM!
VICE HEAD JAILER DOMINO AND I WILL ESCORT YOU THERE!
COME WITH ME. WE'D BETTER HURRY.
EXCUSE ME, VICE ADMIRAL, BUT YOU'LL HAVE TO GO INTO THAT ROOM AND BE SEARCHED.
WHEN PRISONERS ARRIVE HERE, THEY'RE TAKEN INTO THE AREA ON THE OTHER SIDE OF THAT FENCE.
THEIR CLOTHES ARE REMOVED AND THE PRISONERS ARE THROWN INTO A BUBBLING CAULDRON CALLED "THE UNDERWORLD'S LUKEWARM BATH."
IT'S RATHER LIKE A BAPTISM RITUAL...
...AND IT STERILIZES THEM AS WELL.
OF COURSE, THERE ARE MANY DIFFERENT CLASSES OF CRIMINALS.
SOME RECENT ARRIVALS INCLUDE "FIRE FIST" ACE...
...JIMBEI, ONE OF THE SEVEN WARLORDS OF THE SEA...
...AND THE FORMER WARLORD, CROCODILE.
...
THEY'RE JUST A FEW WHO'VE UNDER-GONE OUR BAPTISM RITUAL WITHOUT BATTING AN EYELID. MOST ADMIRABLE.

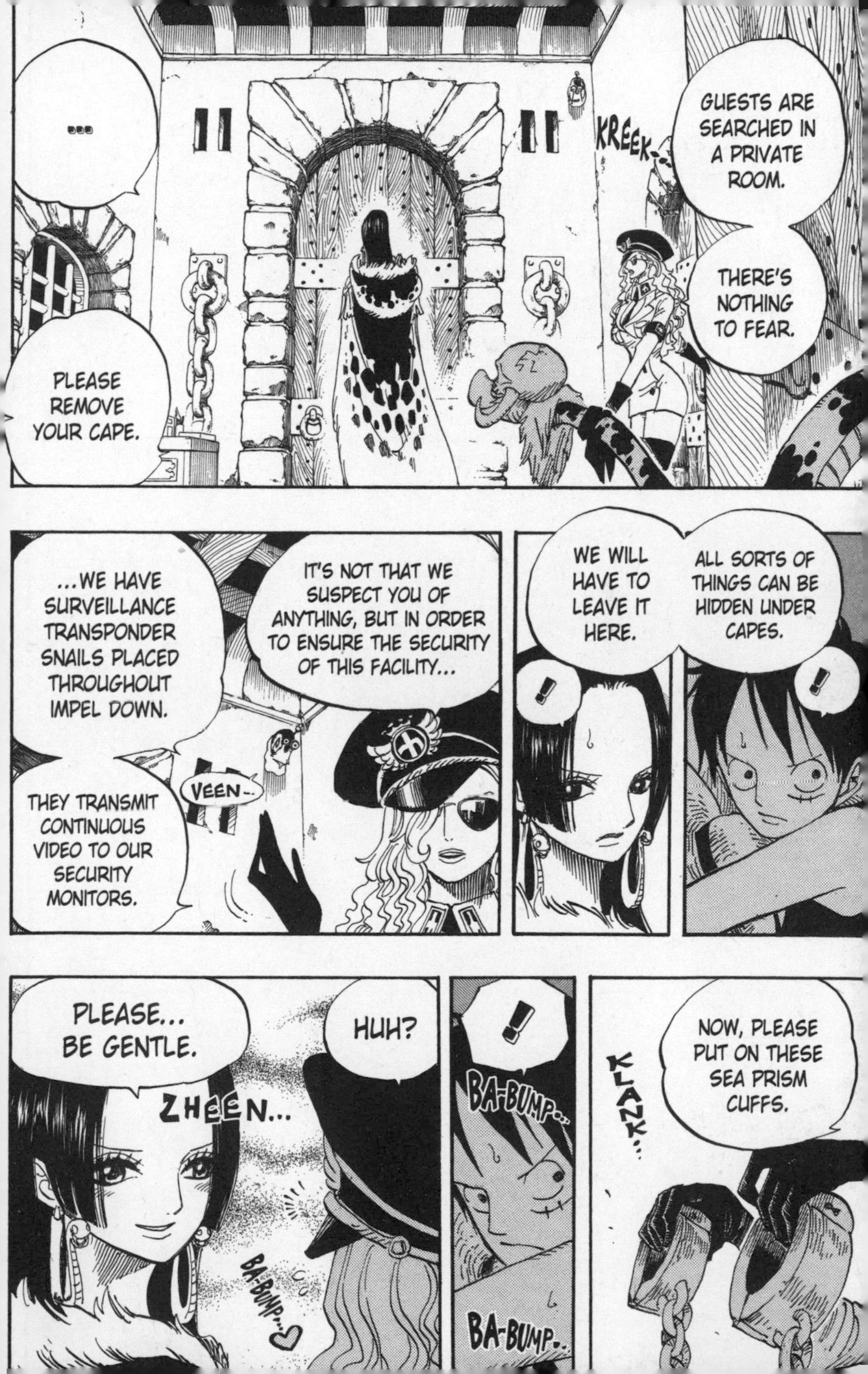
KREEK...
GUESTS ARE SEARCHED IN A PRIVATE ROOM.
THERE'S NOTHING TO FEAR.
...
PLEASE REMOVE YOUR CAPE.
ALL SORTS OF THINGS CAN BE HIDDEN UNDER CAPES.
!
WE WILL HAVE TO LEAVE IT HERE.
!
IT'S NOT THAT WE SUSPECT YOU OF ANYTHING, BUT IN ORDER TO ENSURE THE SECURITY OF THIS FACILITY...
...WE HAVE SURVEILLANCE TRANSPONDER SNAILS PLACED THROUGHOUT IMPEL DOWN.
VEEN...
THEY TRANSMIT CONTINUOUS VIDEO TO OUR SECURITY MONITORS.
NOW, PLEASE PUT ON THESE SEA PRISM CUFFS.
KLANK...
!
BA-BUMP...
BA-BUMP..
HUH?
PLEASE... BE GENTLE.
ZHEEN...
BA-BUMP...♥

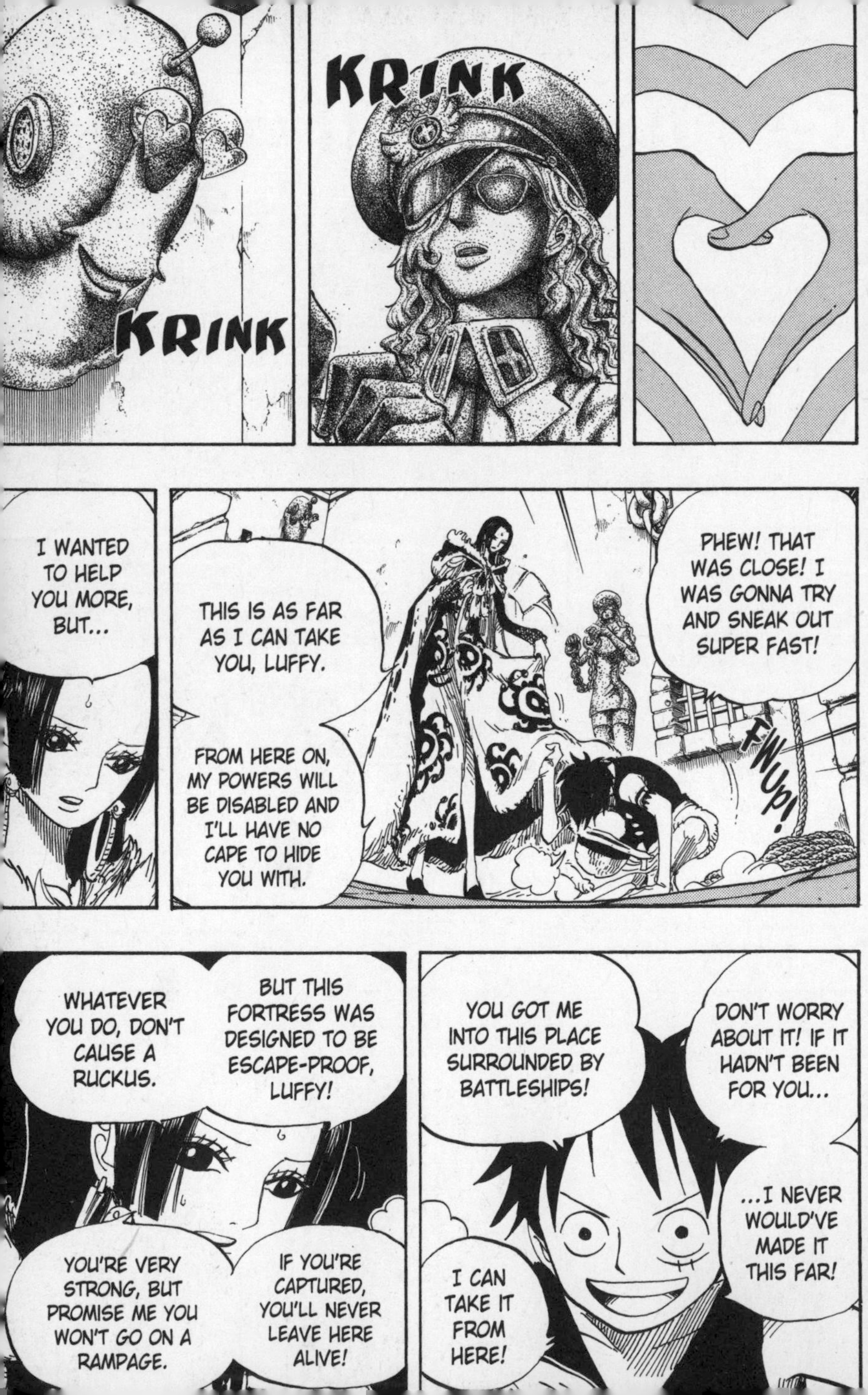
KRINK
KRINK
PHEW! THAT WAS CLOSE! I WAS GONNA TRY AND SNEAK OUT SUPER FAST!
THIS IS AS FAR AS I CAN TAKE YOU, LUFFY.
FWUP!
FROM HERE ON, MY POWERS WILL BE DISABLED AND I'LL HAVE NO CAPE TO HIDE YOU WITH.
I WANTED TO HELP YOU MORE, BUT...
DON'T WORRY ABOUT IT! IF IT HADN'T BEEN FOR YOU...
YOU GOT ME INTO THIS PLACE SURROUNDED BY BATTLESHIPS!
...I NEVER WOULD'VE MADE IT THIS FAR!
I CAN TAKE IT FROM HERE!
BUT THIS FORTRESS WAS DESIGNED TO BE ESCAPE-PROOF, LUFFY!
WHATEVER YOU DO, DON'T CAUSE A RUCKUS.
IF YOU'RE CAPTURED, YOU'LL NEVER LEAVE HERE ALIVE!
YOU'RE VERY STRONG, BUT PROMISE ME YOU WON'T GO ON A RAMPAGE.

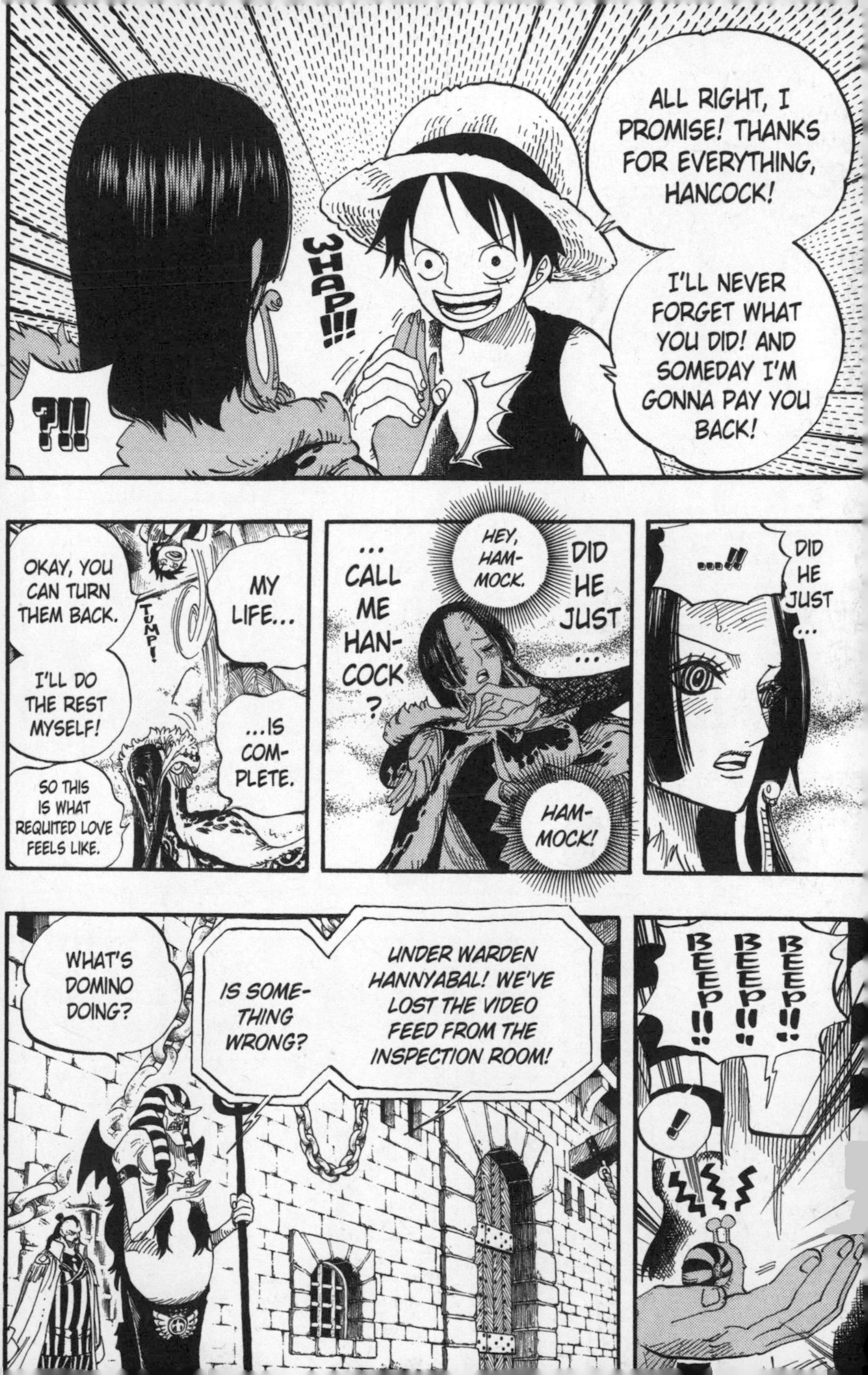
ALL RIGHT, I PROMISE! THANKS FOR EVERYTHING, HANCOCK!
I'LL NEVER FORGET WHAT YOU DID! AND SOMEDAY I'M GONNA PAY YOU BACK!
WHAP!!!
?!!
...!!
DID HE JUST...
HEY, HAM-MOCK.
DID HE JUST...
...CALL ME HAN-COCK?
HAM-MOCK!
MY LIFE...
...IS COM-PLETE.
OKAY, YOU CAN TURN THEM BACK.
TUMP!
I'LL DO THE REST MYSELF!
SO THIS IS WHAT REQUITED LOVE FEELS LIKE.
BEEP!! BEEP!! BEEP!!
!
UNDER WARDEN HANNYABAL! WE'VE LOST THE VIDEO FEED FROM THE INSPECTION ROOM!
IS SOME-THING WRONG?
WHAT'S DOMINO DOING?

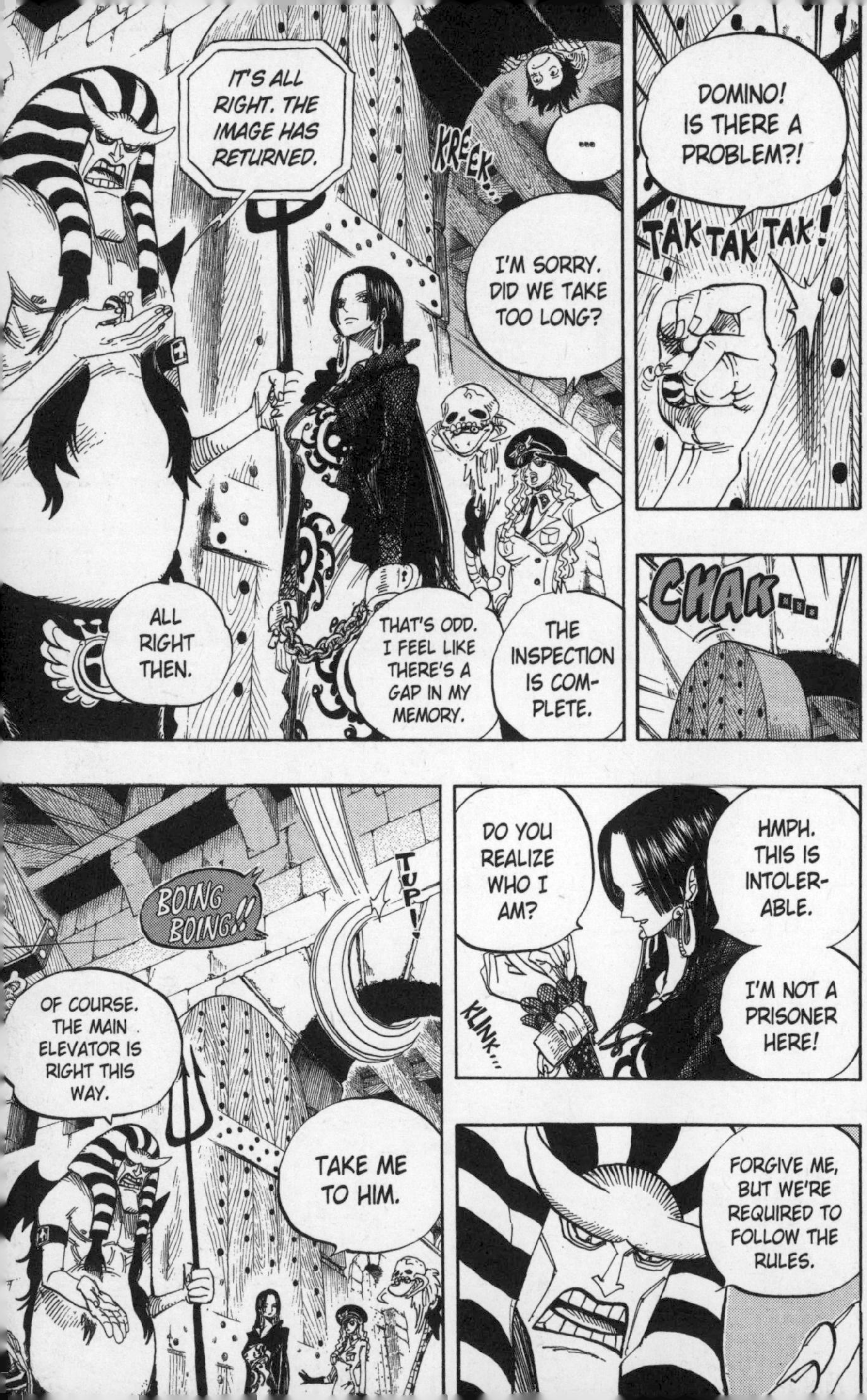
DOMINO! IS THERE A PROBLEM?!
TAK TAK TAK!
CHAK...
...
KREEK...
I'M SORRY. DID WE TAKE TOO LONG?
IT'S ALL RIGHT. THE IMAGE HAS RETURNED.
THE INSPECTION IS COMPLETE.
THAT'S ODD. I FEEL LIKE THERE'S A GAP IN MY MEMORY.
ALL RIGHT THEN.
HMPH. THIS IS INTOLERABLE.
I'M NOT A PRISONER HERE!
DO YOU REALIZE WHO I AM?
KLINK...
FORGIVE ME, BUT WE'RE REQUIRED TO FOLLOW THE RULES.
TUP!
TAKE ME TO HIM.
BOING BOING!!
OF COURSE. THE MAIN ELEVATOR IS RIGHT THIS WAY.

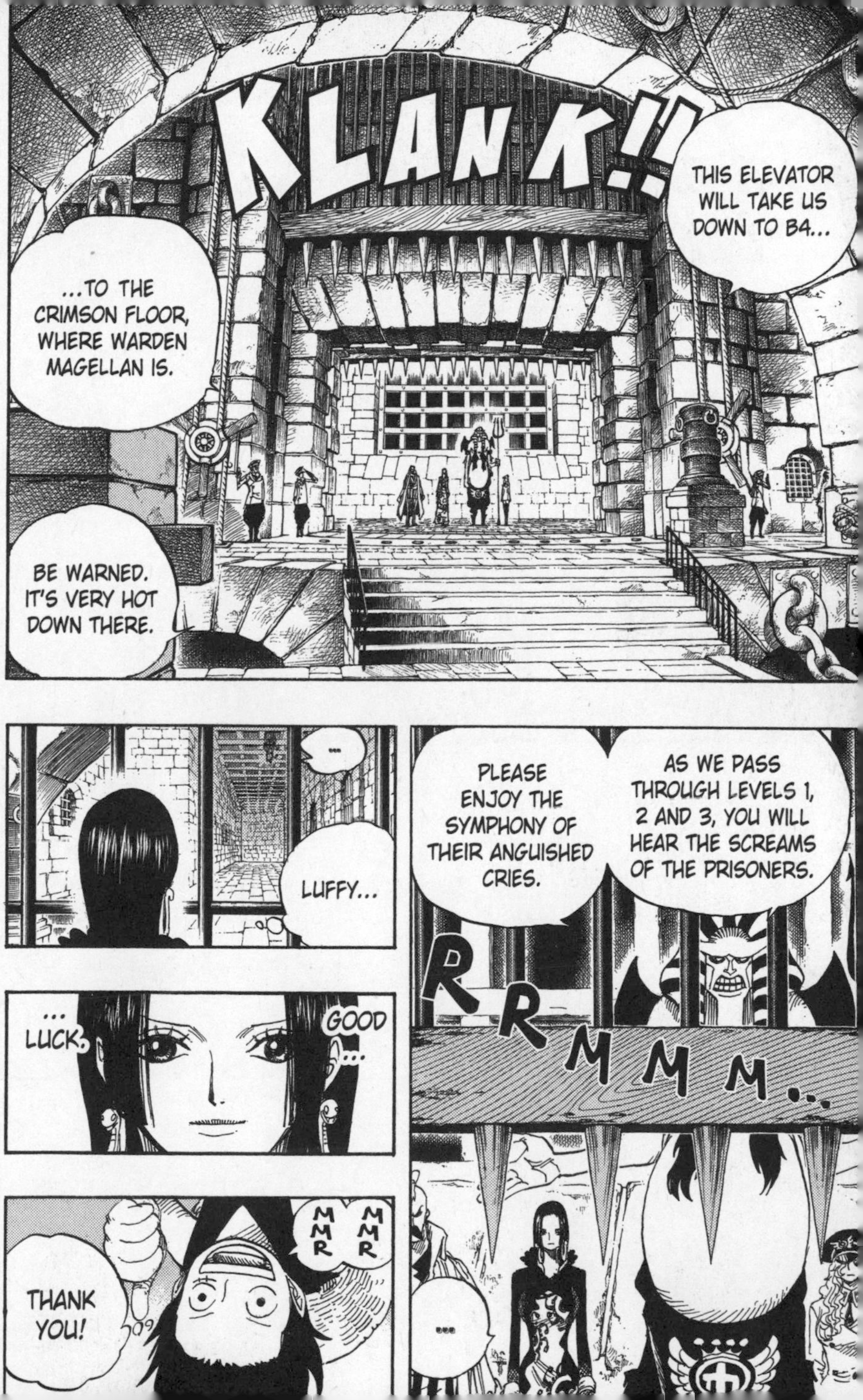
KLANK!!
THIS ELEVATOR WILL TAKE US DOWN TO B4...
...TO THE CRIMSON FLOOR, WHERE WARDEN MAGELLAN IS.
BE WARNED. IT'S VERY HOT DOWN THERE.
AS WE PASS THROUGH LEVELS 1, 2 AND 3, YOU WILL HEAR THE SCREAMS OF THE PRISONERS.
PLEASE ENJOY THE SYMPHONY OF THEIR ANGUISHED CRIES.
RRMMMM..
...
...
LUFFY...
GOOD ...
... LUCK.
MMMR
MMMR
THANK YOU!

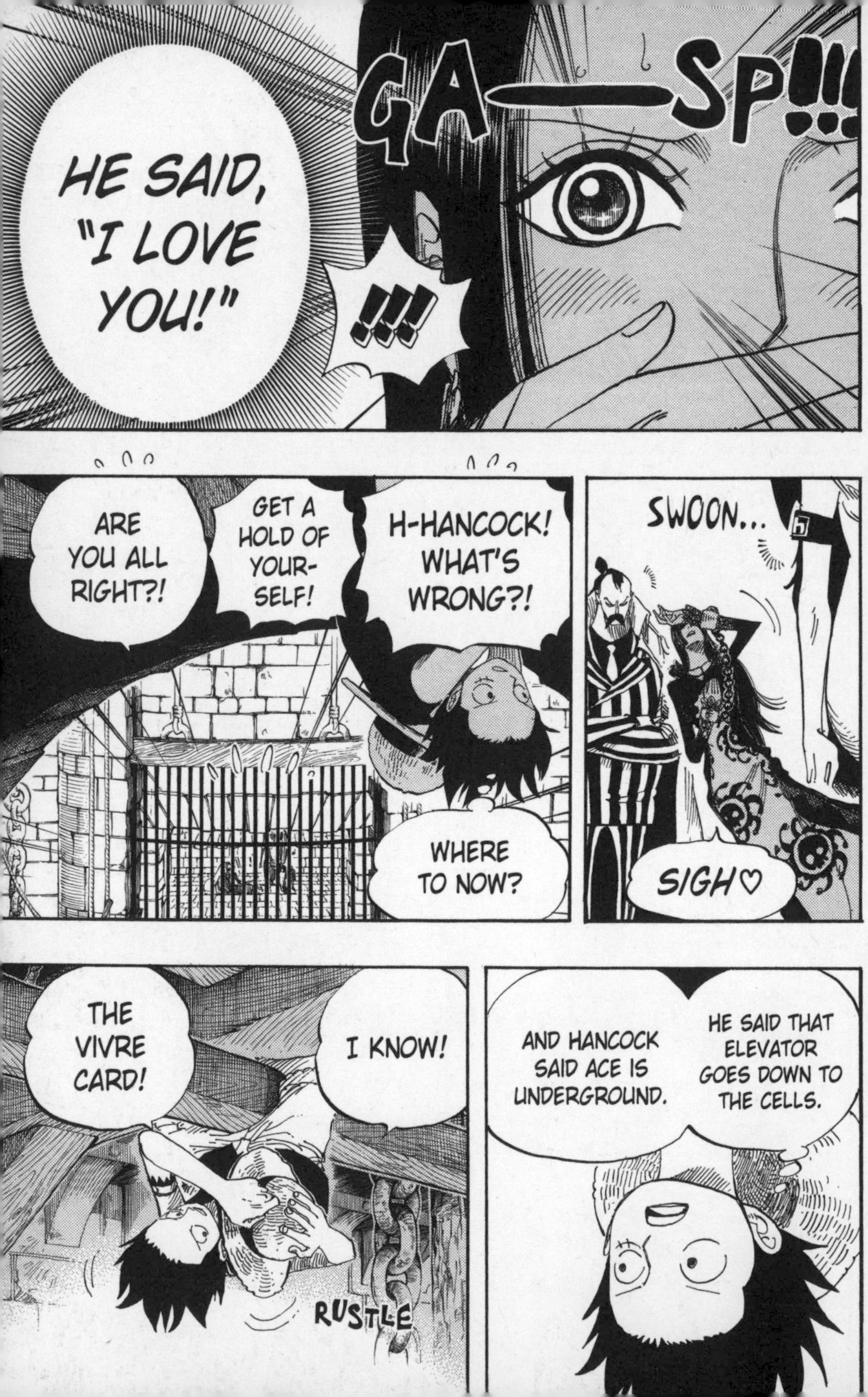
GA—SP!!!
HE SAID, "I LOVE YOU!"
!!!
SWOON...
SIGH♡
H-HANCOCK! WHAT'S WRONG?!
GET A HOLD OF YOURSELF!
ARE YOU ALL RIGHT?!
WHERE TO NOW?
HE SAID THAT ELEVATOR GOES DOWN TO THE CELLS.
AND HANCOCK SAID ACE IS UNDERGROUND.
I KNOW!
THE VIVRE CARD!
RUSTLE

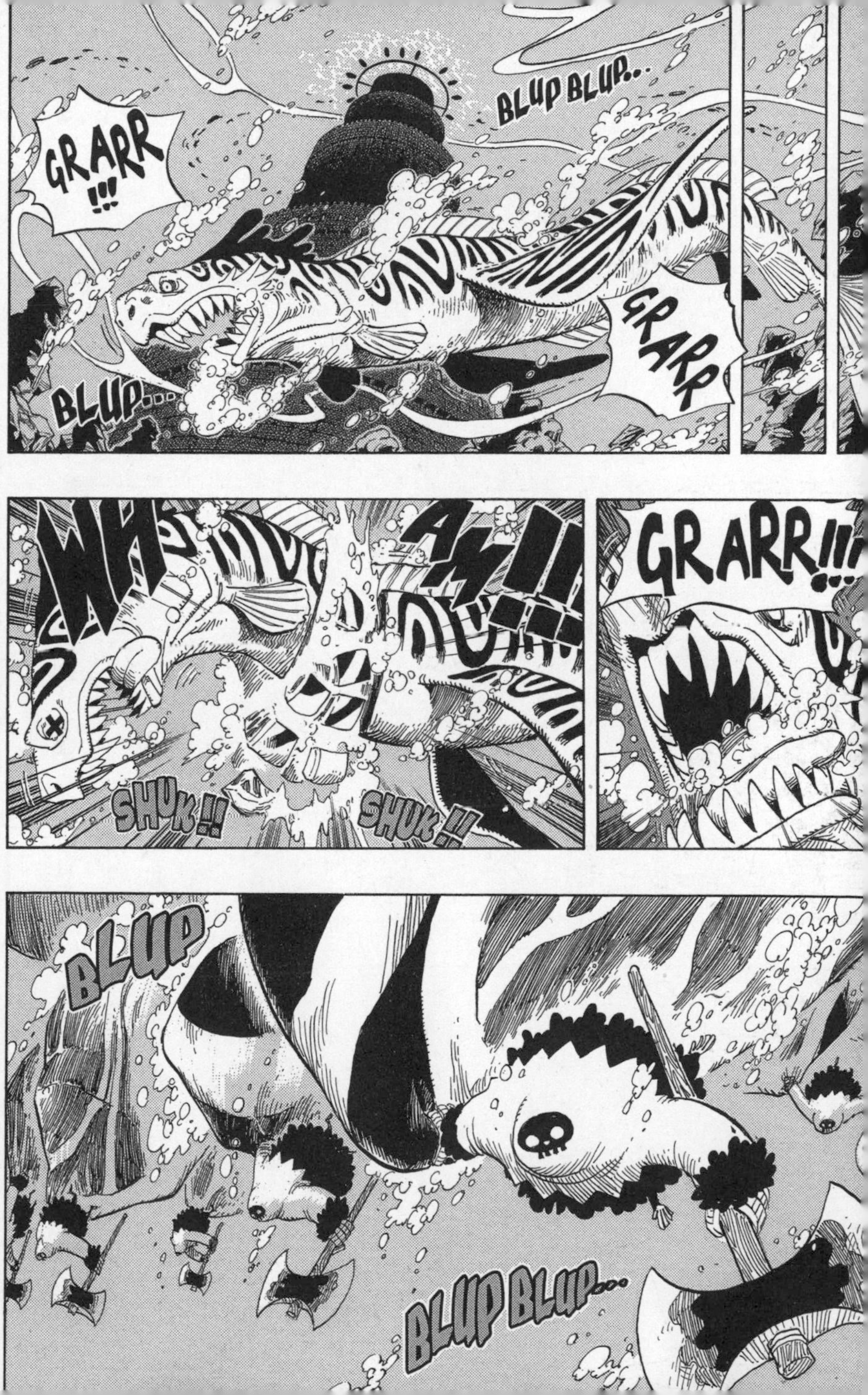
BLUP BLUP...
GRARR
GRARR !!!
BLUP...
GRARR!!!...
AH!!
WH
SHUK!!
SHUK!!
BLUP
BLUP BLUP...

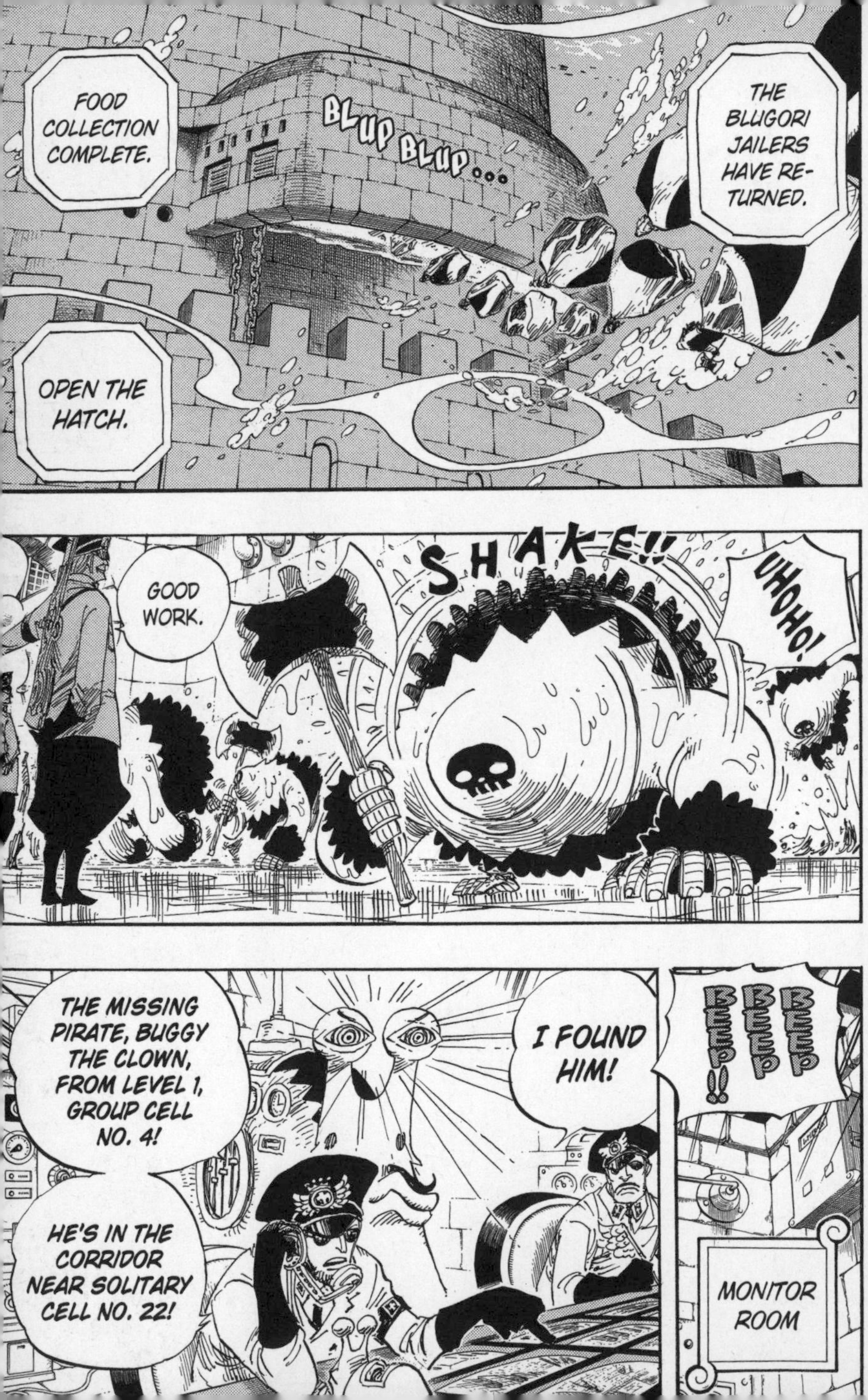
THE BLUGORI JAILERS HAVE RE-TURNED.
BLUP BLUP...
FOOD COLLECTION COMPLETE.
OPEN THE HATCH.
UHOHO!
SHAKE!!
GOOD WORK.
BEEP BEEP BEEP!!
MONITOR ROOM
I FOUND HIM!
THE MISSING PIRATE, BUGGY THE CLOWN, FROM LEVEL 1, GROUP CELL NO. 4!
HE'S IN THE CORRIDOR NEAR SOLITARY CELL NO. 22!

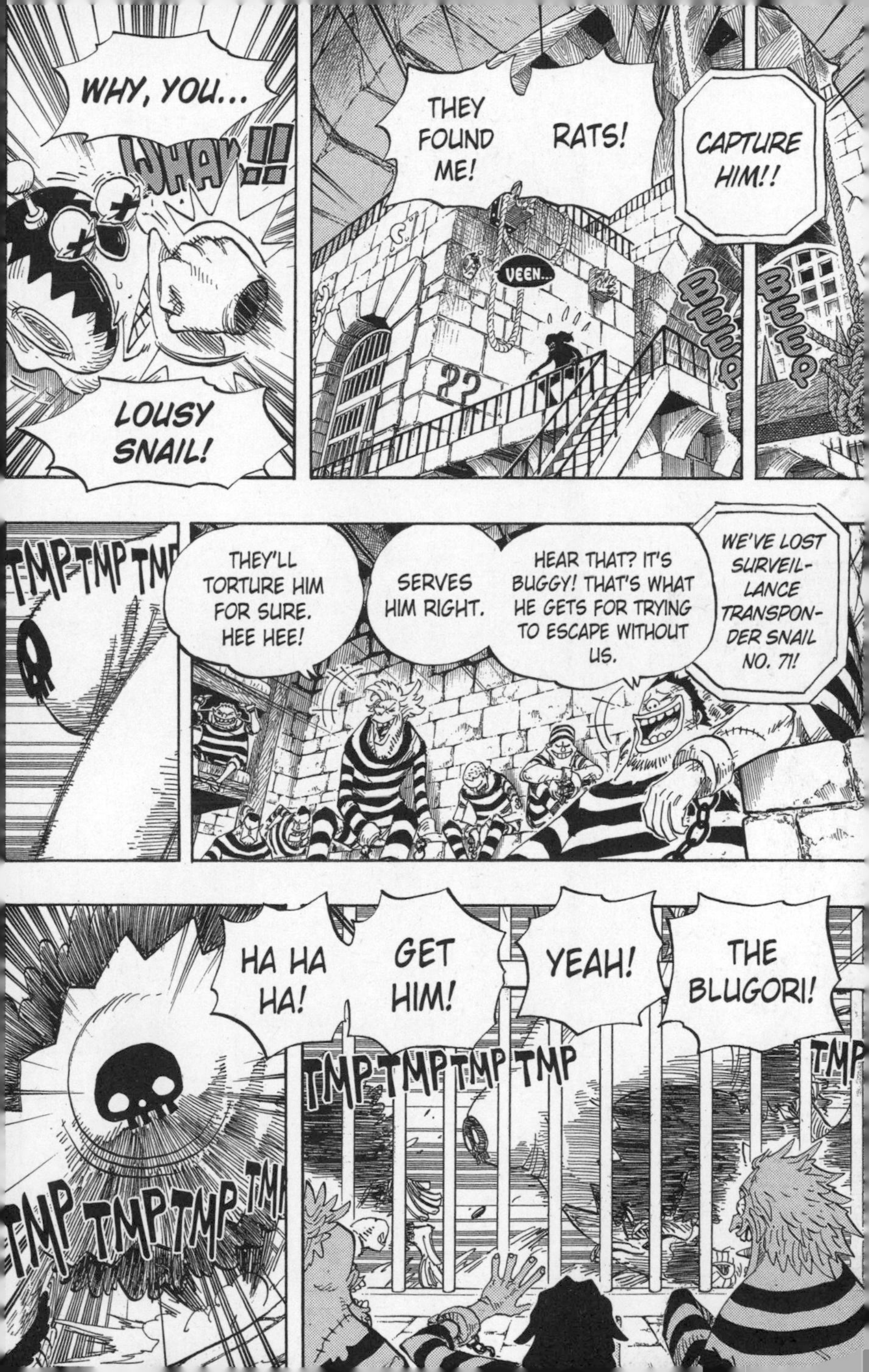
CAPTURE HIM!!
BEEEP
BEEEP
RATS!
THEY FOUND ME!
VEEN...
WHY, YOU...
WHAM!!
LOUSY SNAIL!
WE'VE LOST SURVEIL-LANCE TRANSPON-DER SNAIL NO. 71!
HEAR THAT? IT'S BUGGY! THAT'S WHAT HE GETS FOR TRYING TO ESCAPE WITHOUT US.
SERVES HIM RIGHT.
THEY'LL TORTURE HIM FOR SURE. HEE HEE!
TMP TMP TMP
THE BLUGORI!
YEAH!
GET HIM!
HA HA HA!
TMP
TMP TMP TMP TMP
TMP TMP TMP TMP

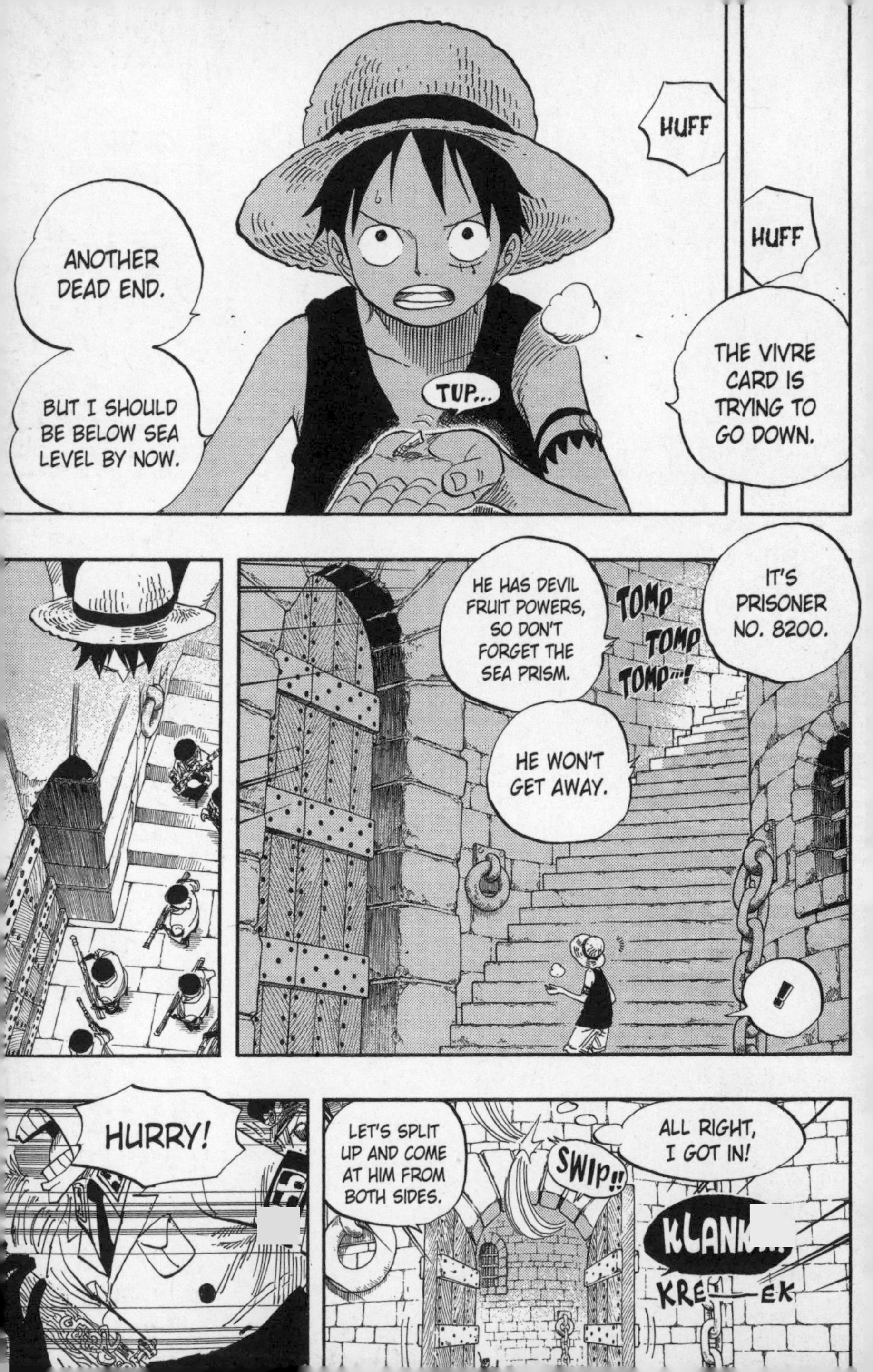
HUFF
HUFF
ANOTHER DEAD END.
BUT I SHOULD BE BELOW SEA LEVEL BY NOW.
TUP...
THE VIVRE CARD IS TRYING TO GO DOWN.
IT'S PRISONER NO. 8200.
TOMP TOMP TOMP...!
HE HAS DEVIL FRUIT POWERS, SO DON'T FORGET THE SEA PRISM.
HE WON'T GET AWAY.
!
ALL RIGHT, I GOT IN!
SWIP!!
LET'S SPLIT UP AND COME AT HIM FROM BOTH SIDES.
KLANK
KRE-EK
HURRY!

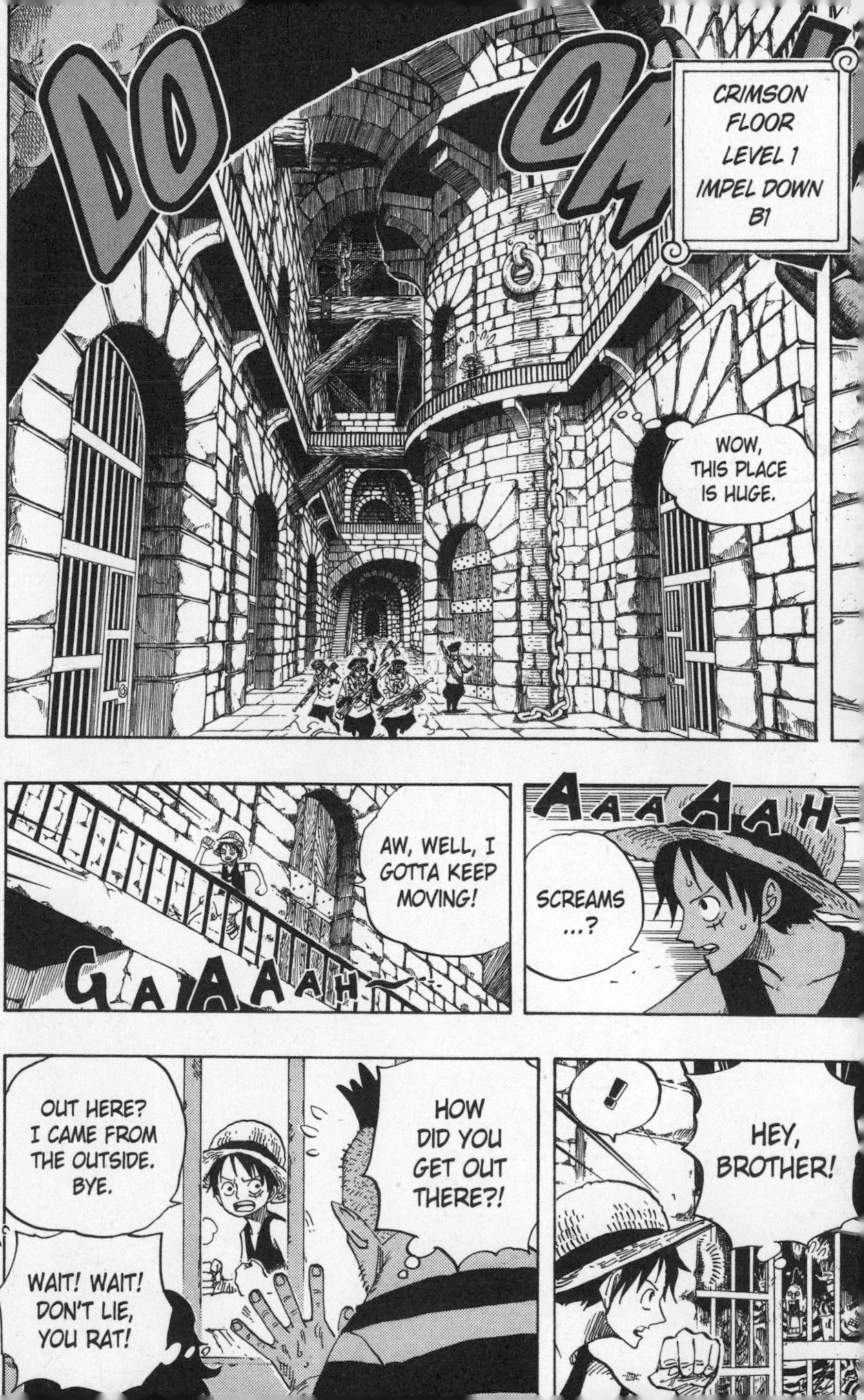
CRIMSON FLOOR LEVEL 1 IMPEL DOWN B1
DO
OM
WOW, THIS PLACE IS HUGE.
AAAAAH—
SCREAMS ...?
AW, WELL, I GOTTA KEEP MOVING!
GAAAAAH
!
HEY, BROTHER!
HOW DID YOU GET OUT THERE?!
OUT HERE? I CAME FROM THE OUTSIDE. BYE.
WAIT! WAIT! DON'T LIE, YOU RAT!

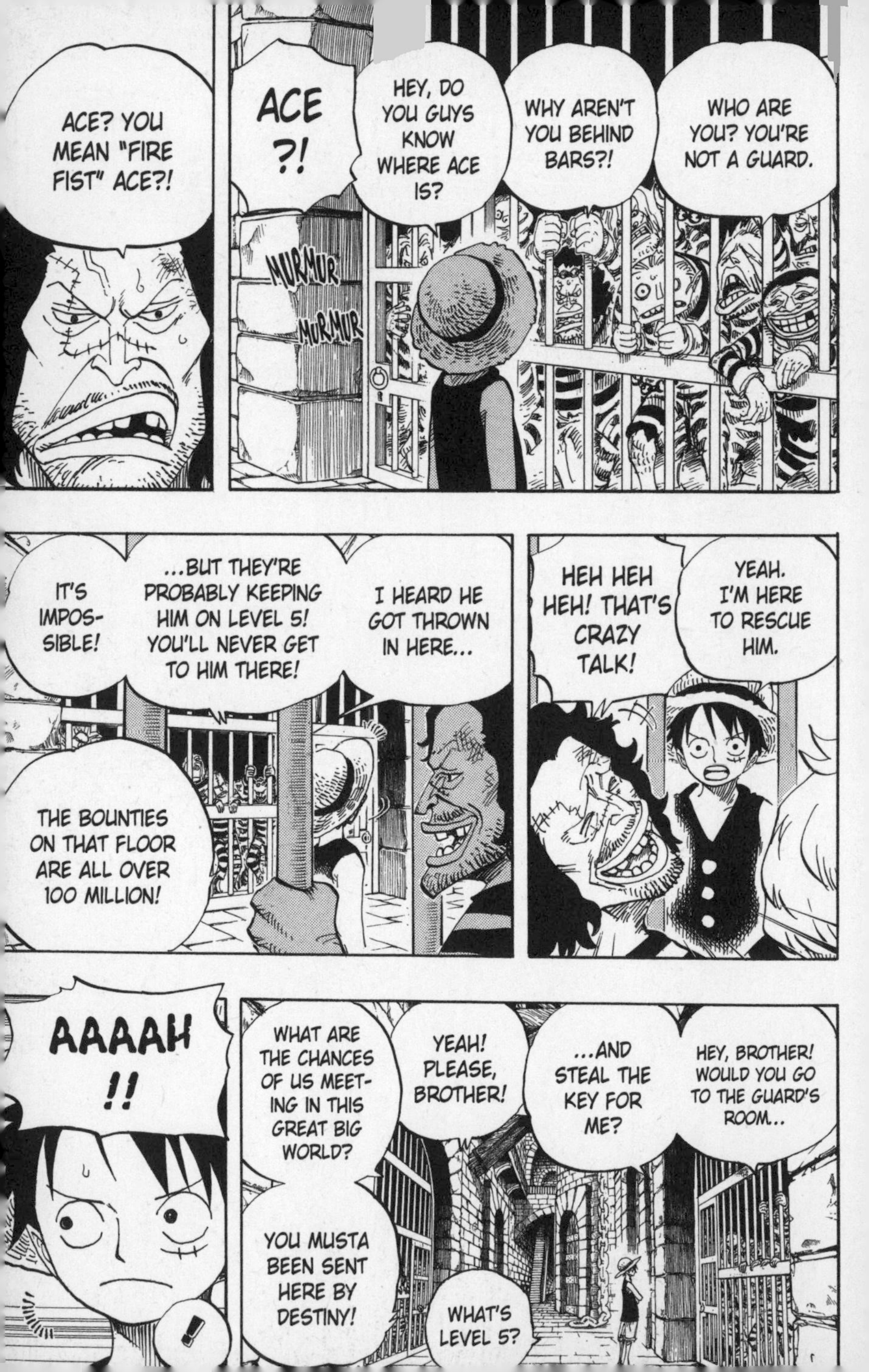
WHO ARE YOU? YOU'RE NOT A GUARD.
WHY AREN'T YOU BEHIND BARS?!
HEY, DO YOU GUYS KNOW WHERE ACE IS?
ACE ?!
MURMUR
MURMUR
ACE? YOU MEAN "FIRE FIST" ACE?!
YEAH. I'M HERE TO RESCUE HIM.
HEH HEH HEH! THAT'S CRAZY TALK!
I HEARD HE GOT THROWN IN HERE...
...BUT THEY'RE PROBABLY KEEPING HIM ON LEVEL 5! YOU'LL NEVER GET TO HIM THERE!
IT'S IMPOS-SIBLE!
THE BOUNTIES ON THAT FLOOR ARE ALL OVER 100 MILLION!
HEY, BROTHER! WOULD YOU GO TO THE GUARD'S ROOM...
...AND STEAL THE KEY FOR ME?
YEAH! PLEASE, BROTHER!
WHAT ARE THE CHANCES OF US MEET-ING IN THIS GREAT BIG WORLD?
YOU MUSTA BEEN SENT HERE BY DESTINY!
WHAT'S LEVEL 5?
AAAAH !!
!

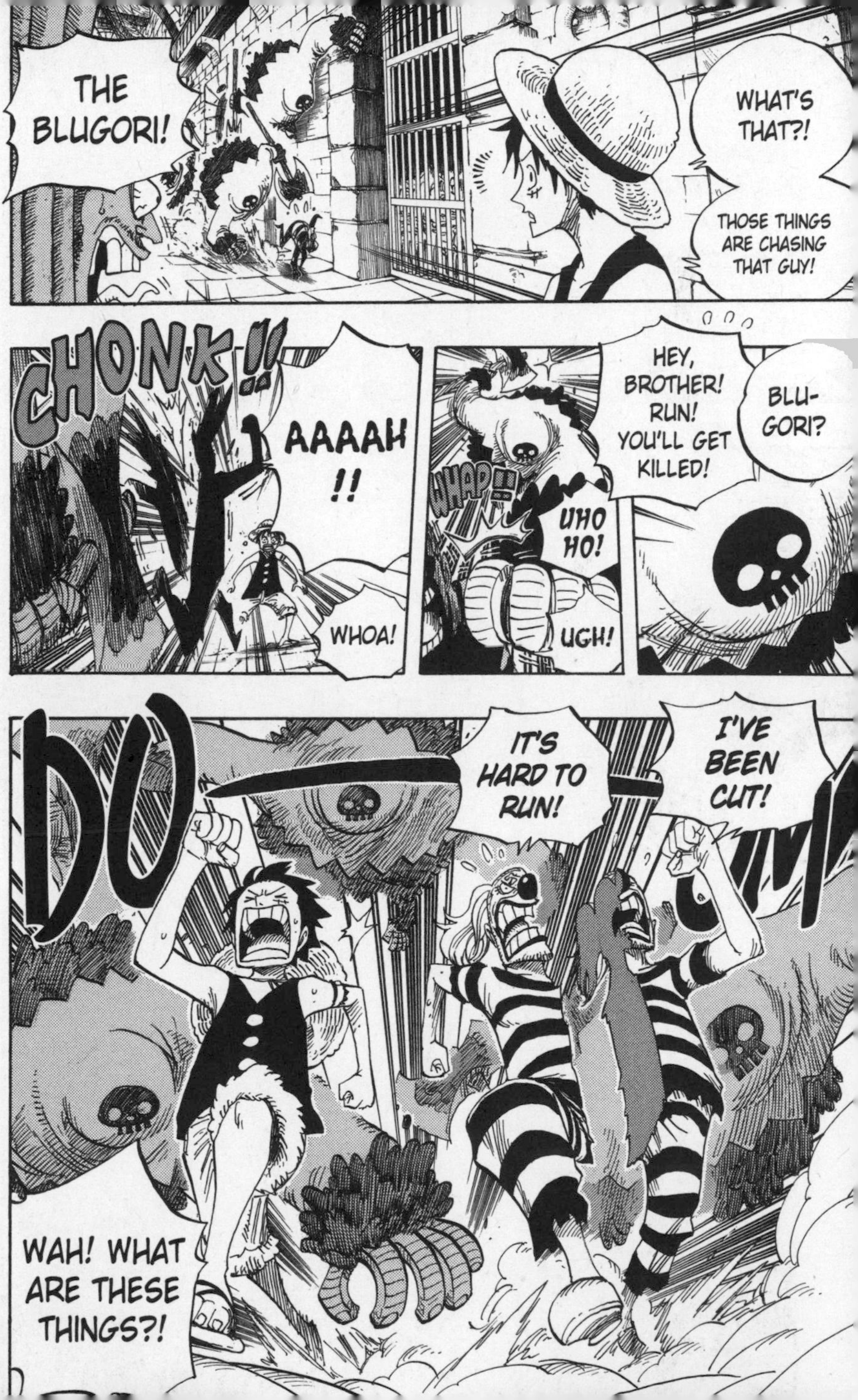
WHAT'S THAT?!
THOSE THINGS ARE CHASING THAT GUY!
THE BLUGORI!
BLU-GORI?
HEY, BROTHER! RUN! YOU'LL GET KILLED!
WHAP!!
UHO HO!
UGH!
CHONK!!
AAAAH !!
WHOA!
I'VE BEEN CUT!
IT'S HARD TO RUN!
DO
WAH! WHAT ARE THESE THINGS?!

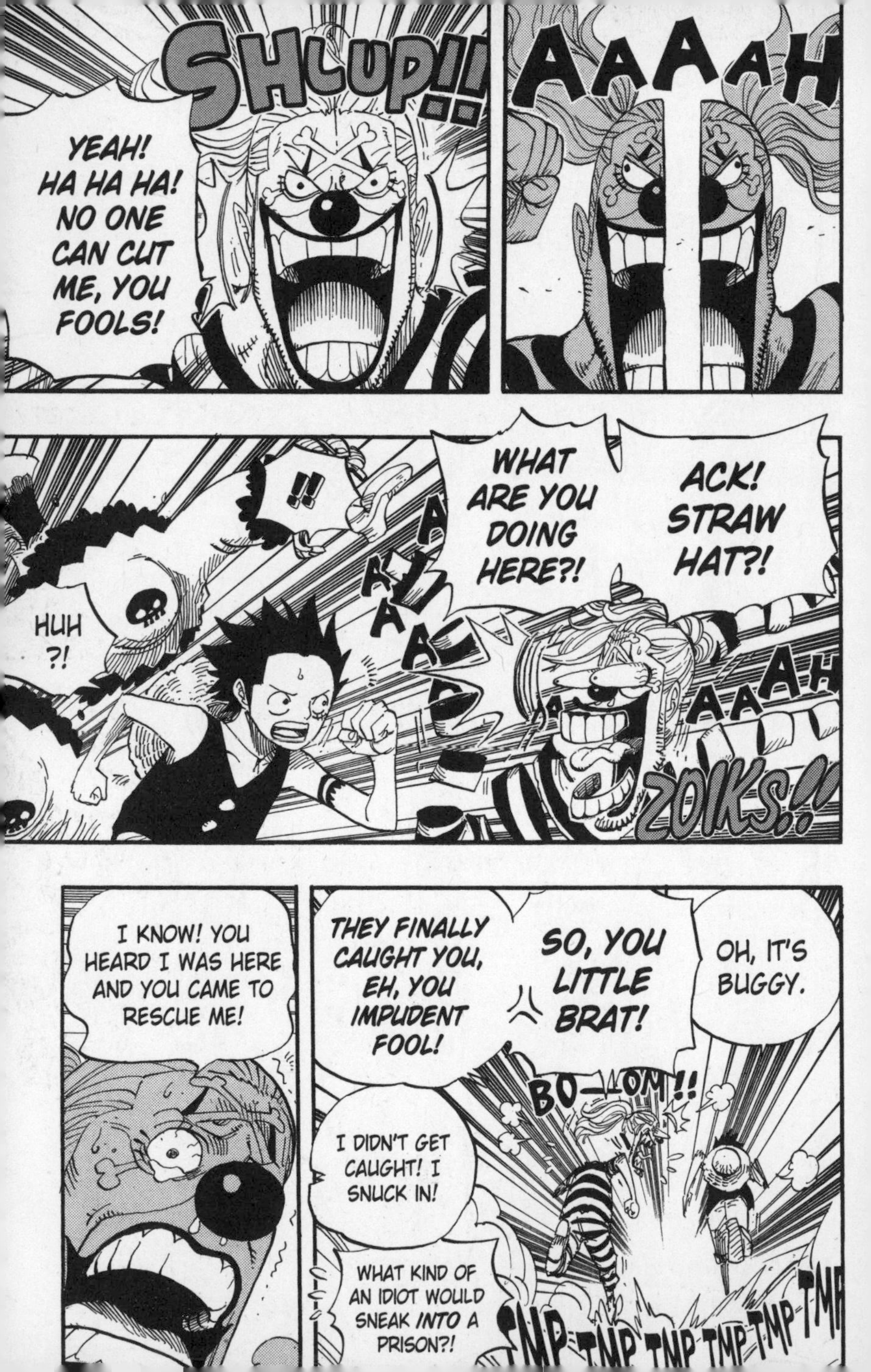
AAAAH
SHLUP!!
YEAH! HA HA HA! NO ONE CAN CUT ME, YOU FOOLS!
ACK! STRAW HAT?!
WHAT ARE YOU DOING HERE?!
AAAAH
ZOIKS!!
!!
HUH ?!
OH, IT'S BUGGY.
SO, YOU LITTLE BRAT!
THEY FINALLY CAUGHT YOU, EH, YOU IMPUDENT FOOL!
BO-OOM!!
I DIDN'T GET CAUGHT! I SNUCK IN!
TMP TMP TMP TMP TMP TMP
WHAT KIND OF AN IDIOT WOULD SNEAK *INTO* A PRISON?!
I KNOW! YOU HEARD I WAS HERE AND YOU CAME TO RESCUE ME!

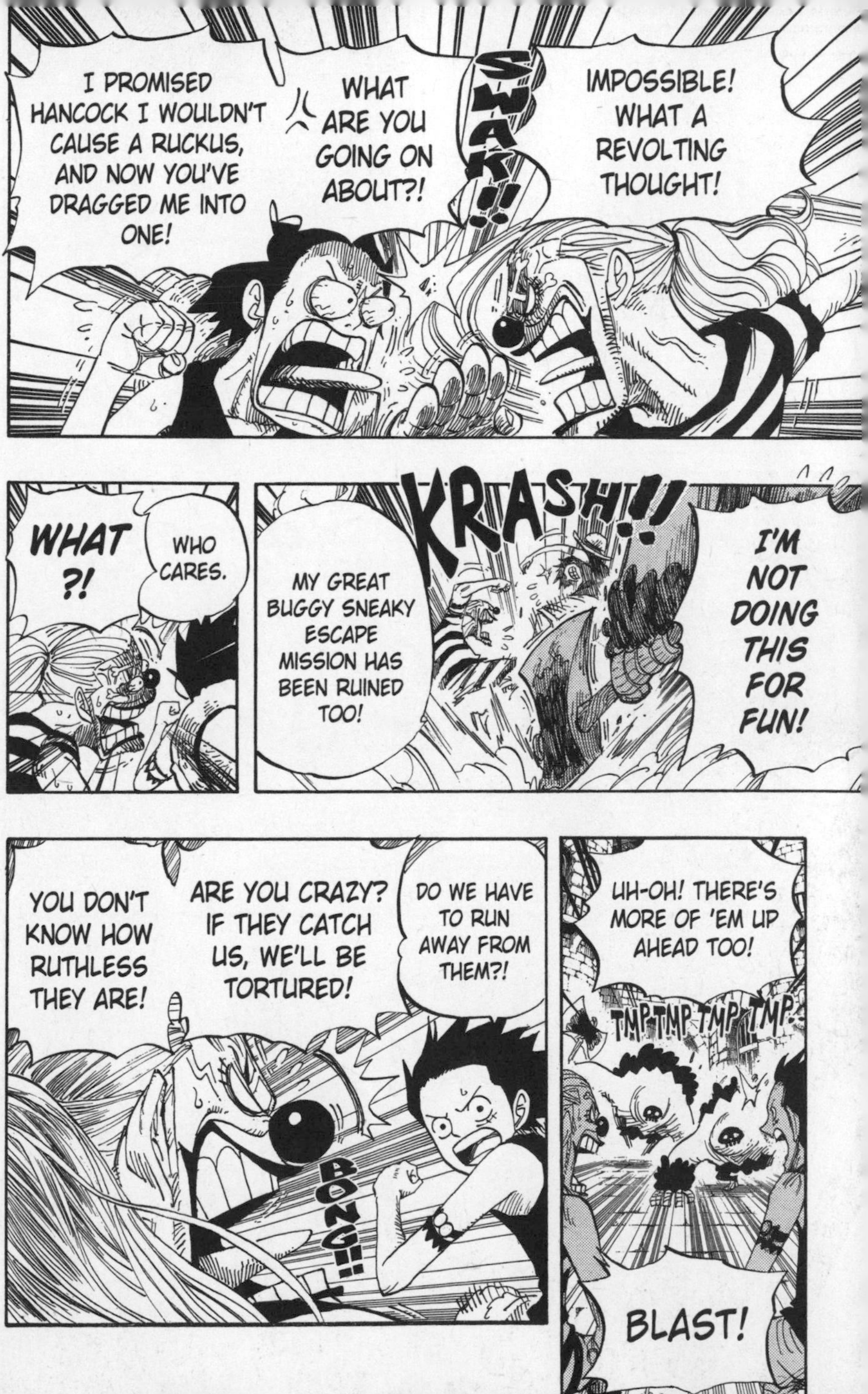
IMPOSSIBLE! WHAT A REVOLTING THOUGHT!
SWAK!!
WHAT ARE YOU GOING ON ABOUT?!
I PROMISED HANCOCK I WOULDN'T CAUSE A RUCKUS, AND NOW YOU'VE DRAGGED ME INTO ONE!
I'M NOT DOING THIS FOR FUN!
KRASH!!
MY GREAT BUGGY SNEAKY ESCAPE MISSION HAS BEEN RUINED TOO!
WHO CARES.
WHAT ?!
UH-OH! THERE'S MORE OF 'EM UP AHEAD TOO!
TMP TMP TMP TMP
BLAST!
DO WE HAVE TO RUN AWAY FROM THEM?!
ARE YOU CRAZY? IF THEY CATCH US, WE'LL BE TORTURED!
YOU DON'T KNOW HOW RUTHLESS THEY ARE!
BONG!!

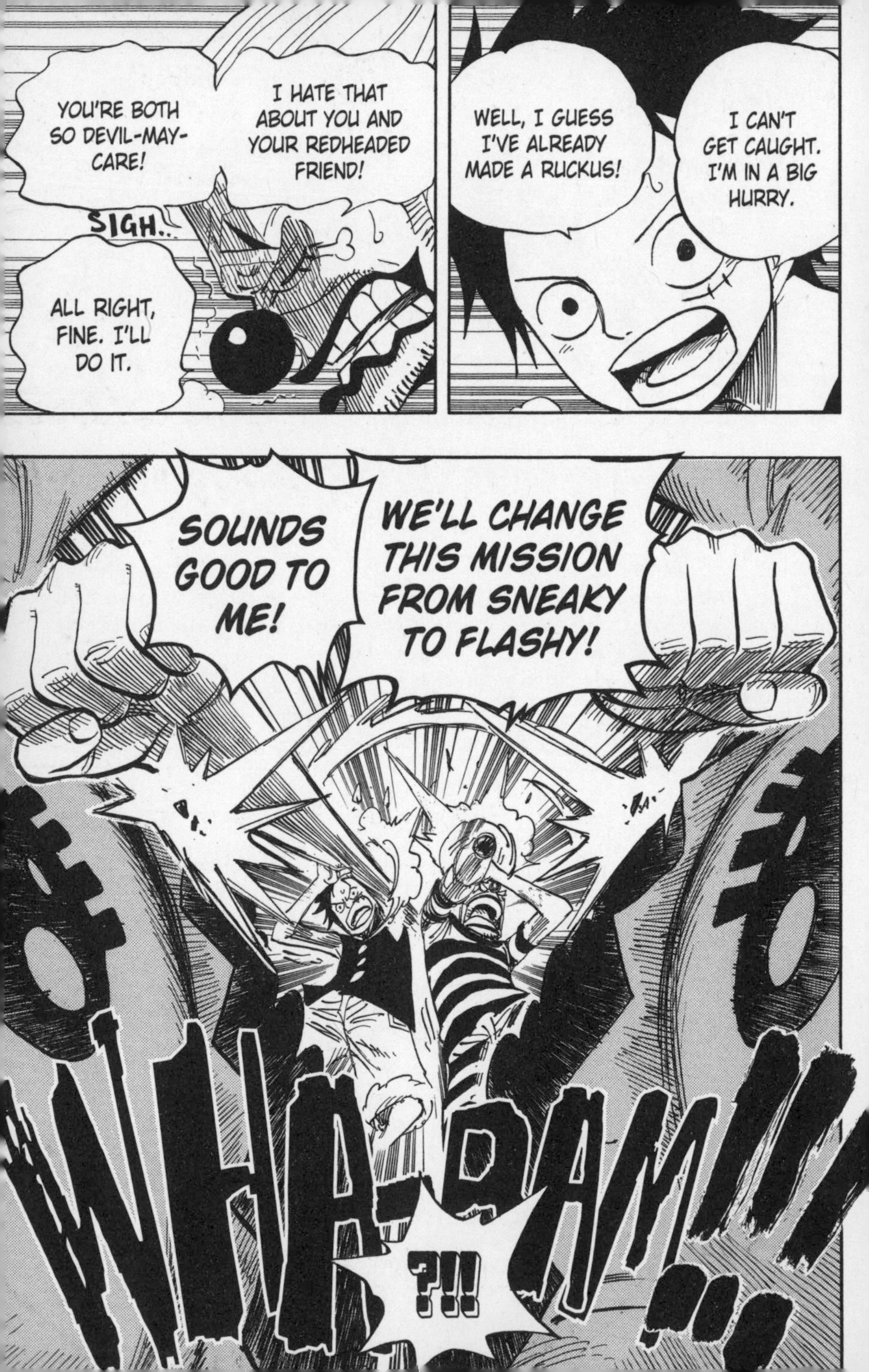
I CAN'T GET CAUGHT. I'M IN A BIG HURRY.
WELL, I GUESS I'VE ALREADY MADE A RUCKUS!
I HATE THAT ABOUT YOU AND YOUR REDHEADED FRIEND!
YOU'RE BOTH SO DEVIL-MAY-CARE!
SIGH...
ALL RIGHT, FINE. I'LL DO IT.
WE'LL CHANGE THIS MISSION FROM SNEAKY TO FLASHY!
SOUNDS GOOD TO ME!
WHA-BAM!!...
?!!

SBS Question Corner

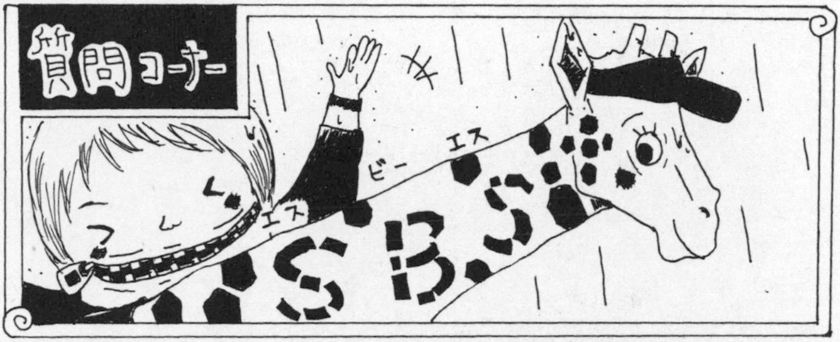
質問コーナー
エス
ビー
エス
SBS

(Yuki, Iwate)

Q: I'm in love with the Snake Princess and all of the Kuja Girls!♡ I'm especially in love with that lady with the cigarette that's wearing only a jacket on top of her bare skin! It seems that the names of the characters of Kuja haven't been shown anywhere. (like the girl taking notes or the members of the Kuja pirates) Please tell me their names!

--Ice Fish

A: They're called the Kuja Girls now? That sounds really nice. They do have names, but I just haven't shown them. I went through my sketchbook and picked them out from there. Go ahead and take a look if you're that interested.

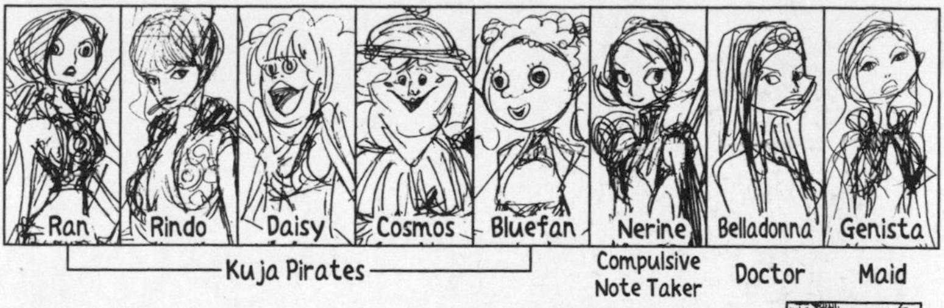
Ran
Rindo
Daisy
Cosmos
Bluefan
Nerine
Belladonna
Genista
Kuja Pirates
Compulsive Note Taker
Doctor
Maid

Q: Oda... If you ate the Clear-Clear Fruit, what would you do?

--Lumberjack

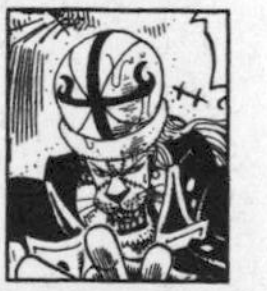

A: Heh!♡ Heh heh...♡ Whoops! Moving on

Good morning afternoon evening night! Hey, Odacchi!

Q: In volume 53, page 193, third panel, I saw Buggy on the newspaper that Grandma Nyon was reading. Did he finally get captured? What happened here?

--Okoge Riceball

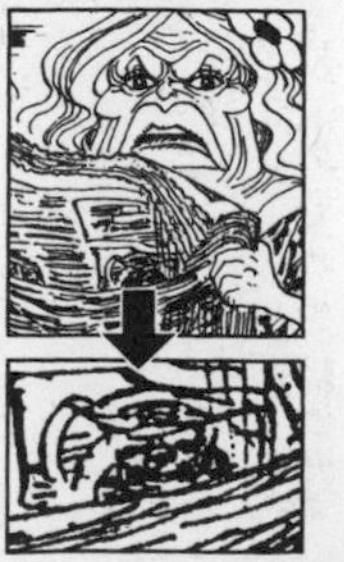

A: Man, nothing gets past these readers... You're right. I did, in fact, draw Buggy. You'll find out why he's on the newspaper when you read this volume! Buggy got caught! He got caught by entering a navy garrison that he thought was a cave with Captain John's treasure. That's what the article says.

Chapter 527:
LEVEL 1: CRIMSON HELL

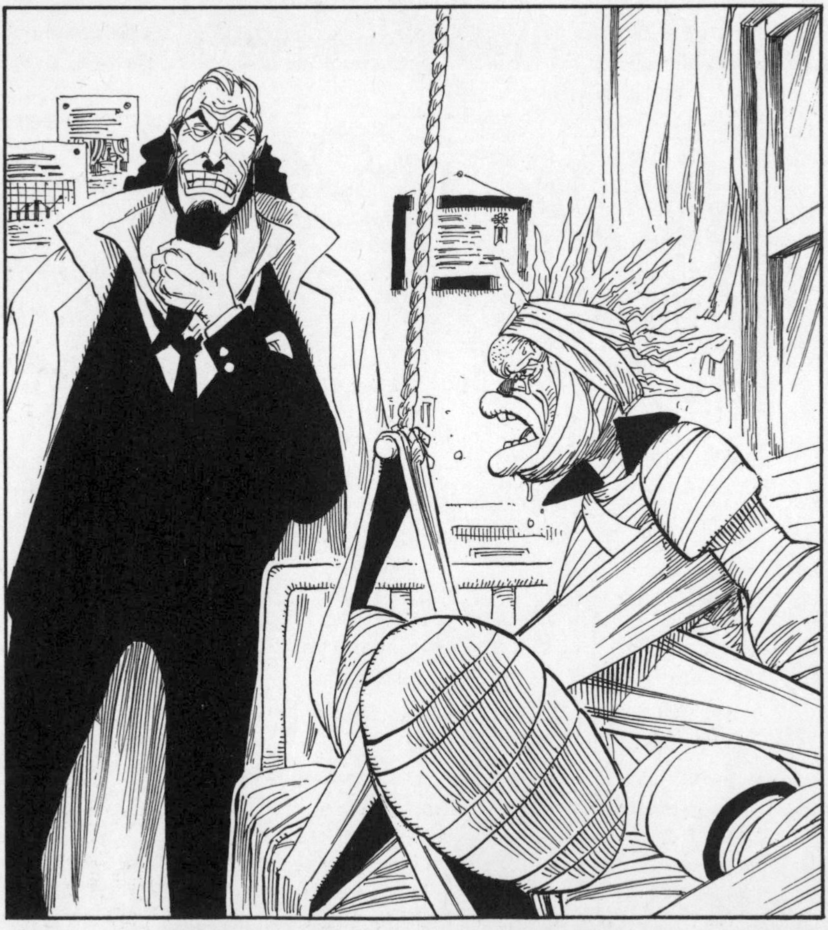

CP9 INDEPENDENT REPORT, VOL. 32:
"FATHER AND SON PLOTTING TO KILL CP9 AGENTS"

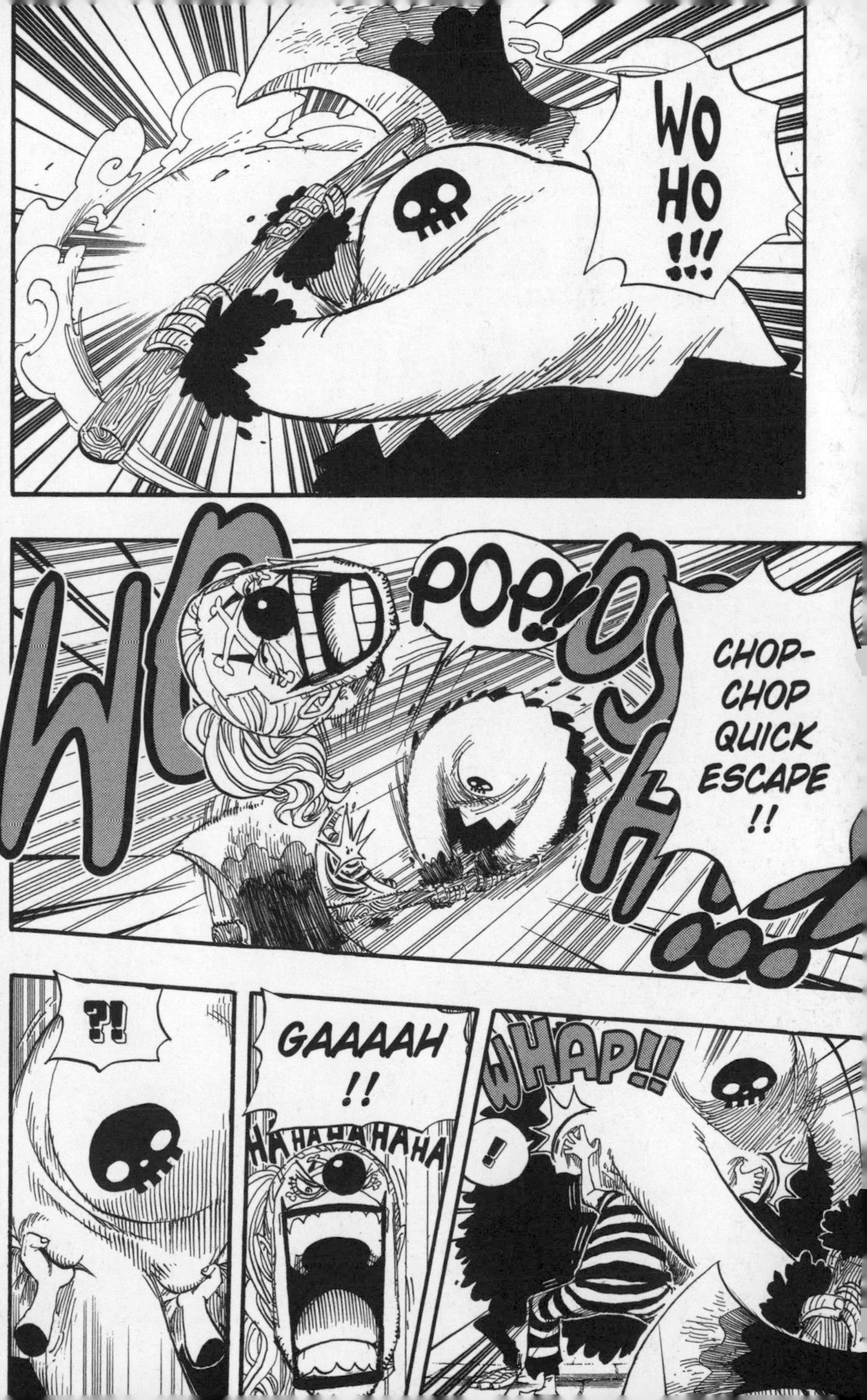
WO HO!!!
CHOP-CHOP QUICK ESCAPE!!
POP!!
WHAP!!
!
GAAAAH!!
HAHAHAHAHA
?!

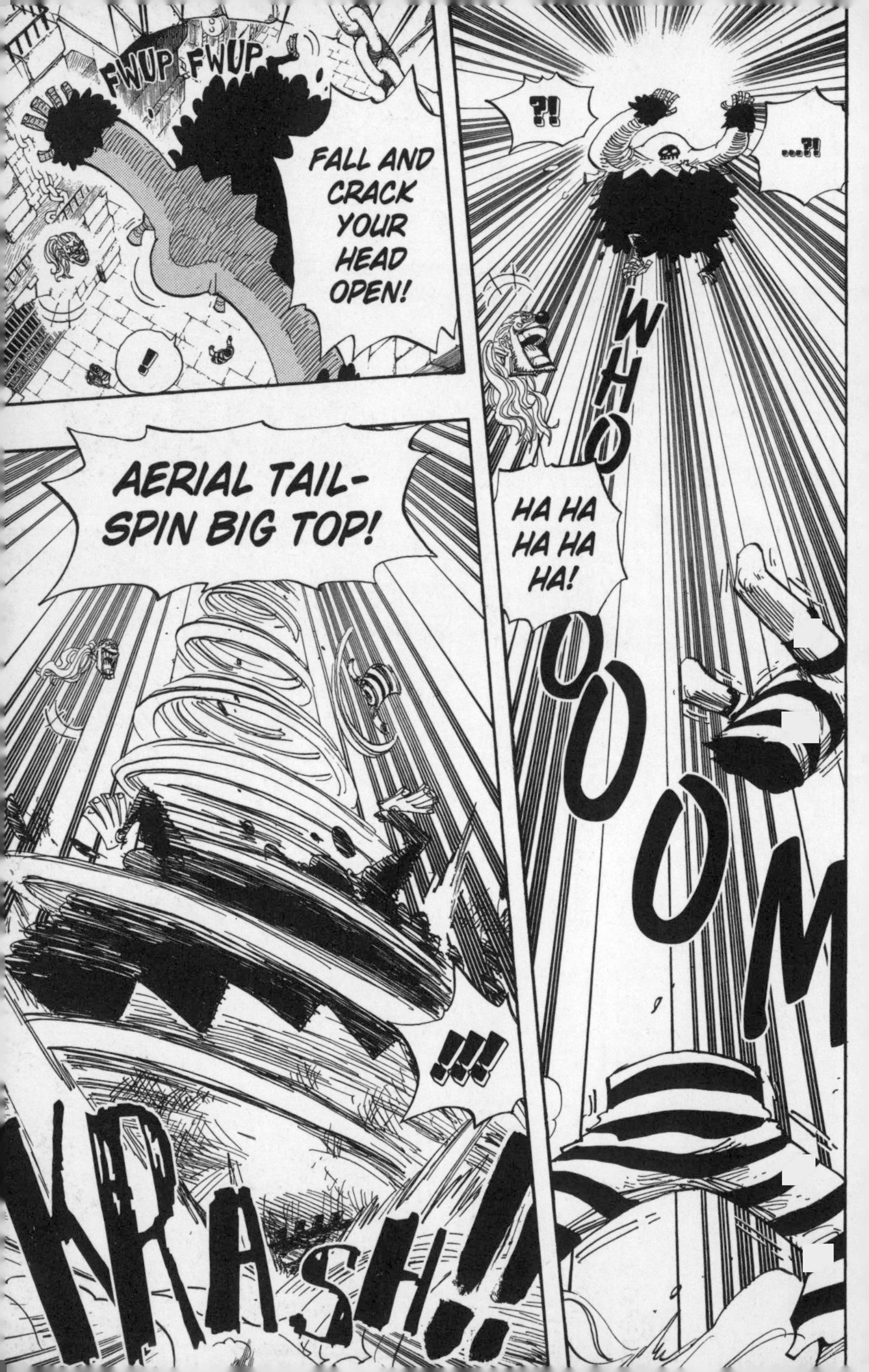
?!
...?!
WHOOOOM
HA HA HA HA HA!
FWUP FWUP
FALL AND CRACK YOUR HEAD OPEN!
!
AERIAL TAIL-SPIN BIG TOP!
!!!
KRASH!!

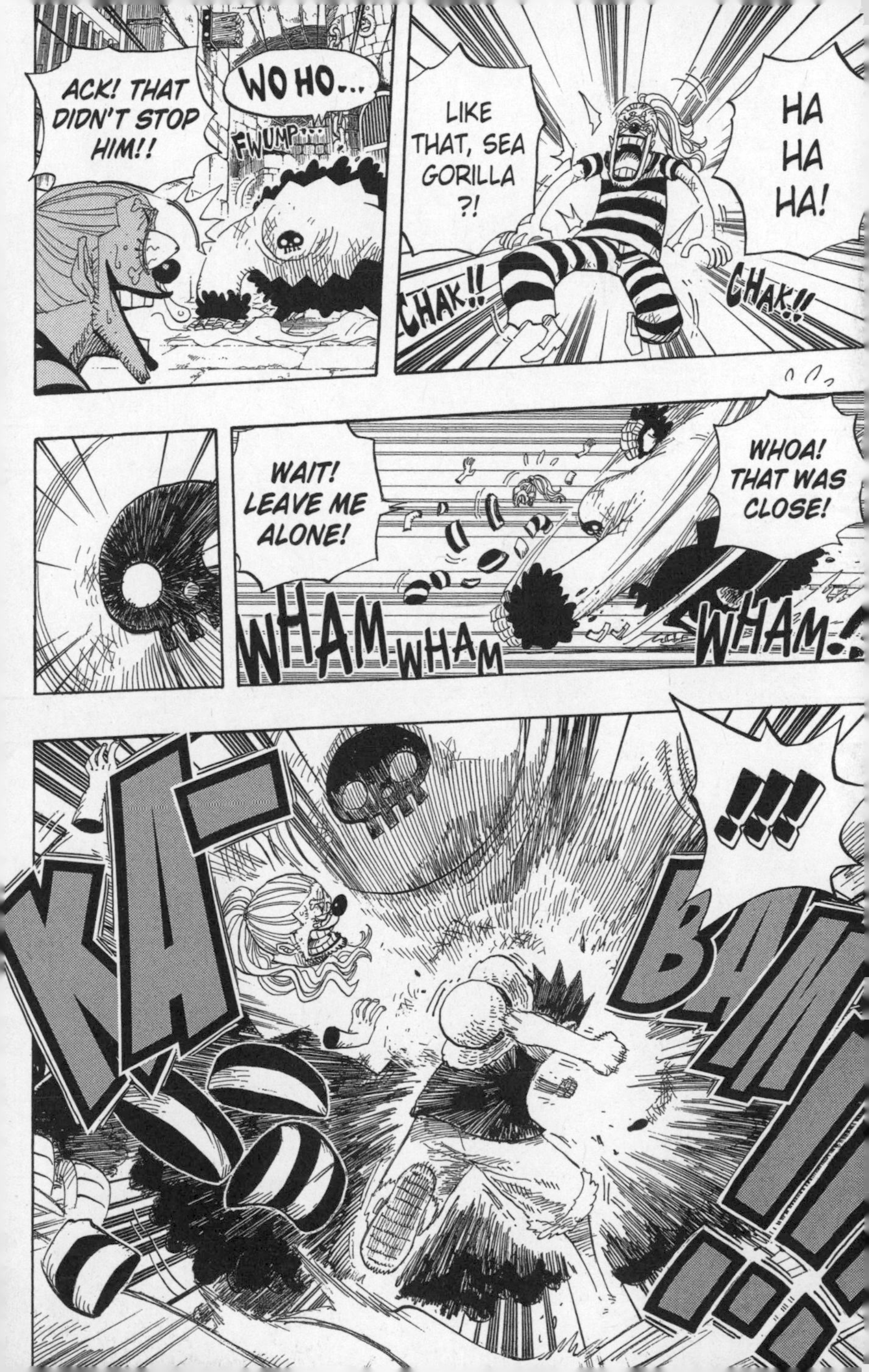
HA HA HA!
LIKE THAT, SEA GORILLA ?!
CHAK!!
CHAK!!
WO HO...
FWUMP...
ACK! THAT DIDN'T STOP HIM!!
WHOA! THAT WAS CLOSE!
WAIT! LEAVE ME ALONE!
WHAM!!
WHAM WHAM
!!!

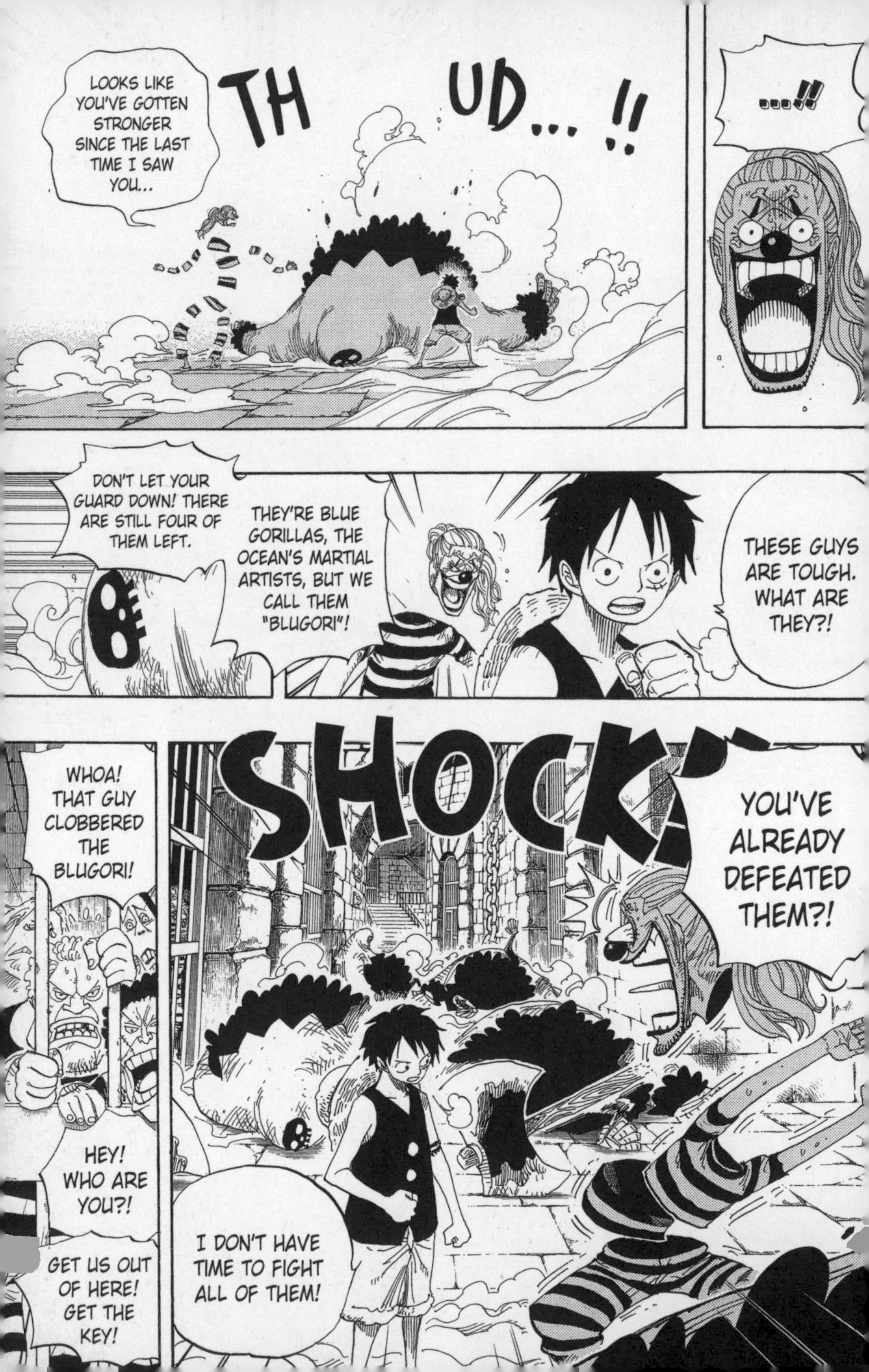
...!!
THUD...!!
LOOKS LIKE YOU'VE GOTTEN STRONGER SINCE THE LAST TIME I SAW YOU...
THESE GUYS ARE TOUGH. WHAT ARE THEY?!
THEY'RE BLUE GORILLAS, THE OCEAN'S MARTIAL ARTISTS, BUT WE CALL THEM "BLUGORI"!
DON'T LET YOUR GUARD DOWN! THERE ARE STILL FOUR OF THEM LEFT.
SHOCK
YOU'VE ALREADY DEFEATED THEM?!
I DON'T HAVE TIME TO FIGHT ALL OF THEM!
WHOA! THAT GUY CLOBBERED THE BLUGORI!
HEY! WHO ARE YOU?!
GET US OUT OF HERE! GET THE KEY!

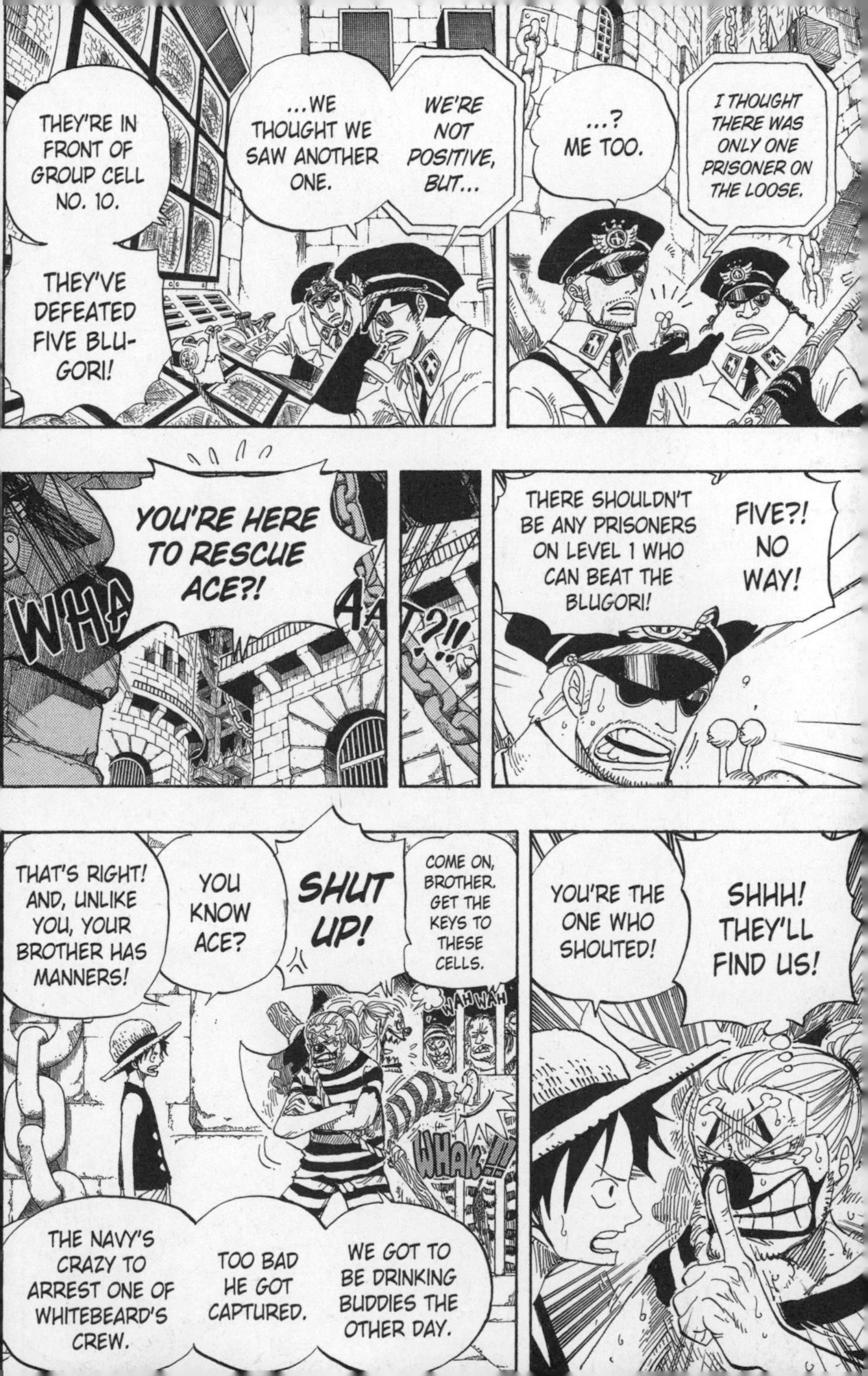
I THOUGHT THERE WAS ONLY ONE PRISONER ON THE LOOSE.
...? ME TOO.
WE'RE NOT POSITIVE, BUT...
...WE THOUGHT WE SAW ANOTHER ONE.
THEY'RE IN FRONT OF GROUP CELL NO. 10.
THEY'VE DEFEATED FIVE BLU-GORI!
FIVE?! NO WAY!
THERE SHOULDN'T BE ANY PRISONERS ON LEVEL 1 WHO CAN BEAT THE BLUGORI!
YOU'RE HERE TO RESCUE ACE?!
WHA
AAT?!!
SHHH! THEY'LL FIND US!
YOU'RE THE ONE WHO SHOUTED!
COME ON, BROTHER. GET THE KEYS TO THESE CELLS.
SHUT UP!
YOU KNOW ACE?
THAT'S RIGHT! AND, UNLIKE YOU, YOUR BROTHER HAS MANNERS!
WAH WAH
WHAK!!
WE GOT TO BE DRINKING BUDDIES THE OTHER DAY.
TOO BAD HE GOT CAPTURED.
THE NAVY'S CRAZY TO ARREST ONE OF WHITEBEARD'S CREW.

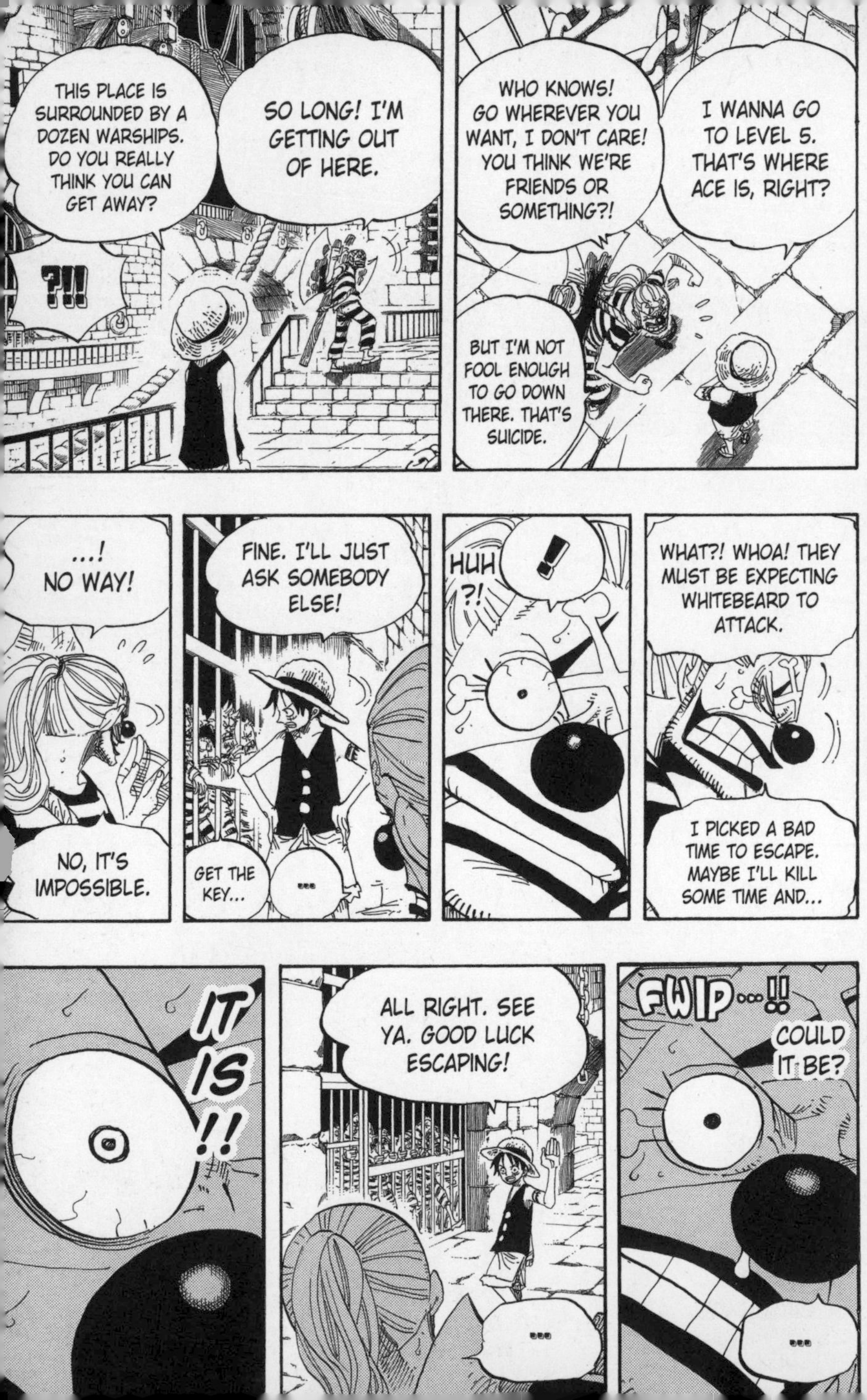
I WANNA GO TO LEVEL 5. THAT'S WHERE ACE IS, RIGHT?
WHO KNOWS! GO WHEREVER YOU WANT, I DON'T CARE! YOU THINK WE'RE FRIENDS OR SOMETHING?!
BUT I'M NOT FOOL ENOUGH TO GO DOWN THERE. THAT'S SUICIDE.
SO LONG! I'M GETTING OUT OF HERE.
THIS PLACE IS SURROUNDED BY A DOZEN WARSHIPS. DO YOU REALLY THINK YOU CAN GET AWAY?
?!!
WHAT?! WHOA! THEY MUST BE EXPECTING WHITEBEARD TO ATTACK.
I PICKED A BAD TIME TO ESCAPE. MAYBE I'LL KILL SOME TIME AND...
!
HUH ?!
FINE. I'LL JUST ASK SOMEBODY ELSE!
...
GET THE KEY...
...! NO WAY!
NO, IT'S IMPOSSIBLE.
FWIP...!!
COULD IT BE?
...
ALL RIGHT. SEE YA. GOOD LUCK ESCAPING!
...
IT IS!!

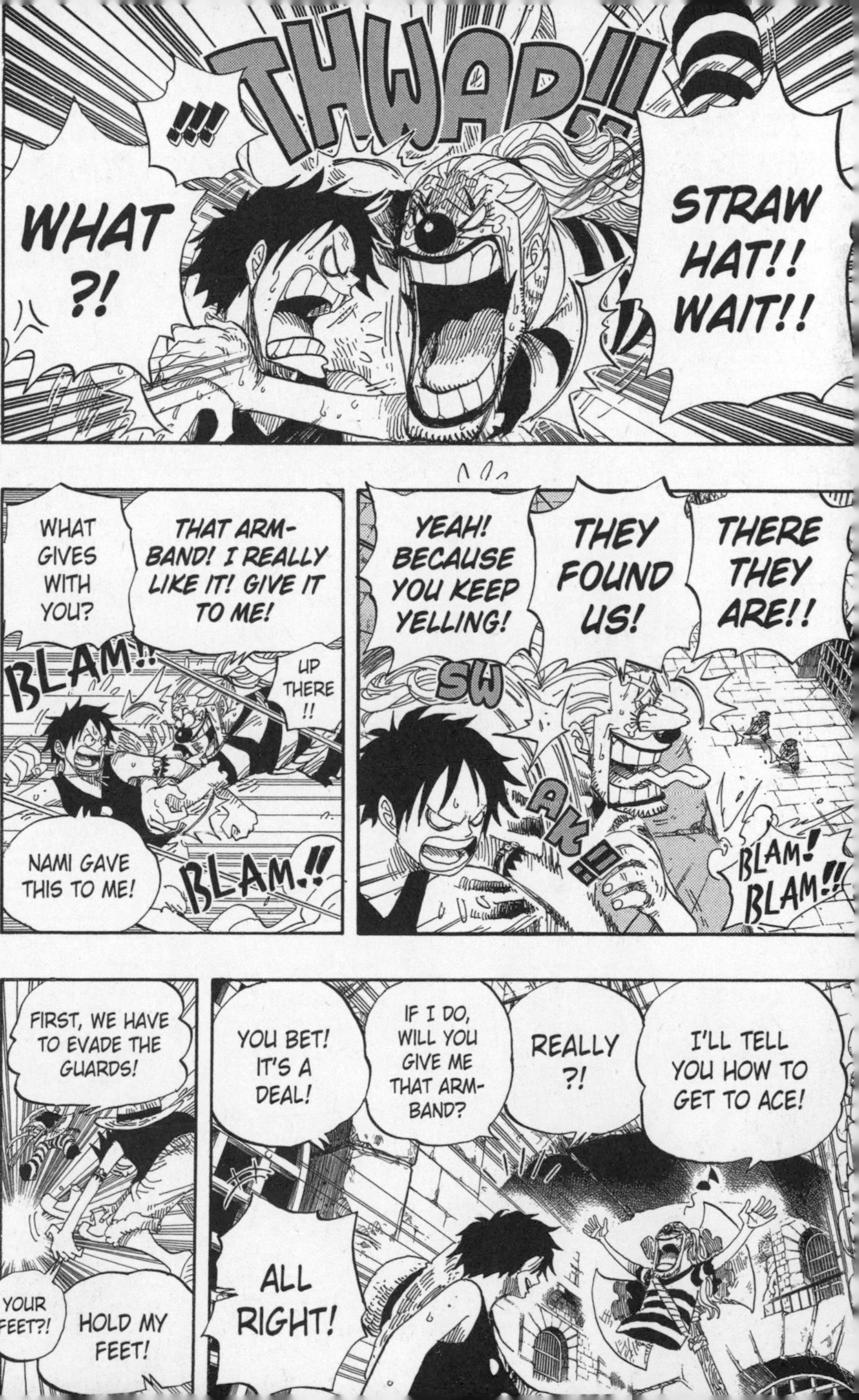
STRAW HAT!! WAIT!!
THWAP!!
!!!
WHAT ?!
THERE THEY ARE!!
THEY FOUND US!
YEAH! BECAUSE YOU KEEP YELLING!
SW
AK!!
BLAM! BLAM!!
THAT ARM-BAND! I REALLY LIKE IT! GIVE IT TO ME!
WHAT GIVES WITH YOU?
UP THERE !!
BLAM!!
NAMI GAVE THIS TO ME!
BLAM!!
I'LL TELL YOU HOW TO GET TO ACE!
REALLY ?!
IF I DO, WILL YOU GIVE ME THAT ARM-BAND?
YOU BET! IT'S A DEAL!
ALL RIGHT!
FIRST, WE HAVE TO EVADE THE GUARDS!
HOLD MY FEET!
YOUR FEET?!

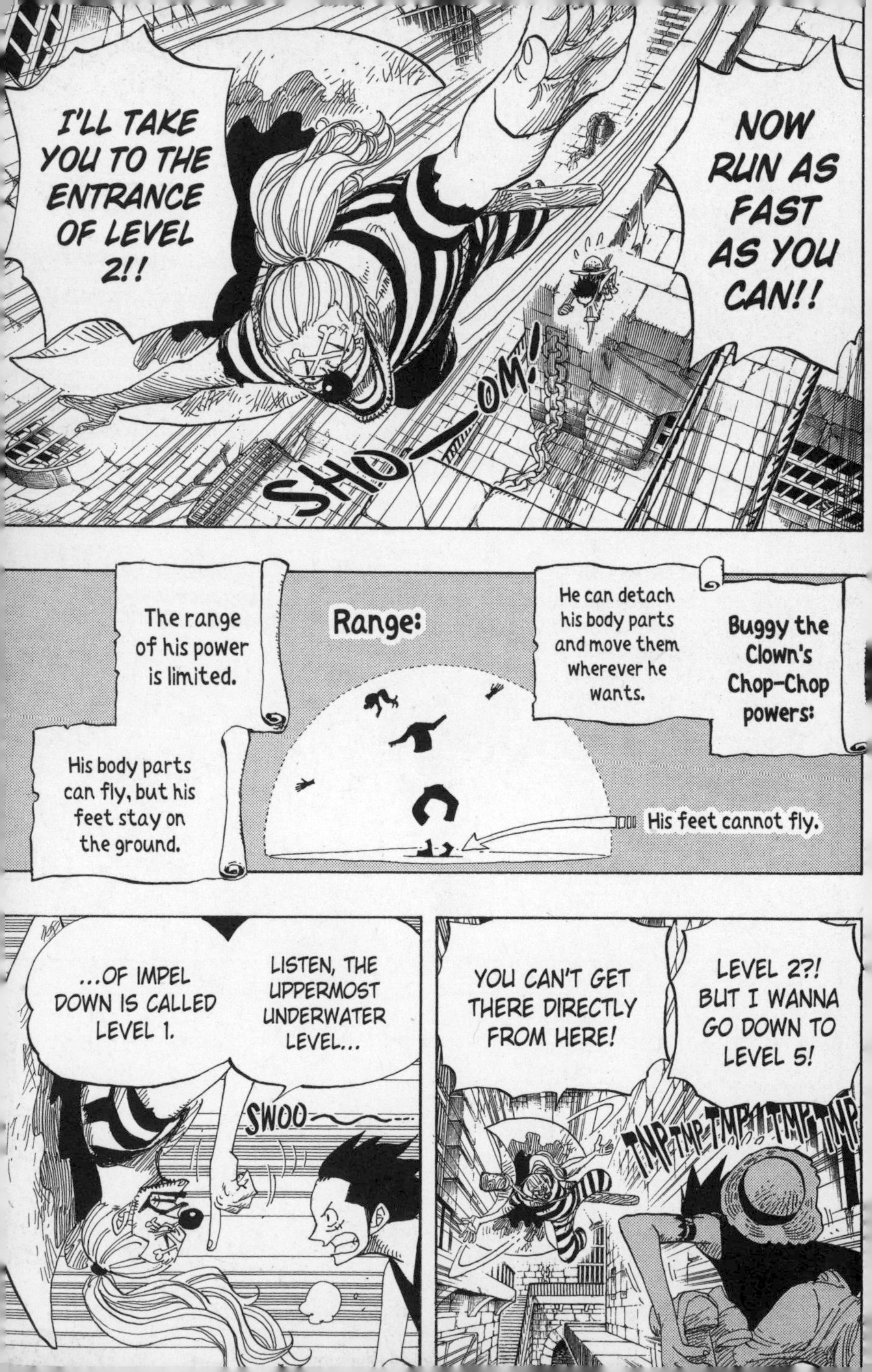
NOW RUN AS FAST AS YOU CAN!!
I'LL TAKE YOU TO THE ENTRANCE OF LEVEL 2!!
SHO—OM!
Buggy the Clown's Chop-Chop powers:
He can detach his body parts and move them wherever he wants.
Range:
The range of his power is limited.
His feet cannot fly.
His body parts can fly, but his feet stay on the ground.
LEVEL 2?! BUT I WANNA GO DOWN TO LEVEL 5!
YOU CAN'T GET THERE DIRECTLY FROM HERE!
TMP TMP TMP TMP TMP
LISTEN, THE UPPERMOST UNDERWATER LEVEL...
...OF IMPEL DOWN IS CALLED LEVEL 1.
SWOO~

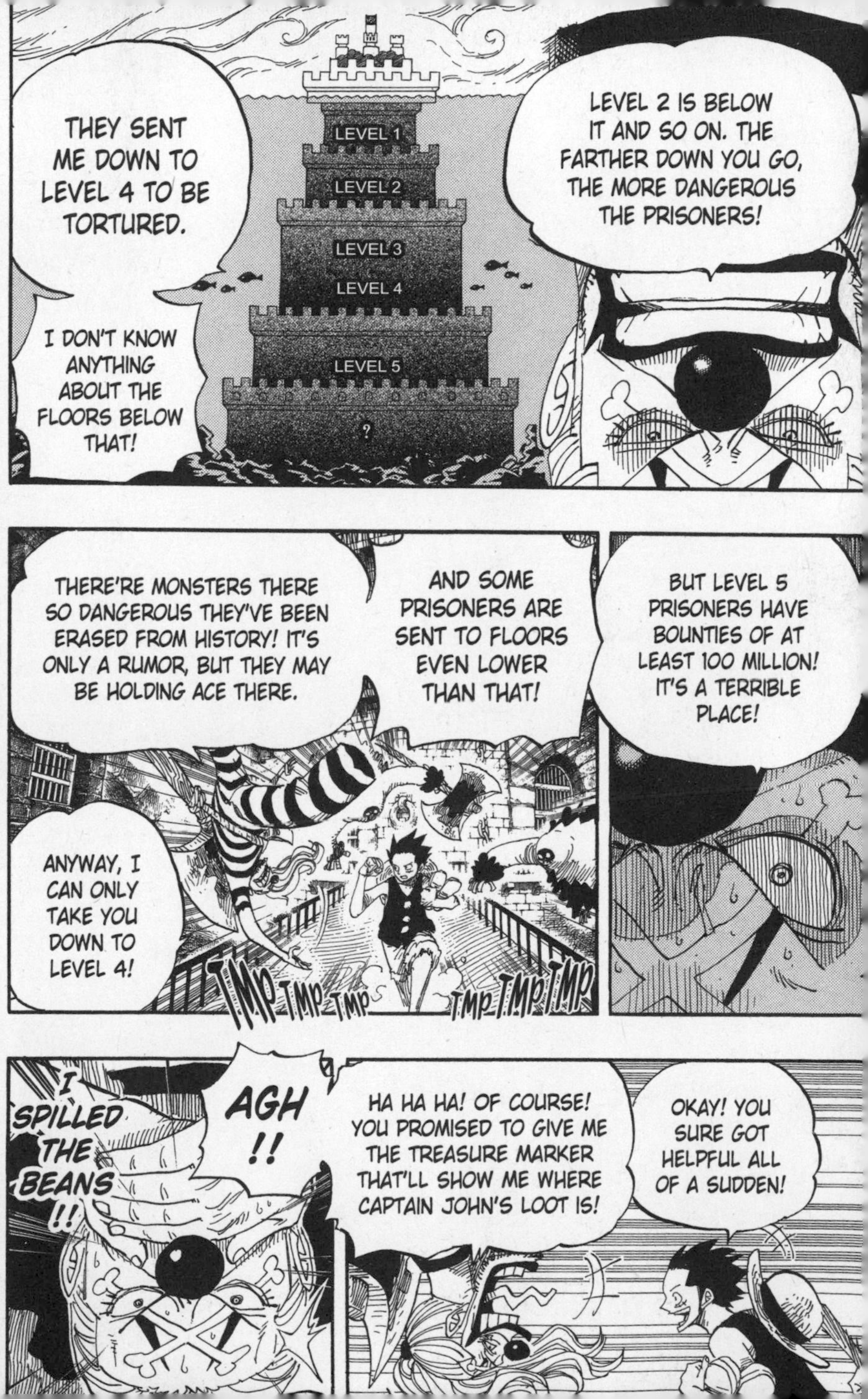

LEVEL 2 IS BELOW IT AND SO ON. THE FARTHER DOWN YOU GO, THE MORE DANGEROUS THE PRISONERS!
LEVEL 1
LEVEL 2
LEVEL 3
LEVEL 4
LEVEL 5
?
THEY SENT ME DOWN TO LEVEL 4 TO BE TORTURED.
I DON'T KNOW ANYTHING ABOUT THE FLOORS BELOW THAT!
BUT LEVEL 5 PRISONERS HAVE BOUNTIES OF AT LEAST 100 MILLION! IT'S A TERRIBLE PLACE!
AND SOME PRISONERS ARE SENT TO FLOORS EVEN LOWER THAN THAT!
THERE'RE MONSTERS THERE SO DANGEROUS THEY'VE BEEN ERASED FROM HISTORY! IT'S ONLY A RUMOR, BUT THEY MAY BE HOLDING ACE THERE.
ANYWAY, I CAN ONLY TAKE YOU DOWN TO LEVEL 4!
TMP TMP TMP TMP TMP TMP
OKAY! YOU SURE GOT HELPFUL ALL OF A SUDDEN!
HA HA HA! OF COURSE! YOU PROMISED TO GIVE ME THE TREASURE MARKER THAT'LL SHOW ME WHERE CAPTAIN JOHN'S LOOT IS!
AGH !!
I SPILLED THE BEANS !!

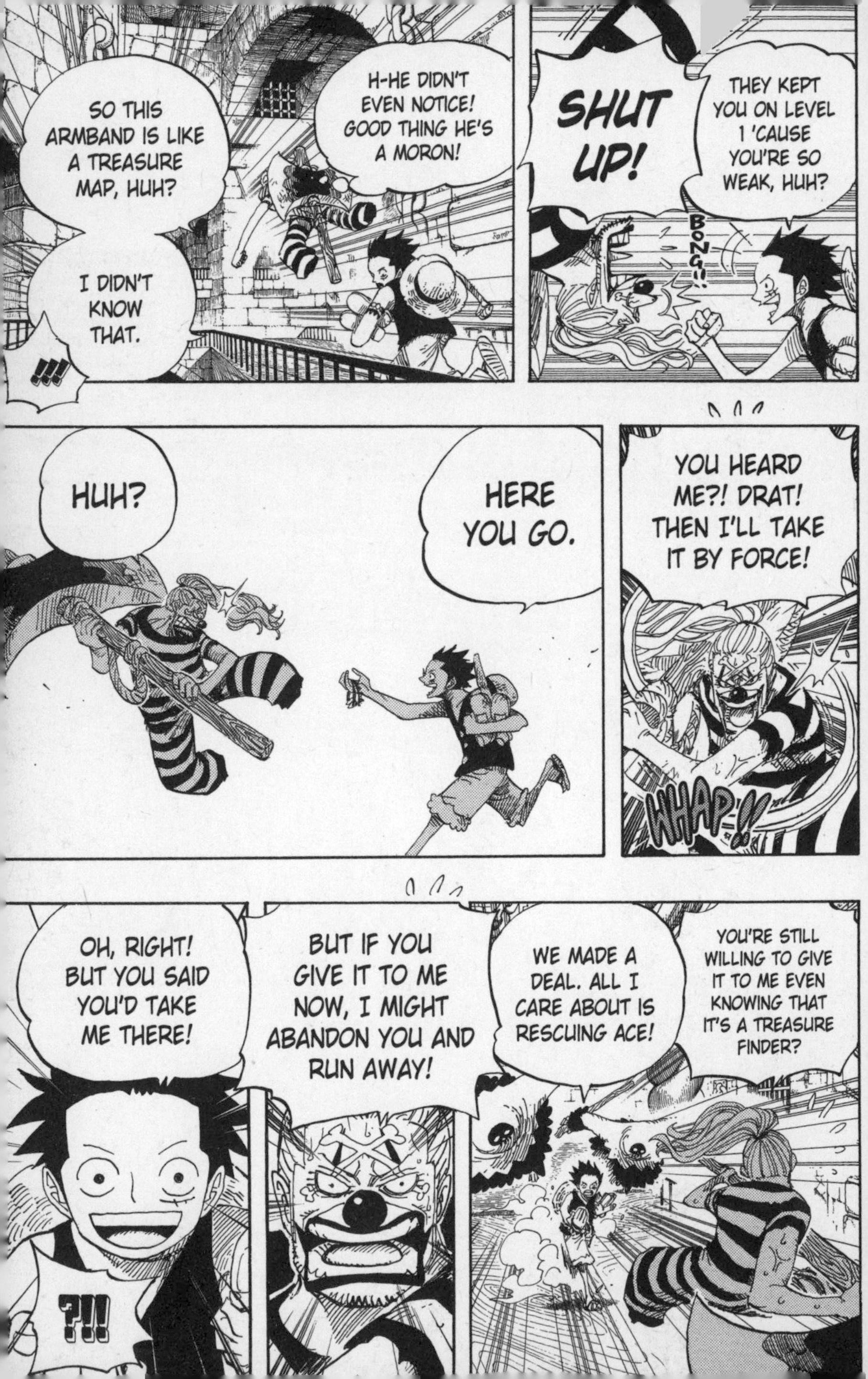

THEY KEPT YOU ON LEVEL 1 'CAUSE YOU'RE SO WEAK, HUH?
SHUT UP!
BONG!!
SO THIS ARMBAND IS LIKE A TREASURE MAP, HUH?
I DIDN'T KNOW THAT.
!!!
H-HE DIDN'T EVEN NOTICE! GOOD THING HE'S A MORON!
YOU HEARD ME?! DRAT! THEN I'LL TAKE IT BY FORCE!
WHAP!!
HERE YOU GO.
HUH?
YOU'RE STILL WILLING TO GIVE IT TO ME EVEN KNOWING THAT IT'S A TREASURE FINDER?
WE MADE A DEAL. ALL I CARE ABOUT IS RESCUING ACE!
BUT IF YOU GIVE IT TO ME NOW, I MIGHT ABANDON YOU AND RUN AWAY!
OH, RIGHT! BUT YOU SAID YOU'D TAKE ME THERE!
?!!

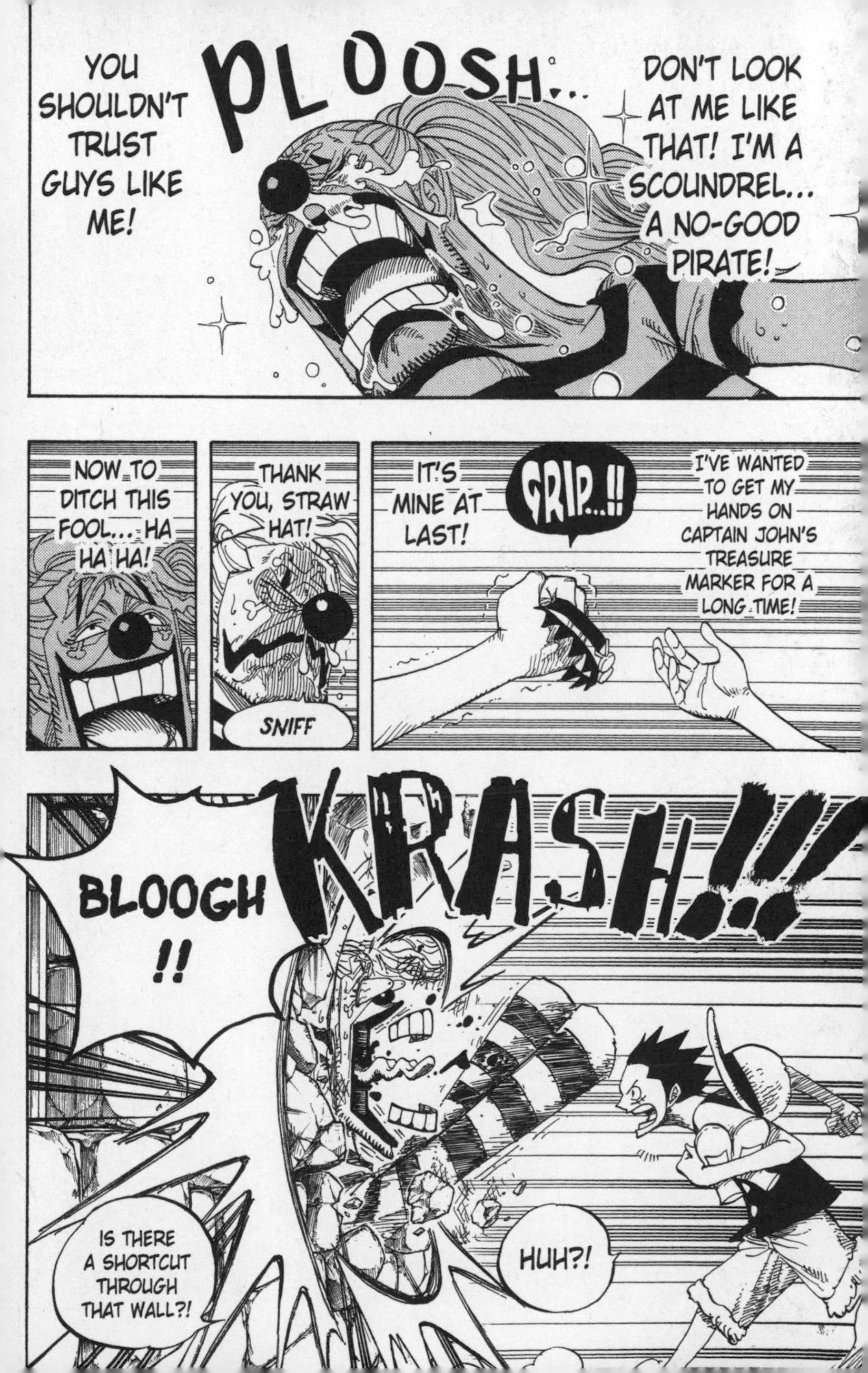
DON'T LOOK AT ME LIKE THAT! I'M A SCOUNDREL... A NO-GOOD PIRATE!
PLOOSH...
YOU SHOULDN'T TRUST GUYS LIKE ME!
I'VE WANTED TO GET MY HANDS ON CAPTAIN JOHN'S TREASURE MARKER FOR A LONG TIME!
GRIP...!!
IT'S MINE AT LAST!
THANK YOU, STRAW HAT!
SNIFF
NOW TO DITCH THIS FOOL... HA HA HA!
KRASH!!!
BLOOGH !!
HUH?!
IS THERE A SHORTCUT THROUGH THAT WALL?!

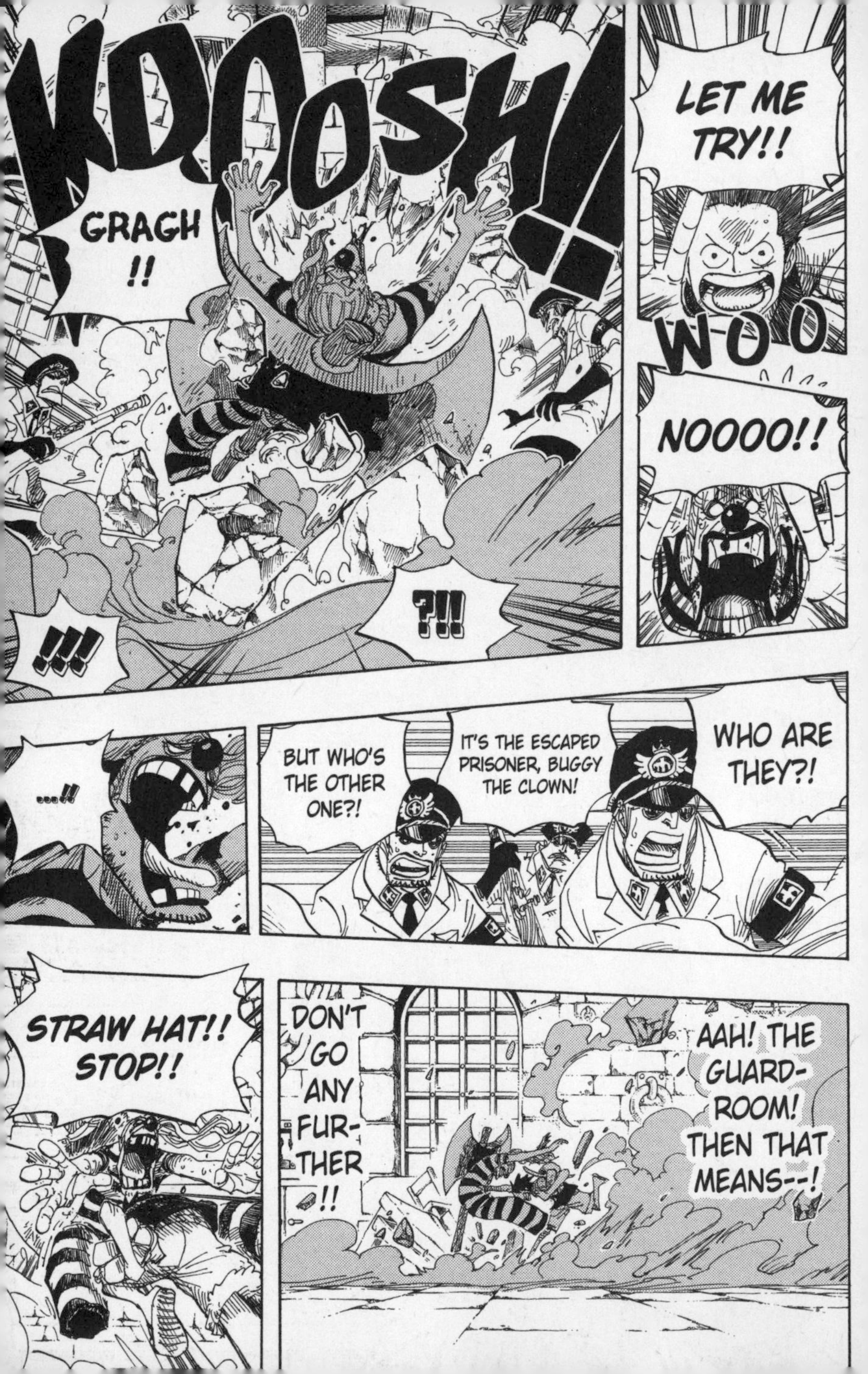
LET ME TRY!!
WOO
NOOOO!!
KDOOSH!!
GRAGH !!
?!!
!!!
WHO ARE THEY?!
IT'S THE ESCAPED PRISONER, BUGGY THE CLOWN!
BUT WHO'S THE OTHER ONE?!
...!!
AAH! THE GUARD-ROOM! THEN THAT MEANS--!
DON'T GO ANY FUR-THER!!
STRAW HAT!! STOP!!

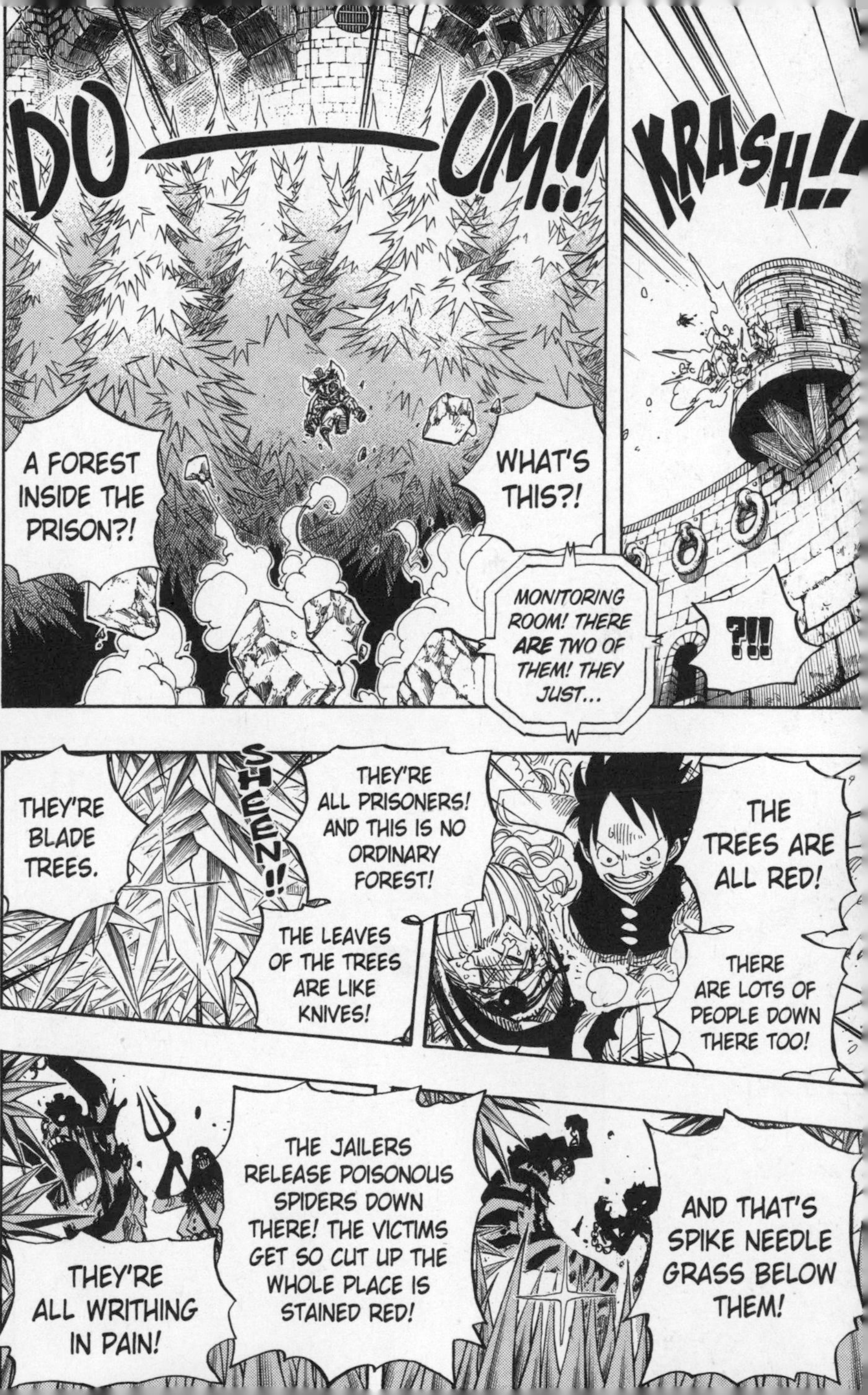
KRASH!!
?!!
MONITORING ROOM! THERE ARE TWO OF THEM! THEY JUST...
DO—OM!!
WHAT'S THIS?!
A FOREST INSIDE THE PRISON?!
THE TREES ARE ALL RED!
THERE ARE LOTS OF PEOPLE DOWN THERE TOO!
THEY'RE ALL PRISONERS! AND THIS IS NO ORDINARY FOREST!
SHEEN!!
THE LEAVES OF THE TREES ARE LIKE KNIVES!
THEY'RE BLADE TREES.
AND THAT'S SPIKE NEEDLE GRASS BELOW THEM!
THE JAILERS RELEASE POISONOUS SPIDERS DOWN THERE! THE VICTIMS GET SO CUT UP THE WHOLE PLACE IS STAINED RED!
THEY'RE ALL WRITHING IN PAIN!

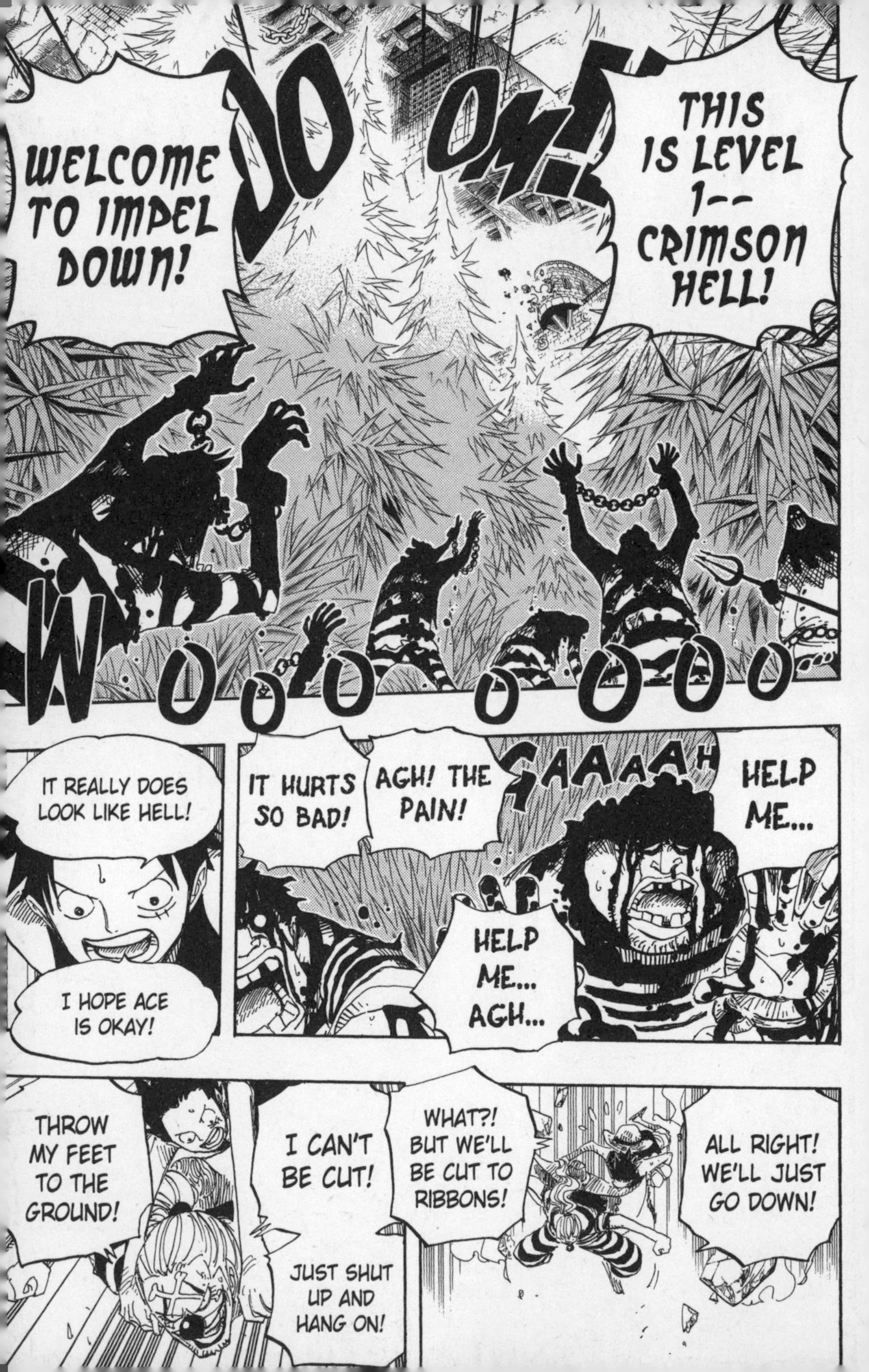
THIS IS LEVEL 1-- CRIMSON HELL!
DOON!
WELCOME TO IMPEL DOWN!
WOOOO OOOO
HELP ME...
GAAAAH
AGH! THE PAIN!
IT HURTS SO BAD!
HELP ME... AGH...
IT REALLY DOES LOOK LIKE HELL!
I HOPE ACE IS OKAY!
ALL RIGHT! WE'LL JUST GO DOWN!
WHAT?! BUT WE'LL BE CUT TO RIBBONS!
I CAN'T BE CUT!
JUST SHUT UP AND HANG ON!
THROW MY FEET TO THE GROUND!

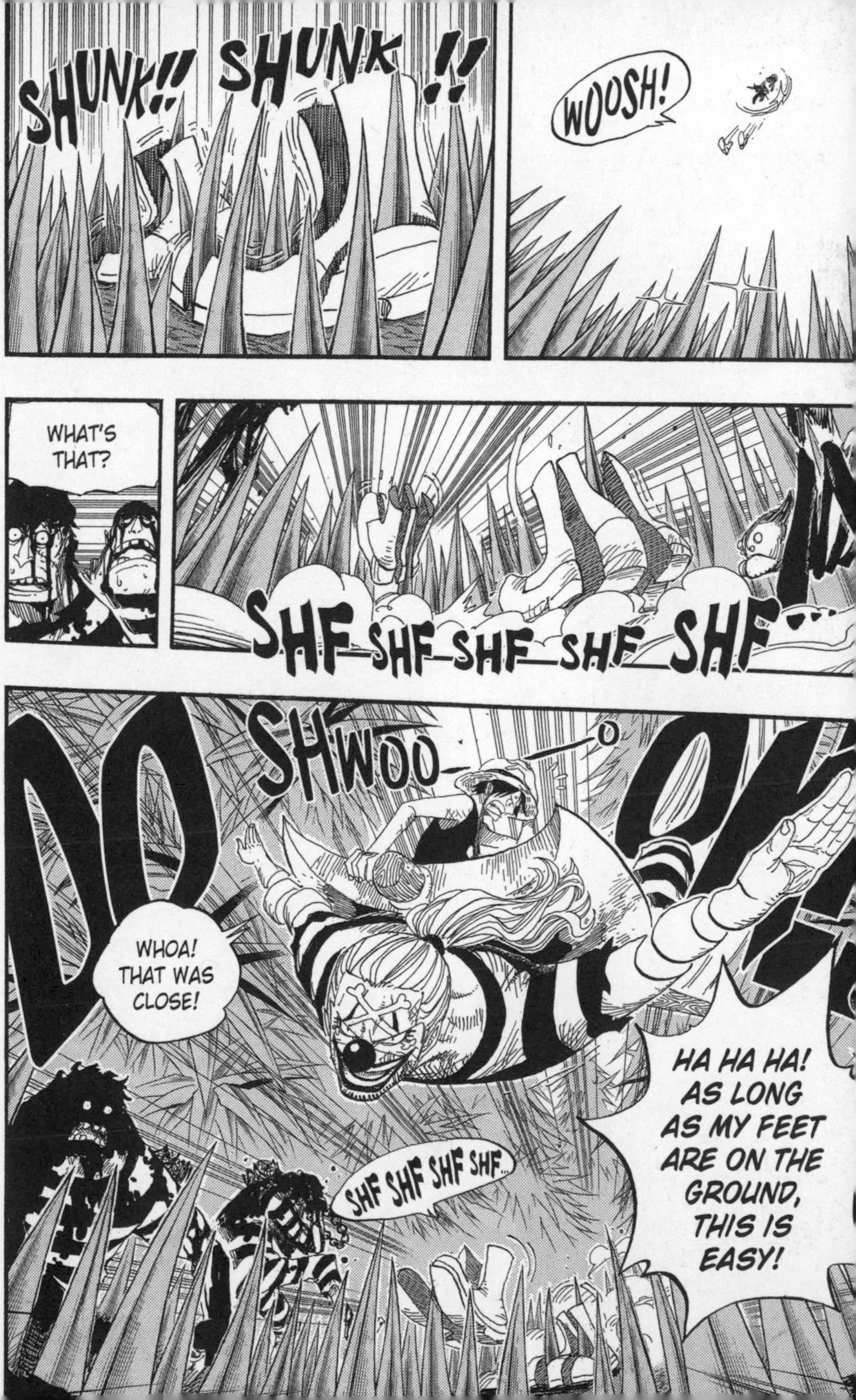
WOOSH!
SHUNK!! SHUNK!!
SHF SHF SHF SHF SHF...
WHAT'S THAT?
SHWOO
HA HA HA! AS LONG AS MY FEET ARE ON THE GROUND, THIS IS EASY!
WHOA! THAT WAS CLOSE!
SHF SHF SHF SHF...

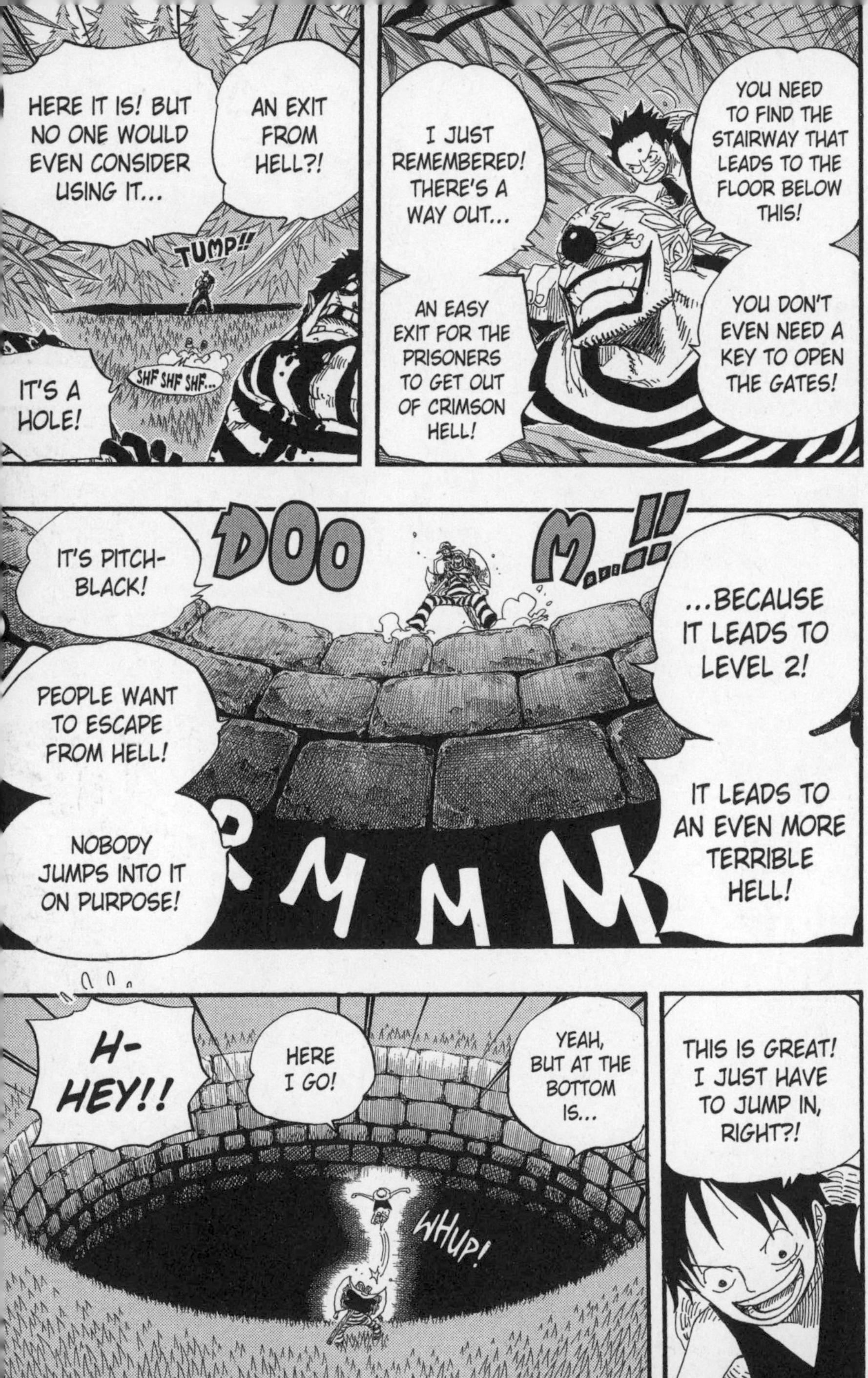
I JUST REMEMBERED! THERE'S A WAY OUT...
YOU NEED TO FIND THE STAIRWAY THAT LEADS TO THE FLOOR BELOW THIS!
AN EASY EXIT FOR THE PRISONERS TO GET OUT OF CRIMSON HELL!
YOU DON'T EVEN NEED A KEY TO OPEN THE GATES!
AN EXIT FROM HELL?!
HERE IT IS! BUT NO ONE WOULD EVEN CONSIDER USING IT...
TUMP!!
SHF SHF SHF...
IT'S A HOLE!
DOOM..!!
IT'S PITCH-BLACK!
PEOPLE WANT TO ESCAPE FROM HELL!
NOBODY JUMPS INTO IT ON PURPOSE!
...BECAUSE IT LEADS TO LEVEL 2!
IT LEADS TO AN EVEN MORE TERRIBLE HELL!
RMMM
THIS IS GREAT! I JUST HAVE TO JUMP IN, RIGHT?!
YEAH, BUT AT THE BOTTOM IS...
HERE I GO!
WHUP!
H-HEY!!

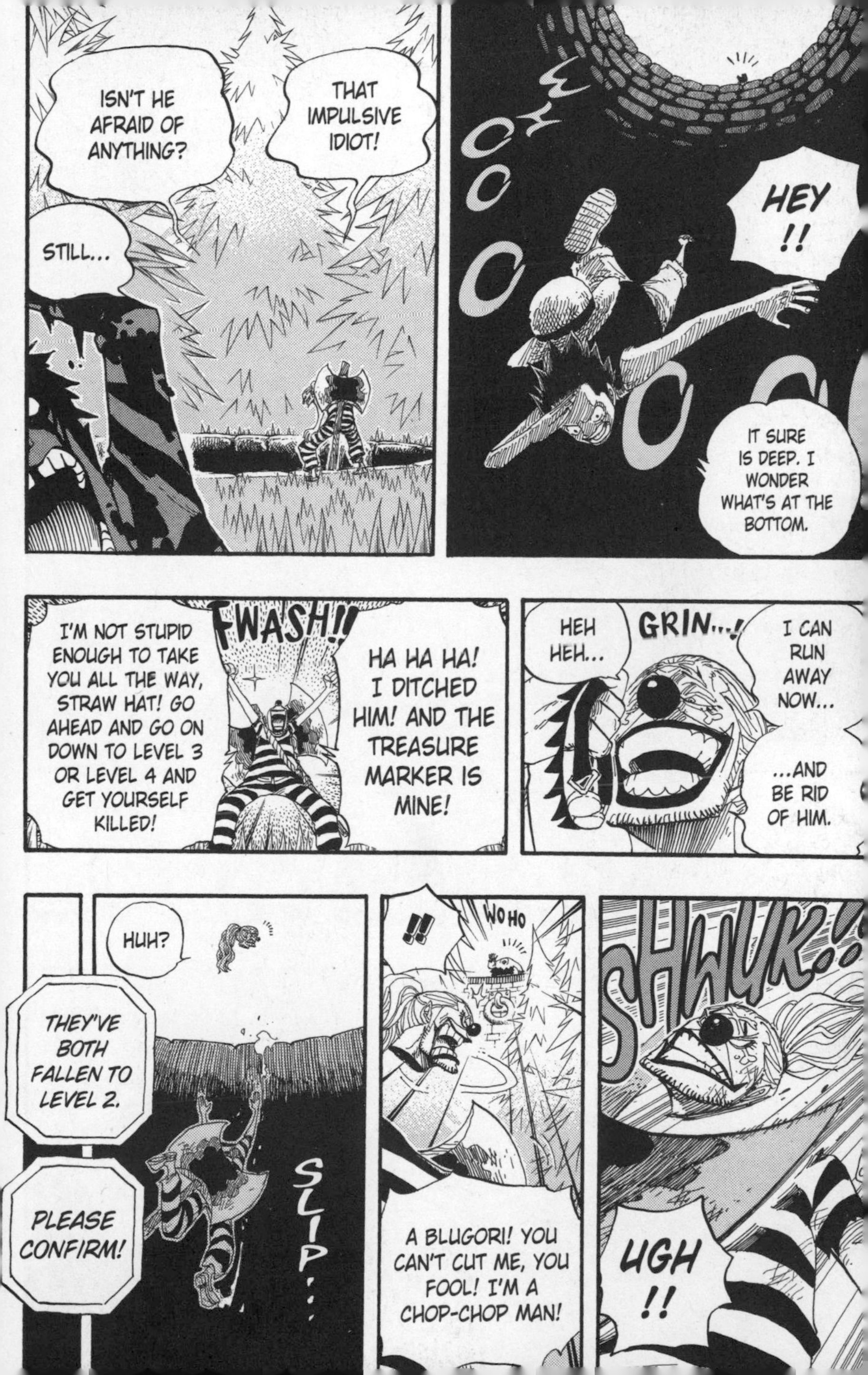
WHOOOOO
HEY!!
IT SURE IS DEEP. I WONDER WHAT'S AT THE BOTTOM.
THAT IMPULSIVE IDIOT!
ISN'T HE AFRAID OF ANYTHING?
STILL...
GRIN...!
HEH HEH...
I CAN RUN AWAY NOW...
...AND BE RID OF HIM.
HA HA HA! I DITCHED HIM! AND THE TREASURE MARKER IS MINE!
FWASH!!
I'M NOT STUPID ENOUGH TO TAKE YOU ALL THE WAY, STRAW HAT! GO AHEAD AND GO ON DOWN TO LEVEL 3 OR LEVEL 4 AND GET YOURSELF KILLED!
SHWUK!!
UGH!!
!!
WOHO
A BLUGORI! YOU CAN'T CUT ME, YOU FOOL! I'M A CHOP-CHOP MAN!
HUH?
THEY'VE BOTH FALLEN TO LEVEL 2.
PLEASE CONFIRM!
SLIP...

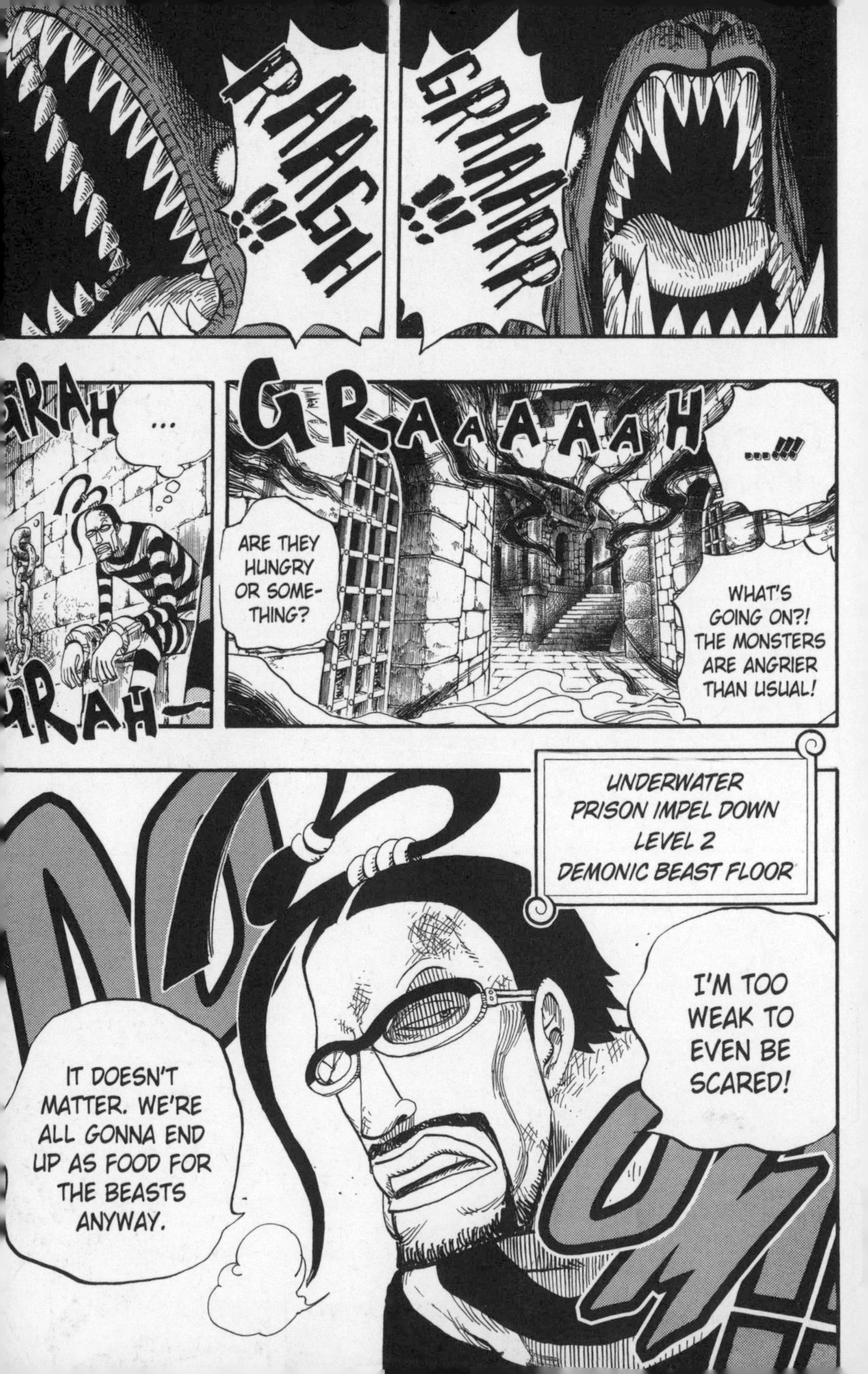
GRAAARRR!!!
RAAGH!!!
GRAAAAAH...!!!
WHAT'S GOING ON?! THE MONSTERS ARE ANGRIER THAN USUAL!
ARE THEY HUNGRY OR SOME-THING?
...
UNDERWATER PRISON IMPEL DOWN LEVEL 2 DEMONIC BEAST FLOOR
I'M TOO WEAK TO EVEN BE SCARED!
IT DOESN'T MATTER. WE'RE ALL GONNA END UP AS FOOD FOR THE BEASTS ANYWAY.

SBS Question Corner

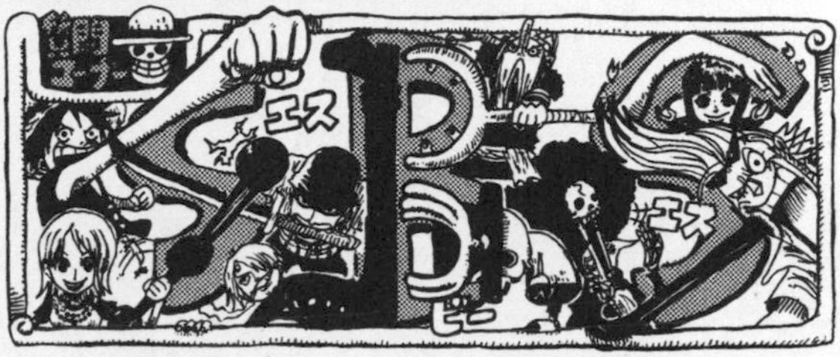

(Ponio, Aichi)

Introducing "One Piece Web"!

Q: Hello, Mr. Oda. This is the first time I've written a letter to you. I always enjoy reading *One Piece*. In a Question Corner in volume 53, you wrote that you wanted to wrap up *One Piece*, so I quickly decided to send this letter to you. Please don't say that. Please don't apologize for making us spend money! I know this is part of the Question Corner, but I don't have a question.

--Smoke

A: You don't?! Anyway, I was surprised to receive lots of letters about what I said in volume 53. I really didn't mean anything significant when I said that! There is an "ideal length of a serialization" I believe, and it's "something that all readers can easily buy." This might be me being selfish as a storywriter, but the "Straw Hat Pirates" are now nine members strong. In the beginning, Luffy went out to sea alone! So readers that read it from the middle don't even know that. I want people to understand what kind of adventures happened or how they got the new crewmembers! But I can't tell them to buy all 50 volumes! I know exactly how small kids' allowances are! That's why I made a lot of summary books that wrap up past stories. Every single time one is released, I asked the publishers to make it as cheap as possible. The two companies, Caramel Mama and Partyware, both did it for me! It's too cheap! Free, in fact! Awesome job! The Japanese website "One Piece Web" has been made! It's a story guide for the entire comic and it'll explain everything that happened in the past! For all the kids that can't buy the books, just read it here! Check it out now! (To the adults, please go buy the books) My earlier statement was just from that. It's not that I'm tired of drawing or anything. What I want to do hasn't changed at all. It's where all sorts of stories come together and "the final chapter is the most fun." The story of One Piece is still in the middle. If you have time, I hope you can read the whole thing through. I'm still challenging myself to create stories that no one has ever read before! Now go check out the website!

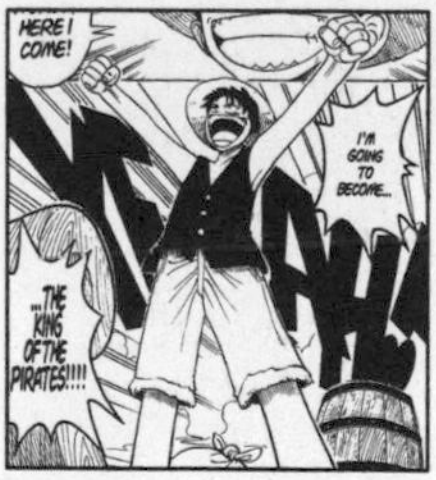
HERE I COME!
I'M GOING TO BECOME...
...THE KING OF THE PIRATES!!!!

One Piece Web http://www.j-onepiece.com
English Website at http://onepiece.viz.com

Chapter 528:

JIMBEI, FIRST SON OF THE SEA

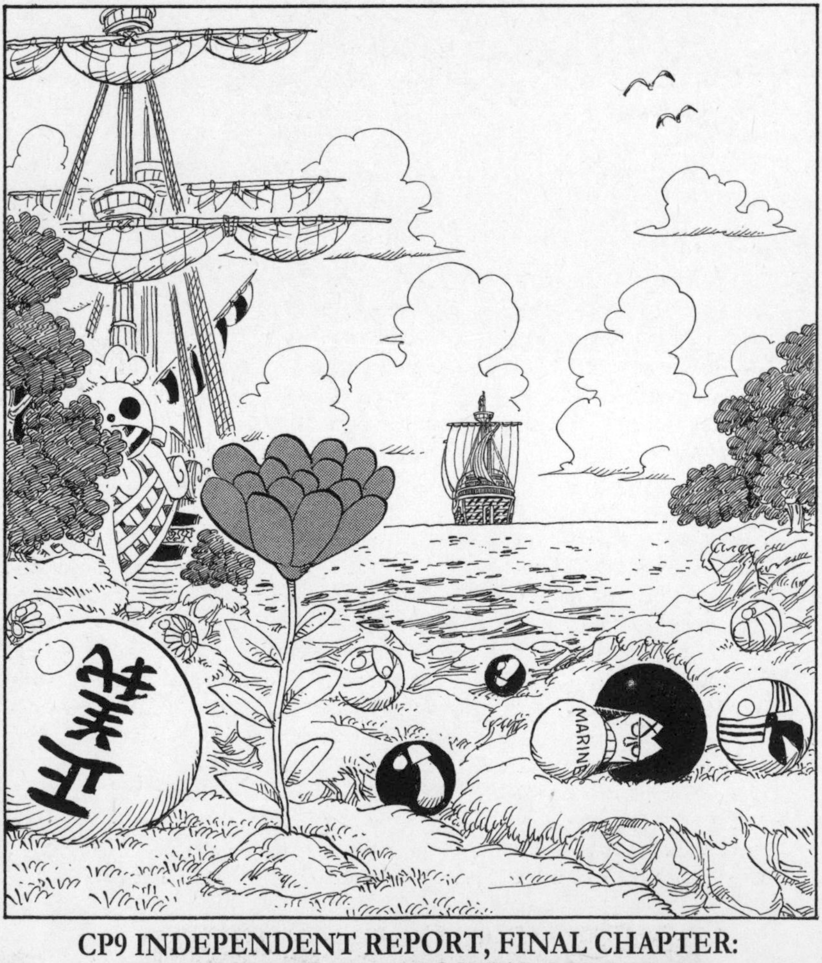
MARINE

TEXT ON BALL SAYS "JUSTICE" --ED.

CP9 INDEPENDENT REPORT, FINAL CHAPTER:
"THE SHIP DISAPPEARS INTO OBLIVION"

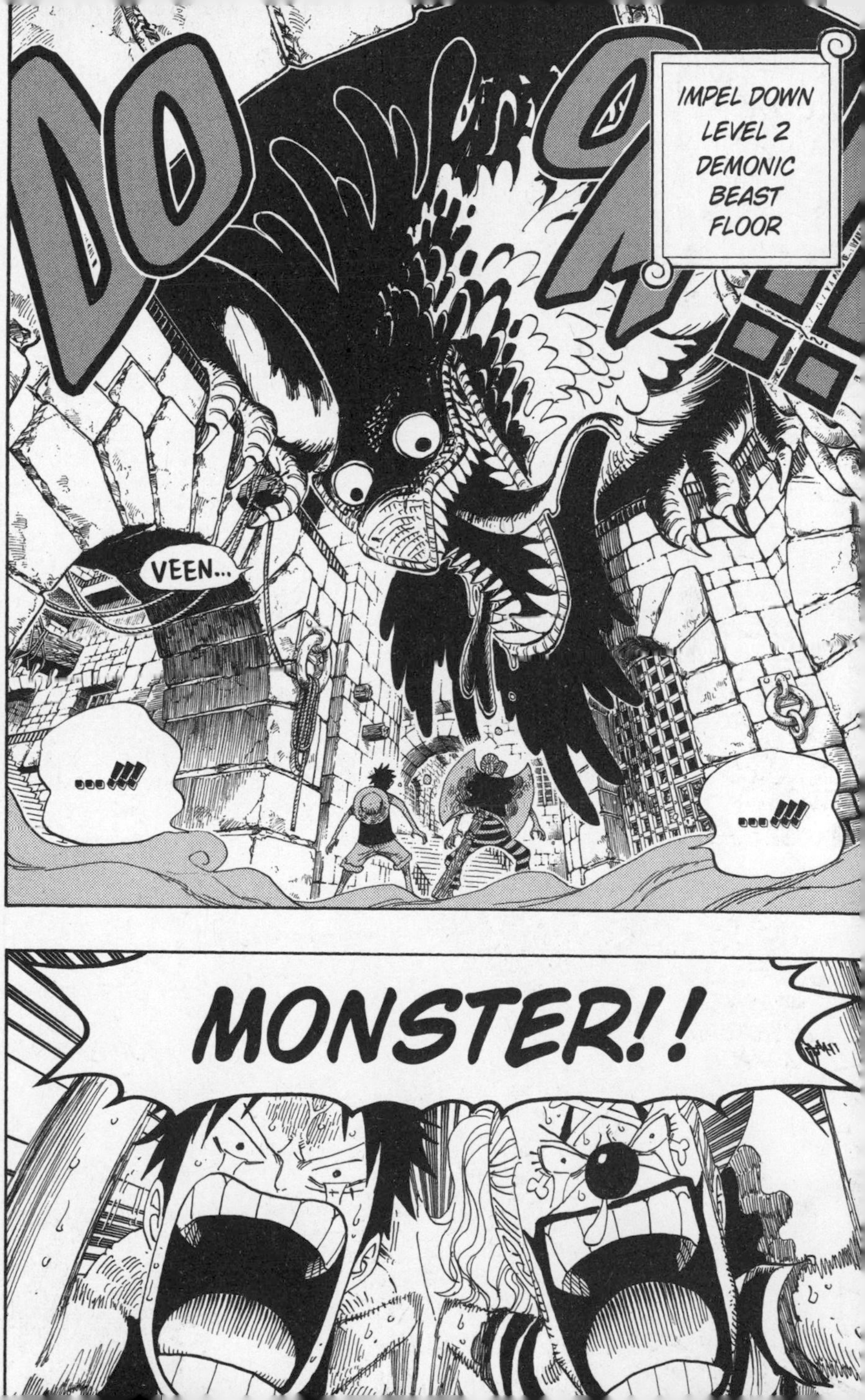
IMPEL DOWN
LEVEL 2
DEMONIC
BEAST
FLOOR
DO
...!!!
VEEN...
...!!!
MONSTER!!

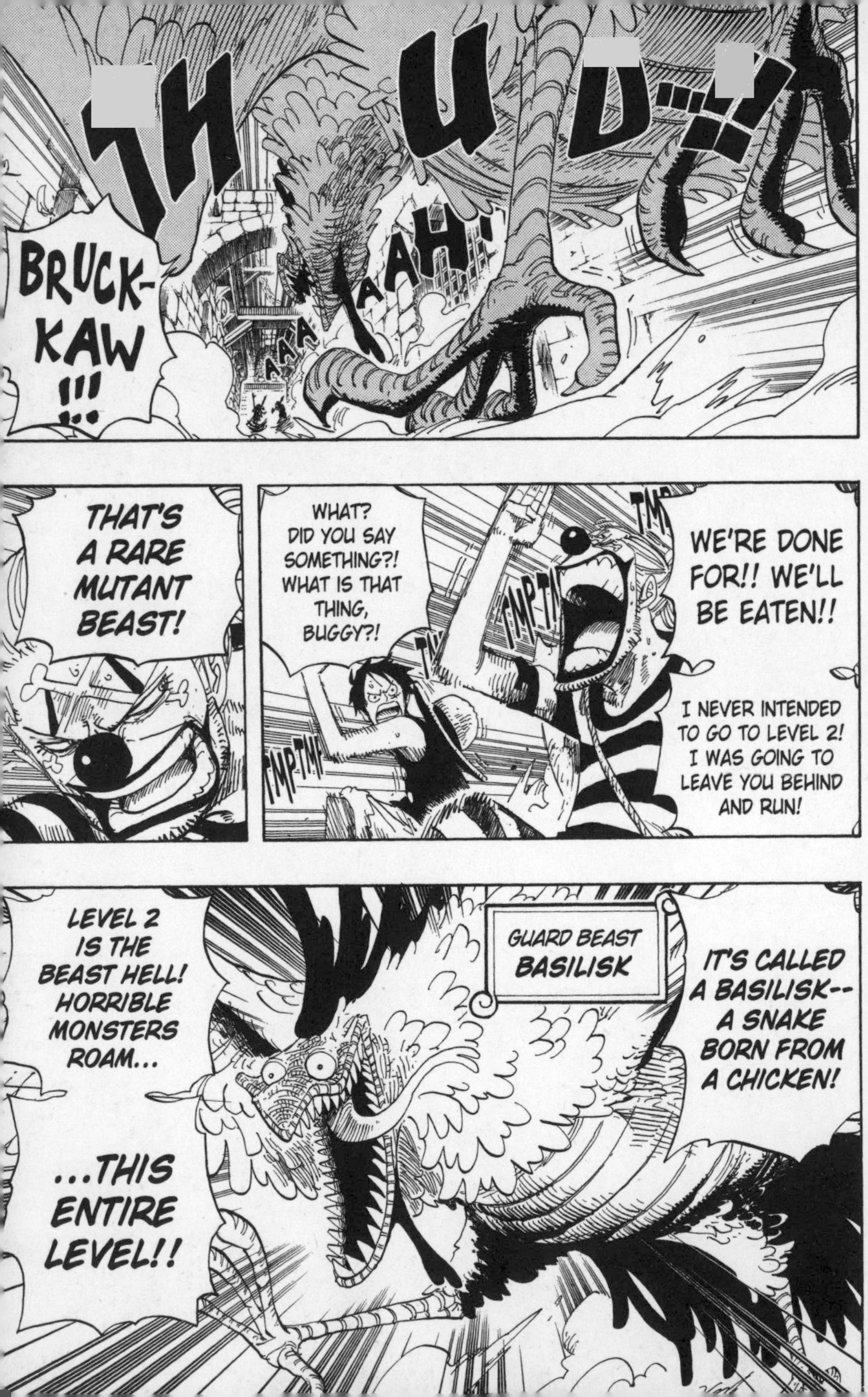
AAAAH!
BRUCK-KAW!!!
WE'RE DONE FOR!! WE'LL BE EATEN!!
I NEVER INTENDED TO GO TO LEVEL 2! I WAS GOING TO LEAVE YOU BEHIND AND RUN!
WHAT? DID YOU SAY SOMETHING?! WHAT IS THAT THING, BUGGY?!
THAT'S A RARE MUTANT BEAST!
IT'S CALLED A BASILISK-- A SNAKE BORN FROM A CHICKEN!
GUARD BEAST BASILISK
LEVEL 2 IS THE BEAST HELL! HORRIBLE MONSTERS ROAM...
...THIS ENTIRE LEVEL!!

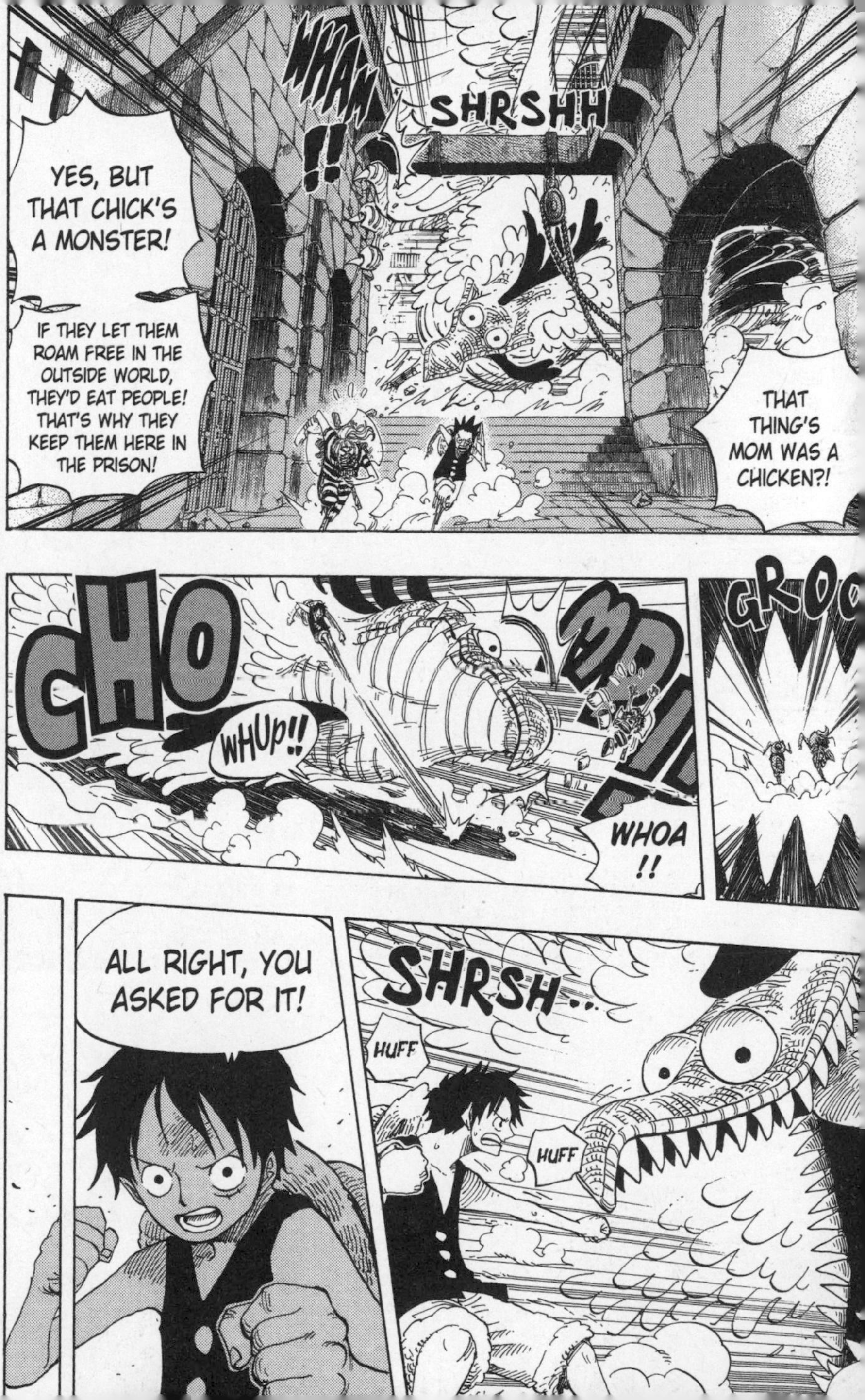
THAT THING'S MOM WAS A CHICKEN?!
YES, BUT THAT CHICK'S A MONSTER!
IF THEY LET THEM ROAM FREE IN THE OUTSIDE WORLD, THEY'D EAT PEOPLE! THAT'S WHY THEY KEEP THEM HERE IN THE PRISON!
SHRSHH
WHAM!!
GROO
WHOA!!
CHO
WHUP!!
HUFF
HUFF
SHRSH...
ALL RIGHT, YOU ASKED FOR IT!

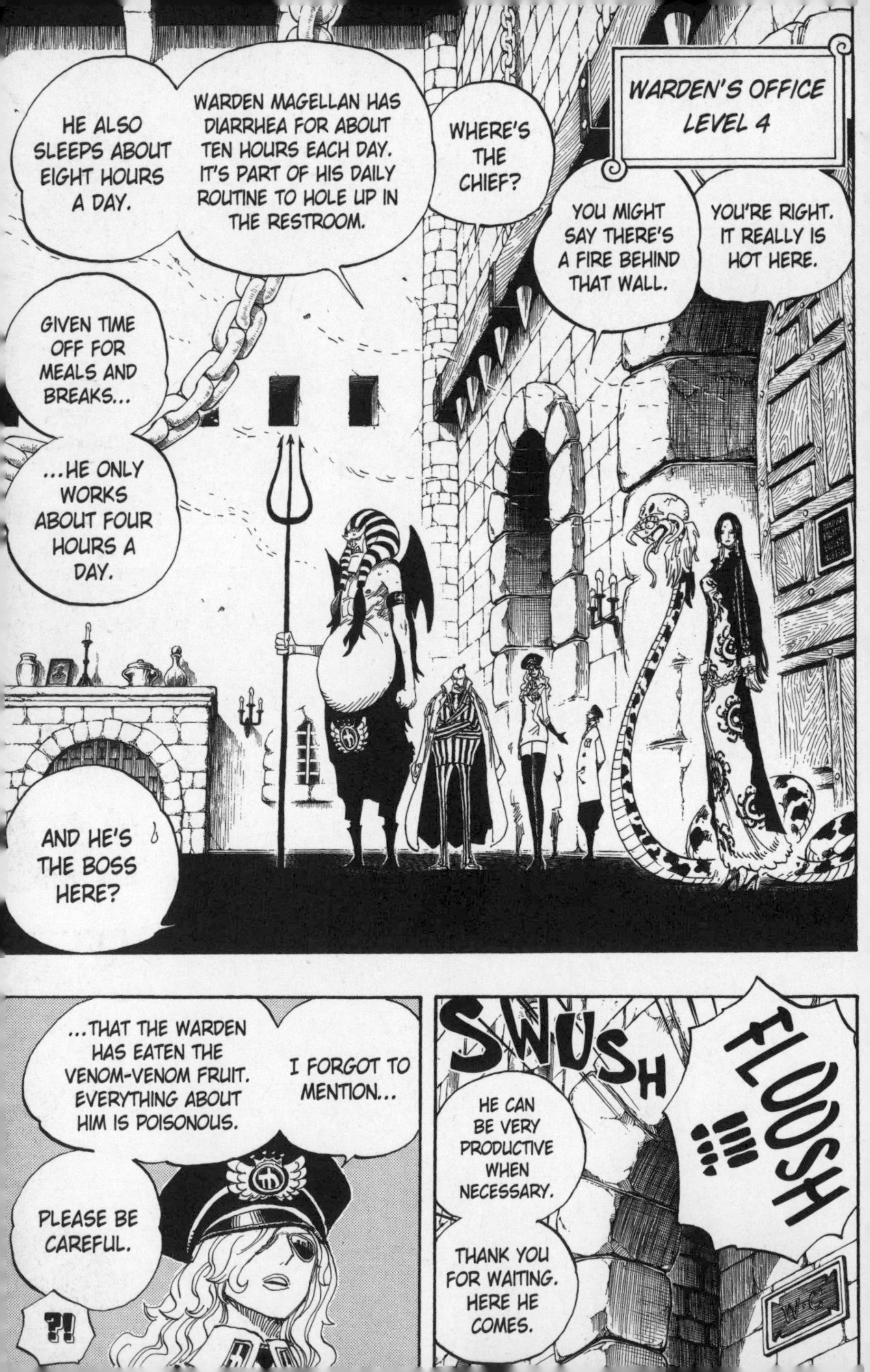
WARDEN'S OFFICE LEVEL 4
YOU'RE RIGHT. IT REALLY IS HOT HERE.
YOU MIGHT SAY THERE'S A FIRE BEHIND THAT WALL.
WHERE'S THE CHIEF?
WARDEN MAGELLAN HAS DIARRHEA FOR ABOUT TEN HOURS EACH DAY. IT'S PART OF HIS DAILY ROUTINE TO HOLE UP IN THE RESTROOM.
HE ALSO SLEEPS ABOUT EIGHT HOURS A DAY.
GIVEN TIME OFF FOR MEALS AND BREAKS...
...HE ONLY WORKS ABOUT FOUR HOURS A DAY.
AND HE'S THE BOSS HERE?
FLOOSH
SWUSH
HE CAN BE VERY PRODUCTIVE WHEN NECESSARY.
THANK YOU FOR WAITING. HERE HE COMES.
I FORGOT TO MENTION...
...THAT THE WARDEN HAS EATEN THE VENOM-VENOM FRUIT. EVERYTHING ABOUT HIM IS POISONOUS.
PLEASE BE CAREFUL.
?!

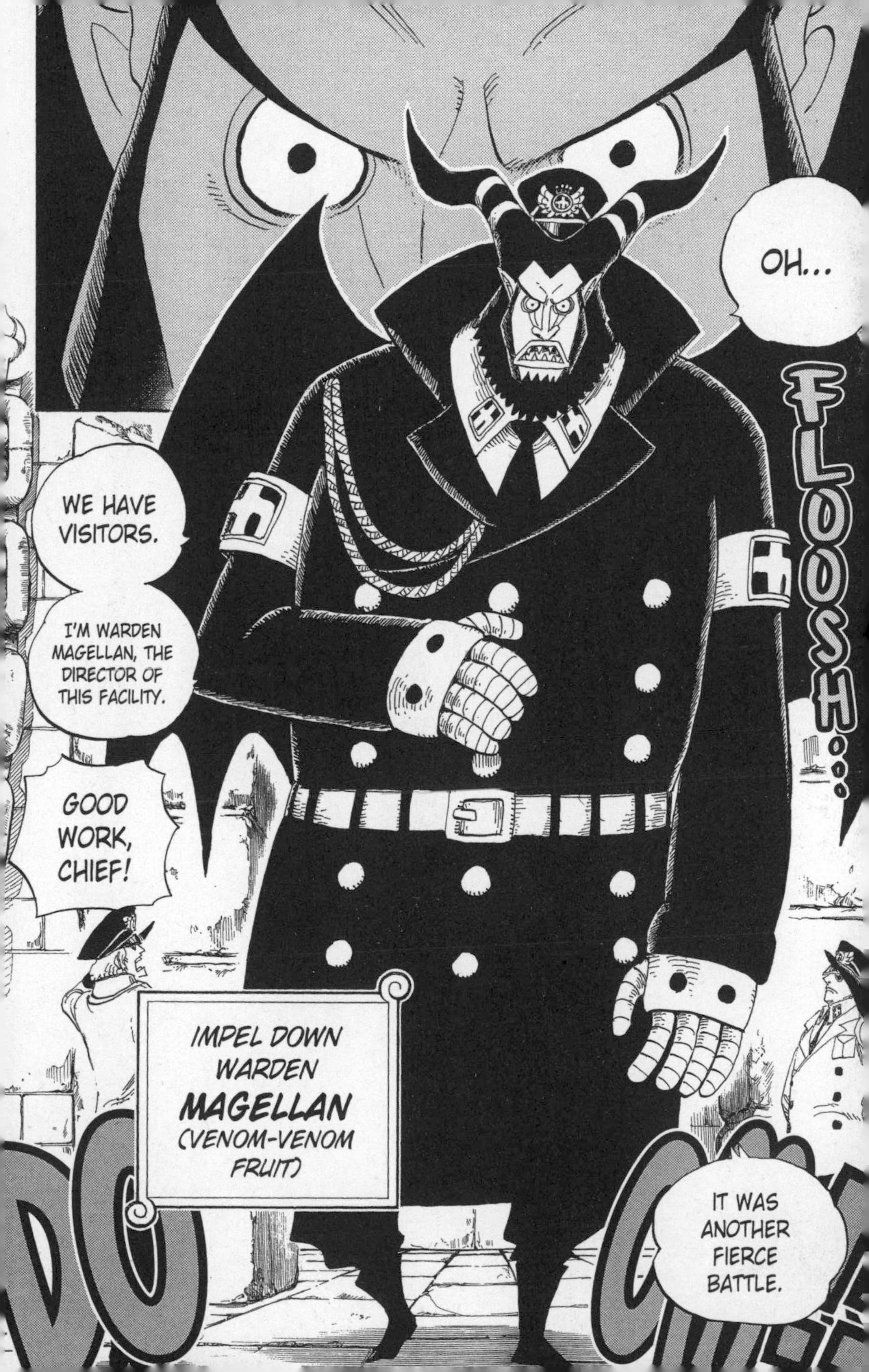
OH...
FLOOSH...
WE HAVE VISITORS.
I'M WARDEN MAGELLAN, THE DIRECTOR OF THIS FACILITY.
GOOD WORK, CHIEF!
IMPEL DOWN WARDEN MAGELLAN (VENOM-VENOM FRUIT)
IT WAS ANOTHER FIERCE BATTLE.

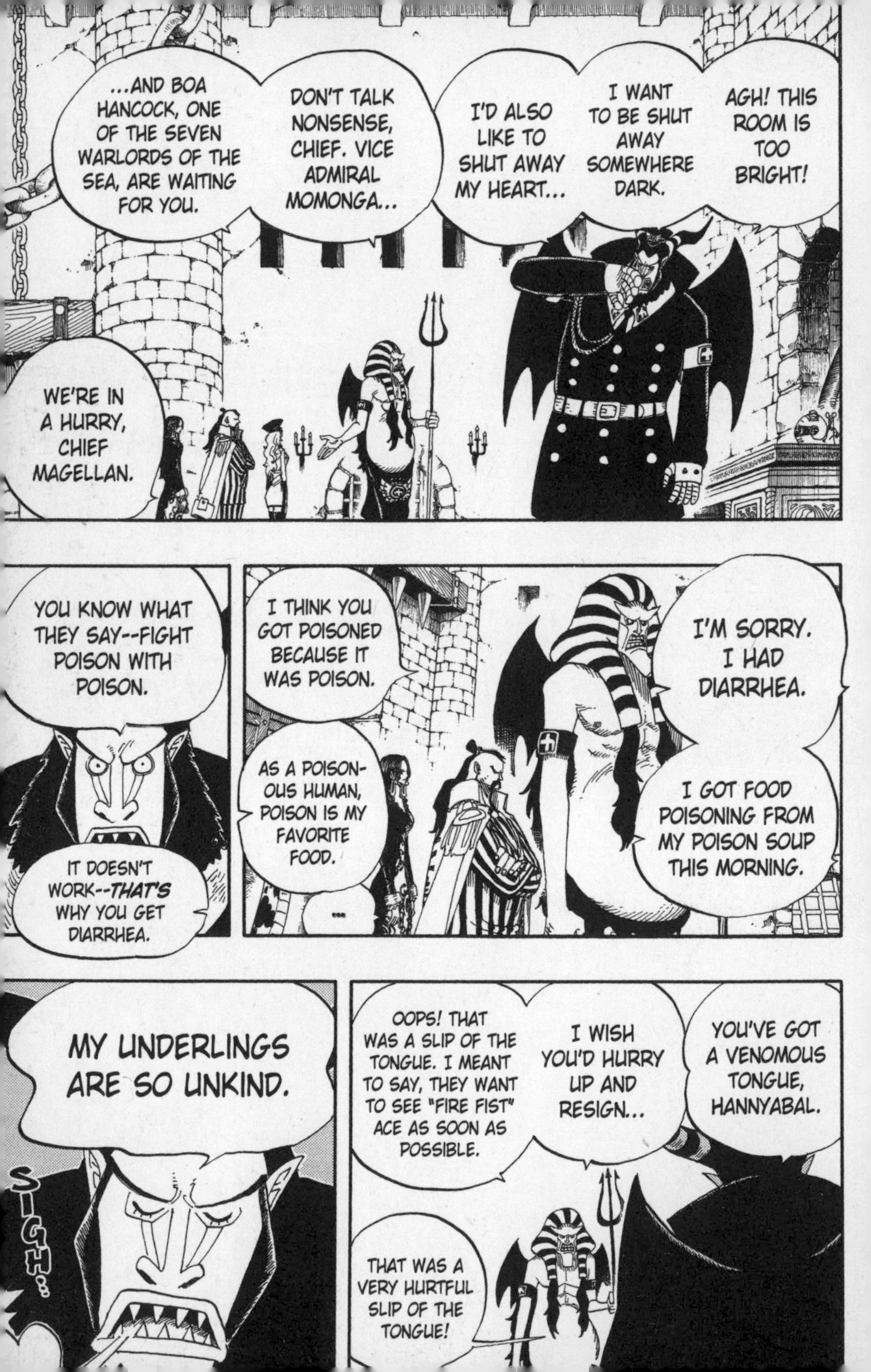
AGH! THIS ROOM IS TOO BRIGHT!
I WANT TO BE SHUT AWAY SOMEWHERE DARK.
I'D ALSO LIKE TO SHUT AWAY MY HEART...
DON'T TALK NONSENSE, CHIEF. VICE ADMIRAL MOMONGA...
...AND BOA HANCOCK, ONE OF THE SEVEN WARLORDS OF THE SEA, ARE WAITING FOR YOU.
WE'RE IN A HURRY, CHIEF MAGELLAN.
I'M SORRY. I HAD DIARRHEA.
I GOT FOOD POISONING FROM MY POISON SOUP THIS MORNING.
I THINK YOU GOT POISONED BECAUSE IT WAS POISON.
AS A POISON-OUS HUMAN, POISON IS MY FAVORITE FOOD.
...
YOU KNOW WHAT THEY SAY--FIGHT POISON WITH POISON.
IT DOESN'T WORK--*THAT'S* WHY YOU GET DIARRHEA.
YOU'VE GOT A VENOMOUS TONGUE, HANNYABAL.
I WISH YOU'D HURRY UP AND RESIGN...
OOPS! THAT WAS A SLIP OF THE TONGUE. I MEANT TO SAY, THEY WANT TO SEE "FIRE FIST" ACE AS SOON AS POSSIBLE.
THAT WAS A VERY HURTFUL SLIP OF THE TONGUE!
MY UNDERLINGS ARE SO UNKIND.
SIGH...

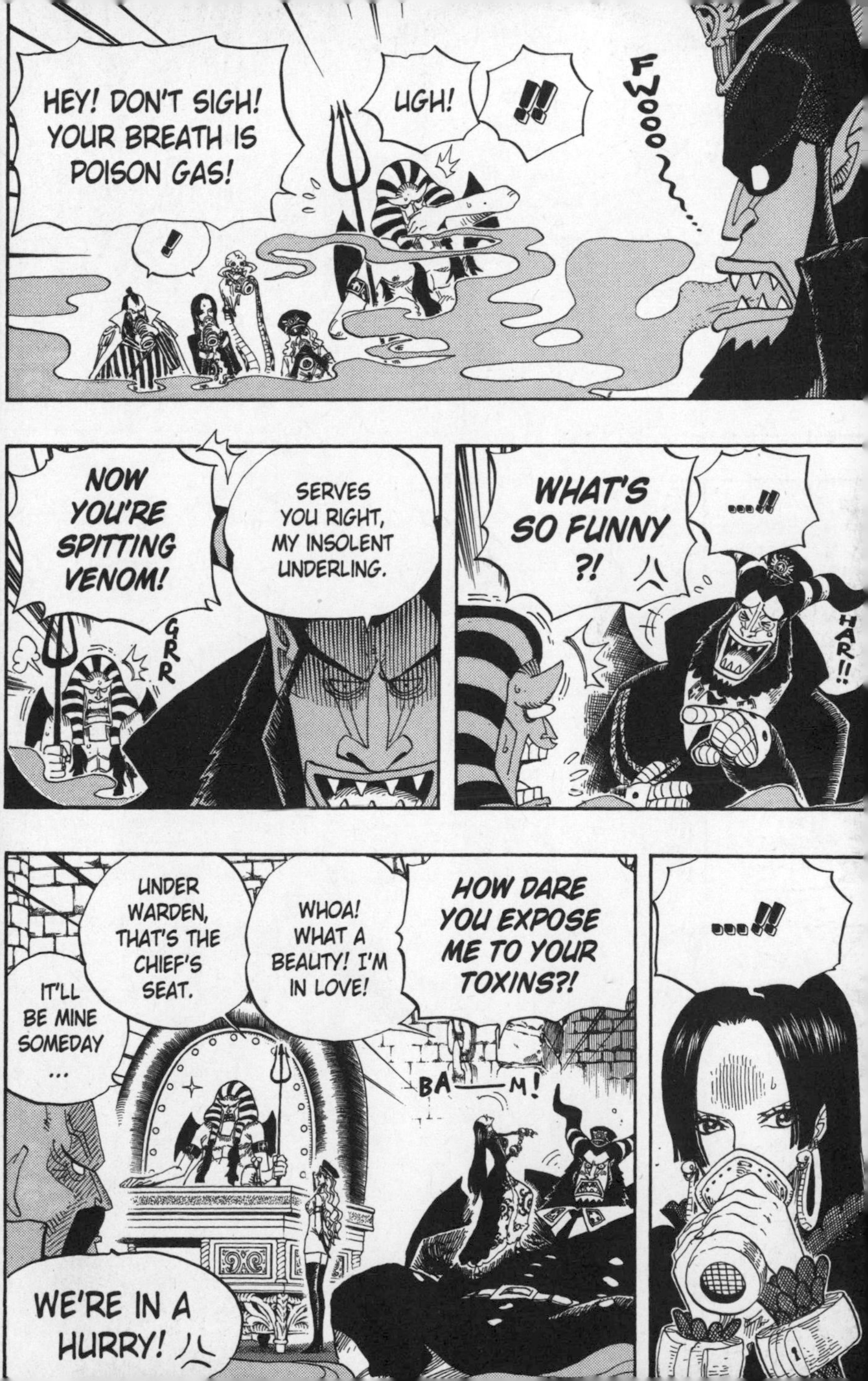
FWOOO
!!
UGH!
HEY! DON'T SIGH! YOUR BREATH IS POISON GAS!
!
...!!
WHAT'S SO FUNNY?!
HAR!!
SERVES YOU RIGHT, MY INSOLENT UNDERLING.
NOW YOU'RE SPITTING VENOM!
GRR
...!!
HOW DARE YOU EXPOSE ME TO YOUR TOXINS?!
WHOA! WHAT A BEAUTY! I'M IN LOVE!
UNDER WARDEN, THAT'S THE CHIEF'S SEAT.
IT'LL BE MINE SOMEDAY ...
BA—M!
WE'RE IN A HURRY!

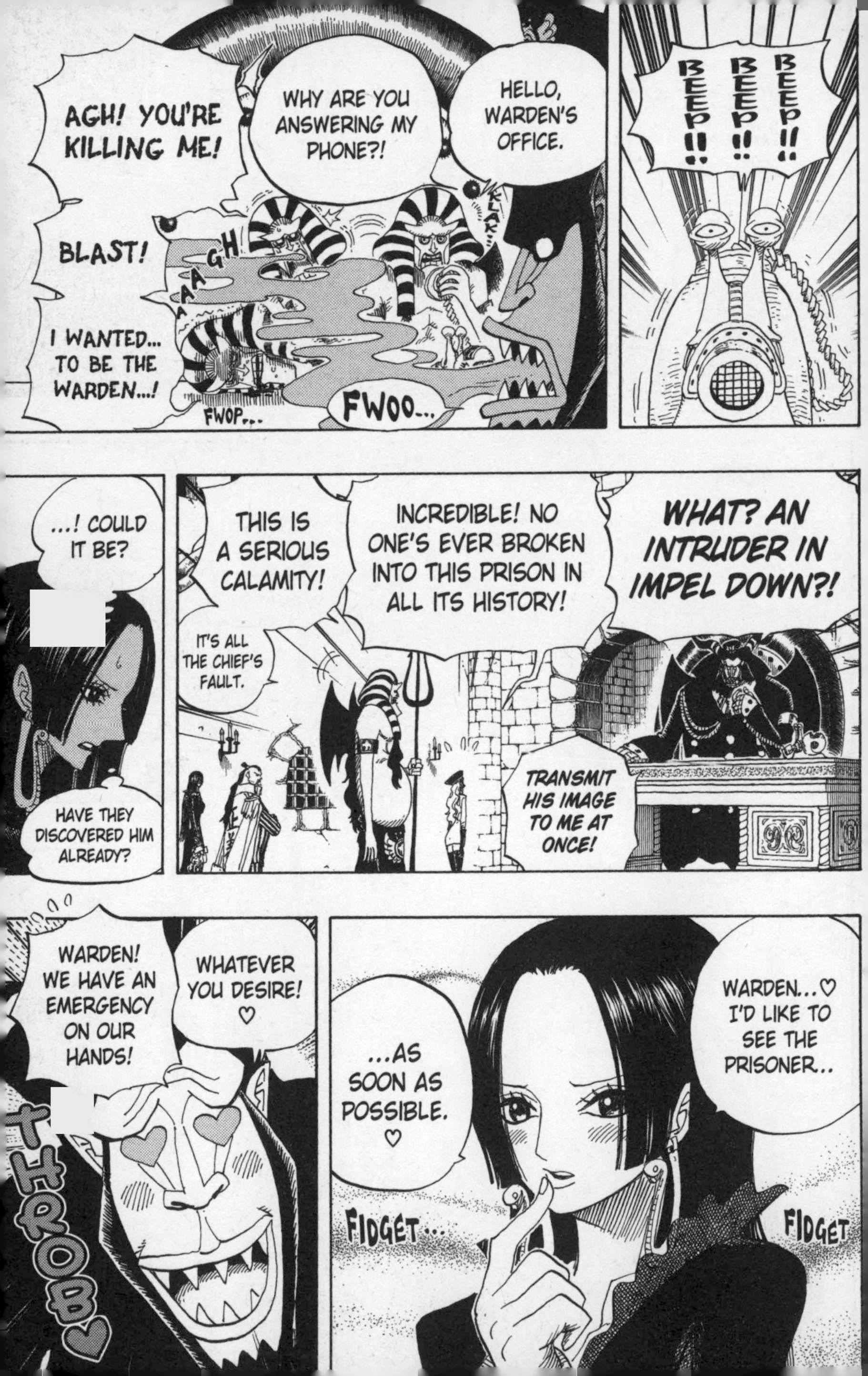
BEEP!! BEEP!! BEEP!!
HELLO, WARDEN'S OFFICE.
KLAK
WHY ARE YOU ANSWERING MY PHONE?!
AGH! YOU'RE KILLING ME!
AAAGH
BLAST!
FWOO...
I WANTED... TO BE THE WARDEN...!
FWOP...
WHAT? AN INTRUDER IN IMPEL DOWN?!
TRANSMIT HIS IMAGE TO ME AT ONCE!
INCREDIBLE! NO ONE'S EVER BROKEN INTO THIS PRISON IN ALL ITS HISTORY!
THIS IS A SERIOUS CALAMITY!
IT'S ALL THE CHIEF'S FAULT.
...! COULD IT BE?
HAVE THEY DISCOVERED HIM ALREADY?
WARDEN...♡ I'D LIKE TO SEE THE PRISONER..
FIDGET
...AS SOON AS POSSIBLE. ♡
FIDGET...
WHATEVER YOU DESIRE! ♡
WARDEN! WE HAVE AN EMERGENCY ON OUR HANDS!
THROB♡

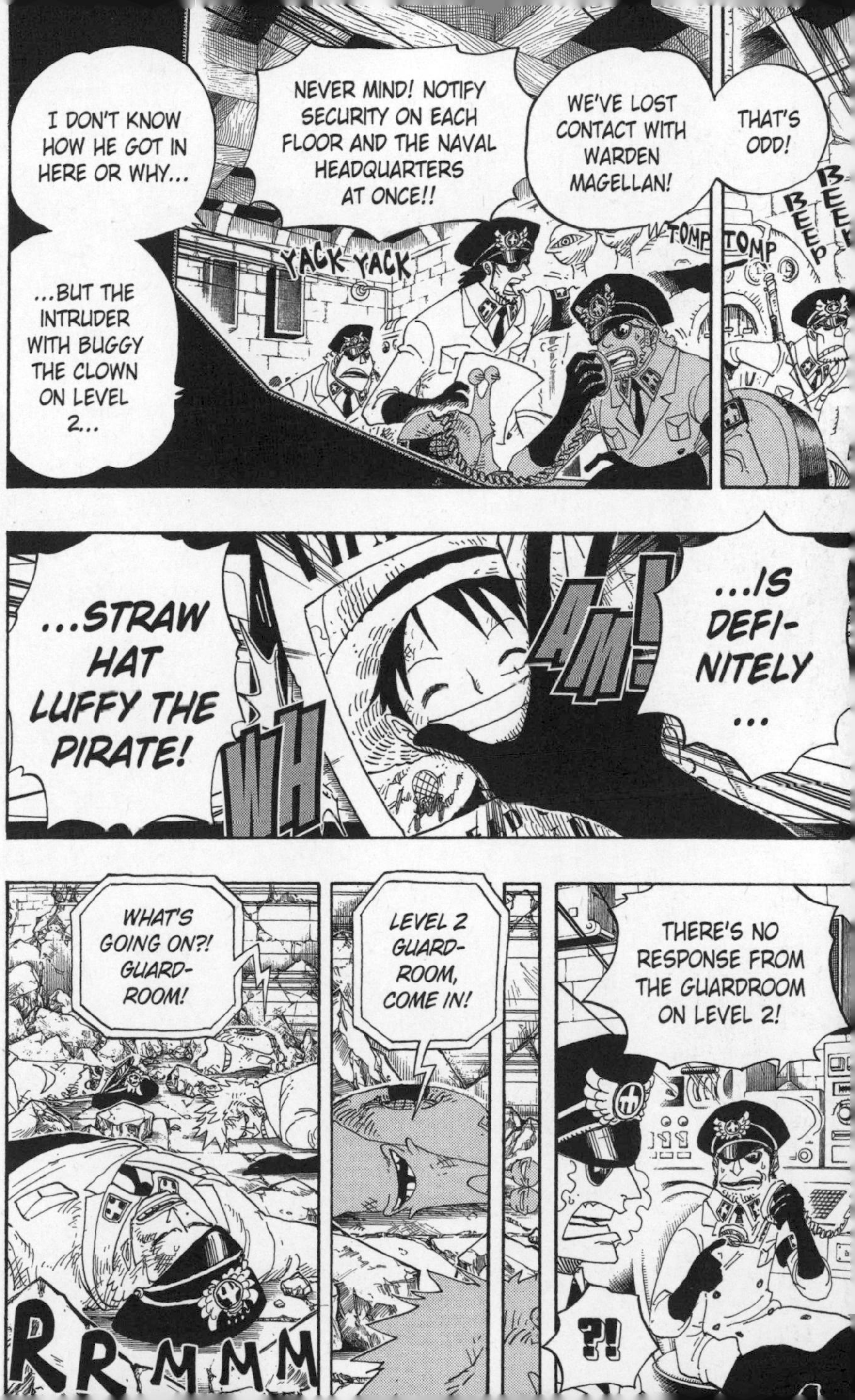
BEEP BEEP
THAT'S ODD!
TOMP TOMP
WE'VE LOST CONTACT WITH WARDEN MAGELLAN!
NEVER MIND! NOTIFY SECURITY ON EACH FLOOR AND THE NAVAL HEADQUARTERS AT ONCE!!
YACK YACK
I DON'T KNOW HOW HE GOT IN HERE OR WHY...
...BUT THE INTRUDER WITH BUGGY THE CLOWN ON LEVEL 2...
...IS DEFINITELY...
WHAM!
...STRAW HAT LUFFY THE PIRATE!
THERE'S NO RESPONSE FROM THE GUARDROOM ON LEVEL 2!
?!
LEVEL 2 GUARDROOM, COME IN!
WHAT'S GOING ON?! GUARDROOM!
RRMMM

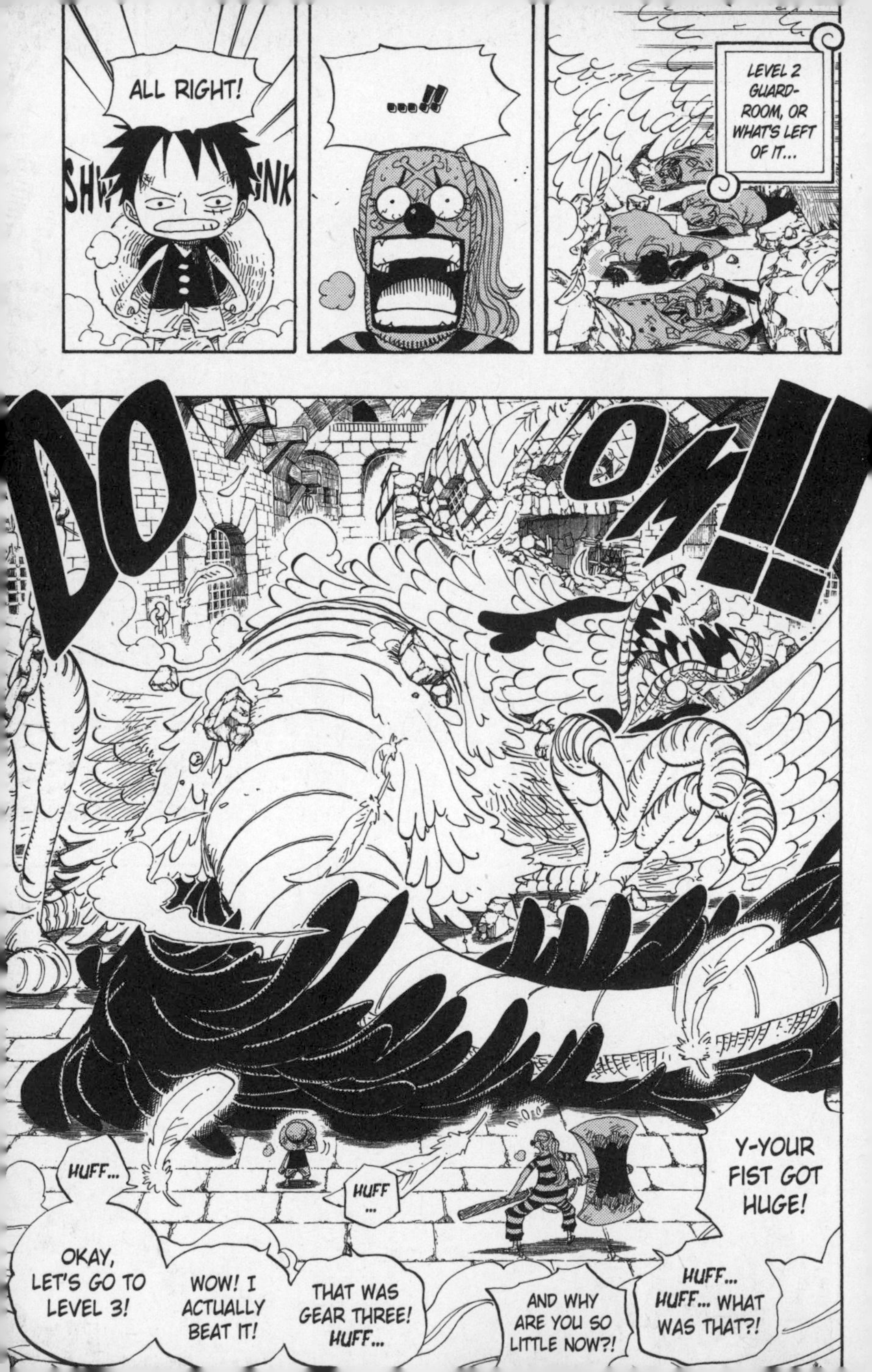
LEVEL 2 GUARD-ROOM, OR WHAT'S LEFT OF IT...
...!!
ALL RIGHT!
SHW
INK
DO
OM!!
Y-YOUR FIST GOT HUGE!
HUFF... HUFF... WHAT WAS THAT?!
AND WHY ARE YOU SO LITTLE NOW?!
HUFF ...
THAT WAS GEAR THREE! HUFF...
HUFF...
WOW! I ACTUALLY BEAT IT!
OKAY, LET'S GO TO LEVEL 3!

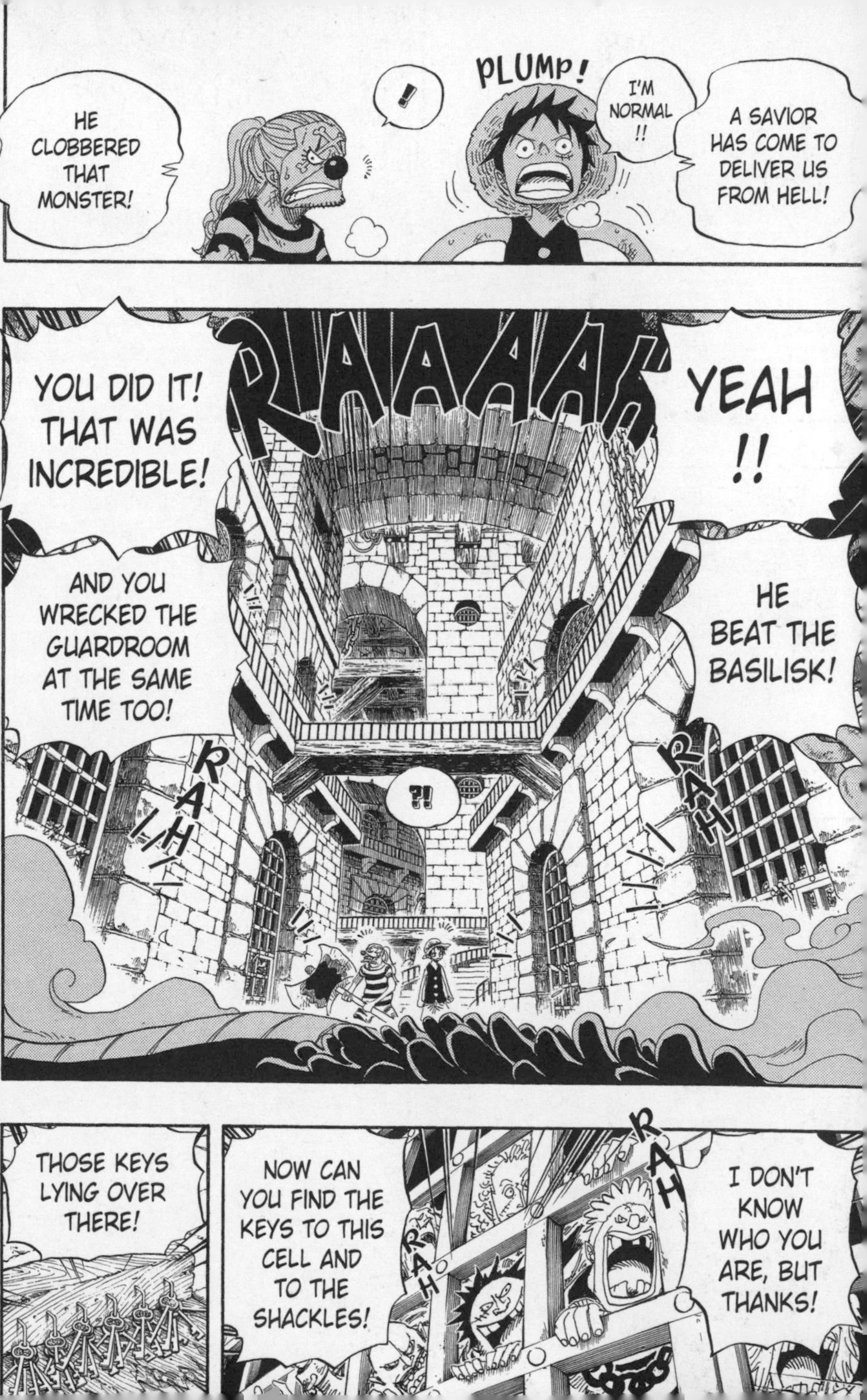
A SAVIOR HAS COME TO DELIVER US FROM HELL!
I'M NORMAL !!
PLUMP!
!
HE CLOBBERED THAT MONSTER!
YEAH !!
RAAAAA
YOU DID IT! THAT WAS INCREDIBLE!
HE BEAT THE BASILISK!
AND YOU WRECKED THE GUARDROOM AT THE SAME TIME TOO!
RAH
?!
RAH
RAH
I DON'T KNOW WHO YOU ARE, BUT THANKS!
RAH
NOW CAN YOU FIND THE KEYS TO THIS CELL AND TO THE SHACKLES!
THOSE KEYS LYING OVER THERE!

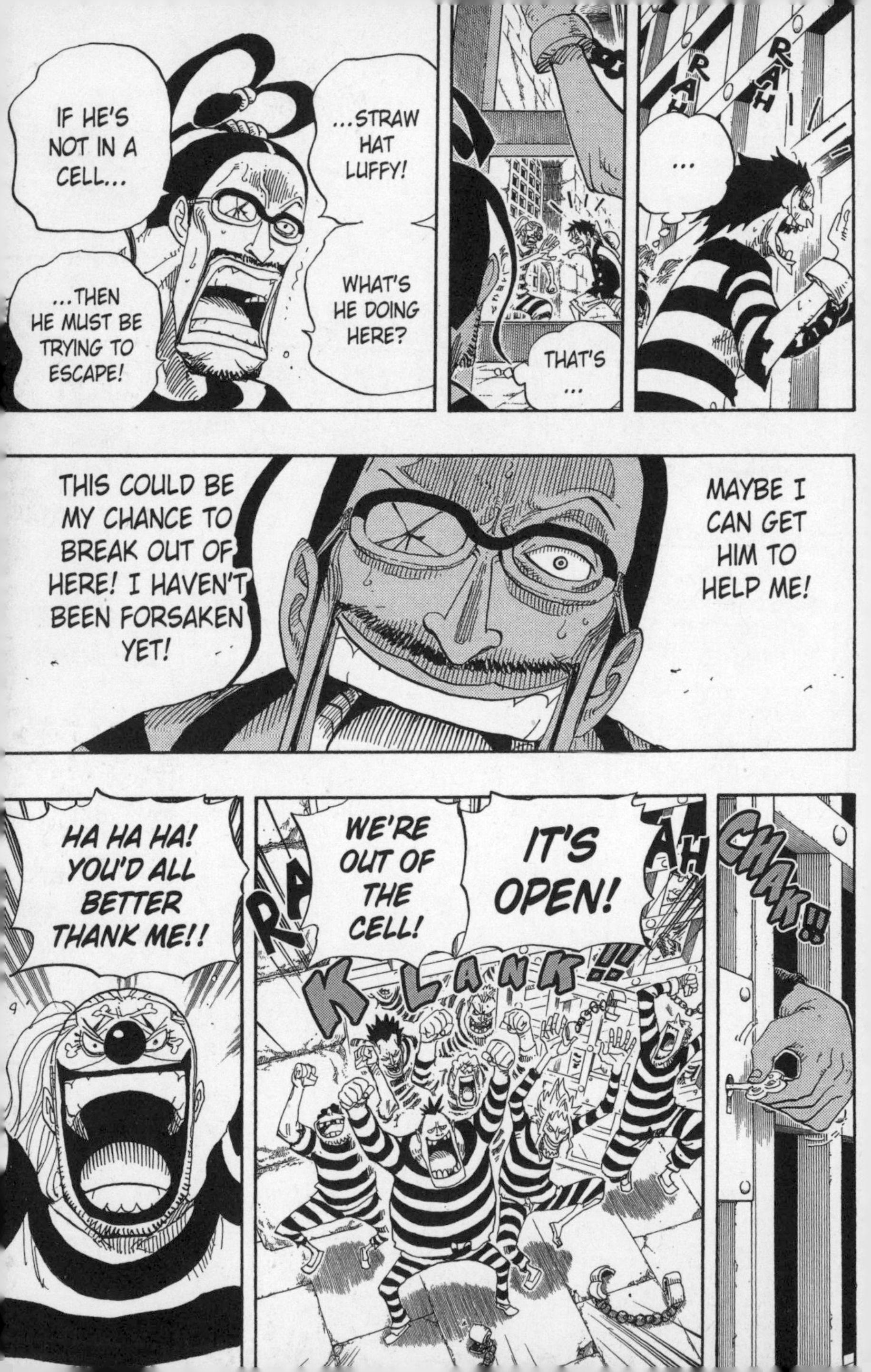
RAH
RAH
...
THAT'S ...
...STRAW HAT LUFFY!
WHAT'S HE DOING HERE?
IF HE'S NOT IN A CELL...
...THEN HE MUST BE TRYING TO ESCAPE!
THIS COULD BE MY CHANCE TO BREAK OUT OF HERE! I HAVEN'T BEEN FORSAKEN YET!
MAYBE I CAN GET HIM TO HELP ME!
CHAK!!
AH
IT'S OPEN!
WE'RE OUT OF THE CELL!
RA
KLANK!!
HA HA HA! YOU'D ALL BETTER THANK ME!!

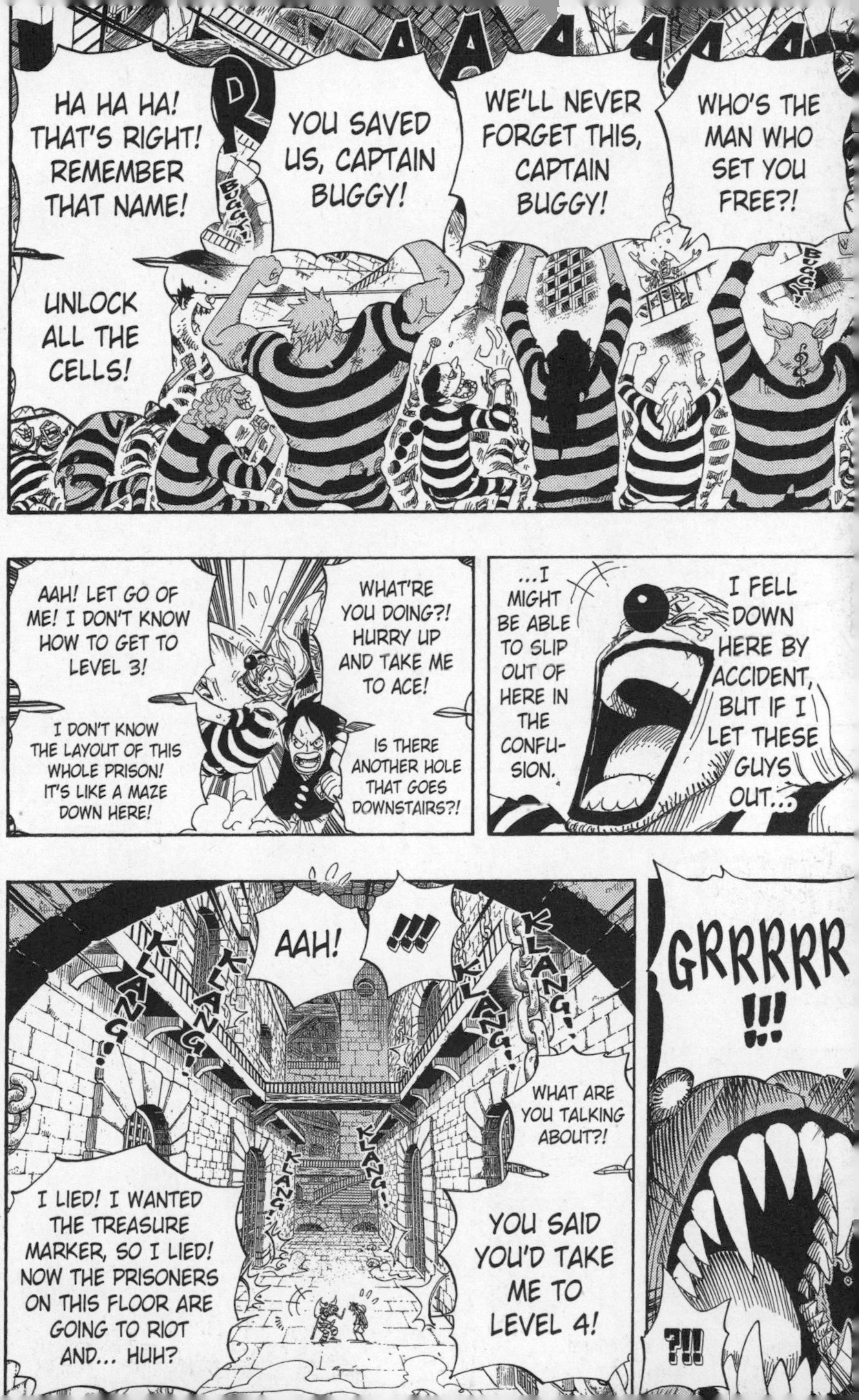
WHO'S THE MAN WHO SET YOU FREE?!
WE'LL NEVER FORGET THIS, CAPTAIN BUGGY!
YOU SAVED US, CAPTAIN BUGGY!
HA HA HA! THAT'S RIGHT! REMEMBER THAT NAME!
UNLOCK ALL THE CELLS!
BUGGY
BUGGY
I FELL DOWN HERE BY ACCIDENT, BUT IF I LET THESE GUYS OUT...
...I MIGHT BE ABLE TO SLIP OUT OF HERE IN THE CONFUSION.
WHAT'RE YOU DOING?! HURRY UP AND TAKE ME TO ACE!
AAH! LET GO OF ME! I DON'T KNOW HOW TO GET TO LEVEL 3!
IS THERE ANOTHER HOLE THAT GOES DOWNSTAIRS?!
I DON'T KNOW THE LAYOUT OF THIS WHOLE PRISON! IT'S LIKE A MAZE DOWN HERE!
GRRRRR!!!
?!!
!!!
AAH!
KLANG!
KLANG!
KLANG!
KLANG!
KLANG!
KLANG!
WHAT ARE YOU TALKING ABOUT?!
YOU SAID YOU'D TAKE ME TO LEVEL 4!
I LIED! I WANTED THE TREASURE MARKER, SO I LIED! NOW THE PRISONERS ON THIS FLOOR ARE GOING TO RIOT AND... HUH?

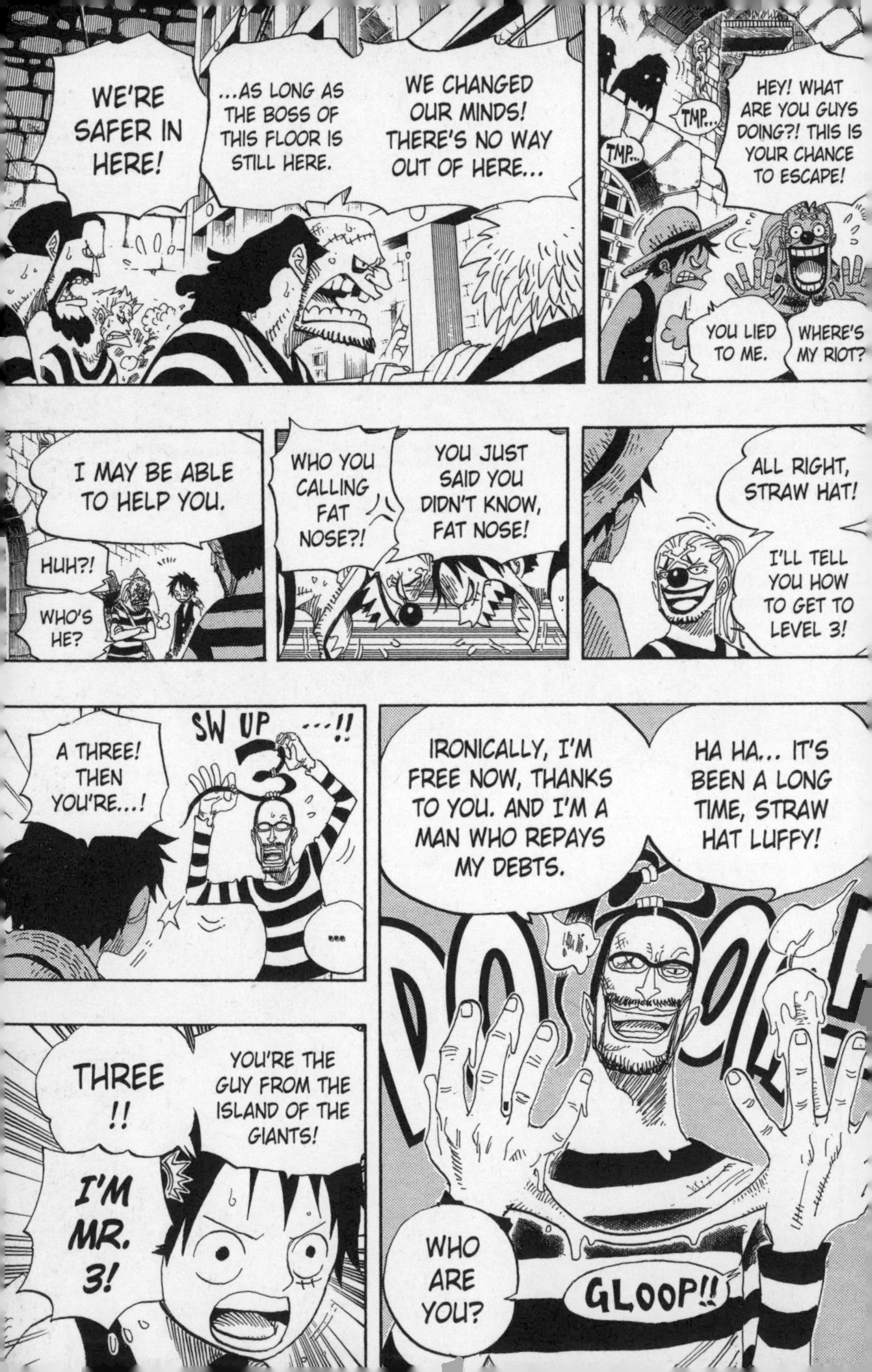
HEY! WHAT ARE YOU GUYS DOING?! THIS IS YOUR CHANCE TO ESCAPE!
TMP...
TMP...
WHERE'S MY RIOT?
YOU LIED TO ME.
WE CHANGED OUR MINDS! THERE'S NO WAY OUT OF HERE...
...AS LONG AS THE BOSS OF THIS FLOOR IS STILL HERE.
WE'RE SAFER IN HERE!
ALL RIGHT, STRAW HAT!
I'LL TELL YOU HOW TO GET TO LEVEL 3!
YOU JUST SAID YOU DIDN'T KNOW, FAT NOSE!
WHO YOU CALLING FAT NOSE?!
I MAY BE ABLE TO HELP YOU.
HUH?!
WHO'S HE?
HA HA... IT'S BEEN A LONG TIME, STRAW HAT LUFFY!
IRONICALLY, I'M FREE NOW, THANKS TO YOU. AND I'M A MAN WHO REPAYS MY DEBTS.
GLOOP!!
WHO ARE YOU?
SW UP
...!!
A THREE! THEN YOU'RE...!
...
YOU'RE THE GUY FROM THE ISLAND OF THE GIANTS!
THREE !!
I'M MR. 3!

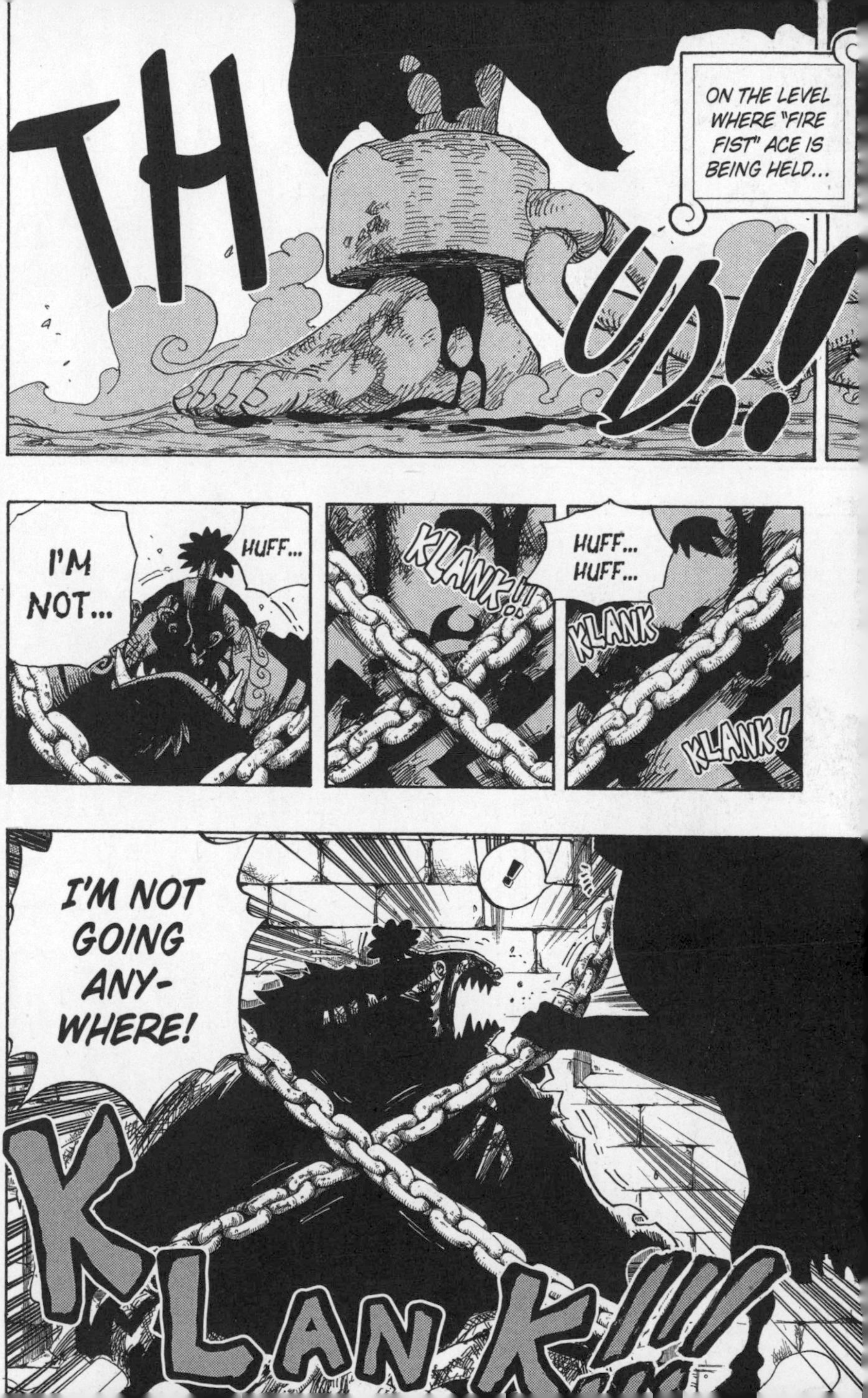
ON THE LEVEL WHERE "FIRE FIST" ACE IS BEING HELD...
THUD!!
HUFF... HUFF...
KLANK
KLANK!
KLANK!!!
HUFF...
I'M NOT...
!
I'M NOT GOING ANYWHERE!
KLANK!!!

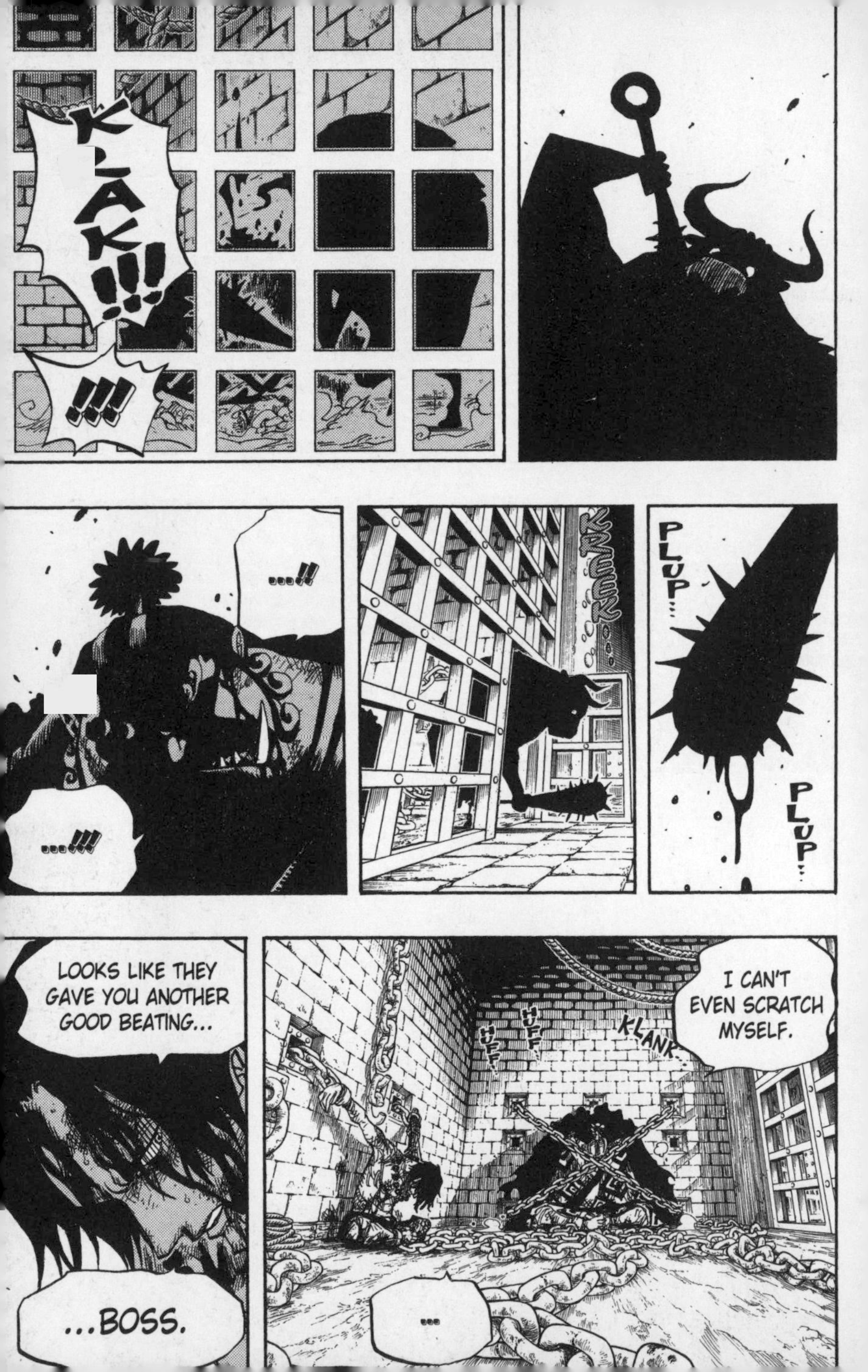
KLAK!!!
!!!!
PLUP...
PLUP...
KREEK...
...!!
...!!!
I CAN'T EVEN SCRATCH MYSELF.
KLANK
HUFF
HUFF
...
LOOKS LIKE THEY GAVE YOU ANOTHER GOOD BEATING...
...BOSS.

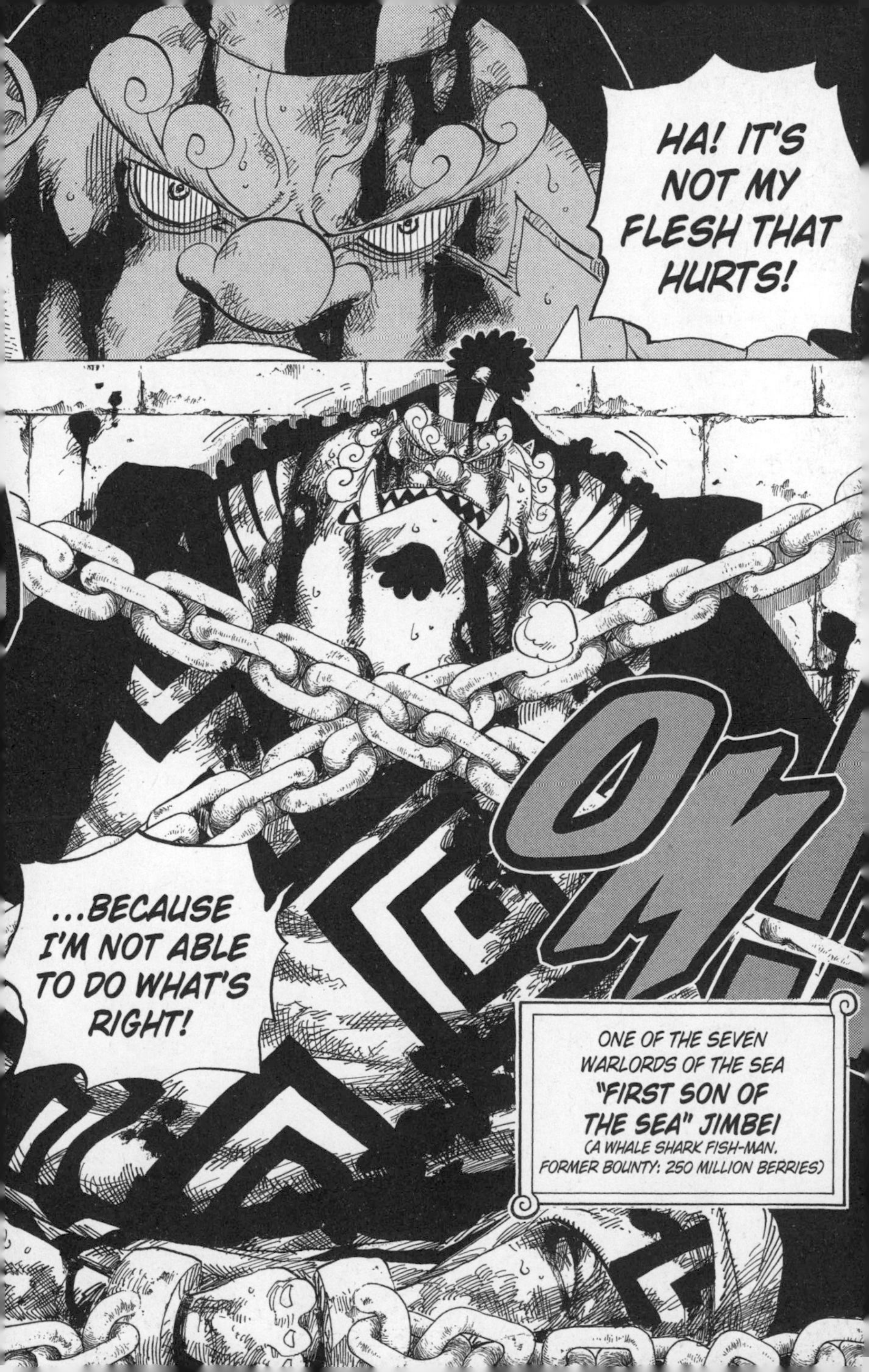
HA! IT'S NOT MY FLESH THAT HURTS!
...BECAUSE I'M NOT ABLE TO DO WHAT'S RIGHT!
ONE OF THE SEVEN WARLORDS OF THE SEA "FIRST SON OF THE SEA" JIMBEI (A WHALE SHARK FISH-MAN. FORMER BOUNTY: 250 MILLION BERRIES)

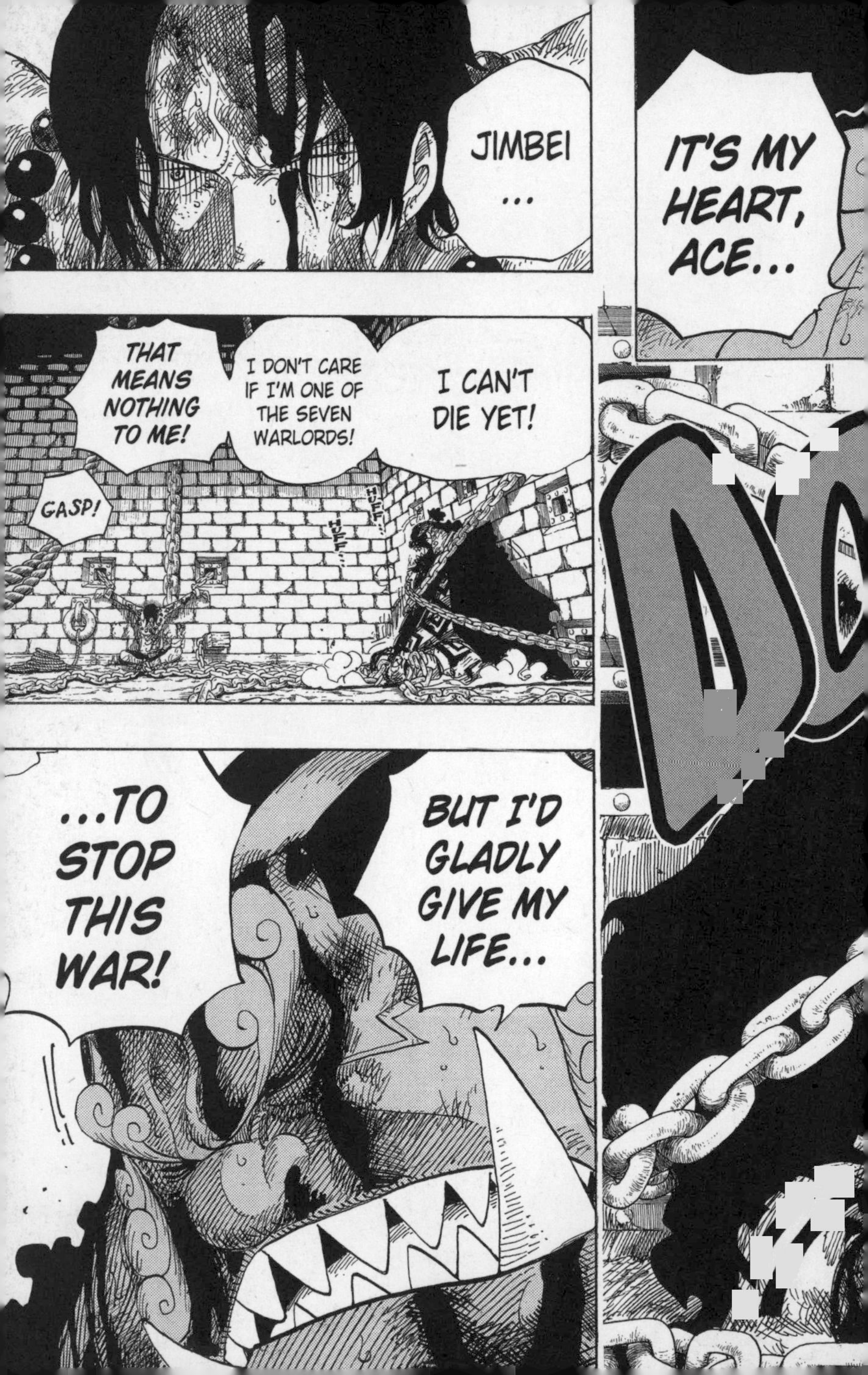
IT'S MY HEART, ACE...
JIMBEI ...
I CAN'T DIE YET!
I DON'T CARE IF I'M ONE OF THE SEVEN WARLORDS!
THAT MEANS NOTHING TO ME!
HUFF... HUFF...
GASP!
BUT I'D GLADLY GIVE MY LIFE...
...TO STOP THIS WAR!

SBS Question Corner

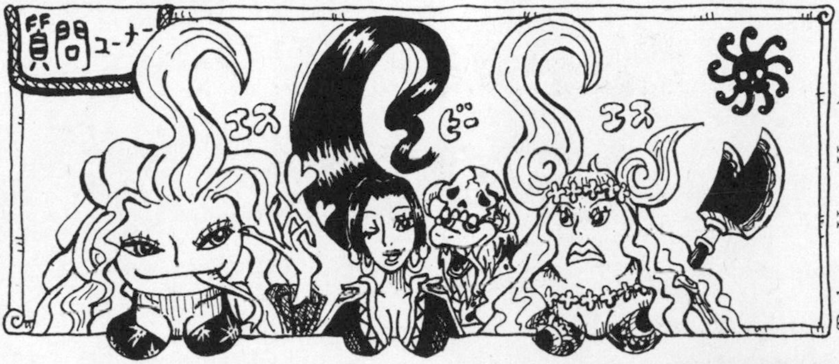
質問コーナー

(Park won-Yong, Korea)

Q: Mr. Oda, Boa Hancock came out on the cover of *Jump* nine years ago! That really surprised me. Is this really her? Please tell me.

--PX-10000

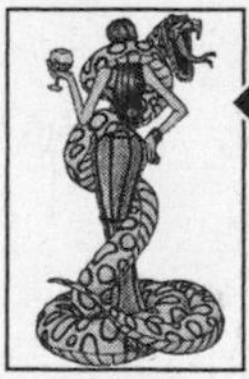

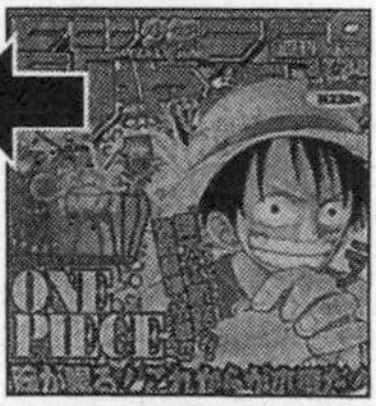
ONE PIECE

A: I'm the one who's surprised! People on the internet noticed this but I completely forgot about it. This picture was in the illustration collection, *Color Walk 2*, but during that time, the crew had just entered the Grand Line. The editors told me to draw the back view of the "enemies that will come." I drew about four, and I remember that Hancock was one of them. When I actually did bring her out in the comic, a lot about her is different, but that design is indeed Warlord Boa Hancock that I thought of nine years ago.

Q: Red light. Green light! I got you! Moss Ball! --Nashi

A: Haha! Zolo got caught! Neener neener neener! Okay.

Q: Hello, Odacchi. I am writing this letter from Liguria. (Liguria is a region of Italy, not Water Seven) I want to know the connections the two agents that went to Ohara with Spandine have with the current CP9 agents. I get the feeling that the guy with the glasses is Kalifa's father. Thank you for making Robin!

--Dario

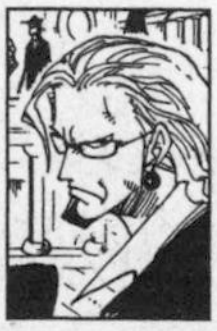

A: Kalifa's dad! You're absolutely right. I didn't give out any hints at all about it. I told my editor at the time about it, but this person (➡) is actually Kalifa's father. Most of the CP9 members are orphans that have been trained by the government, but we thought it might be interesting if among those children are some who belong to a long bloodline of agents. Kumadori's mom isn't one of them, by the way.

Chapter 529:
LEVEL 2: BEAST HELL

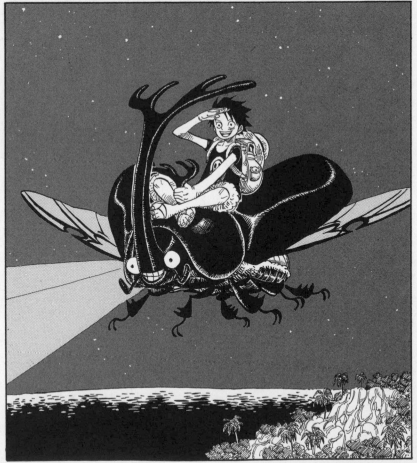

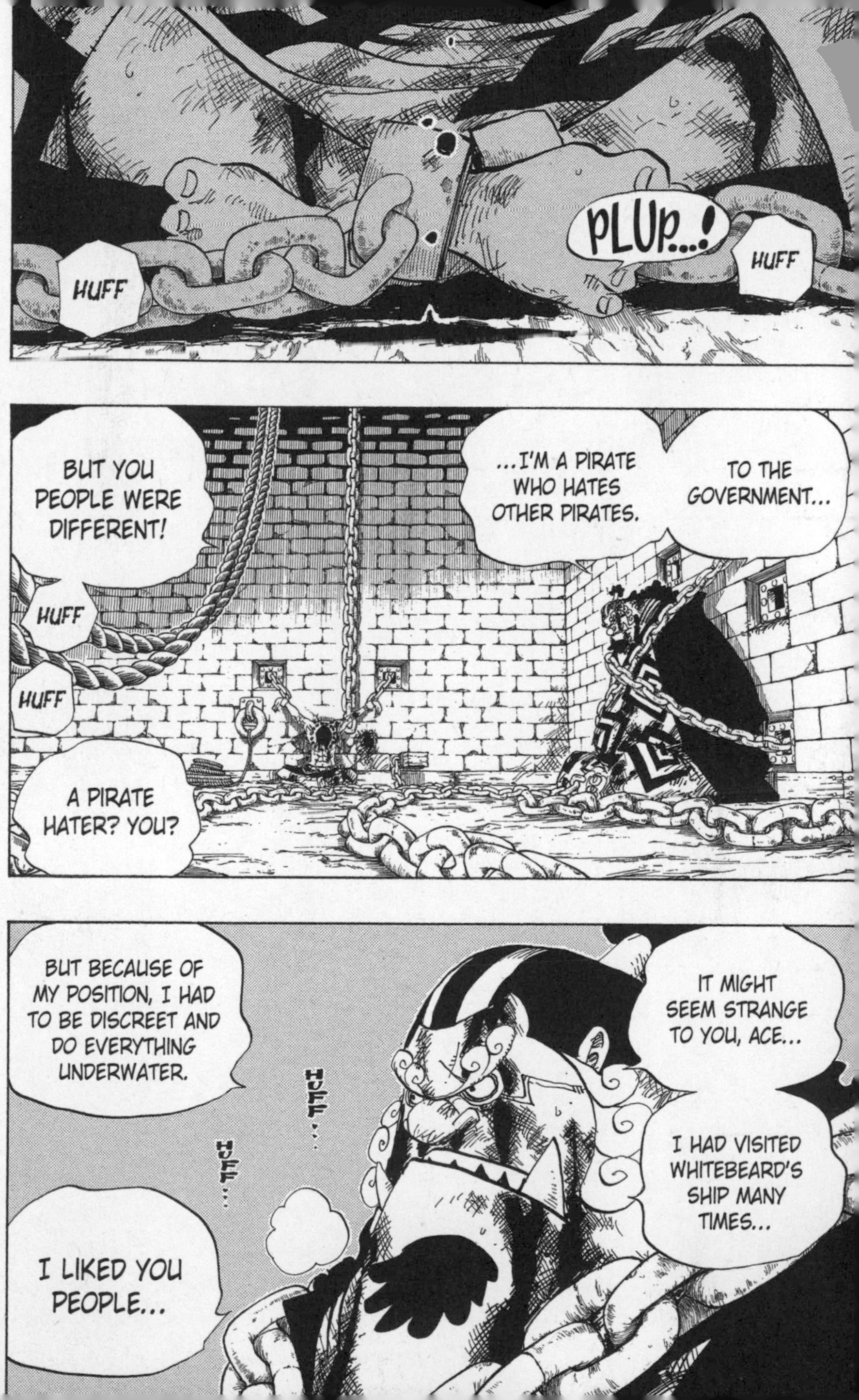
HUFF
PLUP...!
HUFF
TO THE GOVERNMENT...
...I'M A PIRATE WHO HATES OTHER PIRATES.
BUT YOU PEOPLE WERE DIFFERENT!
HUFF
HUFF
A PIRATE HATER? YOU?
IT MIGHT SEEM STRANGE TO YOU, ACE...
I HAD VISITED WHITEBEARD'S SHIP MANY TIMES...
BUT BECAUSE OF MY POSITION, I HAD TO BE DISCREET AND DO EVERYTHING UNDERWATER.
HUFF...
HUFF...
I LIKED YOU PEOPLE...

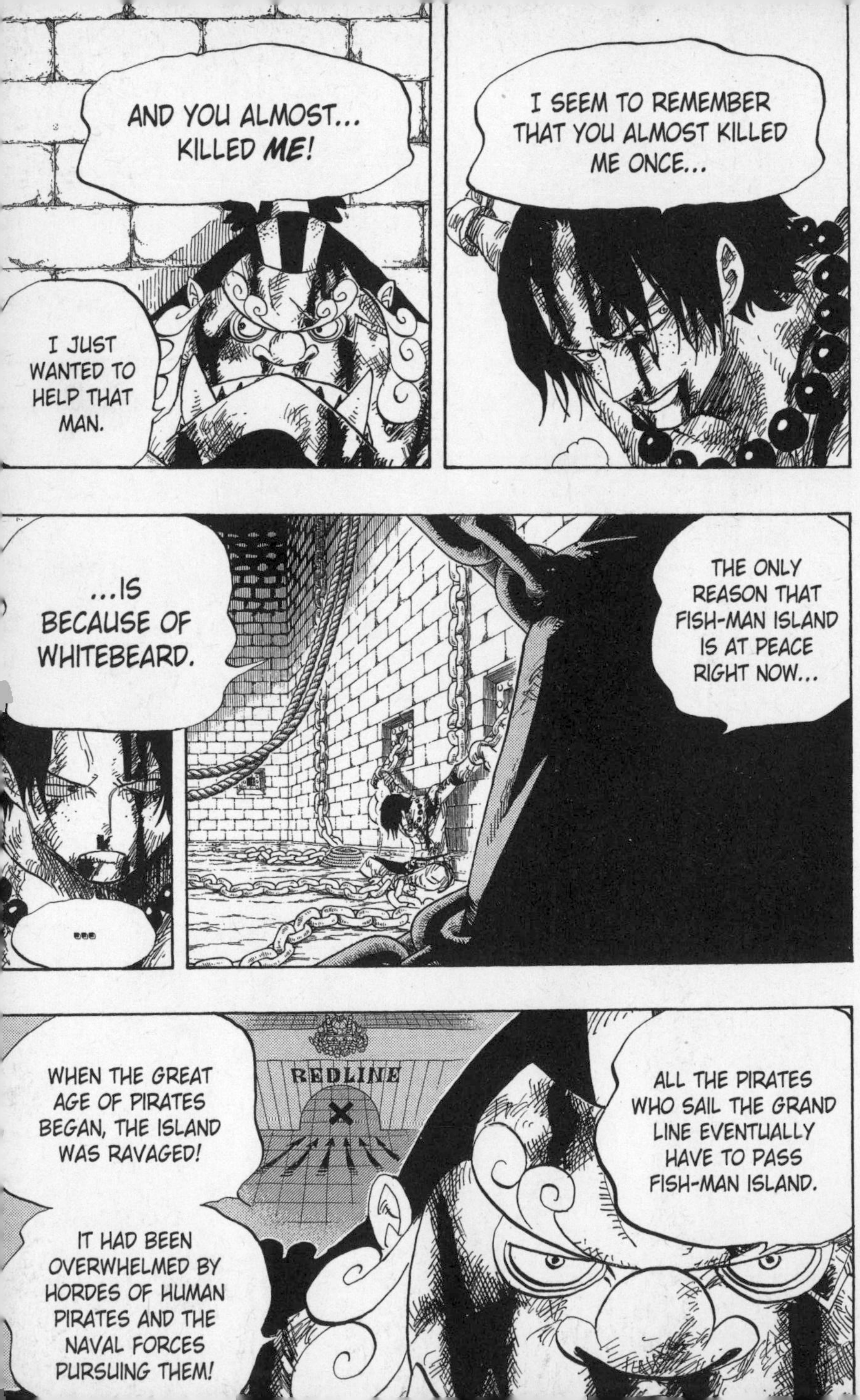
I SEEM TO REMEMBER THAT YOU ALMOST KILLED ME ONCE...
AND YOU ALMOST... KILLED *ME*!
I JUST WANTED TO HELP THAT MAN.
THE ONLY REASON THAT FISH-MAN ISLAND IS AT PEACE RIGHT NOW...
...IS BECAUSE OF WHITEBEARD.
...
ALL THE PIRATES WHO SAIL THE GRAND LINE EVENTUALLY HAVE TO PASS FISH-MAN ISLAND.
REDLINE
WHEN THE GREAT AGE OF PIRATES BEGAN, THE ISLAND WAS RAVAGED!
IT HAD BEEN OVERWHELMED BY HORDES OF HUMAN PIRATES AND THE NAVAL FORCES PURSUING THEM!

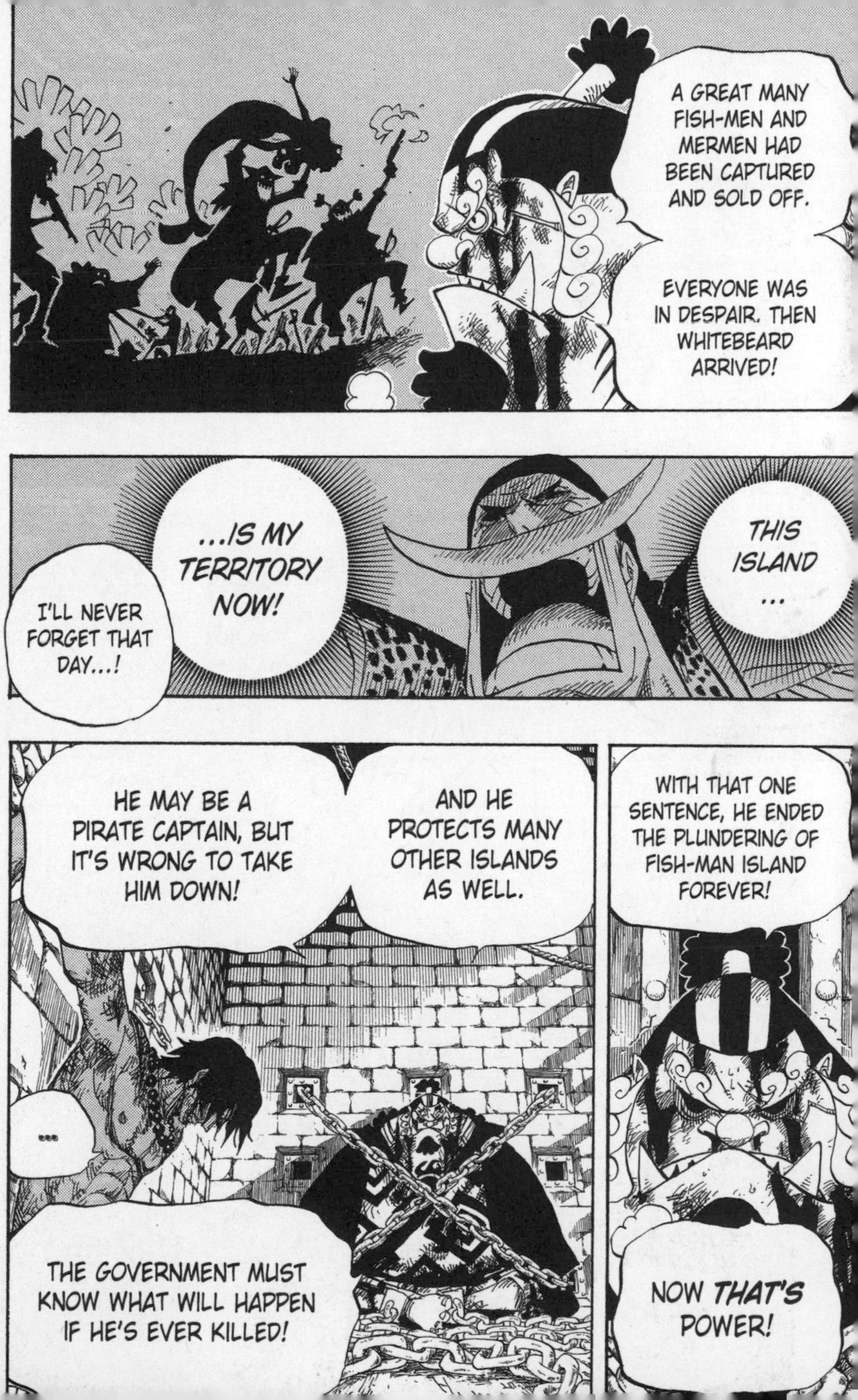
A GREAT MANY FISH-MEN AND MERMEN HAD BEEN CAPTURED AND SOLD OFF.
EVERYONE WAS IN DESPAIR. THEN WHITEBEARD ARRIVED!
THIS ISLAND ...
...IS MY TERRITORY NOW!
I'LL NEVER FORGET THAT DAY...!
WITH THAT ONE SENTENCE, HE ENDED THE PLUNDERING OF FISH-MAN ISLAND FOREVER!
NOW THAT'S POWER!
HE MAY BE A PIRATE CAPTAIN, BUT IT'S WRONG TO TAKE HIM DOWN!
AND HE PROTECTS MANY OTHER ISLANDS AS WELL.
...
THE GOVERNMENT MUST KNOW WHAT WILL HAPPEN IF HE'S EVER KILLED!

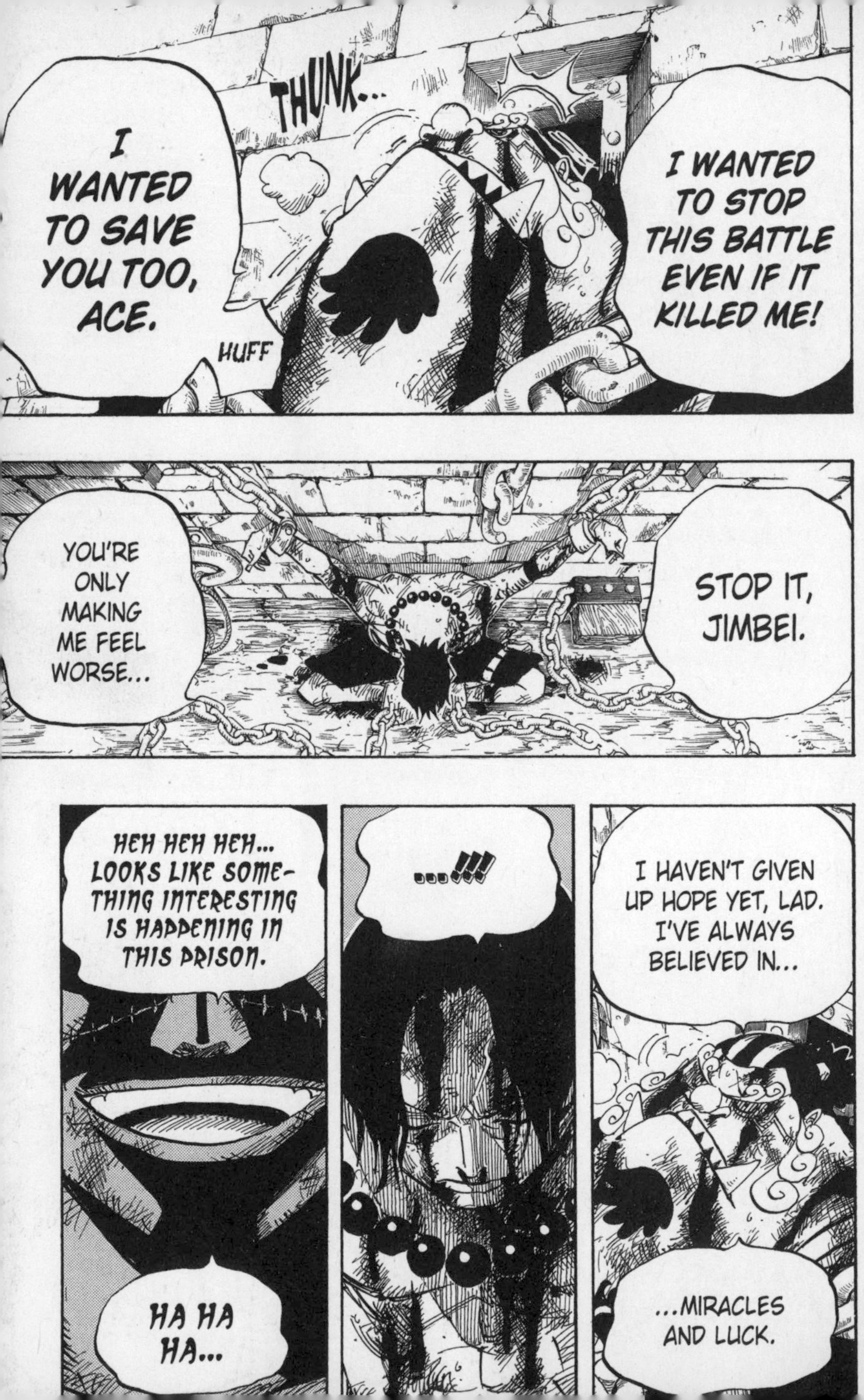
I WANTED TO STOP THIS BATTLE EVEN IF IT KILLED ME!
THUNK...
I WANTED TO SAVE YOU TOO, ACE.
HUFF
STOP IT, JIMBEI.
YOU'RE ONLY MAKING ME FEEL WORSE...
I HAVEN'T GIVEN UP HOPE YET, LAD. I'VE ALWAYS BELIEVED IN...
...MIRACLES AND LUCK.
...!!!
HEH HEH HEH... LOOKS LIKE SOME-THING INTERESTING IS HAPPENING IN THIS PRISON.
HA HA HA...

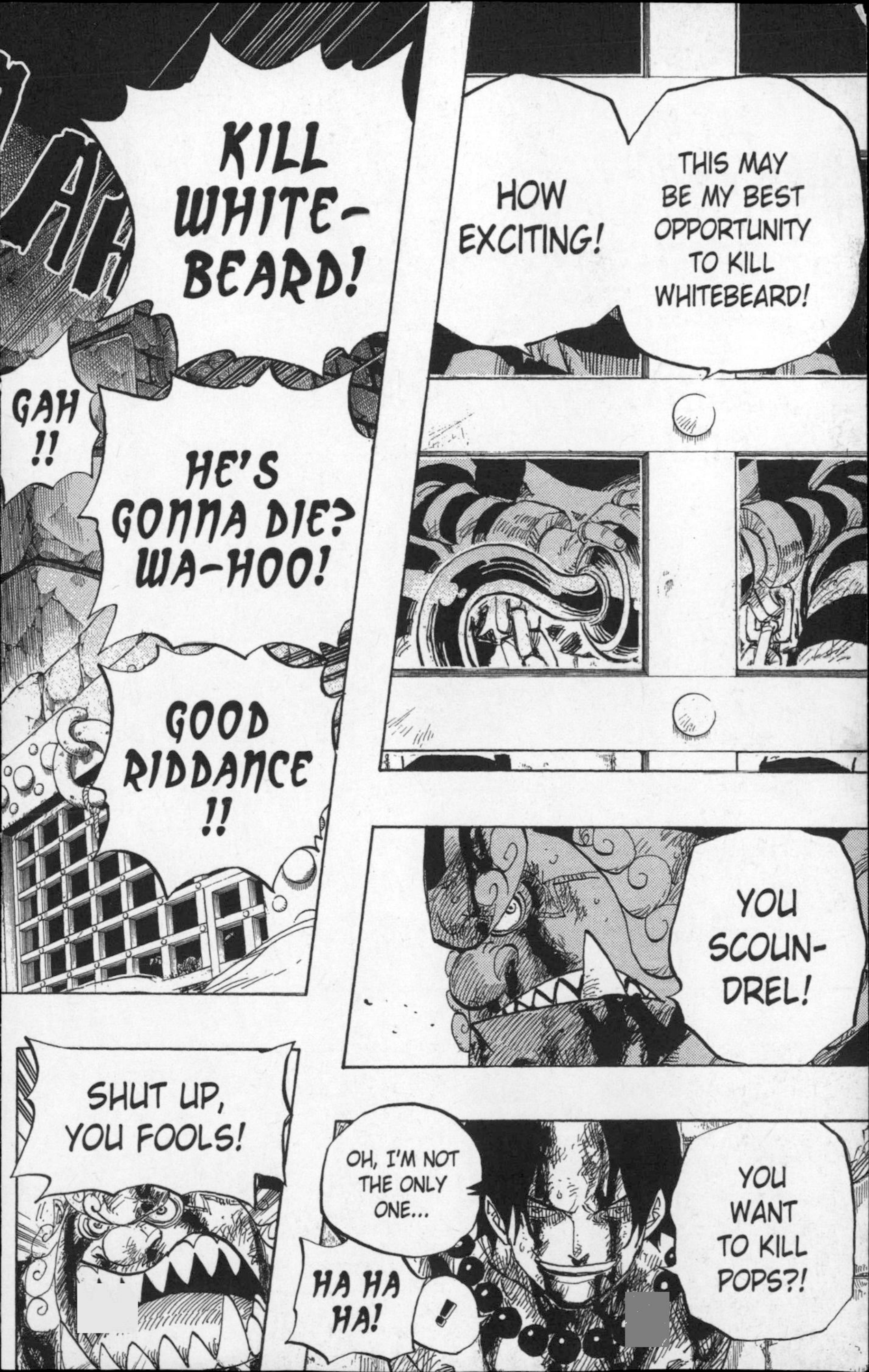
THIS MAY BE MY BEST OPPORTUNITY TO KILL WHITEBEARD!
HOW EXCITING!
YOU SCOUNDREL!
KILL WHITE-BEARD!
GAH!!
HE'S GONNA DIE? WA-HOO!
GOOD RIDDANCE!!
YOU WANT TO KILL POPS?!
OH, I'M NOT THE ONLY ONE...
HA HA HA!
!
SHUT UP, YOU FOOLS!

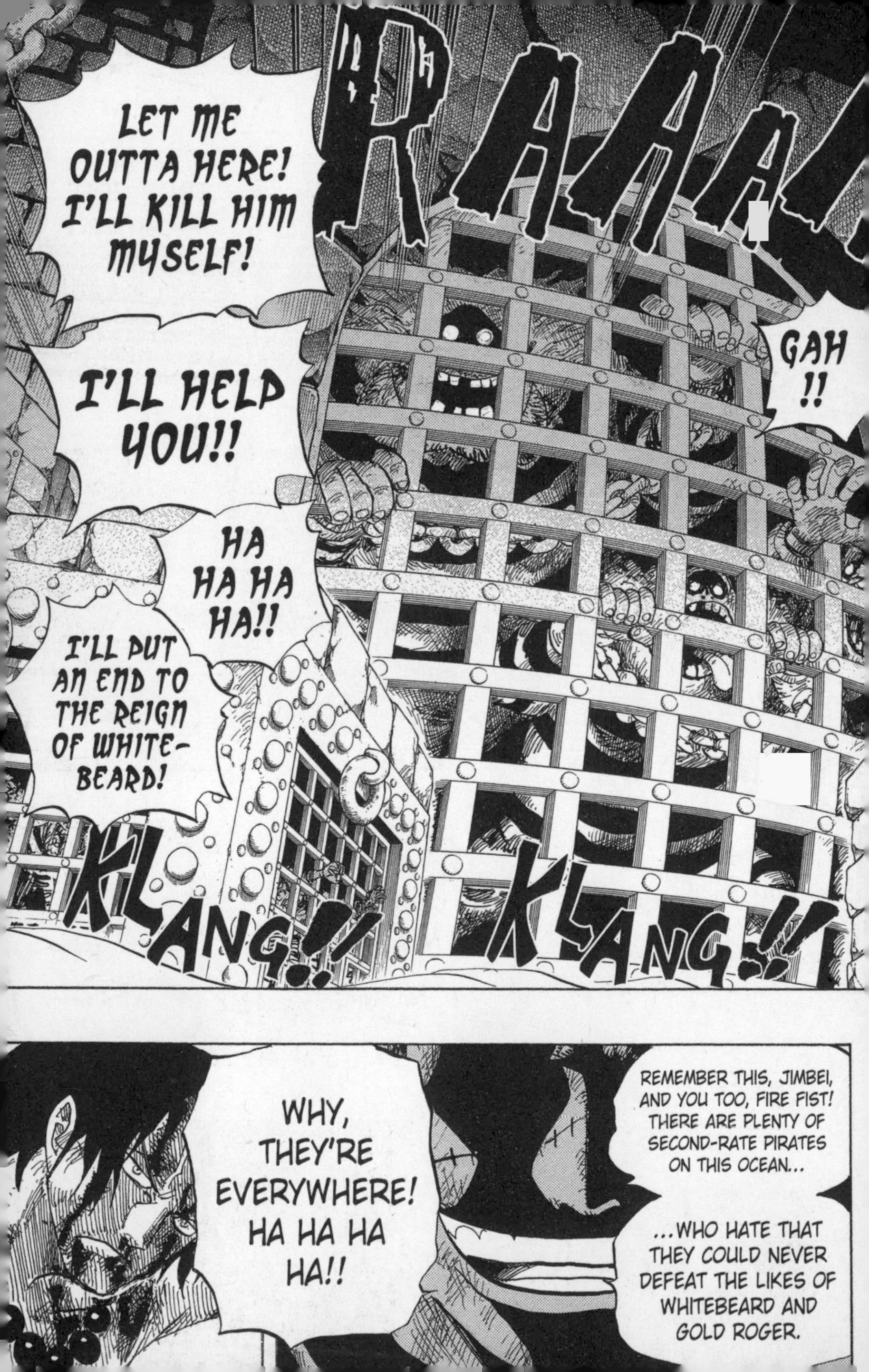
RAAA
GAH!!
LET ME OUTTA HERE! I'LL KILL HIM MYSELF!
I'LL HELP YOU!!
HA HA HA HA!!
I'LL PUT AN END TO THE REIGN OF WHITE-BEARD!
KLANG!!
KLANG!!
REMEMBER THIS, JIMBEI, AND YOU TOO, FIRE FIST! THERE ARE PLENTY OF SECOND-RATE PIRATES ON THIS OCEAN...
...WHO HATE THAT THEY COULD NEVER DEFEAT THE LIKES OF WHITEBEARD AND GOLD ROGER.
WHY, THEY'RE EVERYWHERE! HA HA HA HA!!

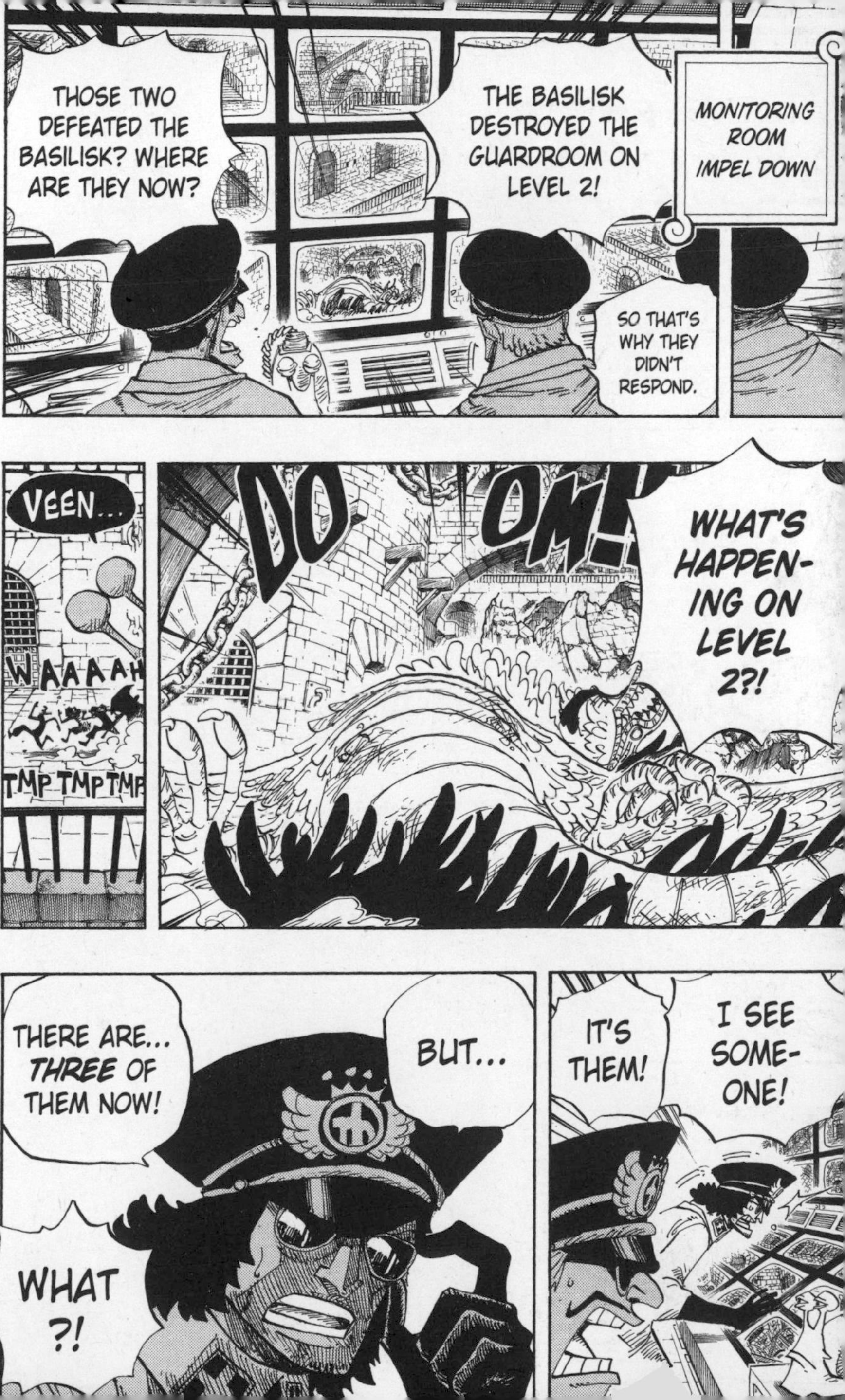
MONITORING ROOM IMPEL DOWN
THE BASILISK DESTROYED THE GUARDROOM ON LEVEL 2!
SO THAT'S WHY THEY DIDN'T RESPOND.
THOSE TWO DEFEATED THE BASILISK? WHERE ARE THEY NOW?
DOOM!!
WHAT'S HAPPEN-ING ON LEVEL 2?!
VEEN...
WAAAAH
TMP TMP TMP
I SEE SOME-ONE!
IT'S THEM!
BUT...
THERE ARE... THREE OF THEM NOW!
WHAT ?!

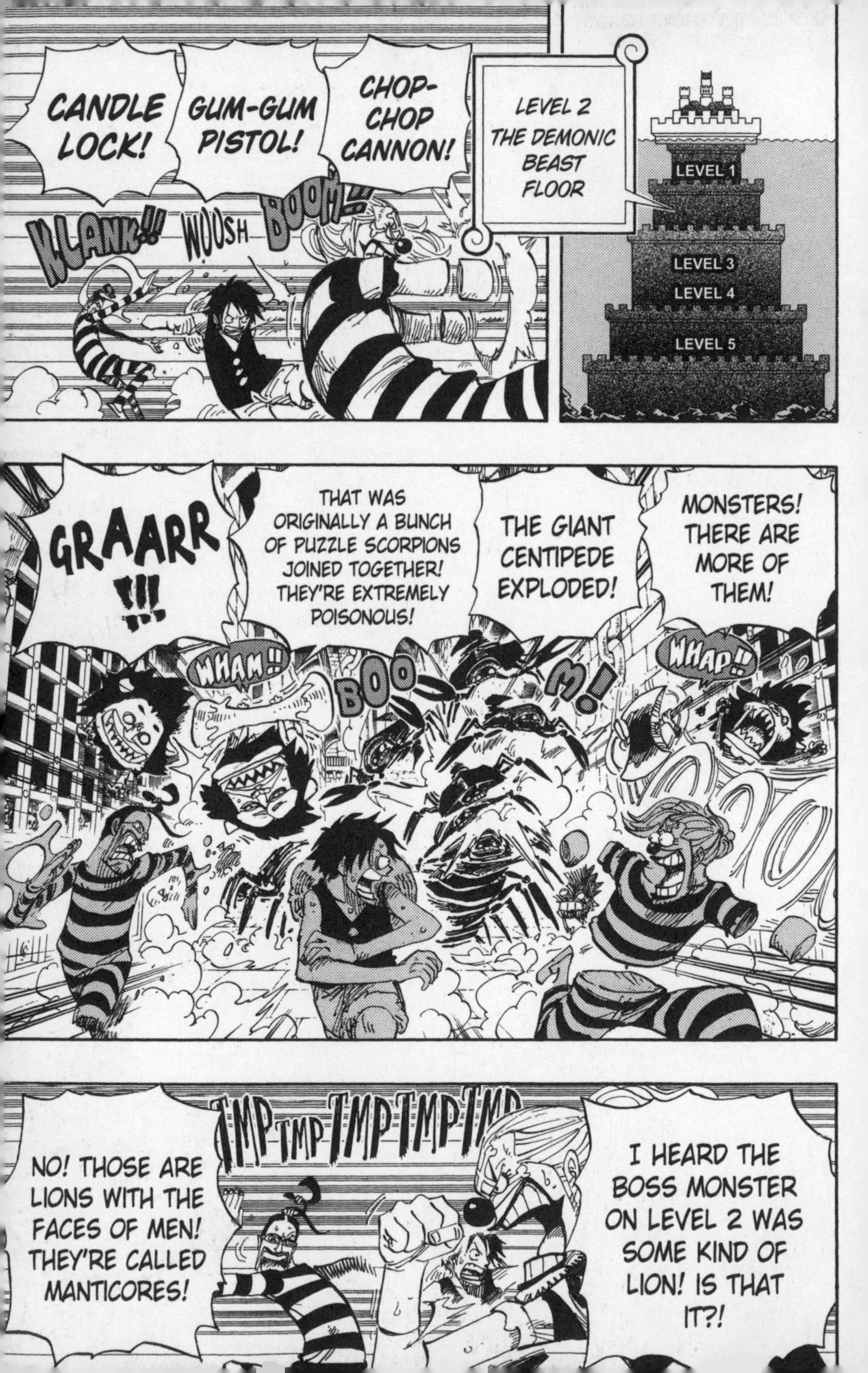
LEVEL 2 THE DEMONIC BEAST FLOOR
LEVEL 1
LEVEL 3
LEVEL 4
LEVEL 5
CHOP-CHOP CANNON!
GUM-GUM PISTOL!
CANDLE LOCK!
BOOM!!
WOOSH
KLANK!!
MONSTERS! THERE ARE MORE OF THEM!
THE GIANT CENTIPEDE EXPLODED!
THAT WAS ORIGINALLY A BUNCH OF PUZZLE SCORPIONS JOINED TOGETHER! THEY'RE EXTREMELY POISONOUS!
GRAARR!!!
WHAP!!
BOOM!
WHAM!!
I HEARD THE BOSS MONSTER ON LEVEL 2 WAS SOME KIND OF LION! IS THAT IT?!
NO! THOSE ARE LIONS WITH THE FACES OF MEN! THEY'RE CALLED MANTICORES!
TMP TMP TMP TMP TMP

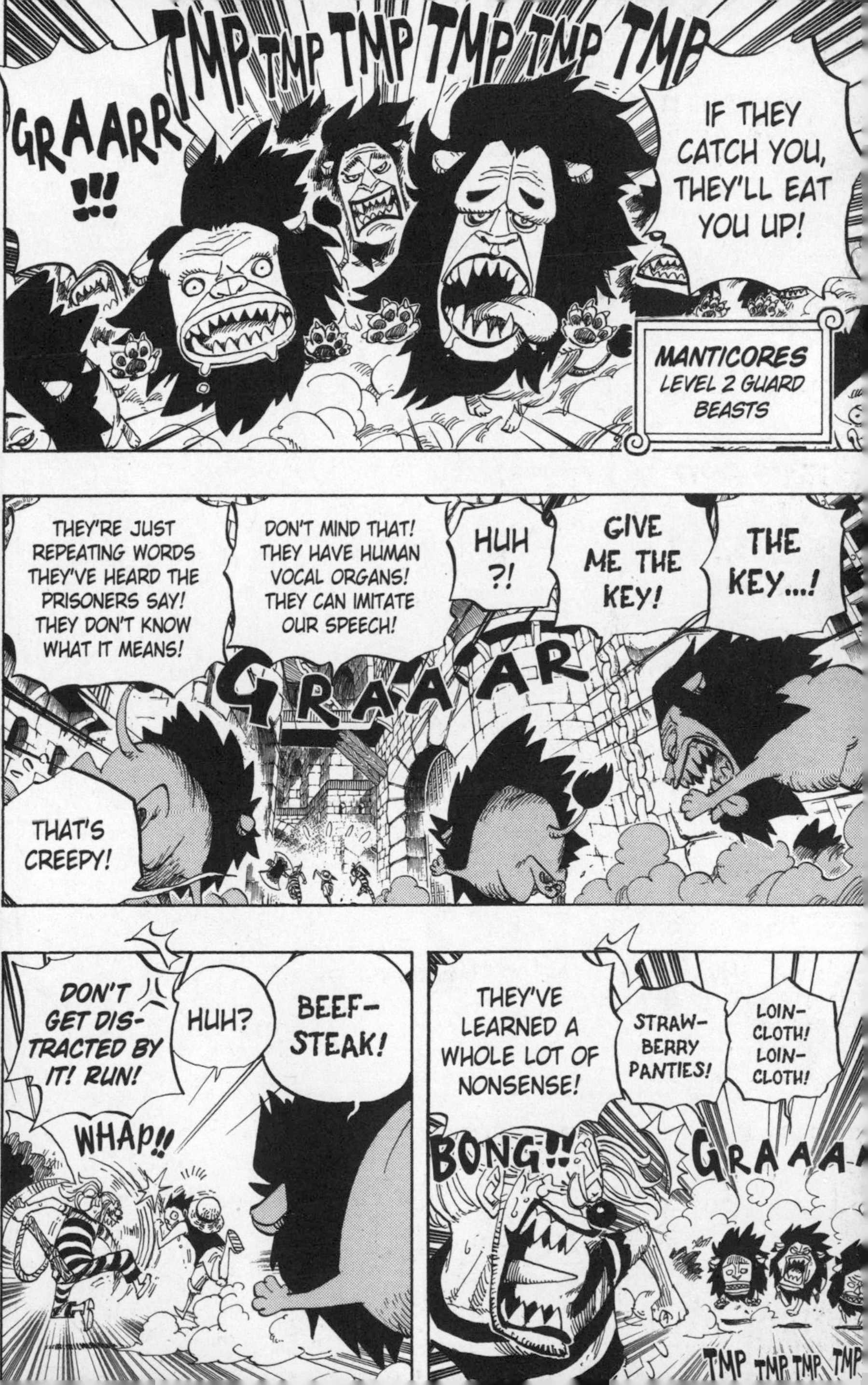
TMP TMP TMP TMP TMP TMP
IF THEY CATCH YOU, THEY'LL EAT YOU UP!
MANTICORES LEVEL 2 GUARD BEASTS
GRAARR!!!
THE KEY...!
GIVE ME THE KEY!
HUH ?!
DON'T MIND THAT! THEY HAVE HUMAN VOCAL ORGANS! THEY CAN IMITATE OUR SPEECH!
THEY'RE JUST REPEATING WORDS THEY'VE HEARD THE PRISONERS SAY! THEY DON'T KNOW WHAT IT MEANS!
GRAAAR
THAT'S CREEPY!
LOIN-CLOTH! LOIN-CLOTH!
STRAW-BERRY PANTIES!
THEY'VE LEARNED A WHOLE LOT OF NONSENSE!
GRAAA
BONG!!
TMP TMP TMP TMP
BEEF-STEAK!
HUH?
DON'T GET DIS-TRACTED BY IT! RUN!
WHAP!!

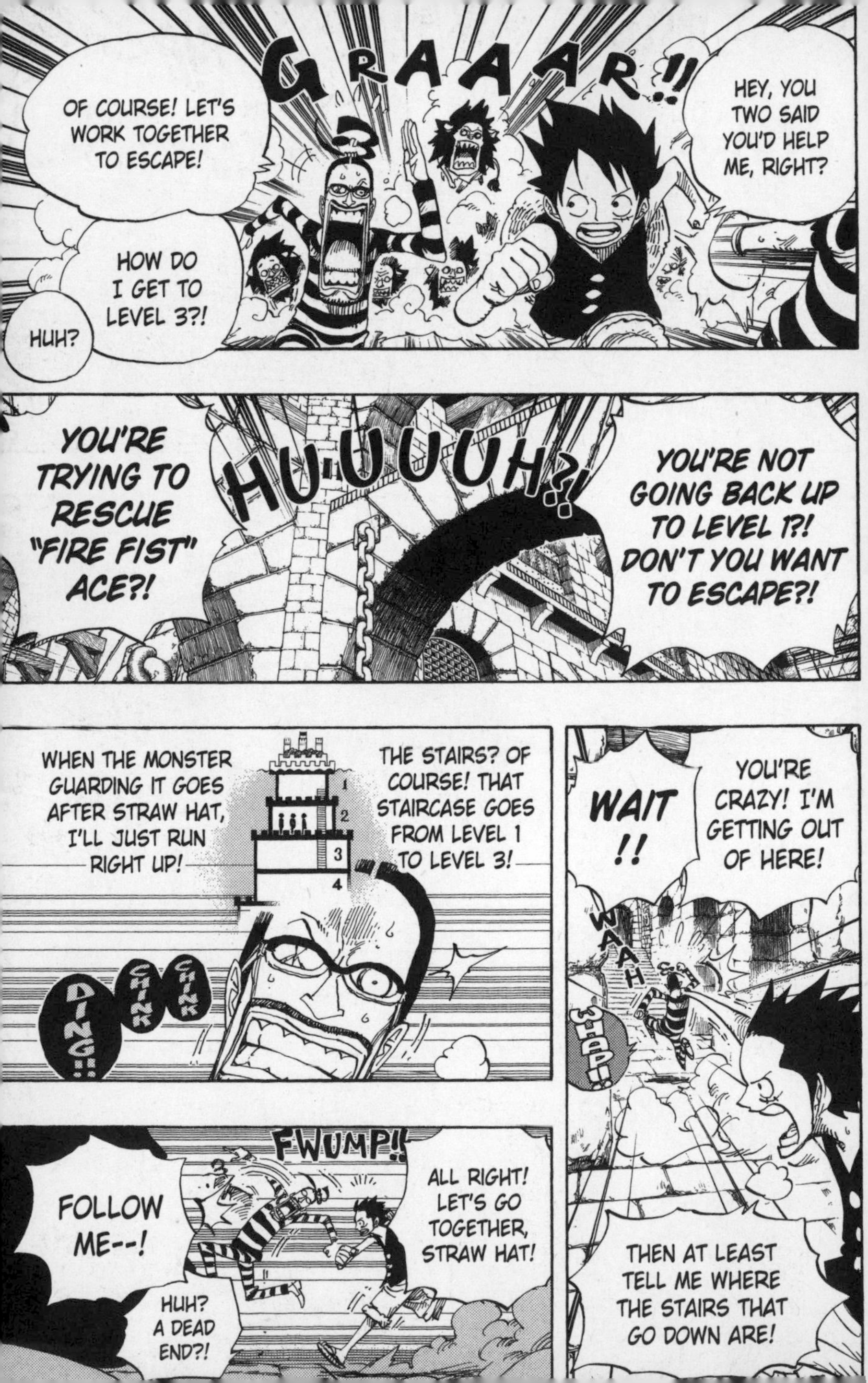
GRAAAR!!
HEY, YOU TWO SAID YOU'D HELP ME, RIGHT?
OF COURSE! LET'S WORK TOGETHER TO ESCAPE!
HOW DO I GET TO LEVEL 3?!
HUH?
YOU'RE NOT GOING BACK UP TO LEVEL 1?! DON'T YOU WANT TO ESCAPE?!
HUUUUH?!
YOU'RE TRYING TO RESCUE "FIRE FIST" ACE?!
YOU'RE CRAZY! I'M GETTING OUT OF HERE!
WAIT !!
WAAAH
THEN AT LEAST TELL ME WHERE THE STAIRS THAT GO DOWN ARE!
THE STAIRS? OF COURSE! THAT STAIRCASE GOES FROM LEVEL 1 TO LEVEL 3!
1
2
3
4
WHEN THE MONSTER GUARDING IT GOES AFTER STRAW HAT, I'LL JUST RUN RIGHT UP!
CHINK
CHINK
DING!!
FWUMP!!
ALL RIGHT! LET'S GO TOGETHER, STRAW HAT!
FOLLOW ME--!
HUH? A DEAD END?!

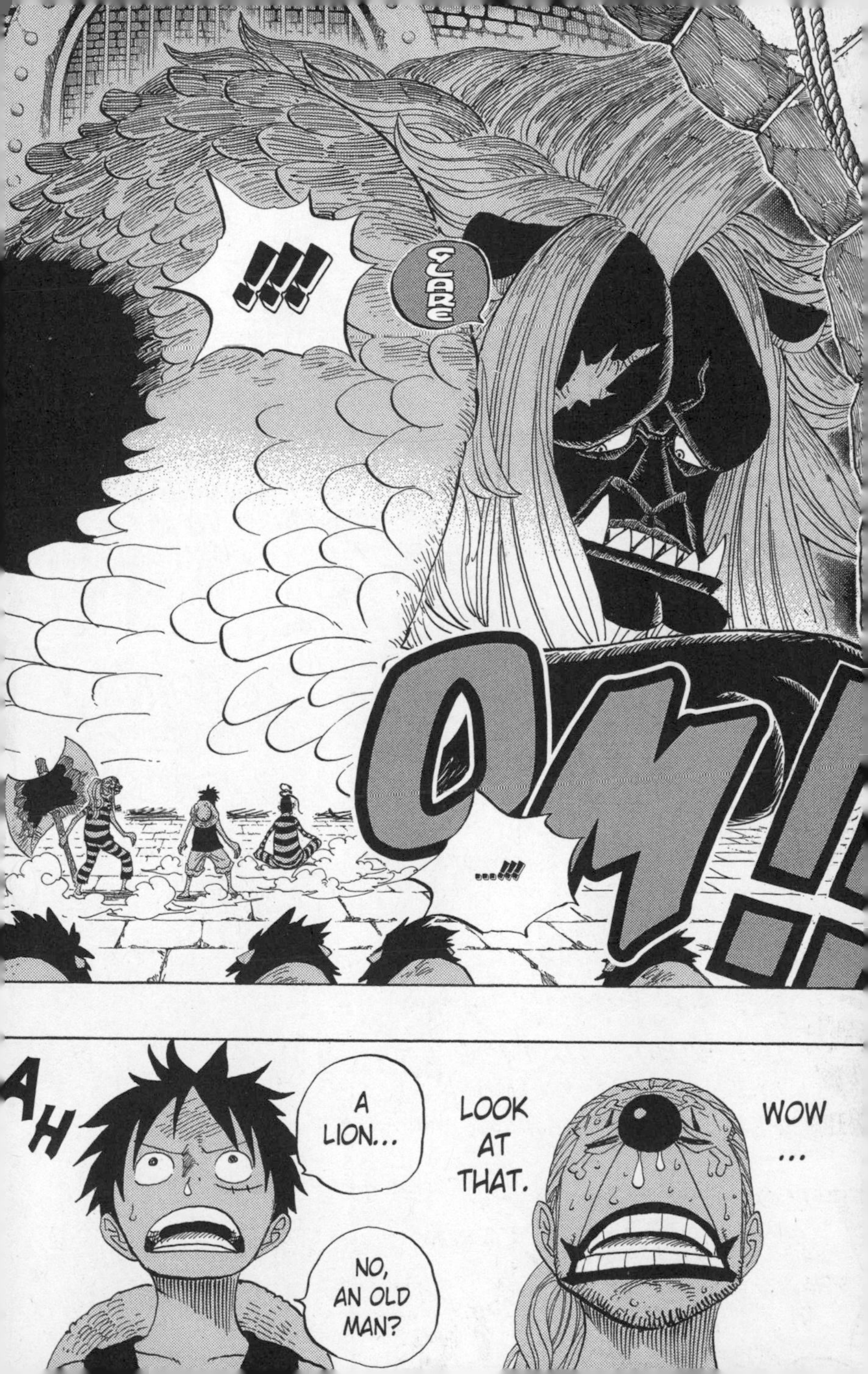
GLARE
!!!
OH!!
...!!!
WOW ...
LOOK AT THAT.
A LION...
NO, AN OLD MAN?
AH

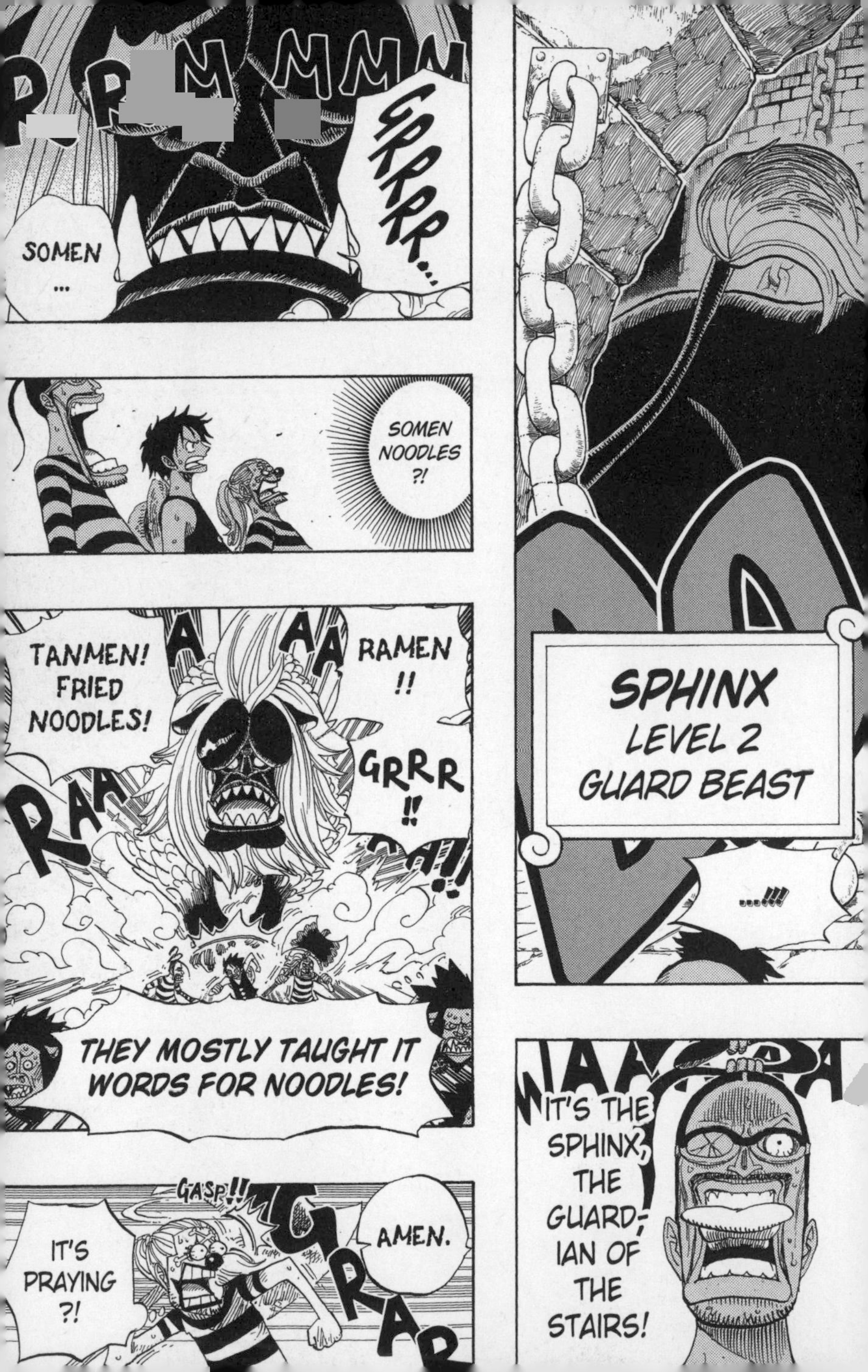
SPHINX
LEVEL 2
GUARD BEAST
...!!!
IT'S THE SPHINX, THE GUARDIAN OF THE STAIRS!
GRRRR...
SOMEN ...
SOMEN NOODLES ?!
RAMEN !!
GRRR !!
TANMEN! FRIED NOODLES!
THEY MOSTLY TAUGHT IT WORDS FOR NOODLES!
AMEN.
GASP!!!
IT'S PRAYING ?!

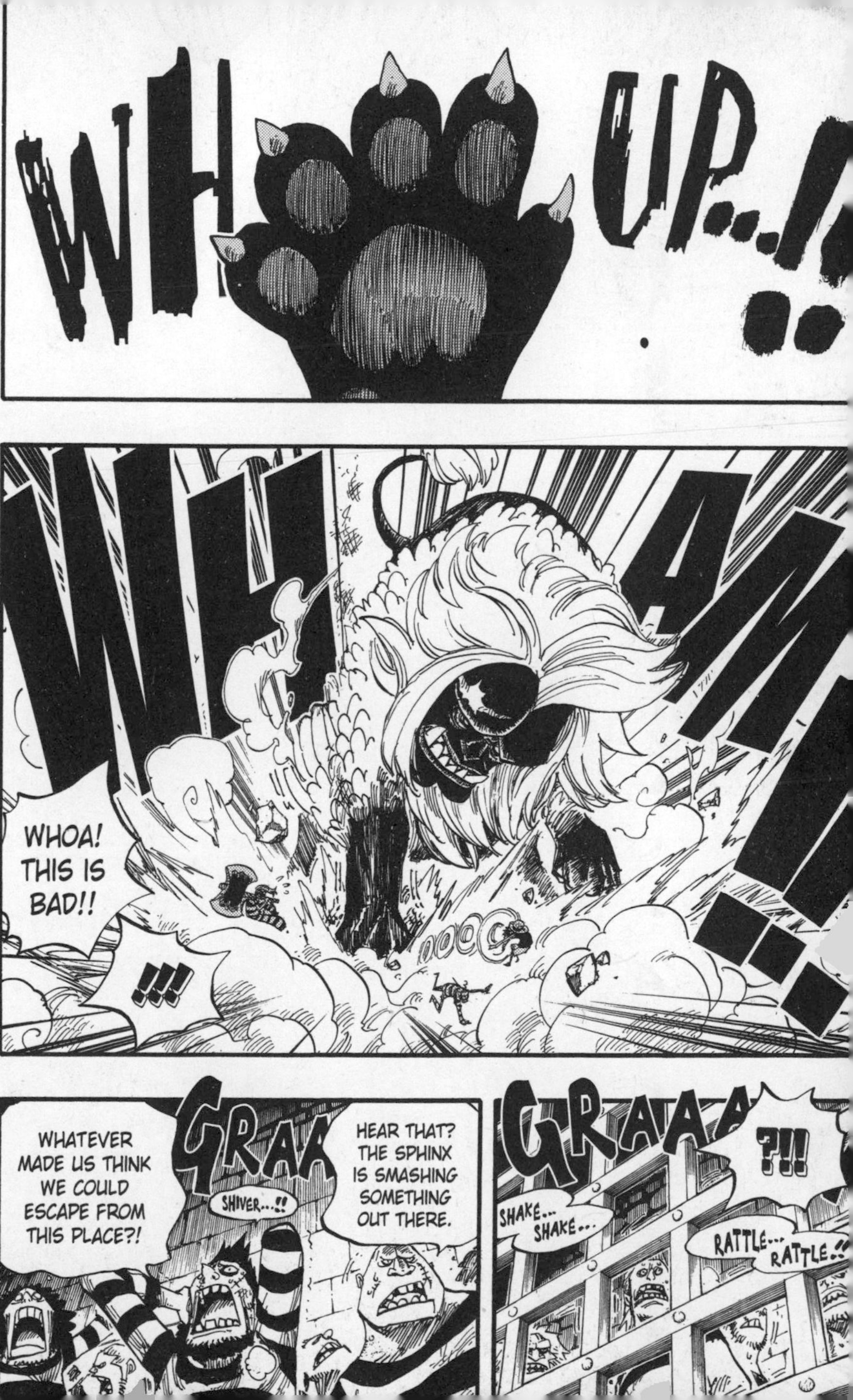
WH UP..!!
WH AM!!
WHOA! THIS IS BAD!!
!!!
GRAAA
?!!
RATTLE... RATTLE..!!
SHAKE... SHAKE...
GRAA
HEAR THAT? THE SPHINX IS SMASHING SOMETHING OUT THERE.
SHIVER...!!
WHATEVER MADE US THINK WE COULD ESCAPE FROM THIS PLACE?!

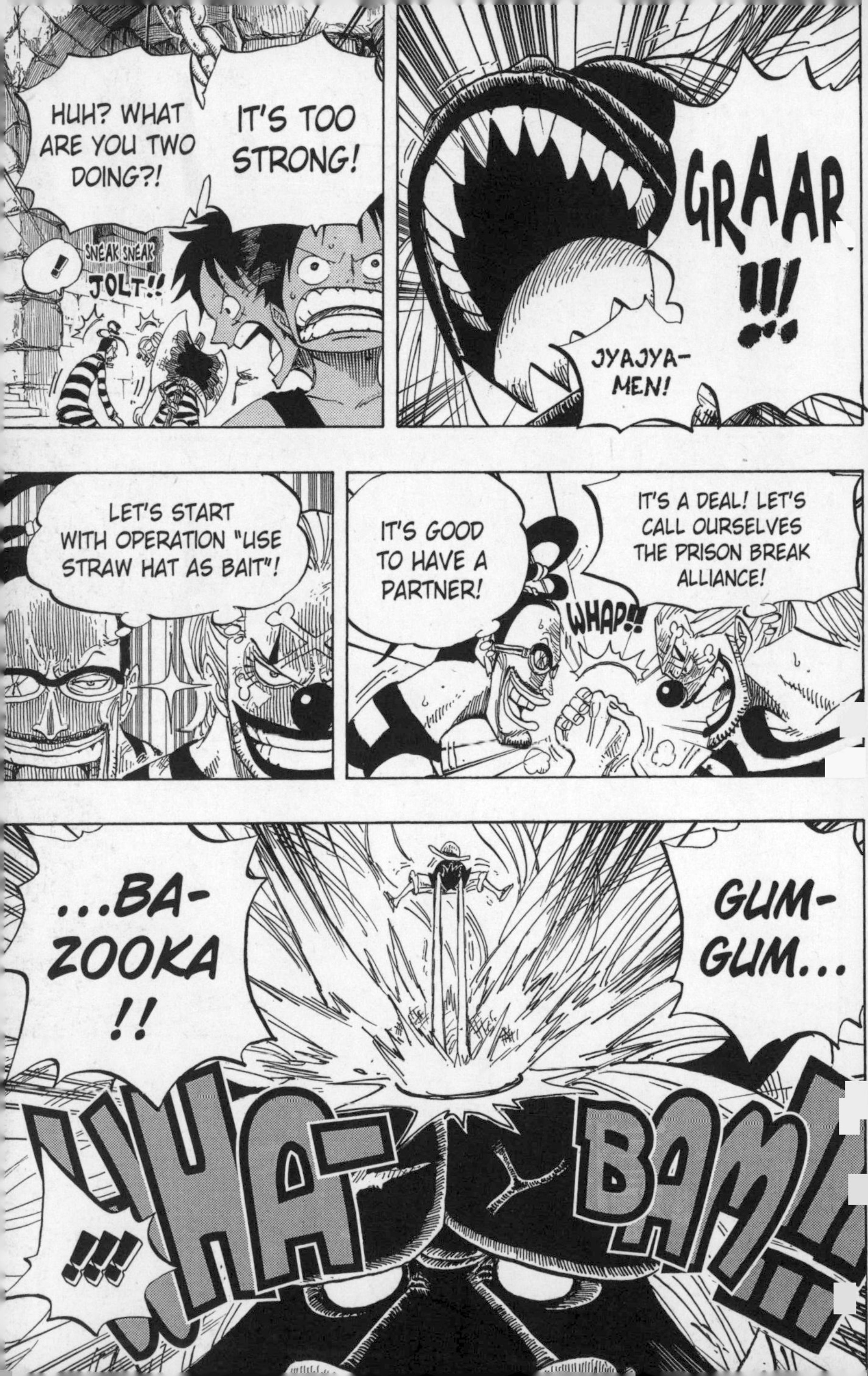
GRAAR!!!
JYAJYA-MEN!
IT'S TOO STRONG!
HUH? WHAT ARE YOU TWO DOING?!
!
SNEAK SNEAK
JOLT!!
IT'S A DEAL! LET'S CALL OURSELVES THE PRISON BREAK ALLIANCE!
IT'S GOOD TO HAVE A PARTNER!
WHAP!!
LET'S START WITH OPERATION "USE STRAW HAT AS BAIT"!
GUM-GUM...
...BA-ZOOKA!!
WHA-BAM!!

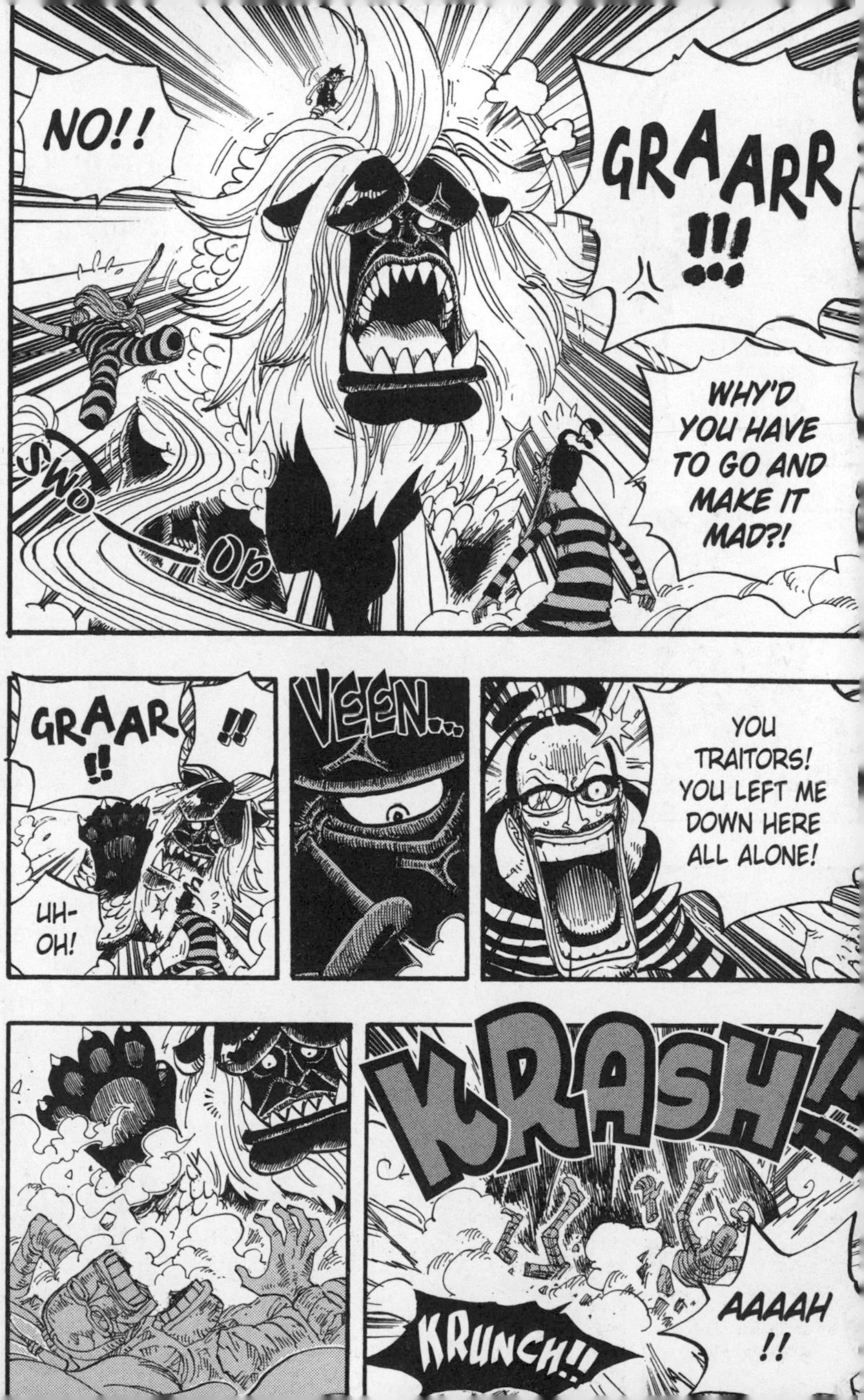
GRAARR!!!
WHY'D YOU HAVE TO GO AND MAKE IT MAD?!
NO!!
SWOOP
YOU TRAITORS! YOU LEFT ME DOWN HERE ALL ALONE!
VEEN...
GRAAR!!!!
UH-OH!
KRASH!!
AAAAH!!
KRUNCH!!

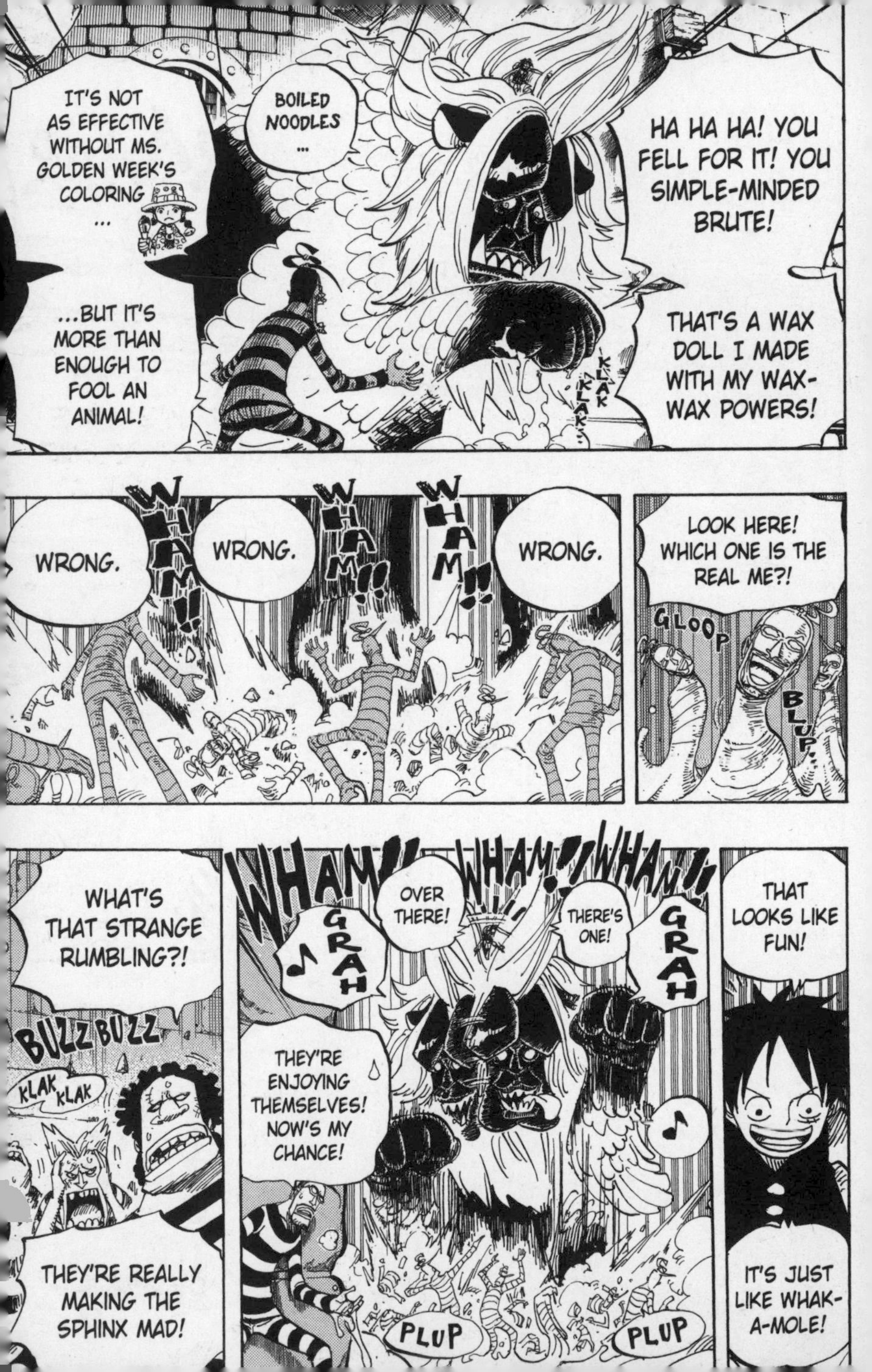
HA HA HA! YOU FELL FOR IT! YOU SIMPLE-MINDED BRUTE!
THAT'S A WAX DOLL I MADE WITH MY WAX-WAX POWERS!
BOILED NOODLES ...
KLAK KLAK
IT'S NOT AS EFFECTIVE WITHOUT MS. GOLDEN WEEK'S COLORING ...
...BUT IT'S MORE THAN ENOUGH TO FOOL AN ANIMAL!
LOOK HERE! WHICH ONE IS THE REAL ME?!
GLOOP
BLUP...
WRONG.
WHAM!!
WRONG.
WHAM!!
WHAM!!
WRONG.
THAT LOOKS LIKE FUN!
IT'S JUST LIKE WHAK-A-MOLE!
WHAM!! WHAM!! WHAM!!
GRAH
THERE'S ONE!
OVER THERE!
GRAH
THEY'RE ENJOYING THEMSELVES! NOW'S MY CHANCE!
PLUP
PLUP
WHAT'S THAT STRANGE RUMBLING?!
BUZZ BUZZ
KLAK KLAK
THEY'RE REALLY MAKING THE SPHINX MAD!

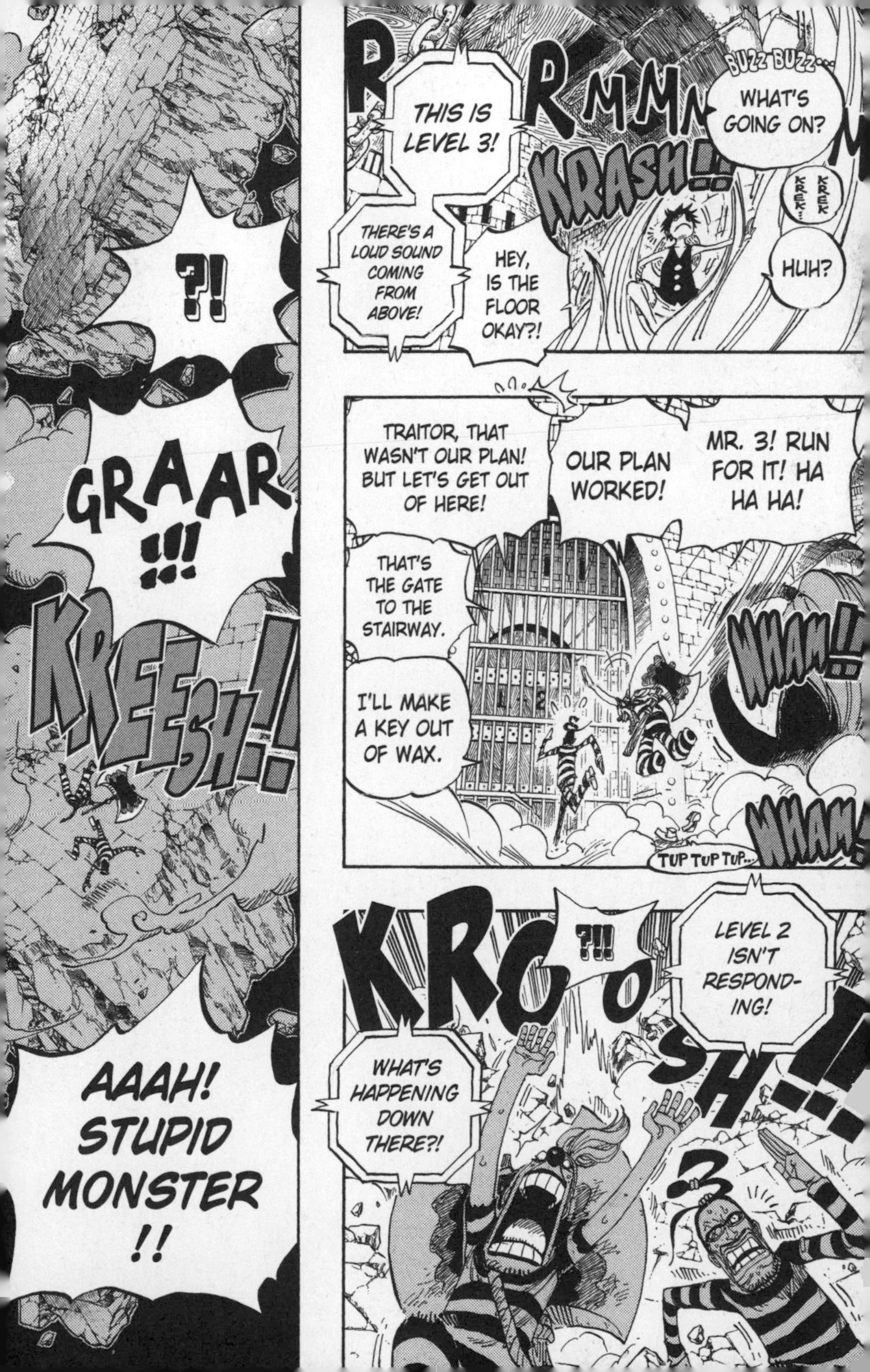
BUZZ BUZZ...
WHAT'S GOING ON?
RRMMMM
KRASH!!
KREK KREK
HUH?
THIS IS LEVEL 3!
HEY, IS THE FLOOR OKAY?!
THERE'S A LOUD SOUND COMING FROM ABOVE!
MR. 3! RUN FOR IT! HA HA HA!
OUR PLAN WORKED!
TRAITOR, THAT WASN'T OUR PLAN! BUT LET'S GET OUT OF HERE!
WHAM!!
THAT'S THE GATE TO THE STAIRWAY.
I'LL MAKE A KEY OUT OF WAX.
WHAM
TUP TUP TUP...
LEVEL 2 ISN'T RESPOND-ING!
?!!
KROOOSH!!
WHAT'S HAPPENING DOWN THERE?!
?!
GRAAR!!!
KREESH!!
AAAH! STUPID MONSTER!!

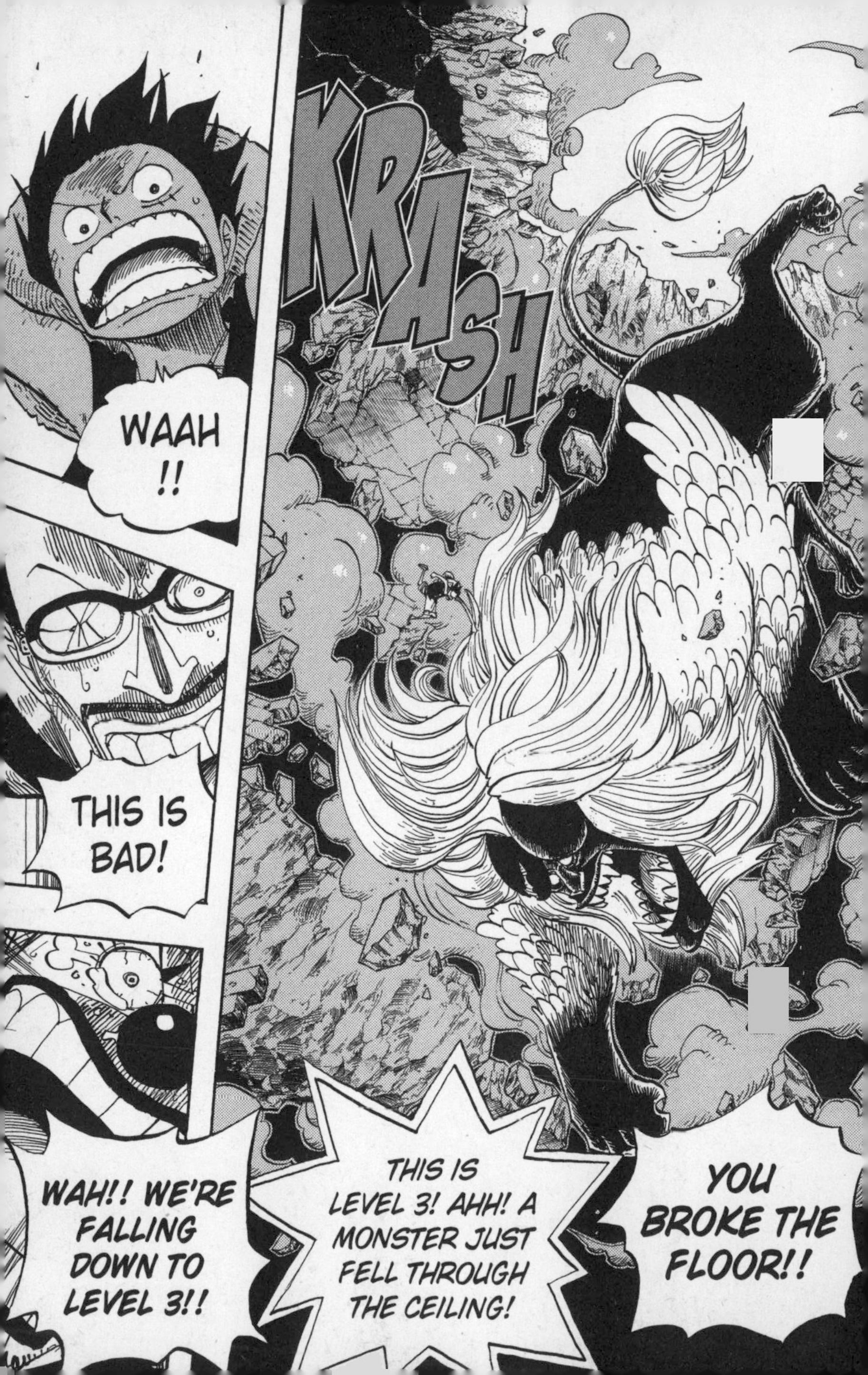
KRASH
YOU BROKE THE FLOOR!!
THIS IS LEVEL 3! AHH! A MONSTER JUST FELL THROUGH THE CEILING!
WAAH !!
THIS IS BAD!
WAH!! WE'RE FALLING DOWN TO LEVEL 3!!

SBS Question Corner

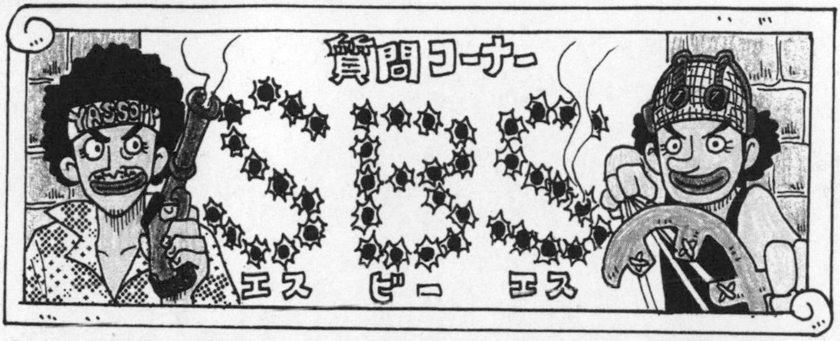
質問コーナー
SBS
エス ビー エス
YASSOP

(Skeleton Yukichi, Iwate)

Q: Hello, Mr. Oda. I just made a discovery about Nami's fighting technique during her battle with Kalifa. Do you remember "Mirage Tempo, Fata Morgana?" According to a book, it said something about the end of the famous witch Morgana. Isn't it something about the mirages that appear in the waters off of Italy? I don't really understand, so please explain. --Rail

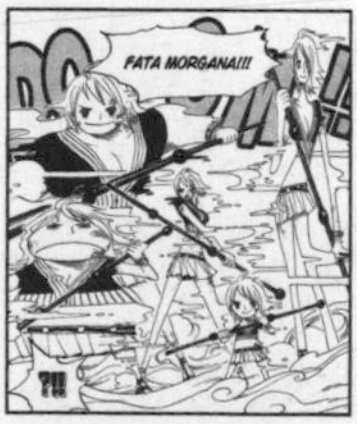
FATA MORGANA!!!
?!!

A: Yes. There are lots of theories about this. Mirages that are seen near Sicily, Italy, are called "Fata Morgana," as in the fairy of illusion. In European legend, there is a witch called Morgana. I don't really know the details either, but you said the book calls it the end of the witch. I've read somewhere that the mirages are caused by Morgana, but either way, the local people who saw the "mirages" blamed them on the doings of the witch.

Q: I became the mother of "Sanji"! (Sanji = three children in Japanese)

--Mother of Three

A: Oh. Congratulations.

Q: Make Hancock's birthday September 2, please. Since September is the 9th month (9 ="Ku" in Japanese) and 2 sounds like "Ja" in Japanese!

--Sun

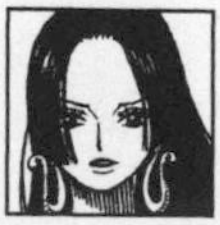

A: Sure.

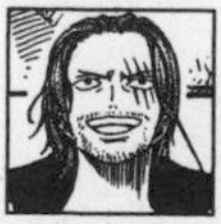

Q: Please choose Shanks's birthday already! "Sha" sounds like "3" and "ks" sounds like "9" in Japanese, so make it March 9! Please, Odacchi! Decide it now! Please! --Pudding

A: Sure. Whatever. Okay, this is the end of the Question Corner. Starting on page 166 is the Question Corner of the voice actors! This is a weird way to end this!

Chapter 530:
FROM ONE HELL TO ANOTHER

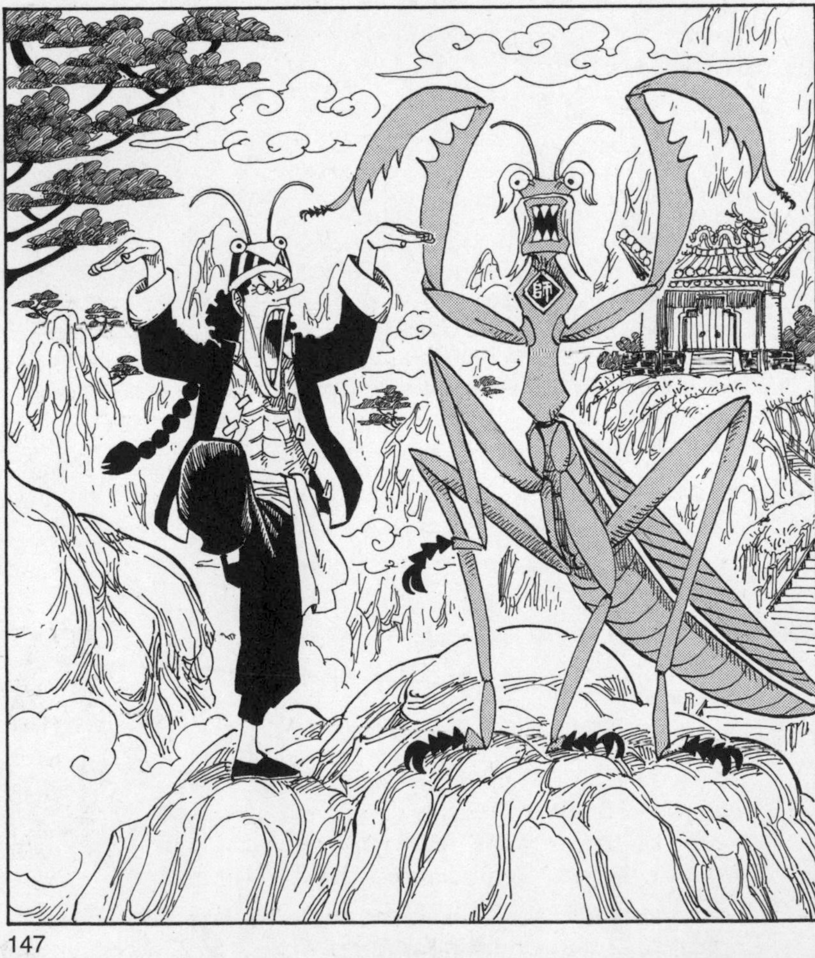

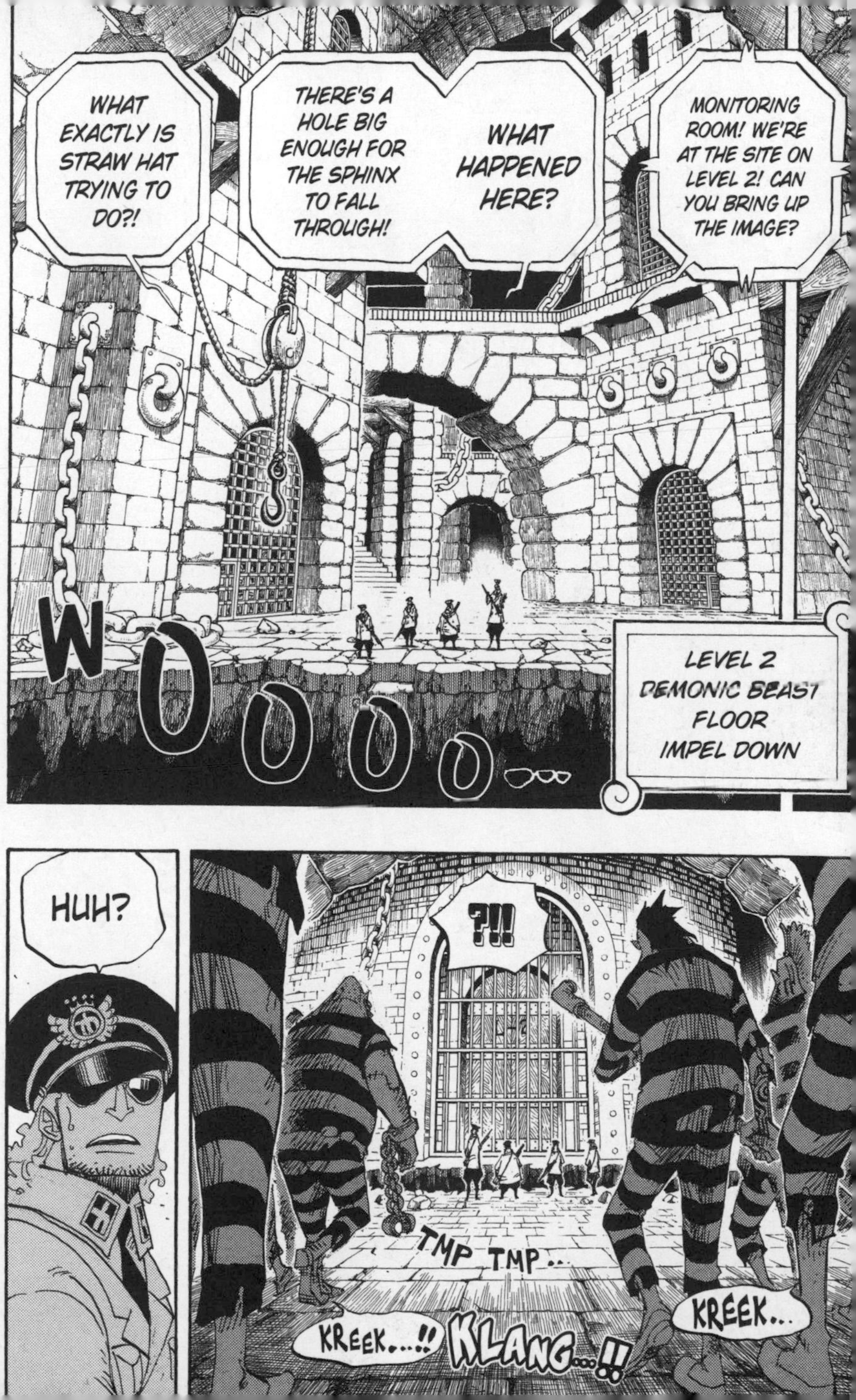
MONITORING ROOM! WE'RE AT THE SITE ON LEVEL 2! CAN YOU BRING UP THE IMAGE?
WHAT HAPPENED HERE?
THERE'S A HOLE BIG ENOUGH FOR THE SPHINX TO FALL THROUGH!
WHAT EXACTLY IS STRAW HAT TRYING TO DO?!
LEVEL 2 DEMONIC BEAST FLOOR IMPEL DOWN
WOOOOO...
?!!
TMP TMP..
KREEK...
KLANG...!!
KREEK...!!
HUH?

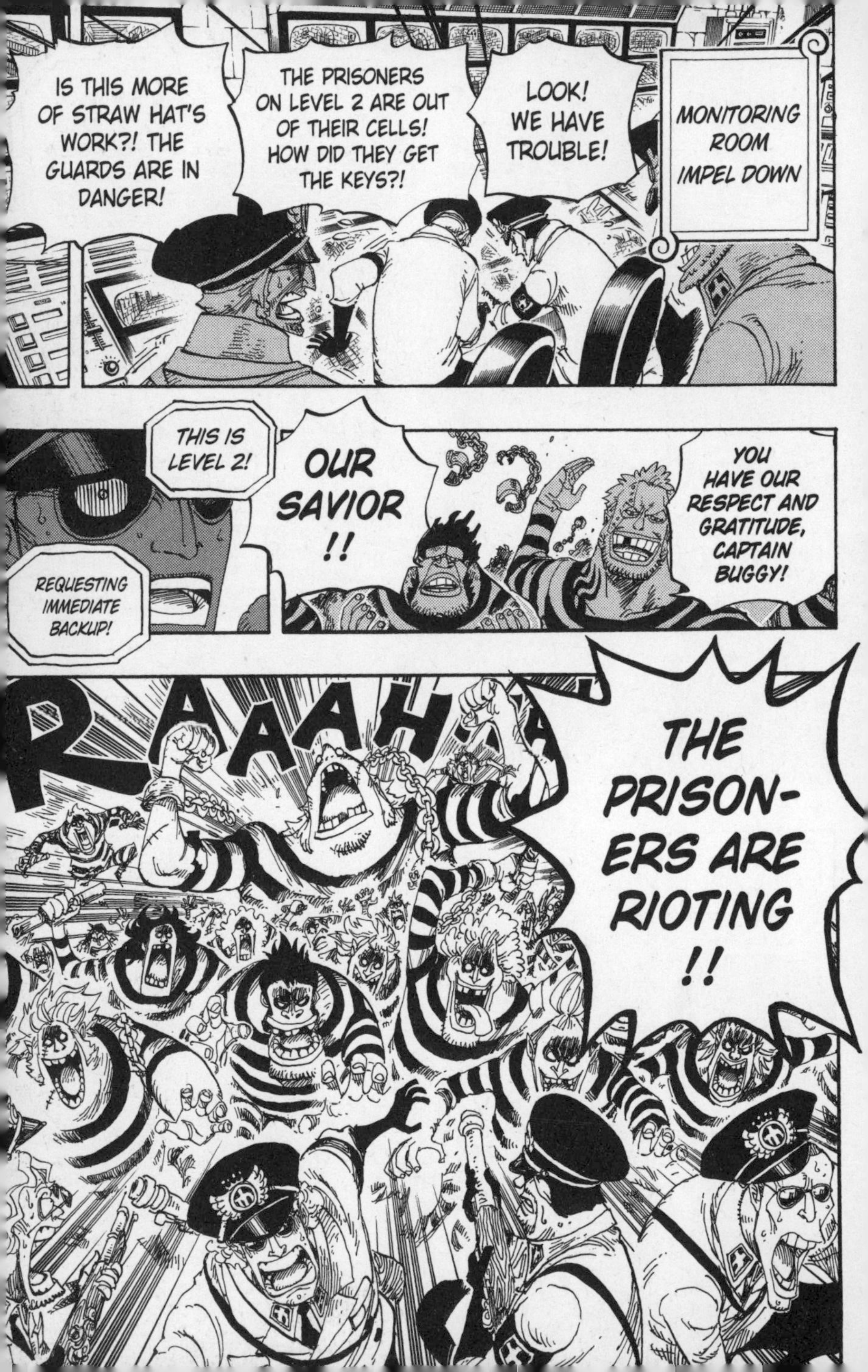
MONITORING ROOM IMPEL DOWN
LOOK! WE HAVE TROUBLE!
THE PRISONERS ON LEVEL 2 ARE OUT OF THEIR CELLS! HOW DID THEY GET THE KEYS?!
IS THIS MORE OF STRAW HAT'S WORK?! THE GUARDS ARE IN DANGER!
YOU HAVE OUR RESPECT AND GRATITUDE, CAPTAIN BUGGY!
OUR SAVIOR!!
THIS IS LEVEL 2!
REQUESTING IMMEDIATE BACKUP!
THE PRISON-ERS ARE RIOTING!!
RAAHA

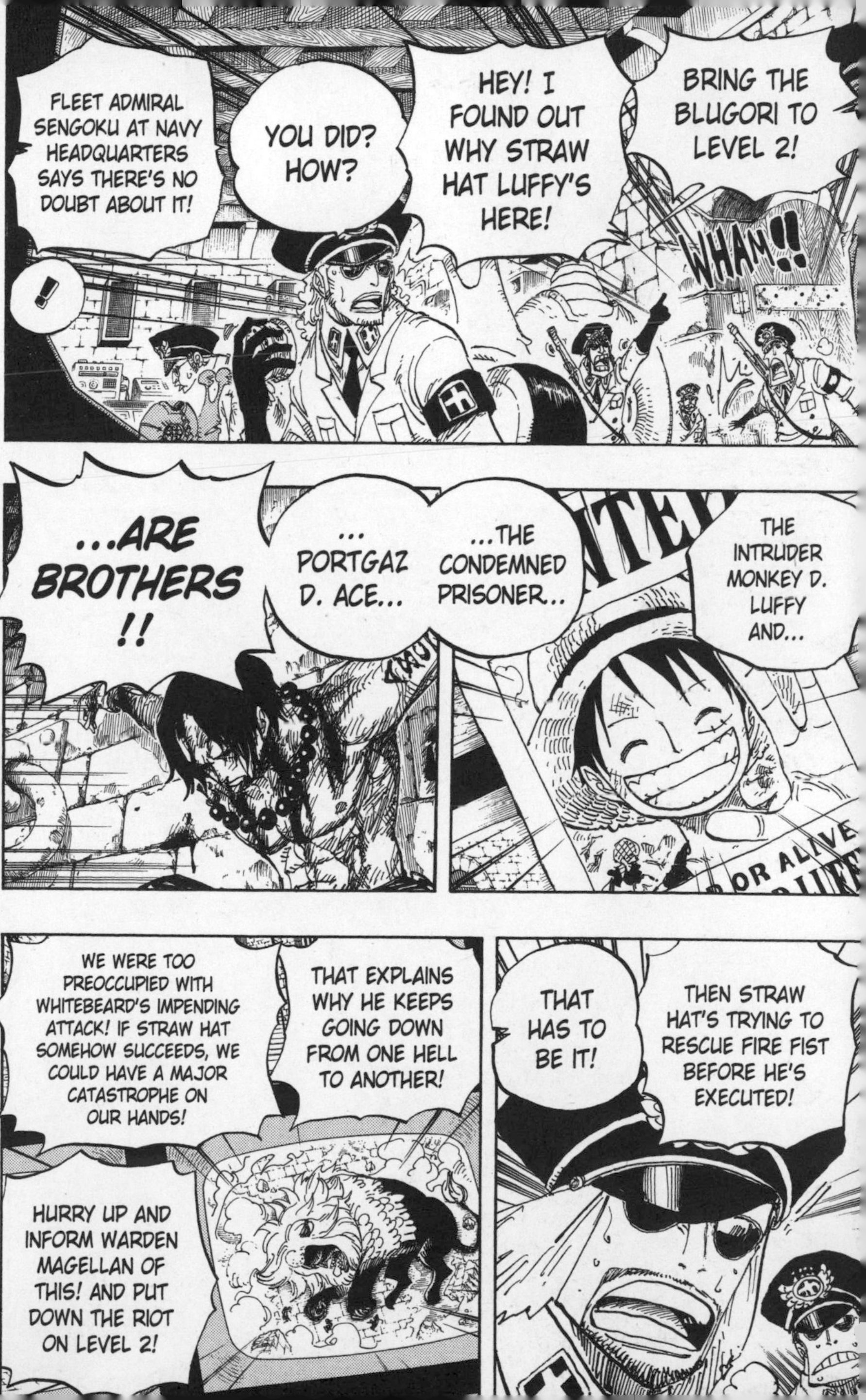
BRING THE BLUGORI TO LEVEL 2!
WHAM!!
HEY! I FOUND OUT WHY STRAW HAT LUFFY'S HERE!
YOU DID? HOW?
FLEET ADMIRAL SENGOKU AT NAVY HEADQUARTERS SAYS THERE'S NO DOUBT ABOUT IT!
!
THE INTRUDER MONKEY D. LUFFY AND...
...THE CONDEMNED PRISONER...
... PORTGAZ D. ACE...
...ARE BROTHERS !!
THEN STRAW HAT'S TRYING TO RESCUE FIRE FIST BEFORE HE'S EXECUTED!
THAT HAS TO BE IT!
THAT EXPLAINS WHY HE KEEPS GOING DOWN FROM ONE HELL TO ANOTHER!
WE WERE TOO PREOCCUPIED WITH WHITEBEARD'S IMPENDING ATTACK! IF STRAW HAT SOMEHOW SUCCEEDS, WE COULD HAVE A MAJOR CATASTROPHE ON OUR HANDS!
HURRY UP AND INFORM WARDEN MAGELLAN OF THIS! AND PUT DOWN THE RIOT ON LEVEL 2!

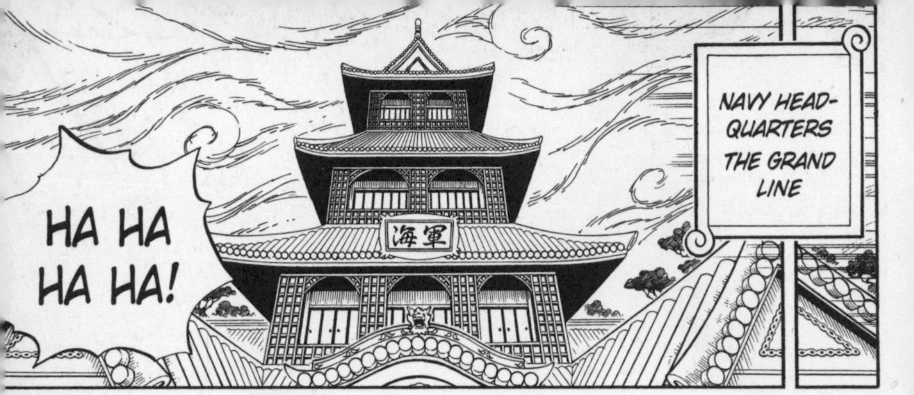
NAVY HEAD-QUARTERS THE GRAND LINE
HA HA HA HA!

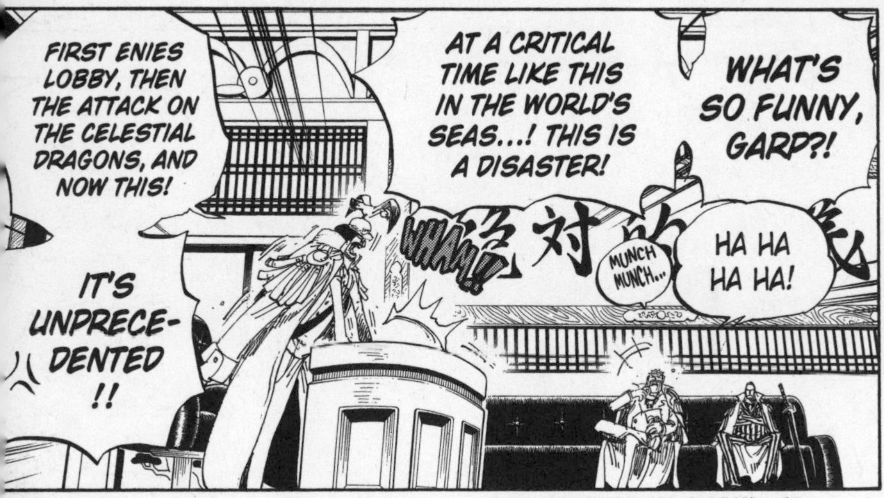
WHAT'S SO FUNNY, GARP?!
AT A CRITICAL TIME LIKE THIS IN THE WORLD'S SEAS...! THIS IS A DISASTER!
FIRST ENIES LOBBY, THEN THE ATTACK ON THE CELESTIAL DRAGONS, AND NOW THIS!
HA HA HA HA!
MUNCH MUNCH...
WHAM!!
IT'S UNPRECE-DENTED!!

SIGN SAYS "ABSOLUTE JUSTICE" --ED.

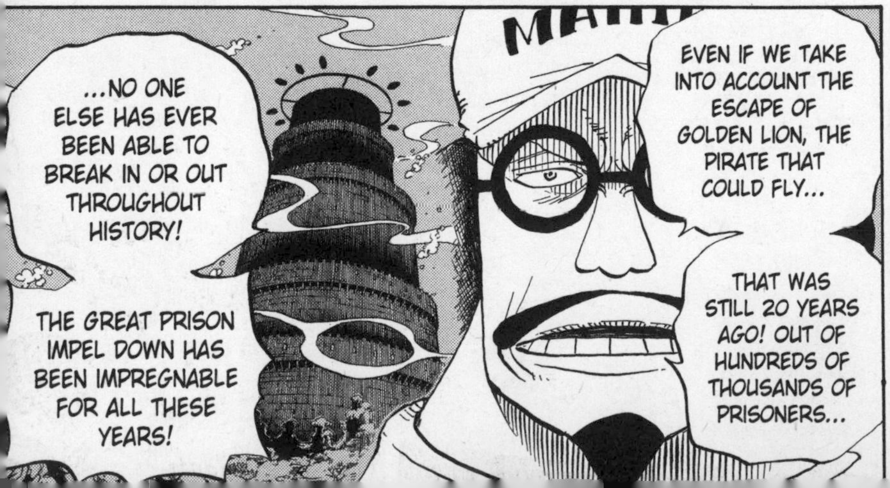
EVEN IF WE TAKE INTO ACCOUNT THE ESCAPE OF GOLDEN LION, THE PIRATE THAT COULD FLY...
THAT WAS STILL 20 YEARS AGO! OUT OF HUNDREDS OF THOUSANDS OF PRISONERS...
...NO ONE ELSE HAS EVER BEEN ABLE TO BREAK IN OR OUT THROUGHOUT HISTORY!
THE GREAT PRISON IMPEL DOWN HAS BEEN IMPREGNABLE FOR ALL THESE YEARS!

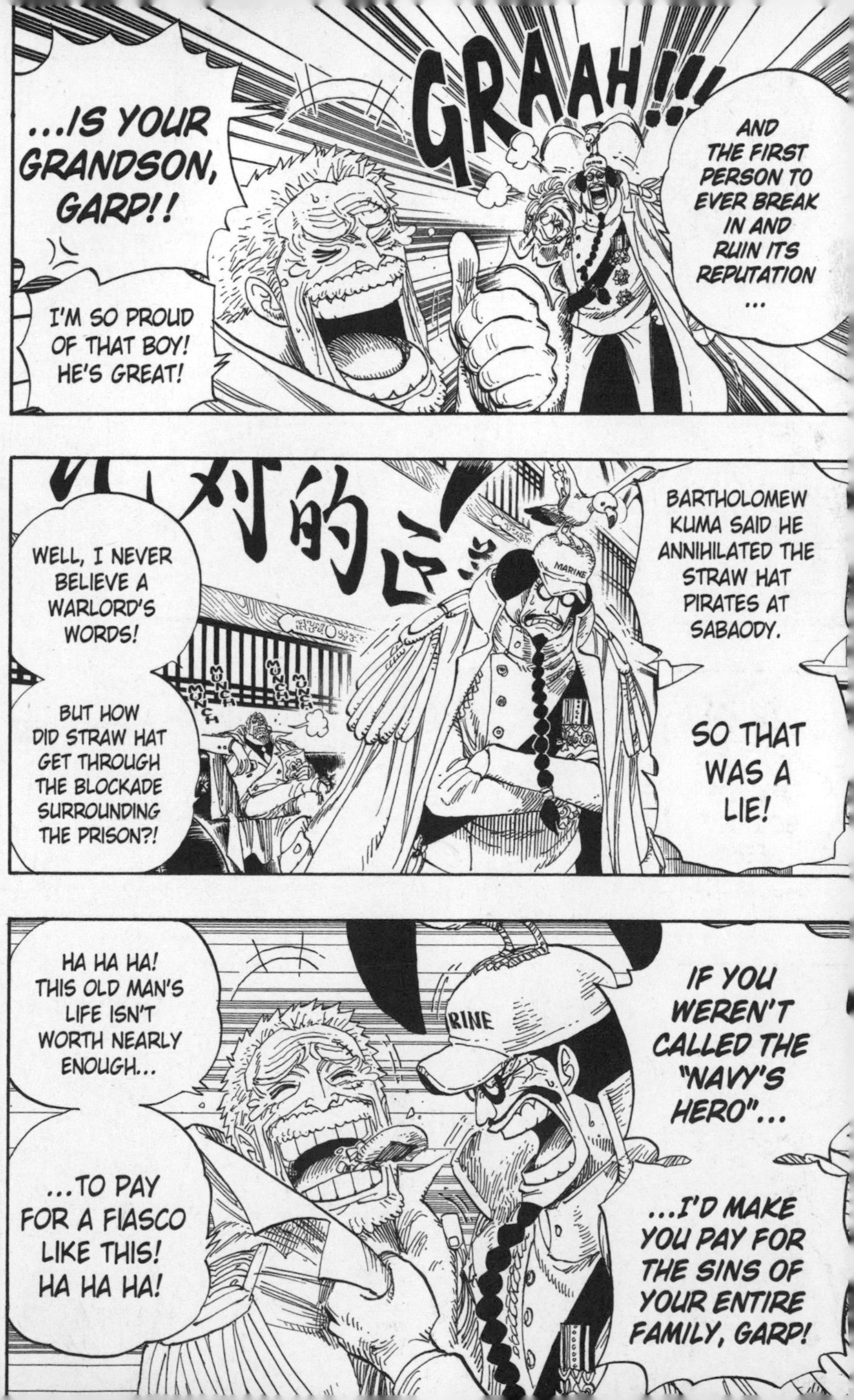
AND THE FIRST PERSON TO EVER BREAK IN AND RUIN ITS REPUTATION...
GRAAH!!!
...IS YOUR GRANDSON, GARP!!
I'M SO PROUD OF THAT BOY! HE'S GREAT!
BARTHOLOMEW KUMA SAID HE ANNIHILATED THE STRAW HAT PIRATES AT SABAODY.
SO THAT WAS A LIE!
MARINE
WELL, I NEVER BELIEVE A WARLORD'S WORDS!
MUNCH MUNCH MUNCH MUNCH
BUT HOW DID STRAW HAT GET THROUGH THE BLOCKADE SURROUNDING THE PRISON?!
IF YOU WEREN'T CALLED THE "NAVY'S HERO"...
...I'D MAKE YOU PAY FOR THE SINS OF YOUR ENTIRE FAMILY, GARP!
HA HA HA! THIS OLD MAN'S LIFE ISN'T WORTH NEARLY ENOUGH...
...TO PAY FOR A FIASCO LIKE THIS! HA HA HA!

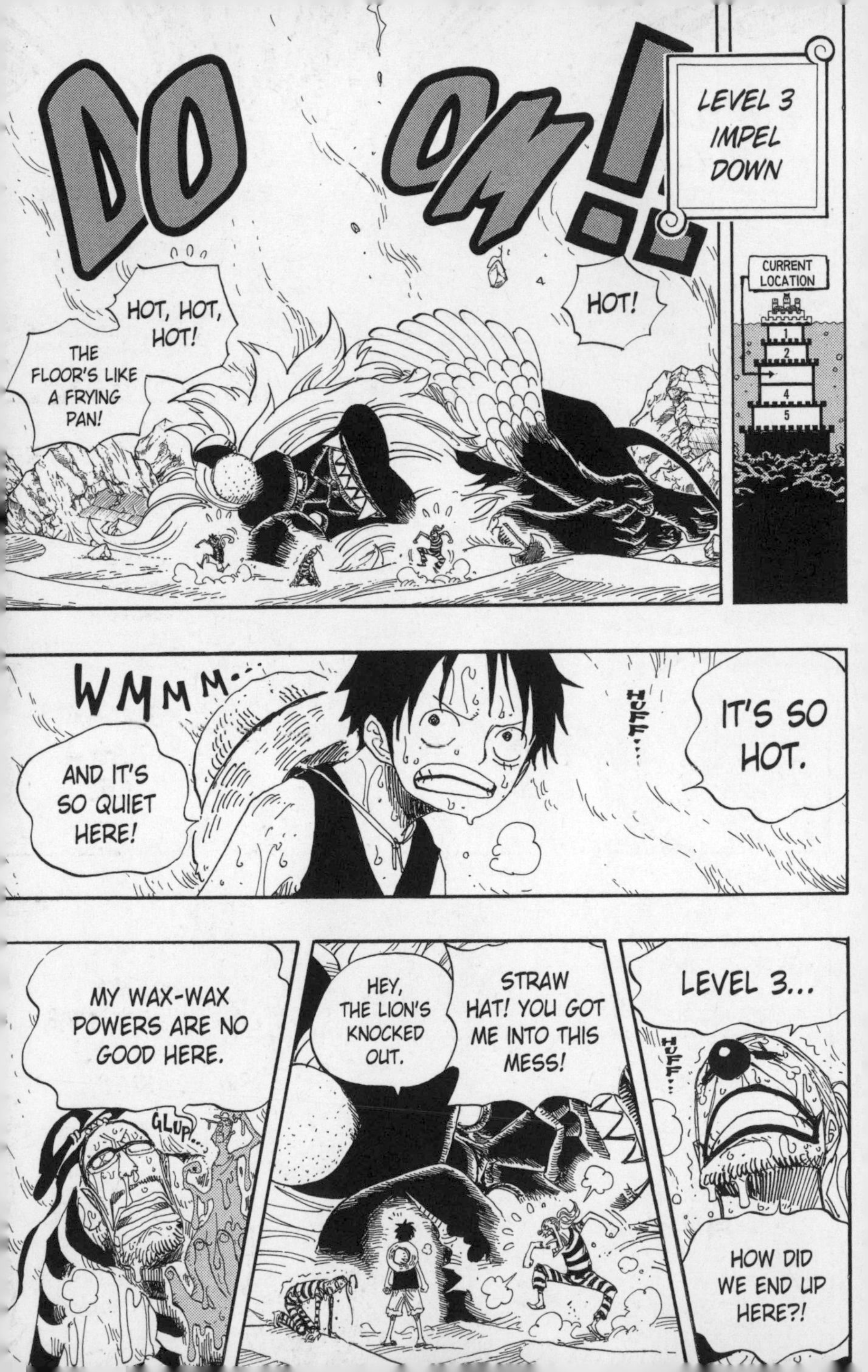
LEVEL 3 IMPEL DOWN
CURRENT LOCATION
1
2
4
5
DOOM!!
HOT!
HOT, HOT, HOT!
THE FLOOR'S LIKE A FRYING PAN!
IT'S SO HOT.
HUFF...
WMMM...
AND IT'S SO QUIET HERE!
LEVEL 3...
HUFF...
HOW DID WE END UP HERE?!
STRAW HAT! YOU GOT ME INTO THIS MESS!
HEY, THE LION'S KNOCKED OUT.
MY WAX-WAX POWERS ARE NO GOOD HERE.
GLUP...

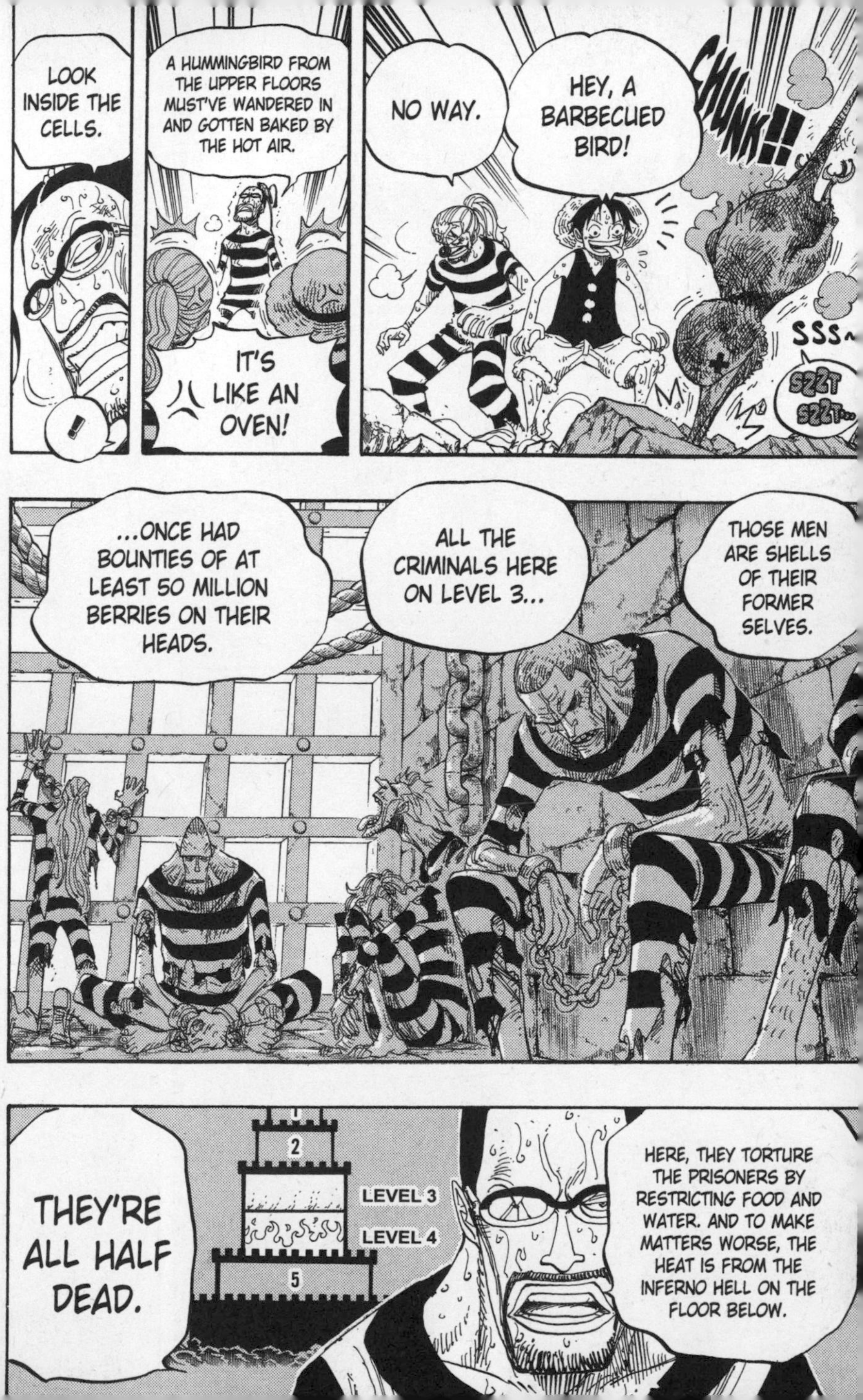
CHUNK!!
HEY, A BARBECUED BIRD!
NO WAY.
SSS~
SZZT SZZT...
A HUMMINGBIRD FROM THE UPPER FLOORS MUST'VE WANDERED IN AND GOTTEN BAKED BY THE HOT AIR.
IT'S LIKE AN OVEN!
LOOK INSIDE THE CELLS.
!
THOSE MEN ARE SHELLS OF THEIR FORMER SELVES.
ALL THE CRIMINALS HERE ON LEVEL 3...
...ONCE HAD BOUNTIES OF AT LEAST 50 MILLION BERRIES ON THEIR HEADS.
HERE, THEY TORTURE THE PRISONERS BY RESTRICTING FOOD AND WATER. AND TO MAKE MATTERS WORSE, THE HEAT IS FROM THE INFERNO HELL ON THE FLOOR BELOW.
1
2
LEVEL 3
LEVEL 4
5
THEY'RE ALL HALF DEAD.

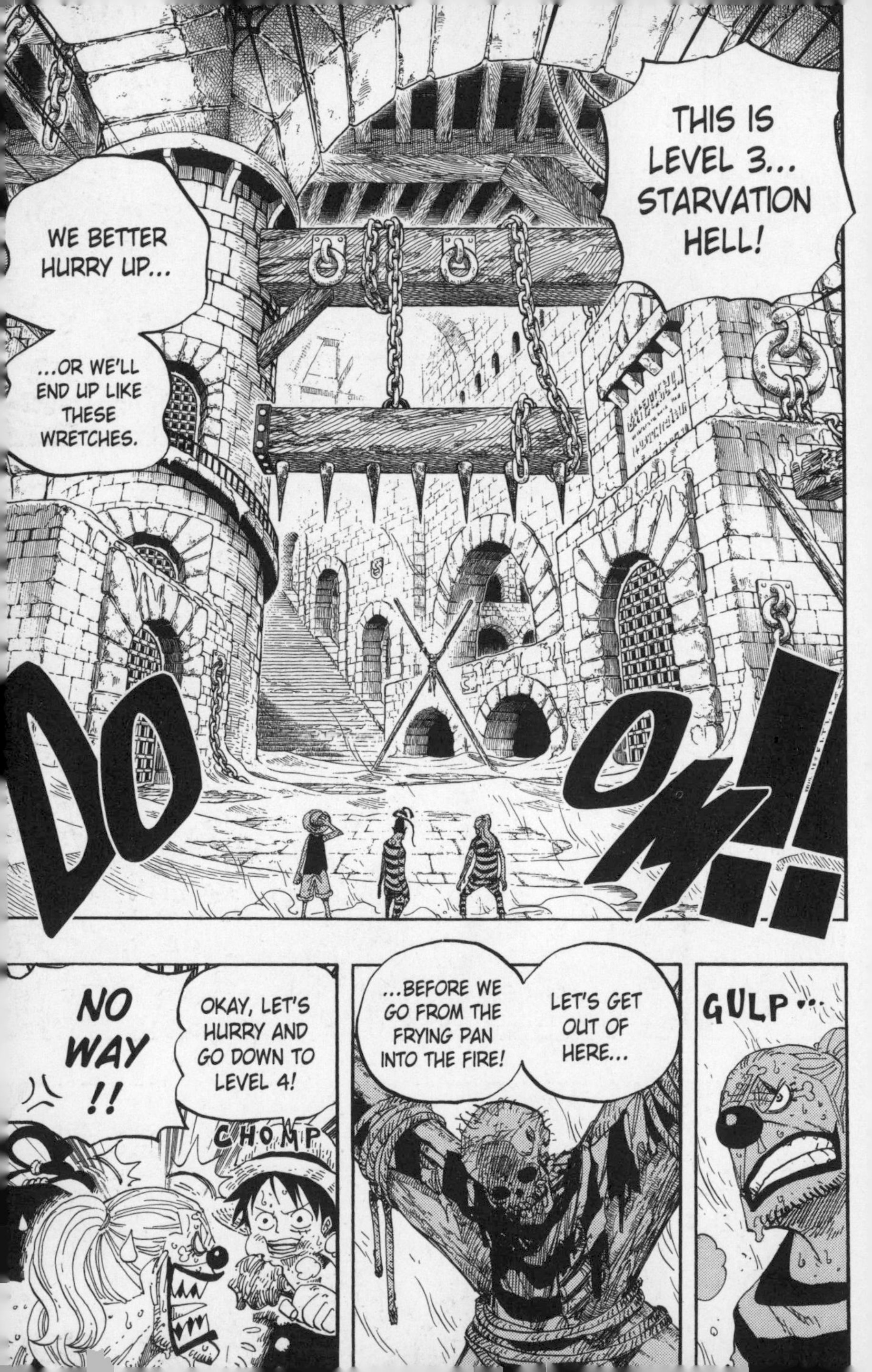
THIS IS LEVEL 3... STARVATION HELL!
WE BETTER HURRY UP...
...OR WE'LL END UP LIKE THESE WRETCHES.
DOOM!!
GULP...
LET'S GET OUT OF HERE...
...BEFORE WE GO FROM THE FRYING PAN INTO THE FIRE!
OKAY, LET'S HURRY AND GO DOWN TO LEVEL 4!
NO WAY!!
CHOMP

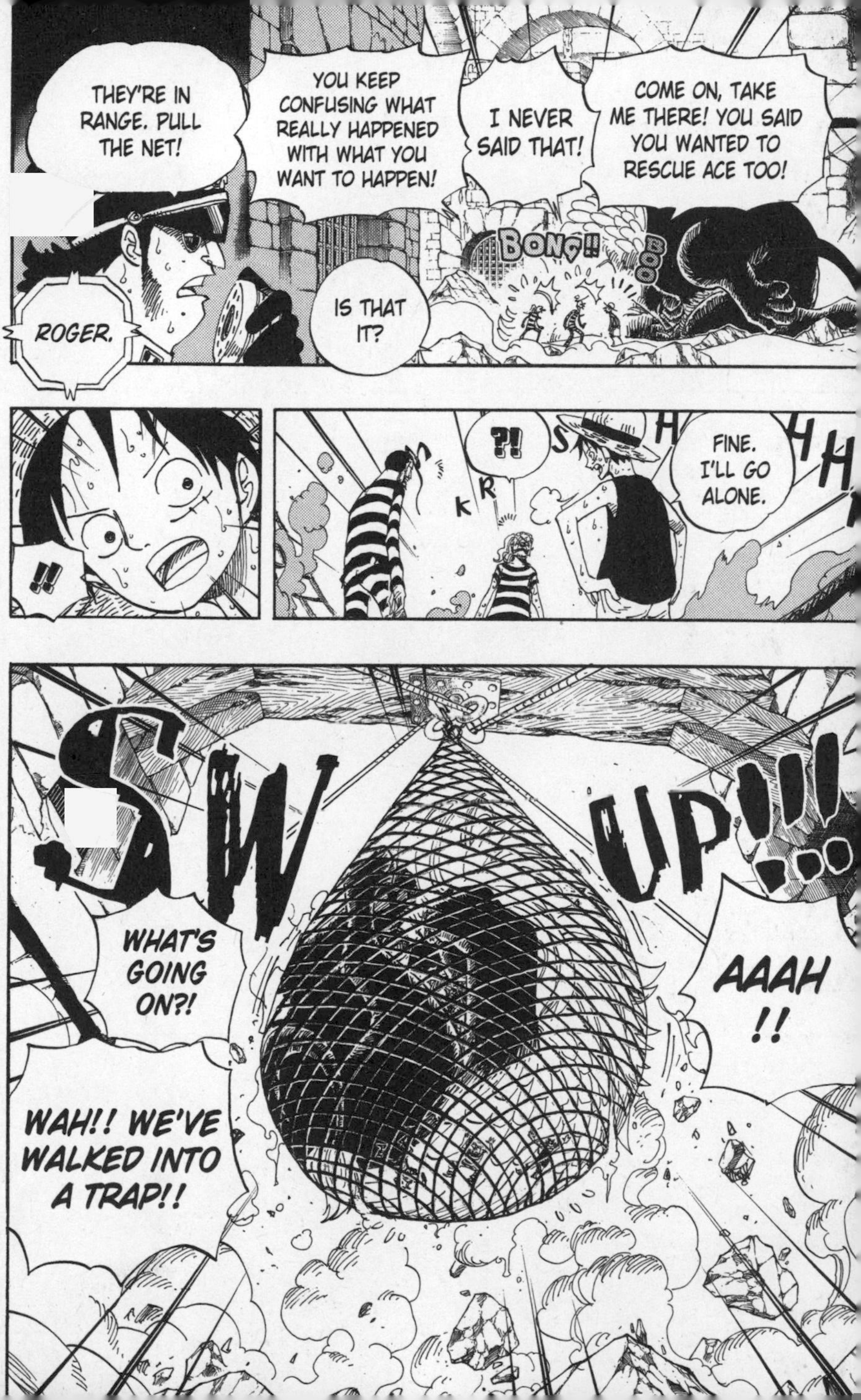
COME ON, TAKE ME THERE! YOU SAID YOU WANTED TO RESCUE ACE TOO!
I NEVER SAID THAT!
BONG!!
BOO
YOU KEEP CONFUSING WHAT REALLY HAPPENED WITH WHAT YOU WANT TO HAPPEN!
IS THAT IT?
THEY'RE IN RANGE. PULL THE NET!
ROGER.
FINE. I'LL GO ALONE.
SHHHH
KR
?!
!!
SWUP!!!
AAAH!!
WHAT'S GOING ON?!
WAH!! WE'VE WALKED INTO A TRAP!!

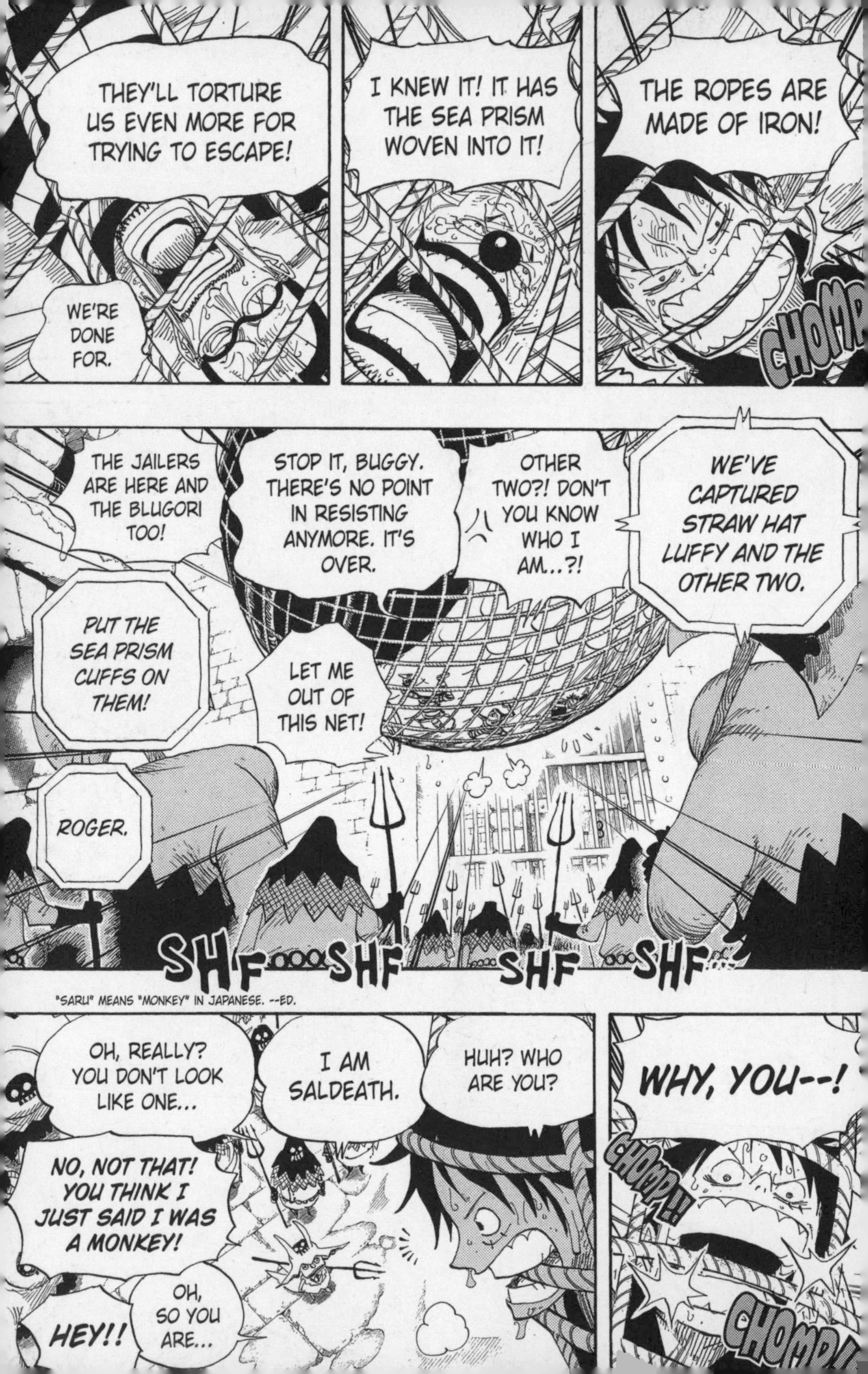
THE ROPES ARE MADE OF IRON!
CHOMP
I KNEW IT! IT HAS THE SEA PRISM WOVEN INTO IT!
THEY'LL TORTURE US EVEN MORE FOR TRYING TO ESCAPE!
WE'RE DONE FOR.
WE'VE CAPTURED STRAW HAT LUFFY AND THE OTHER TWO.
OTHER TWO?! DON'T YOU KNOW WHO I AM...?!
STOP IT, BUGGY. THERE'S NO POINT IN RESISTING ANYMORE. IT'S OVER.
THE JAILERS ARE HERE AND THE BLUGORI TOO!
LET ME OUT OF THIS NET!
PUT THE SEA PRISM CUFFS ON THEM!
ROGER.
SHF SHF SHF SHF
WHY, YOU--!
CHOMP!!
CHOMP!!
HUH? WHO ARE YOU?
I AM SALDEATH.
OH, REALLY? YOU DON'T LOOK LIKE ONE...
NO, NOT THAT! YOU THINK I JUST SAID I WAS A MONKEY!
OH, SO YOU ARE...
HEY!!

"SARU" MEANS "MONKEY" IN JAPANESE. --ED.

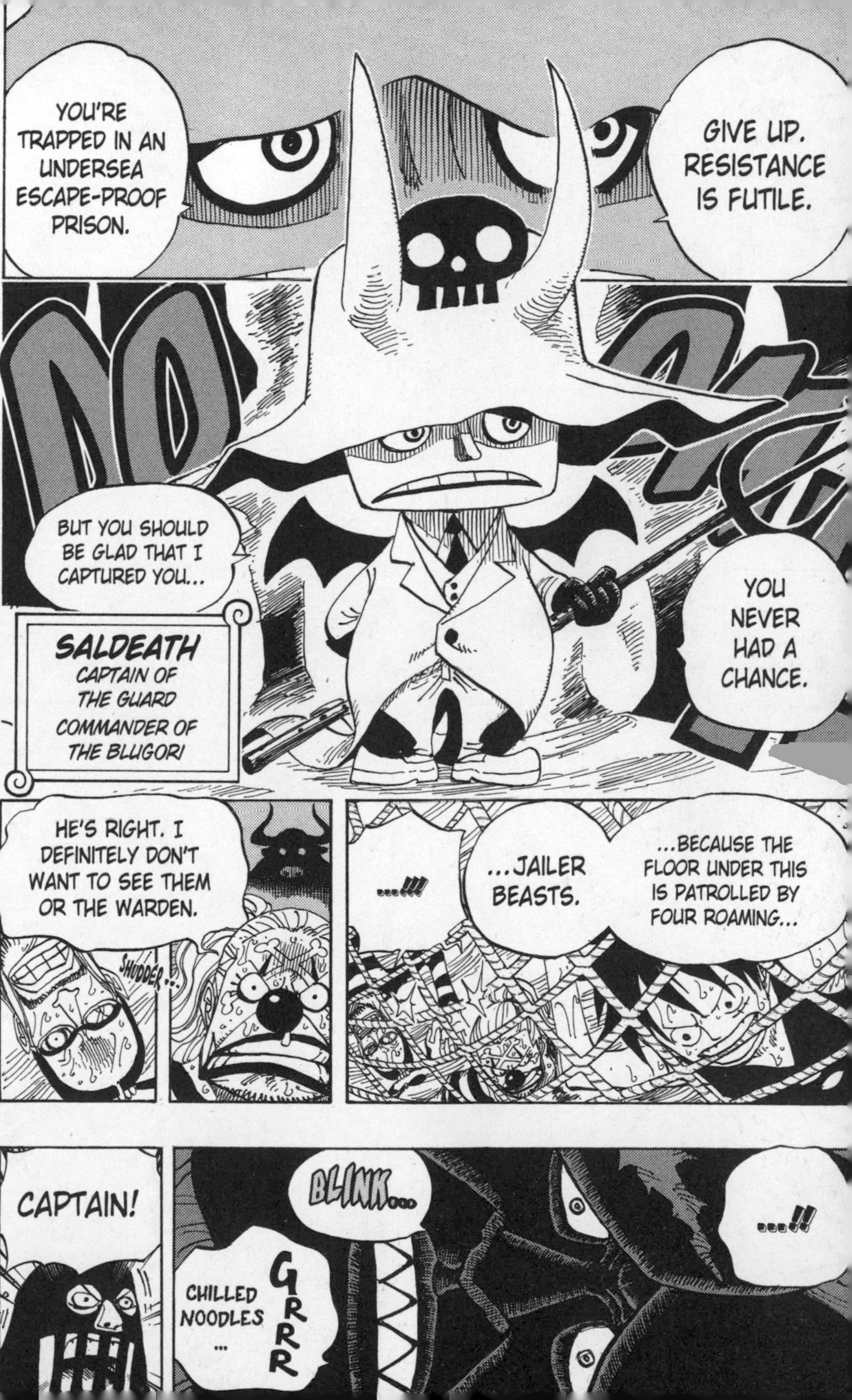
GIVE UP. RESISTANCE IS FUTILE.
YOU'RE TRAPPED IN AN UNDERSEA ESCAPE-PROOF PRISON.
YOU NEVER HAD A CHANCE.
BUT YOU SHOULD BE GLAD THAT I CAPTURED YOU...
SALDEATH
CAPTAIN OF THE GUARD
COMMANDER OF THE BLUGORI
...BECAUSE THE FLOOR UNDER THIS IS PATROLLED BY FOUR ROAMING...
...JAILER BEASTS.
...!!!
HE'S RIGHT. I DEFINITELY DON'T WANT TO SEE THEM OR THE WARDEN.
SHUDDER...
...!!
BLINK...
GRRR
CHILLED NOODLES ...
CAPTAIN!

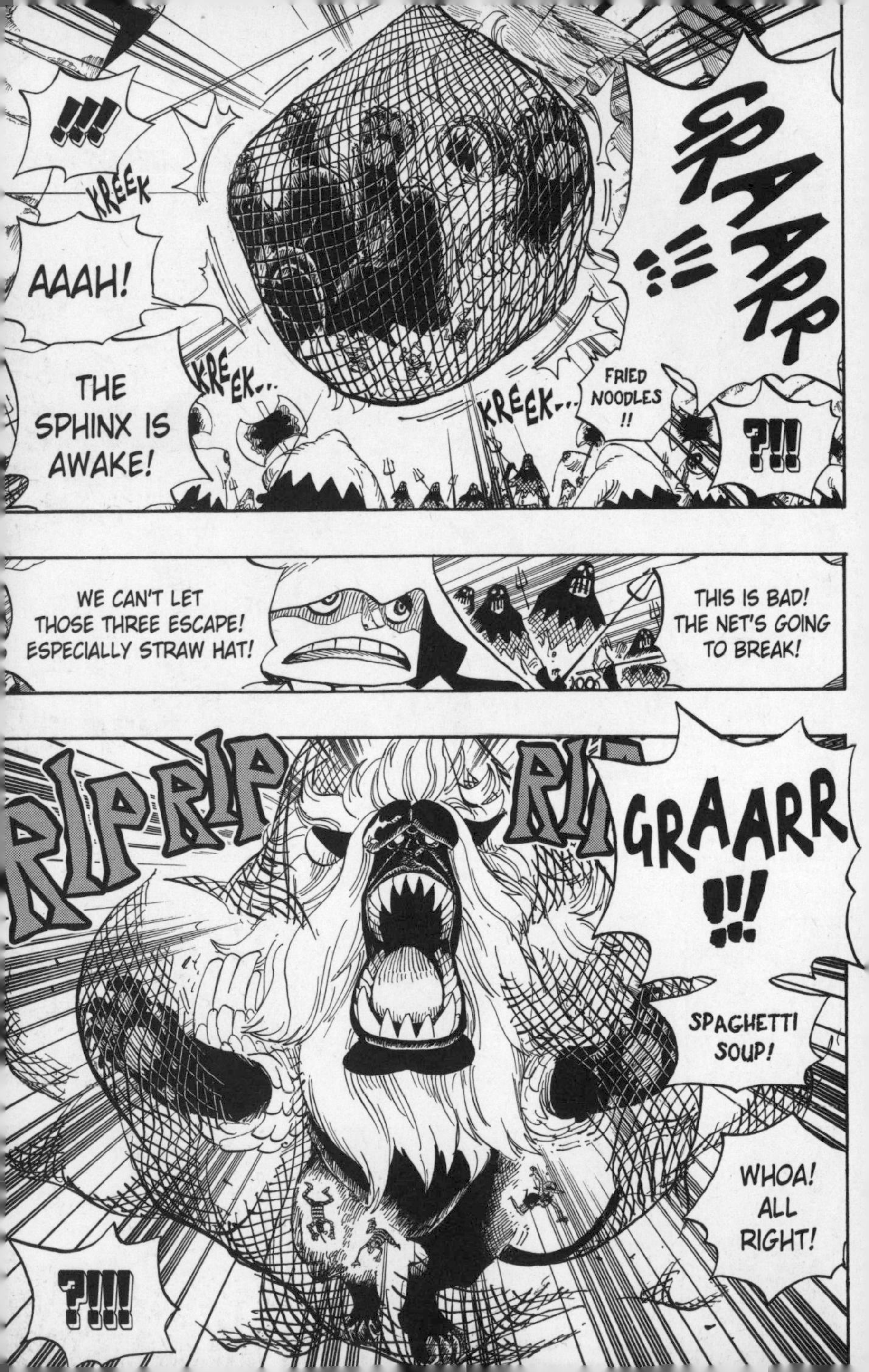
GRAARR
?!!
FRIED NOODLES !!
KREEK...
!!!
KREEK
AAAH!
KREEK...
THE SPHINX IS AWAKE!
THIS IS BAD! THE NET'S GOING TO BREAK!
WE CAN'T LET THOSE THREE ESCAPE! ESPECIALLY STRAW HAT!
GRAARR !!!
RIPRIPRIP RI
SPAGHETTI SOUP!
WHOA! ALL RIGHT!
?!!!

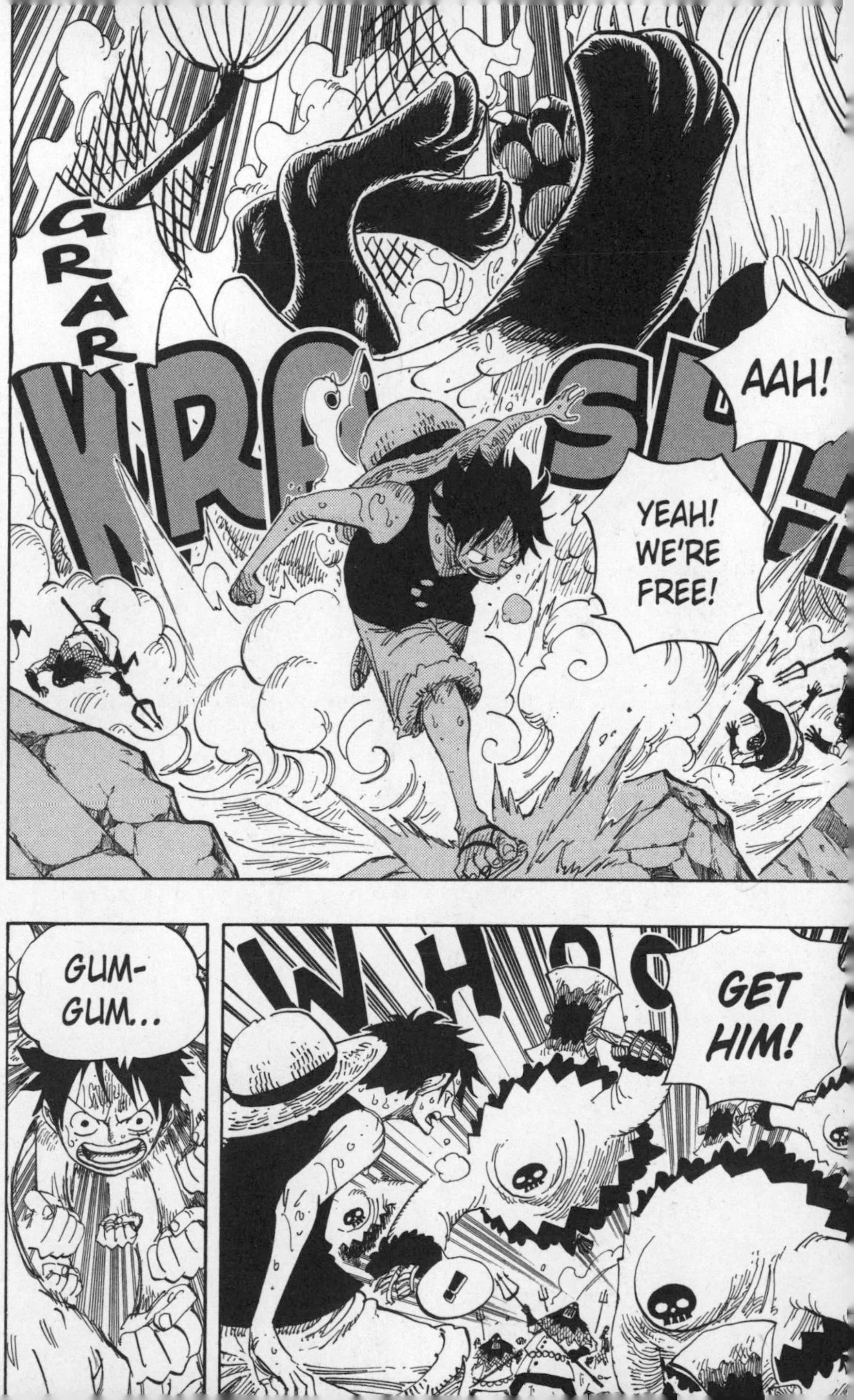
AAH!
YEAH! WE'RE FREE!
GRAR
GET HIM!
!
GUM-GUM...

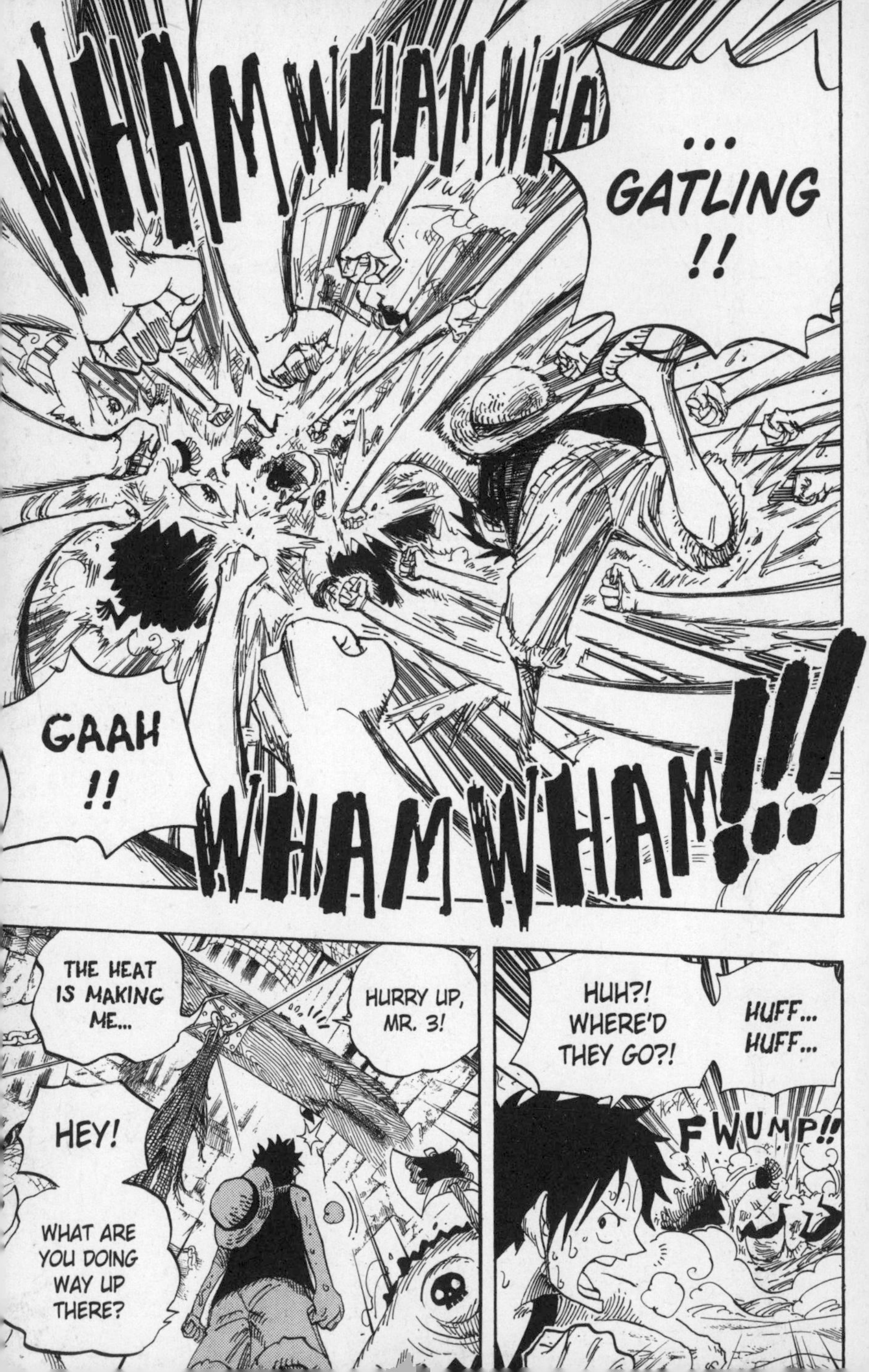
... GATLING !!
WHAM WHAM WHA
GAAH !!
WHAM WHAM!!!
HUFF... HUFF...
HUH?! WHERE'D THEY GO?!
FWUMP!!
HURRY UP, MR. 3!
THE HEAT IS MAKING ME...
HEY!
WHAT ARE YOU DOING WAY UP THERE?

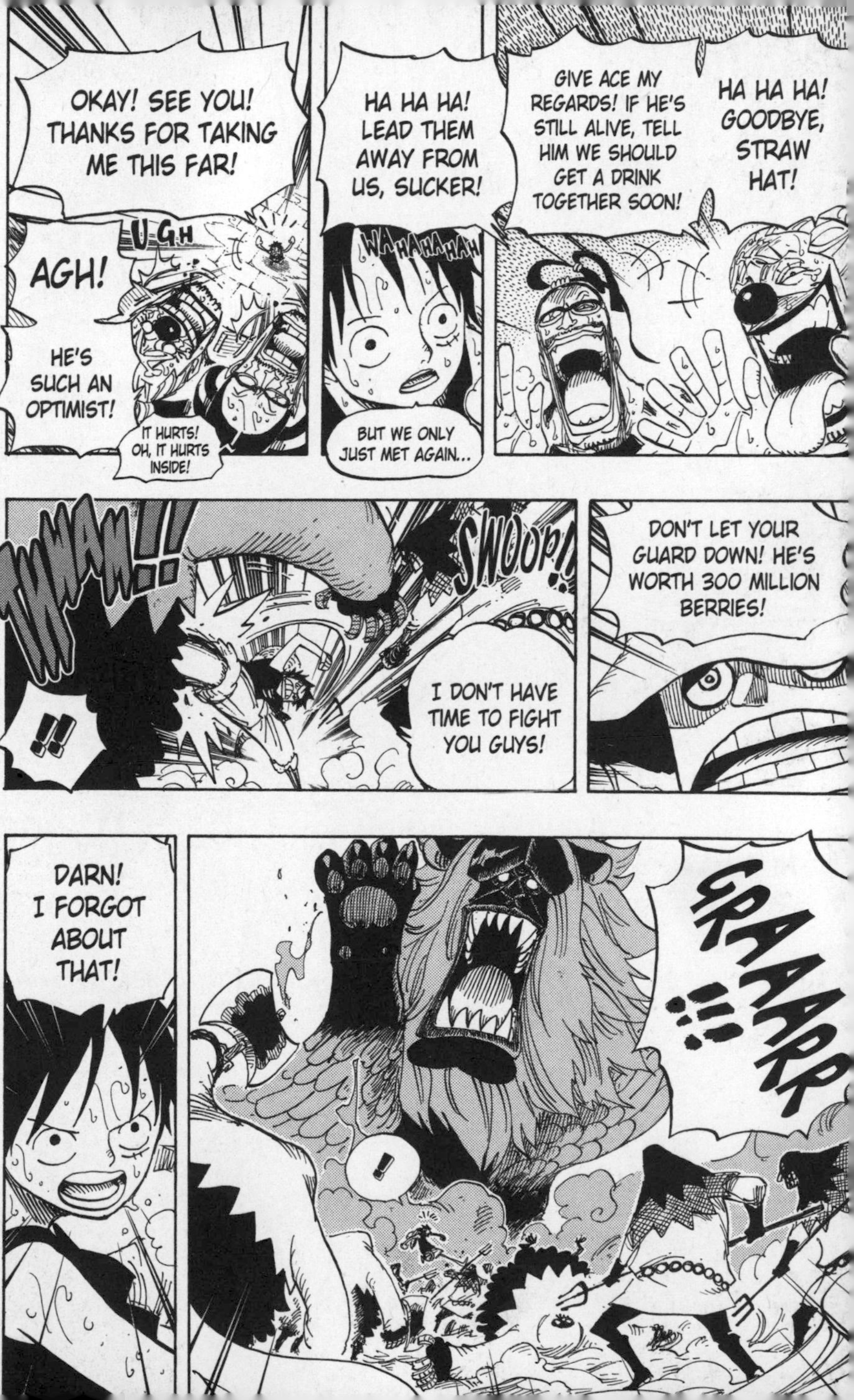
HA HA HA! GOODBYE, STRAW HAT!
GIVE ACE MY REGARDS! IF HE'S STILL ALIVE, TELL HIM WE SHOULD GET A DRINK TOGETHER SOON!
HA HA HA! LEAD THEM AWAY FROM US, SUCKER!
WAHAHAHAHAH
BUT WE ONLY JUST MET AGAIN...
OKAY! SEE YOU! THANKS FOR TAKING ME THIS FAR!
UGH
AGH!
HE'S SUCH AN OPTIMIST!
IT HURTS! OH, IT HURTS INSIDE!
DON'T LET YOUR GUARD DOWN! HE'S WORTH 300 MILLION BERRIES!
SWOOP!!
I DON'T HAVE TIME TO FIGHT YOU GUYS!
THWAM!!
!!
GRAAARR!!
!
DARN! I FORGOT ABOUT THAT!

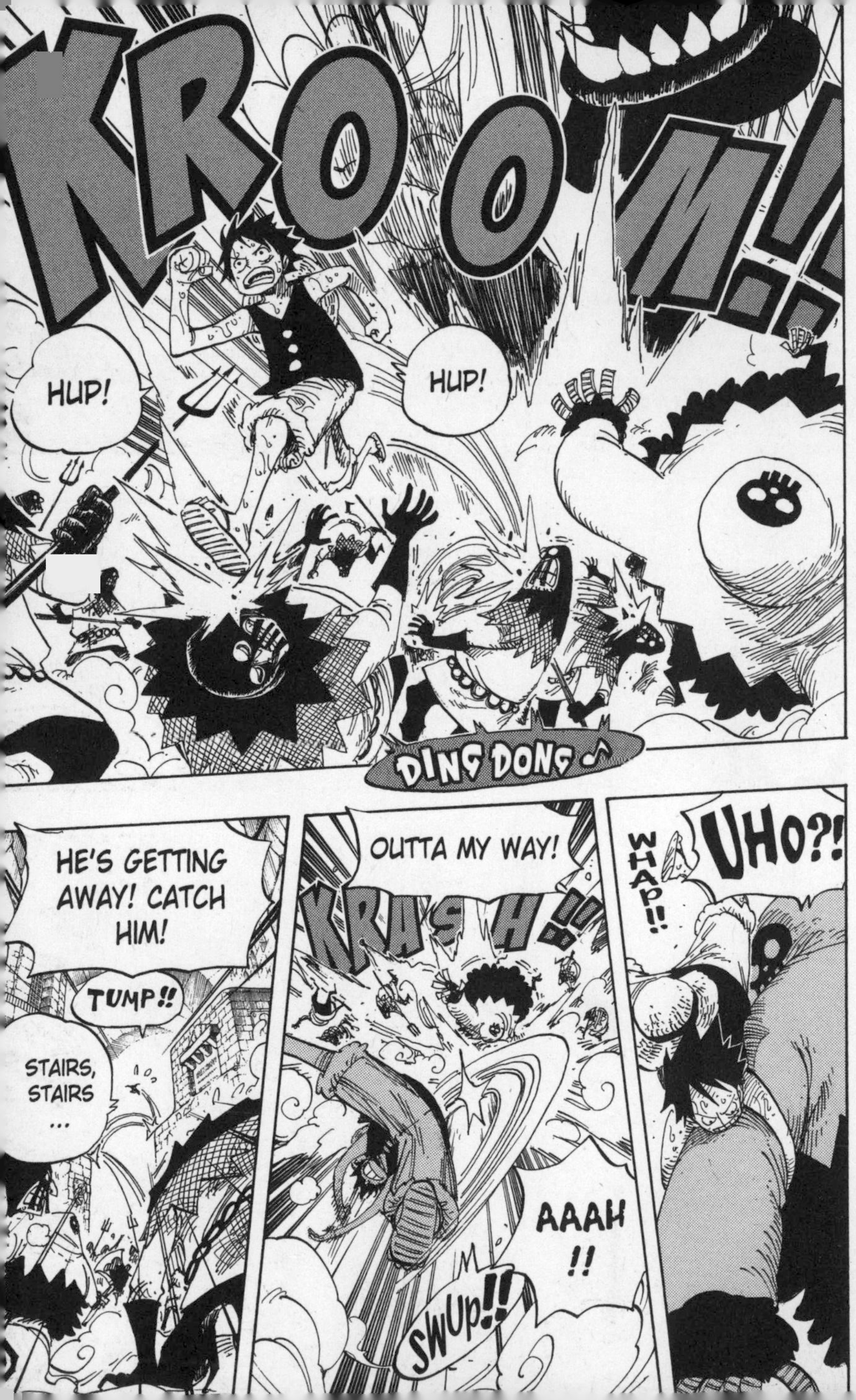
KROOM!!
HUP!
HUP!
DING DONG ♪
UHO?!
WHAP!!
OUTTA MY WAY!
KRASH!!
AAAH!!
SWUP!!
HE'S GETTING AWAY! CATCH HIM!
TUMP!!
STAIRS, STAIRS ...

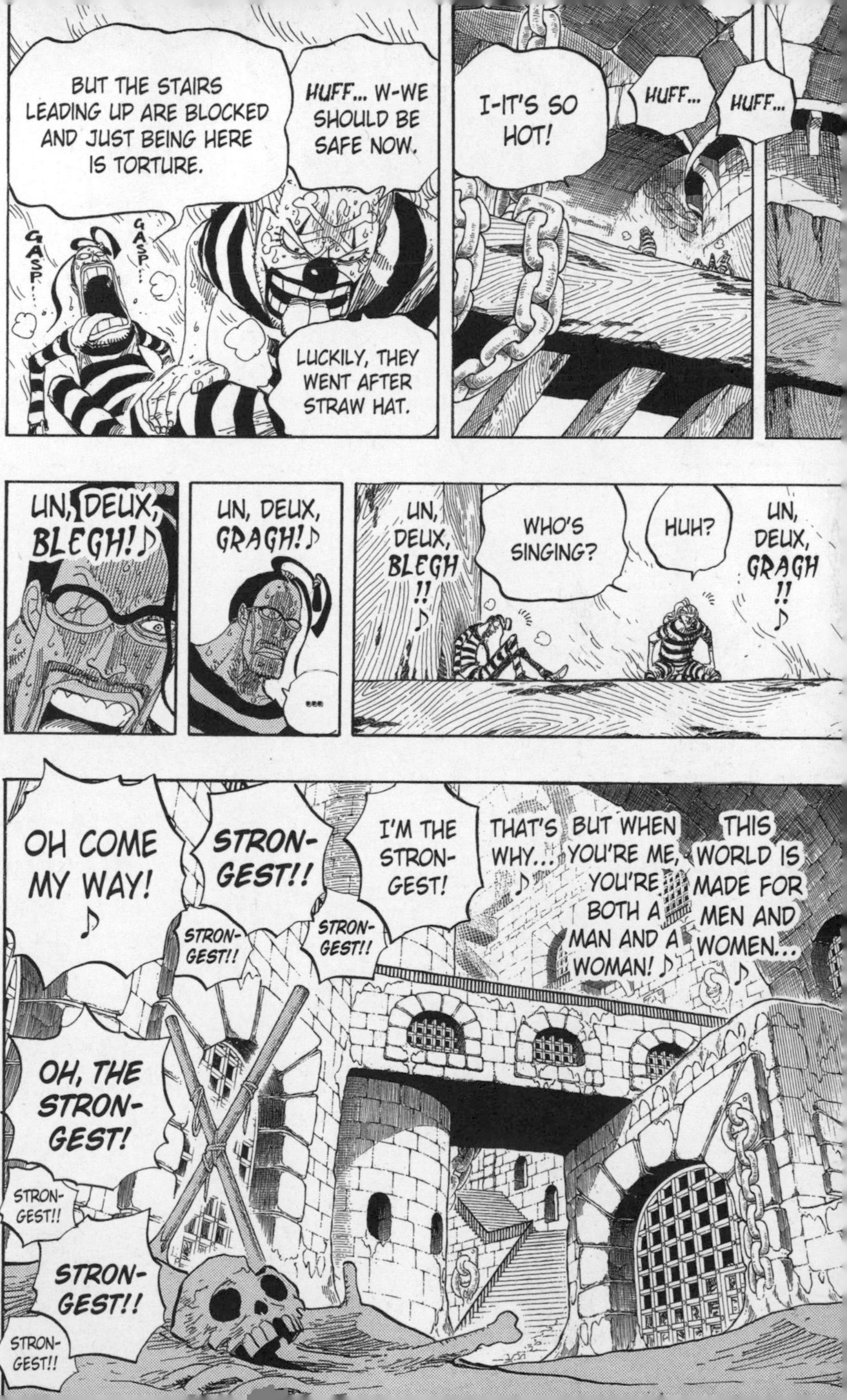
HUFF...
HUFF...
I-IT'S SO HOT!
HUFF... W-WE SHOULD BE SAFE NOW.
BUT THE STAIRS LEADING UP ARE BLOCKED AND JUST BEING HERE IS TORTURE.
GASP...
GASP...
LUCKILY, THEY WENT AFTER STRAW HAT.
UN, DEUX, GRAGH!! ♪
HUH?
WHO'S SINGING?
UN, DEUX, BLEGH!! ♪
UN, DEUX, GRAGH!♪
...
UN, DEUX, BLEGH!♪
THIS WORLD IS MADE FOR MEN AND WOMEN... ♪
BUT WHEN YOU'RE ME, YOU'RE BOTH A MAN AND A WOMAN! ♪
THAT'S WHY... ♪
I'M THE STRON-GEST!
STRON-GEST!!
STRON-GEST!!
STRON-GEST!!
OH COME MY WAY! ♪
OH, THE STRON-GEST!
STRON-GEST!!
STRON-GEST!!
STRON-GEST!!

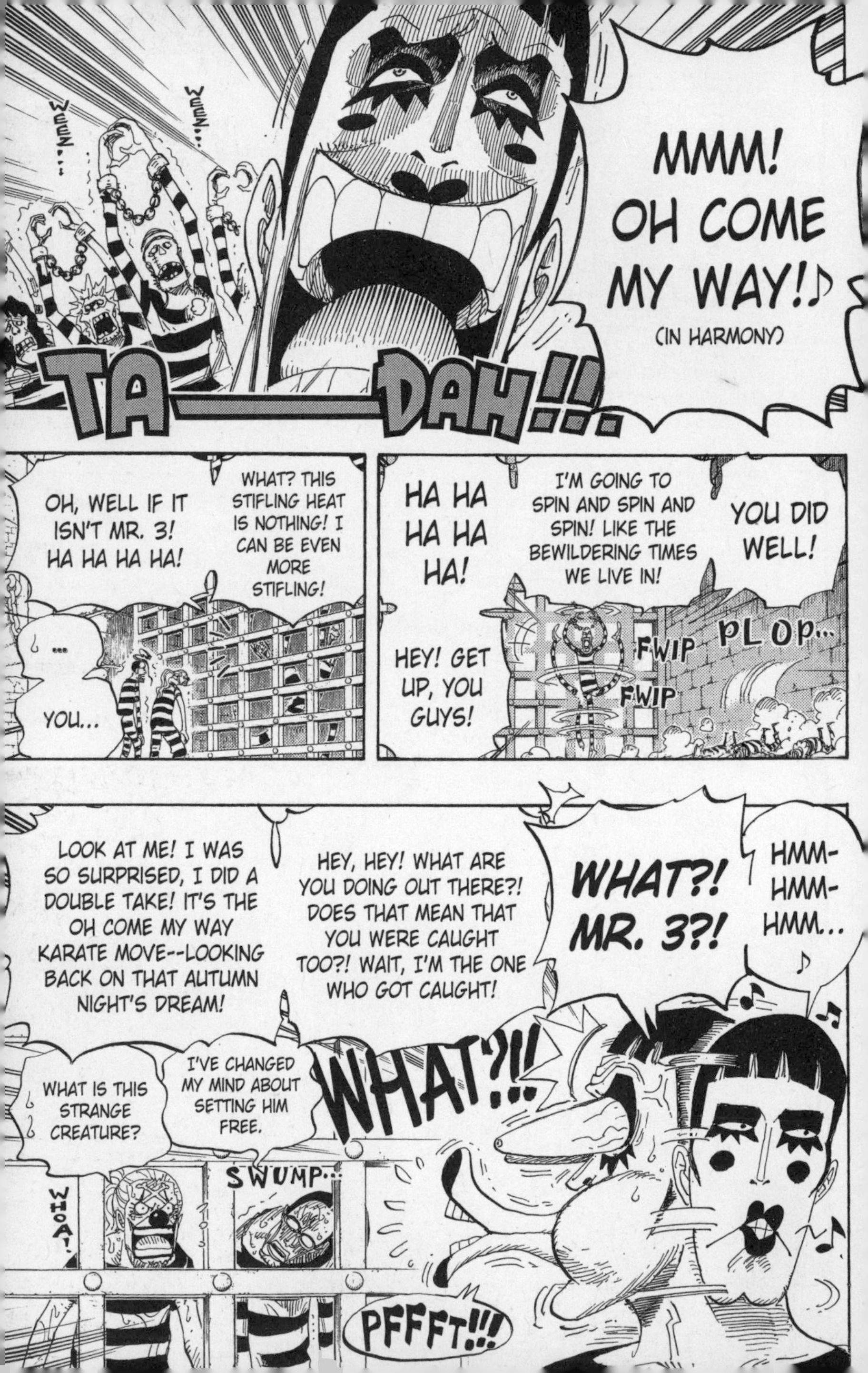
MMM! OH COME MY WAY!♪
(IN HARMONY)
TA—DAH!!!
WEEZ...
WEEZ...
YOU DID WELL!
I'M GOING TO SPIN AND SPIN AND SPIN! LIKE THE BEWILDERING TIMES WE LIVE IN!
HA HA HA HA HA!
HEY! GET UP, YOU GUYS!
PLOP...
FWIP
FWIP
WHAT? THIS STIFLING HEAT IS NOTHING! I CAN BE EVEN MORE STIFLING!
OH, WELL IF IT ISN'T MR. 3! HA HA HA HA!
...
YOU...
HMM-HMM-HMM...♪
WHAT?! MR. 3?!
HEY, HEY! WHAT ARE YOU DOING OUT THERE?! DOES THAT MEAN THAT YOU WERE CAUGHT TOO?! WAIT, I'M THE ONE WHO GOT CAUGHT!
LOOK AT ME! I WAS SO SURPRISED, I DID A DOUBLE TAKE! IT'S THE OH COME MY WAY KARATE MOVE--LOOKING BACK ON THAT AUTUMN NIGHT'S DREAM!
WHAT?!!
I'VE CHANGED MY MIND ABOUT SETTING HIM FREE.
WHAT IS THIS STRANGE CREATURE?
SWUMP...
WHOA!
PFFFT!!!

SBS Question Corner

VOICE ACTRESS FOR NAMI, AKEMI OKAMURA!

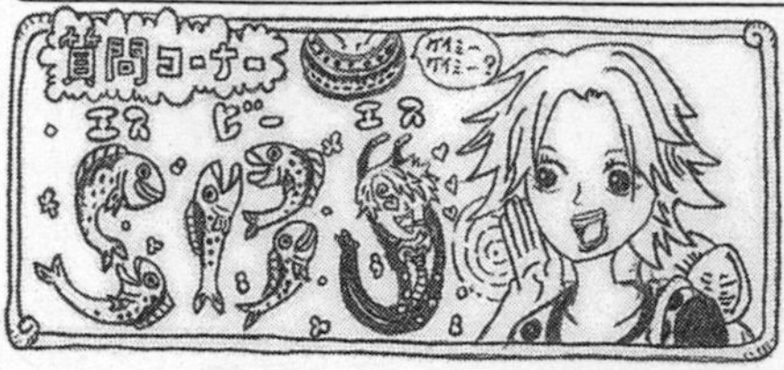
SBS
(Tomofuni Kawakami, Tottori)

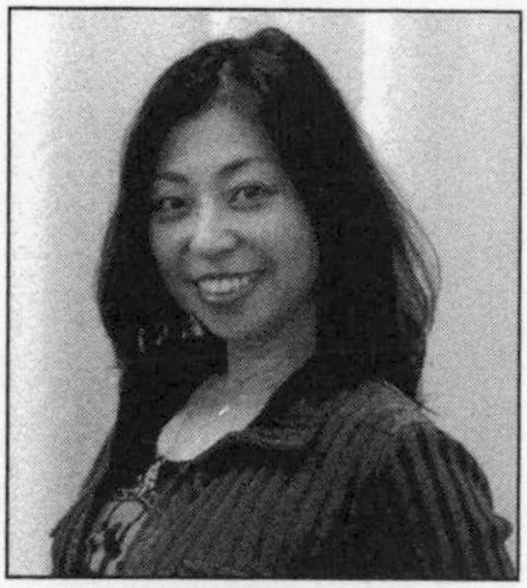

HDYD?! (How do you do?) This is now the third Question Corner for the voice actors! It always ends up being a really nice read, but all the other voice actors complain because they'll have to top the previous Question Corner! Now then. Today we have the voice actor for the navigator, Nami! Let me say this first to the readers. You're sending in way too many perverted questions! Can you be a little more considerate since I have to go through them?! Okay, let's go on! Our wonderful lady Akemi Okamura is in the house!

Oda(O): Here is Okamura! Please gracefully introduce yourself!

Akemi(A): Hello. This is Akemi Okamura, always with a smile.

O: Good intro! Yes, I love it when you guys take this seriously. By the way, do you know what SBS stands for? I'm hoping for a cute answer.

A: Sure thing. (S)tupidity (B)ashed (S)illy.♡

O: That's scary! I introduced you as a sweet lady! Are you going to disappoint all the readers who are young boys?!

A: Oh, that wasn't good? Okay, one more time then. (S)illy (B)oys (S)lapped.♡

O: You're still going to beat them, aren't you?! Whatever! Okay, let's just start this.

A: Sure thing.♡

The Question Corner with Okamura continued on page 206! ☞

PREVIEW FOR NEXT VOICE ACTOR'S SBS

Next time and the one after that will be with these two!

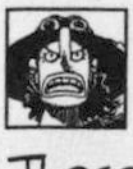 Usopp (Kappei Yamaguchi) 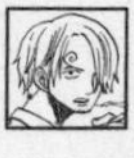 Sanji (Hiroaki Hirata)

These two are veteran voice actors, and you know exactly how they are!

Chapter 531:
LEVEL 3: STARVATION HELL

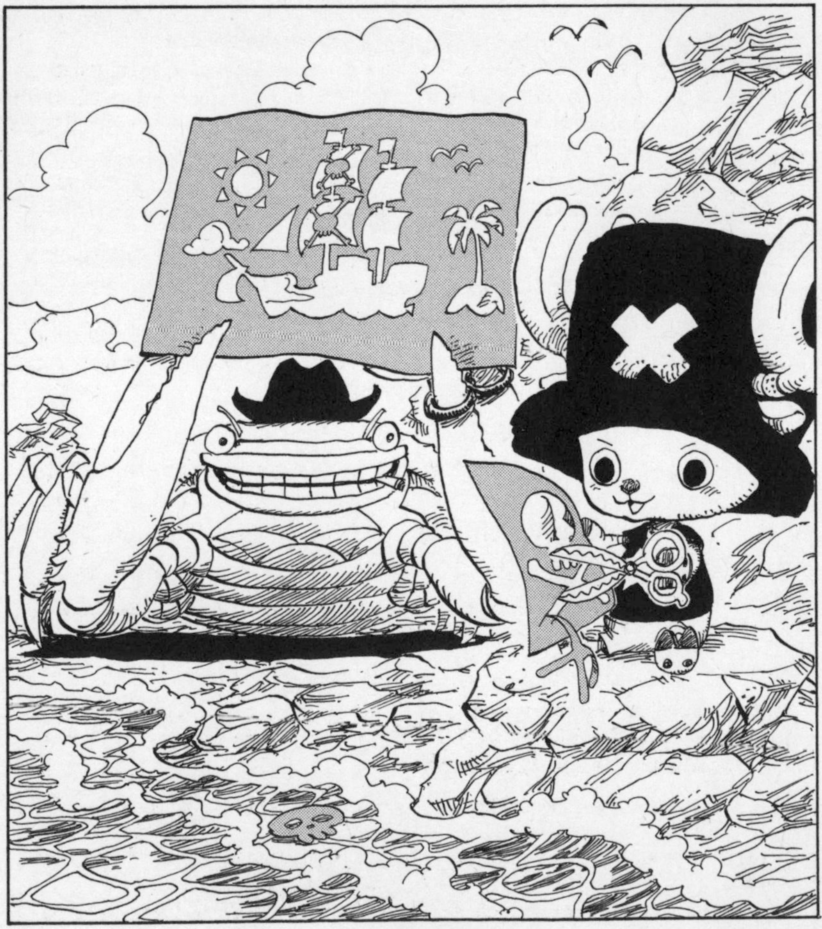

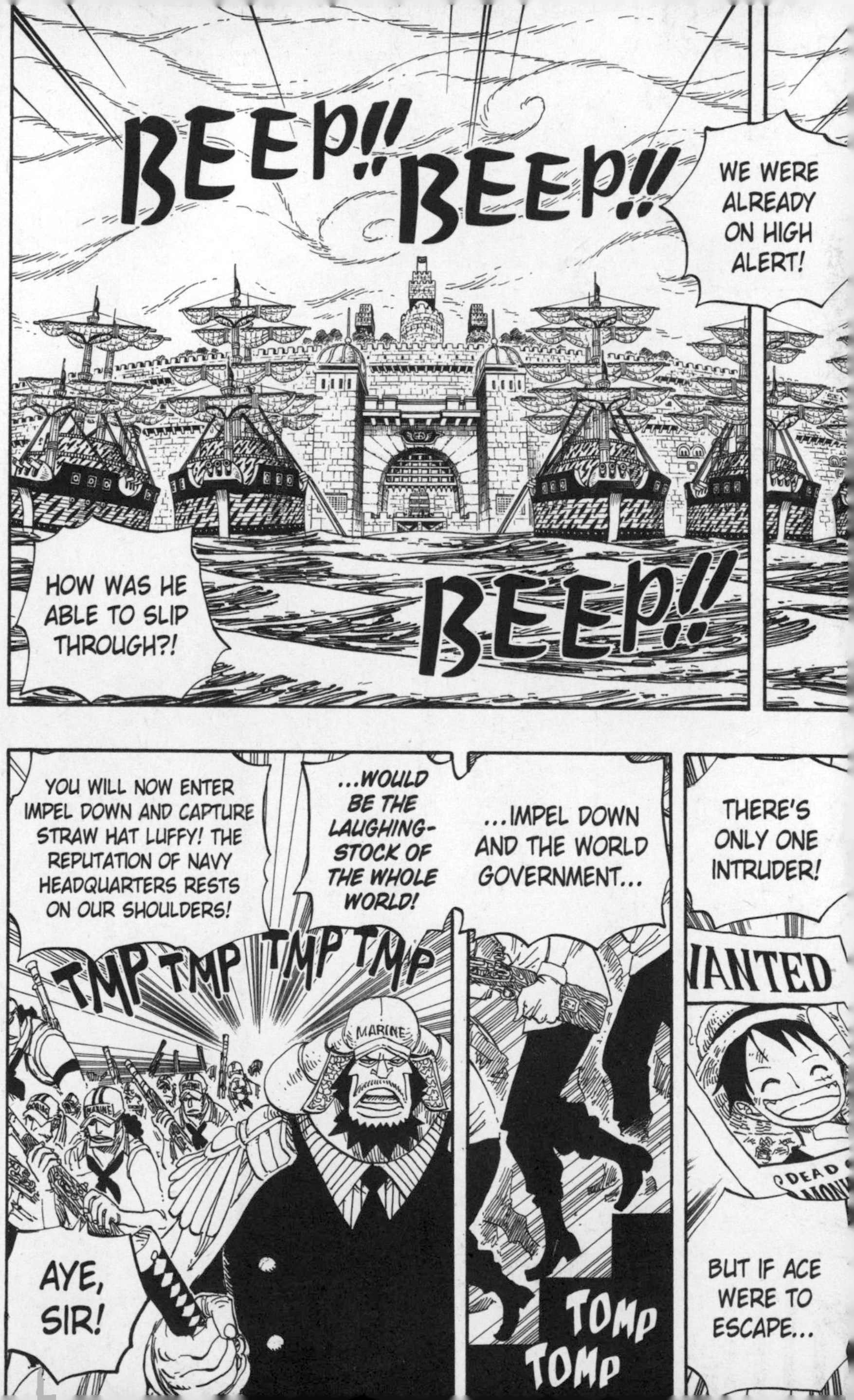
WE WERE ALREADY ON HIGH ALERT!
BEEP!! BEEP!!
BEEP!!
HOW WAS HE ABLE TO SLIP THROUGH?!
THERE'S ONLY ONE INTRUDER!
WANTED
DEAD
BUT IF ACE WERE TO ESCAPE...
...IMPEL DOWN AND THE WORLD GOVERNMENT...
TOMP TOMP
...WOULD BE THE LAUGHING-STOCK OF THE WHOLE WORLD!
YOU WILL NOW ENTER IMPEL DOWN AND CAPTURE STRAW HAT LUFFY! THE REPUTATION OF NAVY HEADQUARTERS RESTS ON OUR SHOULDERS!
TMP TMP TMP TMP
MARINE
AYE, SIR!

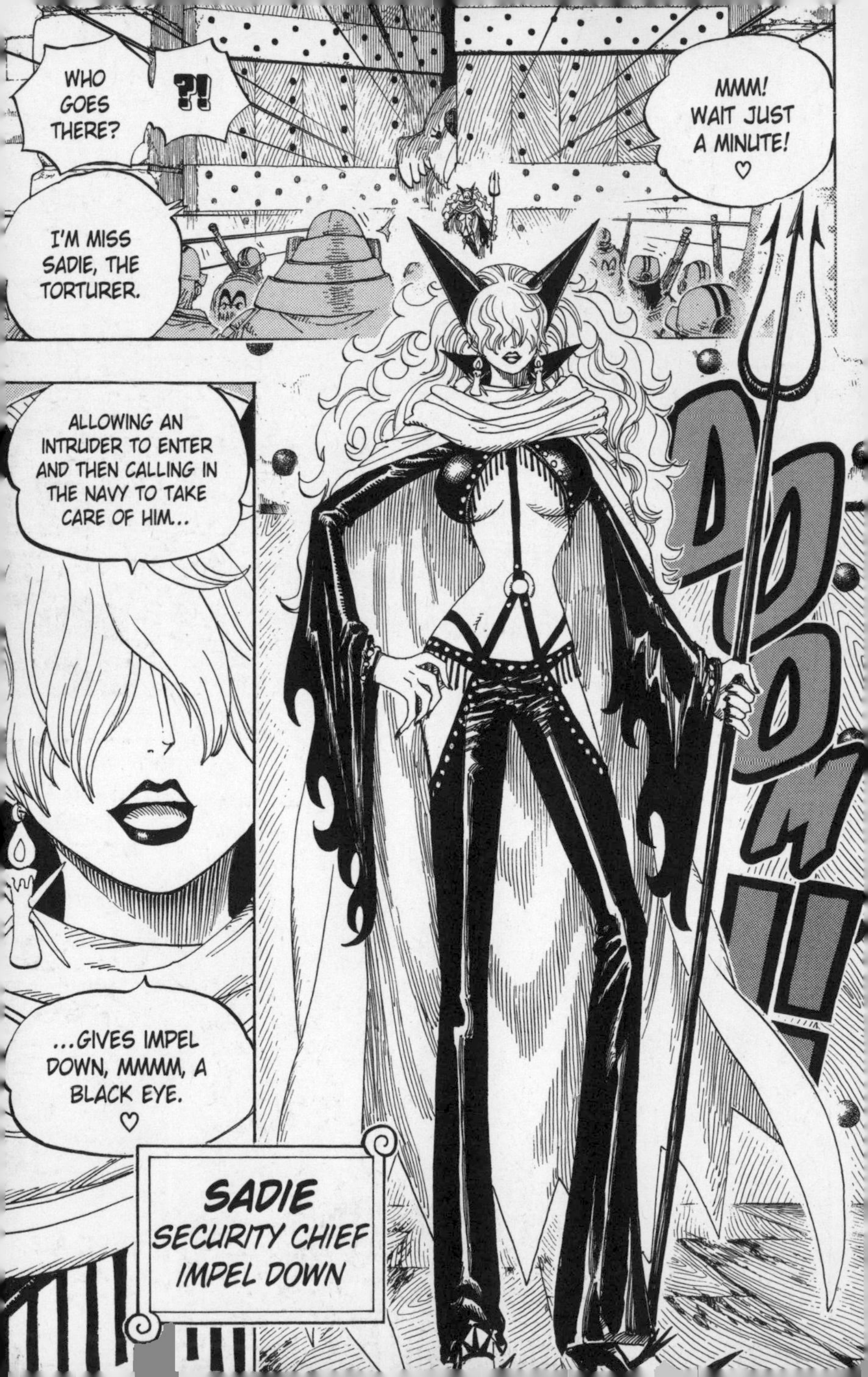
MMM! WAIT JUST A MINUTE! ♡
?!
WHO GOES THERE?
I'M MISS SADIE, THE TORTURER.
DOOM!!
SADIE
SECURITY CHIEF
IMPEL DOWN
ALLOWING AN INTRUDER TO ENTER AND THEN CALLING IN THE NAVY TO TAKE CARE OF HIM...
...GIVES IMPEL DOWN, MMMM, A BLACK EYE. ♡

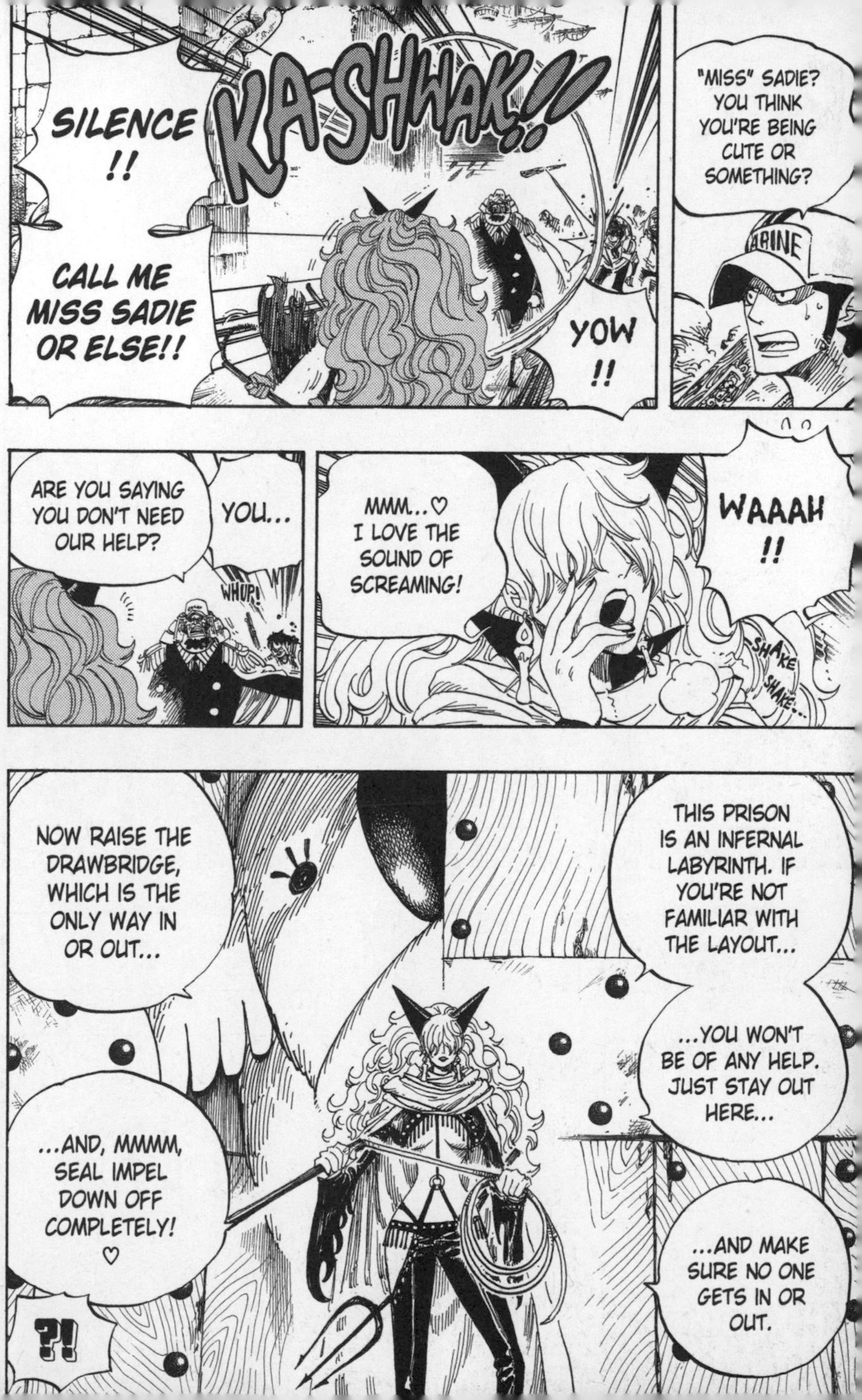
"MISS" SADIE? YOU THINK YOU'RE BEING CUTE OR SOMETHING?
KA-SHWAK!!
SILENCE!!
YOW!!
CALL ME MISS SADIE OR ELSE!!
WAAAH!!
MMM...♡ I LOVE THE SOUND OF SCREAMING!
SHAKE SHAKE...
YOU...
ARE YOU SAYING YOU DON'T NEED OUR HELP?
WHUP!
THIS PRISON IS AN INFERNAL LABYRINTH. IF YOU'RE NOT FAMILIAR WITH THE LAYOUT...
NOW RAISE THE DRAWBRIDGE, WHICH IS THE ONLY WAY IN OR OUT...
...YOU WON'T BE OF ANY HELP. JUST STAY OUT HERE...
...AND, MMMM, SEAL IMPEL DOWN OFF COMPLETELY! ♡
...AND MAKE SURE NO ONE GETS IN OR OUT.
?!

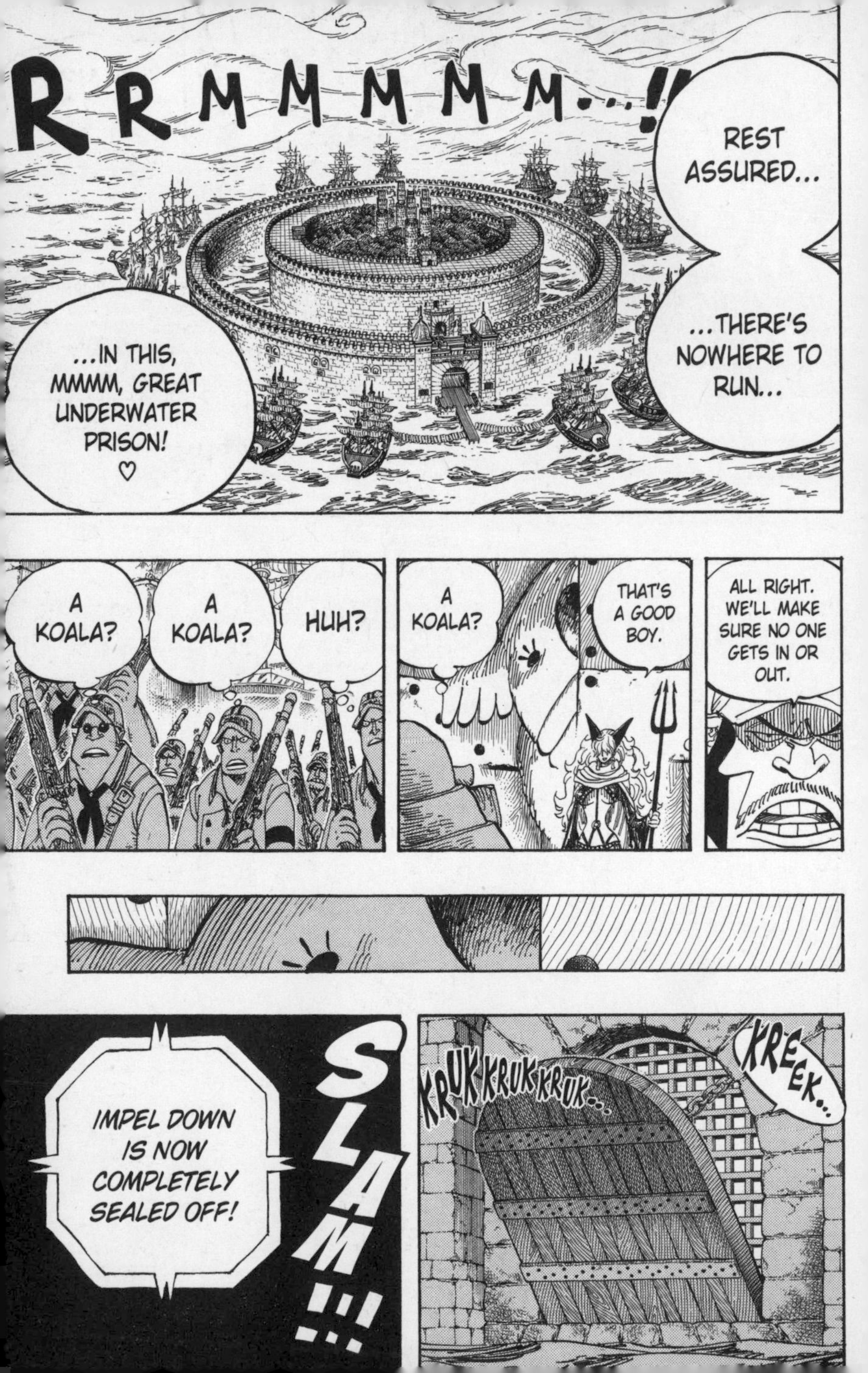
RRMMMMM...!!
REST ASSURED... ...THERE'S NOWHERE TO RUN...
...IN THIS, MMMM, GREAT UNDERWATER PRISON! ♡
ALL RIGHT. WE'LL MAKE SURE NO ONE GETS IN OR OUT.
THAT'S A GOOD BOY.
A KOALA?
HUH?
A KOALA?
A KOALA?
KREEK...
KRUK KRUK KRUK...
SLAM!!!
IMPEL DOWN IS NOW COMPLETELY SEALED OFF!

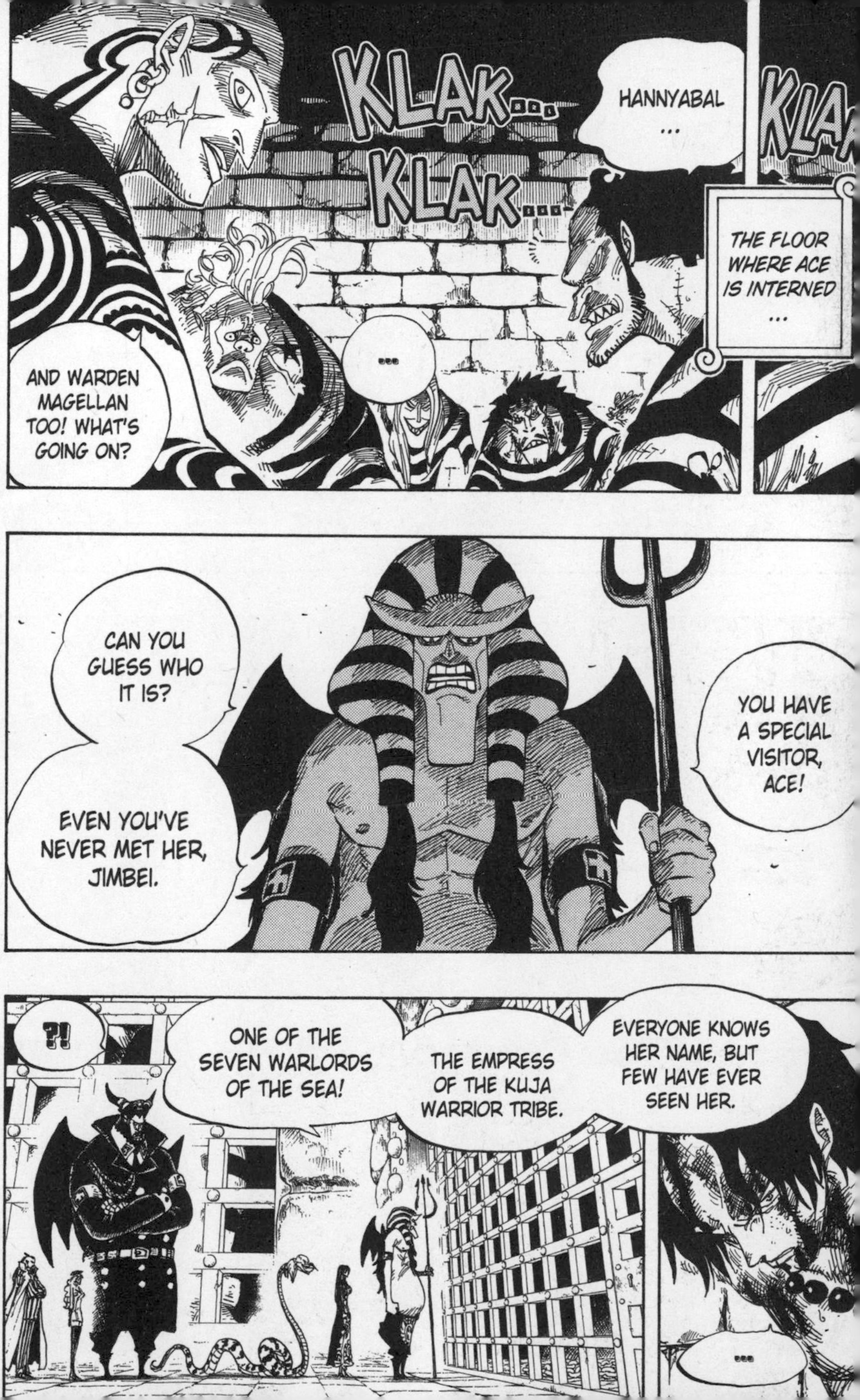
KLAK
THE FLOOR WHERE ACE IS INTERNED ...
HANNYABAL ...
KLAK... KLAK...
...
AND WARDEN MAGELLAN TOO! WHAT'S GOING ON?
YOU HAVE A SPECIAL VISITOR, ACE!
CAN YOU GUESS WHO IT IS?
EVEN YOU'VE NEVER MET HER, JIMBEI.
EVERYONE KNOWS HER NAME, BUT FEW HAVE EVER SEEN HER.
THE EMPRESS OF THE KUJA WARRIOR TRIBE.
ONE OF THE SEVEN WARLORDS OF THE SEA!
?!
...

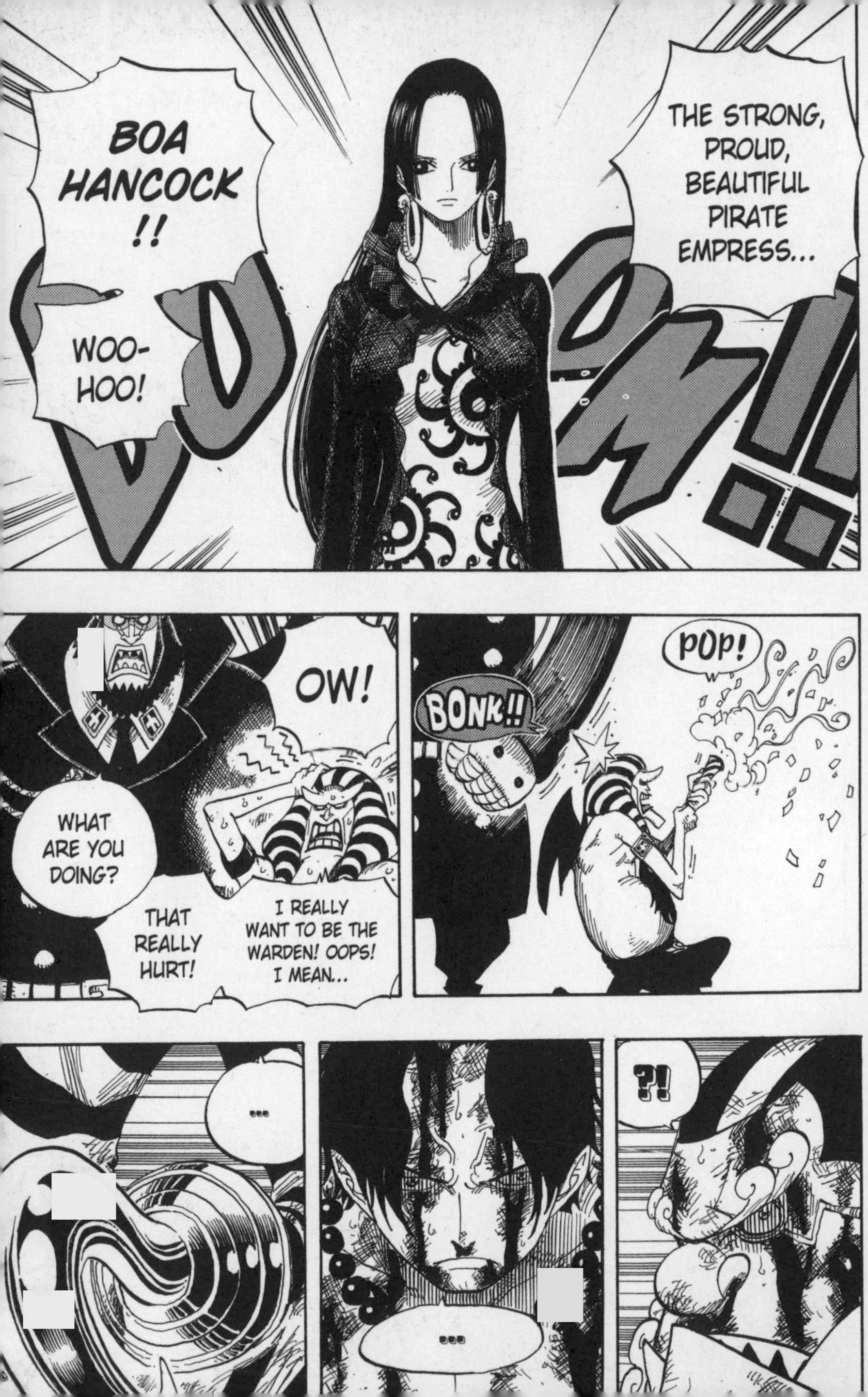
THE STRONG, PROUD, BEAUTIFUL PIRATE EMPRESS...
BOA HANCOCK!!
WOO-HOO!
POP!
BONK!!
OW!
WHAT ARE YOU DOING?
I REALLY WANT TO BE THE WARDEN! OOPS! I MEAN...
THAT REALLY HURT!
?!
...
...

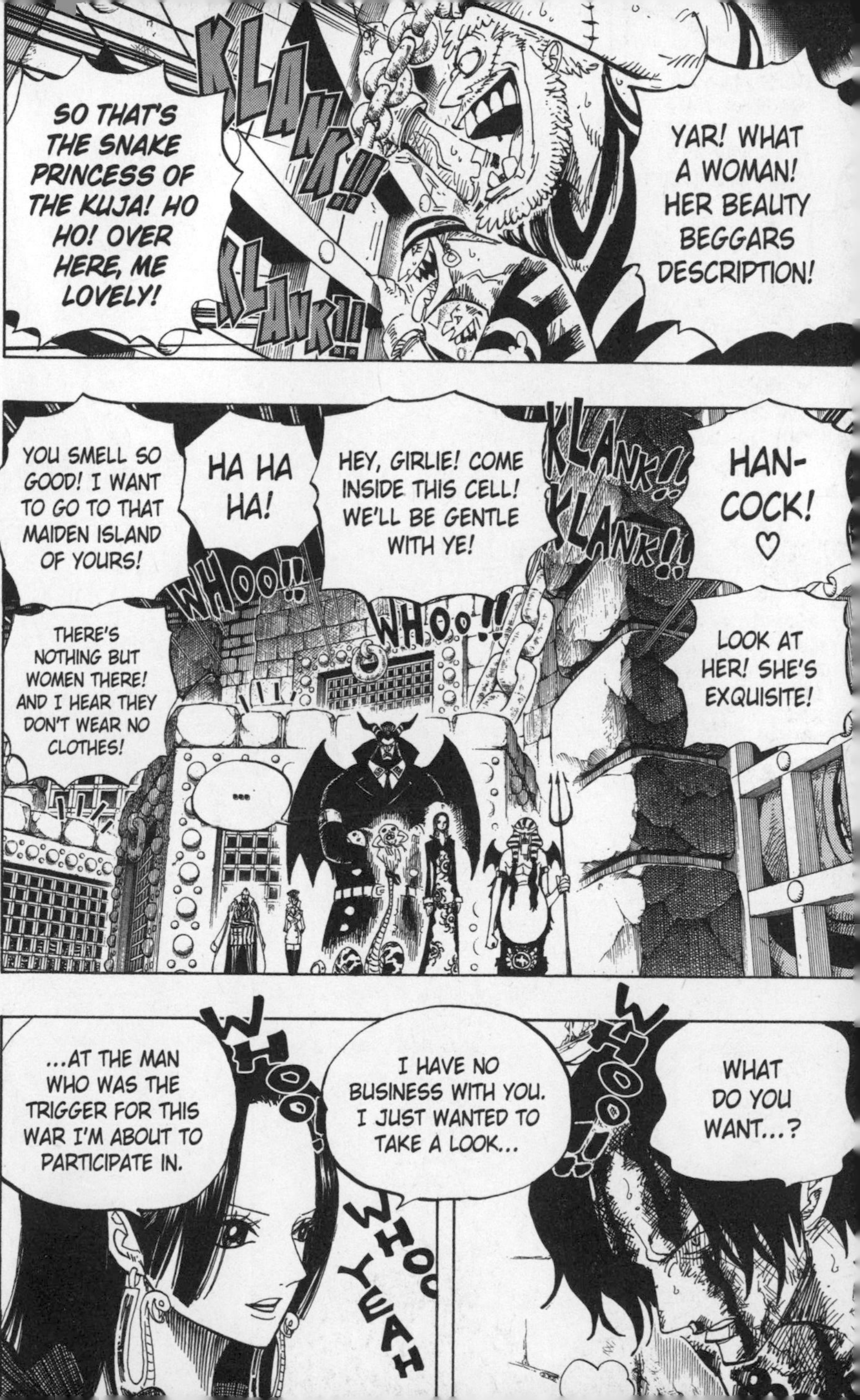
YAR! WHAT A WOMAN! HER BEAUTY BEGGARS DESCRIPTION!
KLANK!!
SLANK!!
SO THAT'S THE SNAKE PRINCESS OF THE KUJA! HO HO! OVER HERE, ME LOVELY!
HAN-COCK! ♡
KLANK!!
KLANK!!
HEY, GIRLIE! COME INSIDE THIS CELL! WE'LL BE GENTLE WITH YE!
HA HA HA!
YOU SMELL SO GOOD! I WANT TO GO TO THAT MAIDEN ISLAND OF YOURS!
LOOK AT HER! SHE'S EXQUISITE!
WHOO!!
WHOO!!
THERE'S NOTHING BUT WOMEN THERE! AND I HEAR THEY DON'T WEAR NO CLOTHES!
...
WHAT DO YOU WANT...?
WHOO!!
I HAVE NO BUSINESS WITH YOU. I JUST WANTED TO TAKE A LOOK...
WHOO!
...AT THE MAN WHO WAS THE TRIGGER FOR THIS WAR I'M ABOUT TO PARTICIPATE IN.
WHOO
YEAH

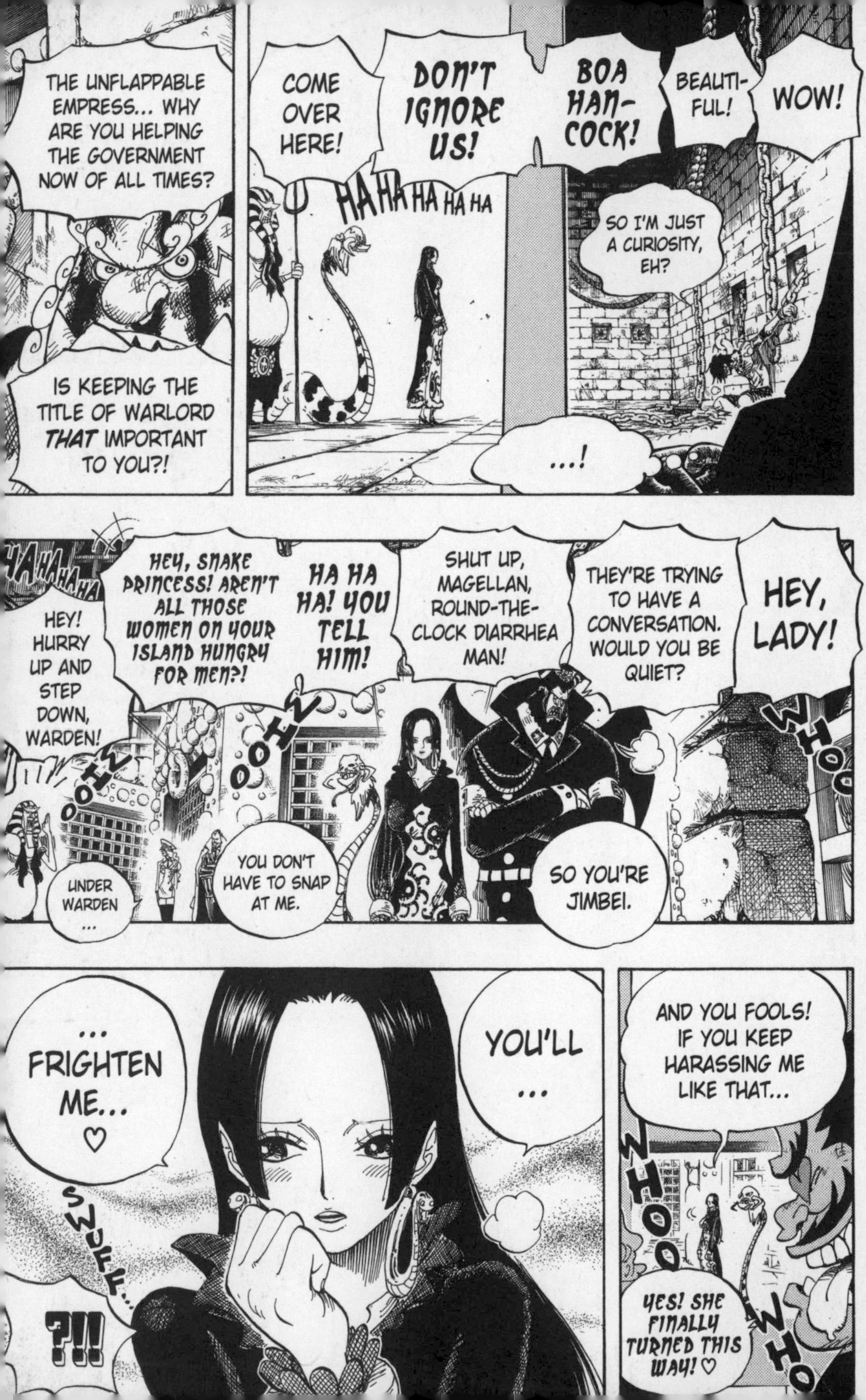
WOW!
BEAUTIFUL!
BOA HANCOCK!
SO I'M JUST A CURIOSITY, EH?
...!
DON'T IGNORE US!
COME OVER HERE!
HA HA HA HA HA
THE UNFLAPPABLE EMPRESS... WHY ARE YOU HELPING THE GOVERNMENT NOW OF ALL TIMES?
IS KEEPING THE TITLE OF WARLORD *THAT* IMPORTANT TO YOU?!
HEY, LADY!
THEY'RE TRYING TO HAVE A CONVERSATION. WOULD YOU BE QUIET?
SHUT UP, MAGELLAN, ROUND-THE-CLOCK DIARRHEA MAN!
HA HA HA! YOU TELL HIM!
HEY, SNAKE PRINCESS! AREN'T ALL THOSE WOMEN ON YOUR ISLAND HUNGRY FOR MEN?!
HAHAHAHA
HEY! HURRY UP AND STEP DOWN, WARDEN!
WHOO
SO YOU'RE JIMBEI.
YOU DON'T HAVE TO SNAP AT ME.
WHOOOHN
WHOOO
UNDER WARDEN ...
AND YOU FOOLS! IF YOU KEEP HARASSING ME LIKE THAT...
WHOOO
YES! SHE FINALLY TURNED THIS WAY! ♡
WHO
YOU'LL ...
... FRIGHTEN ME... ♡
SWUFF...
?!!

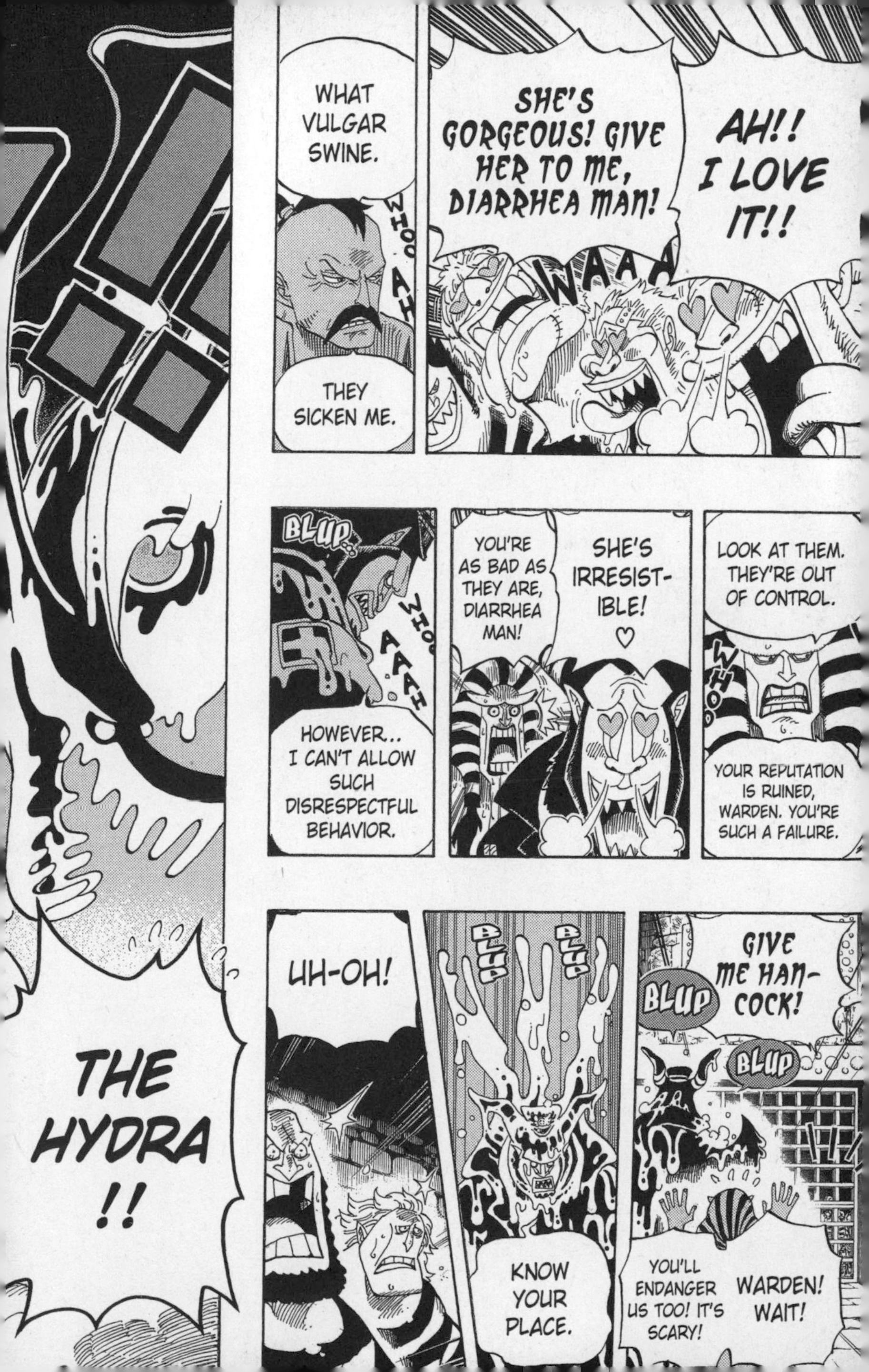

AH!! I LOVE IT!!
SHE'S GORGEOUS! GIVE HER TO ME, DIARRHEA MAN!
WAAAA
WHAT VULGAR SWINE.
WHOOAH
THEY SICKEN ME.
LOOK AT THEM. THEY'RE OUT OF CONTROL.
WHO
YOUR REPUTATION IS RUINED, WARDEN. YOU'RE SUCH A FAILURE.
SHE'S IRRESISTIBLE! ♡
YOU'RE AS BAD AS THEY ARE, DIARRHEA MAN!
BLUP
WHOOAAAH
HOWEVER... I CAN'T ALLOW SUCH DISRESPECTFUL BEHAVIOR.
GIVE ME HANCOCK!
BLUP
BLUP
WARDEN! WAIT!
YOU'LL ENDANGER US TOO! IT'S SCARY!
BLUP
BLUP
KNOW YOUR PLACE.
UH-OH!
THE HYDRA!!

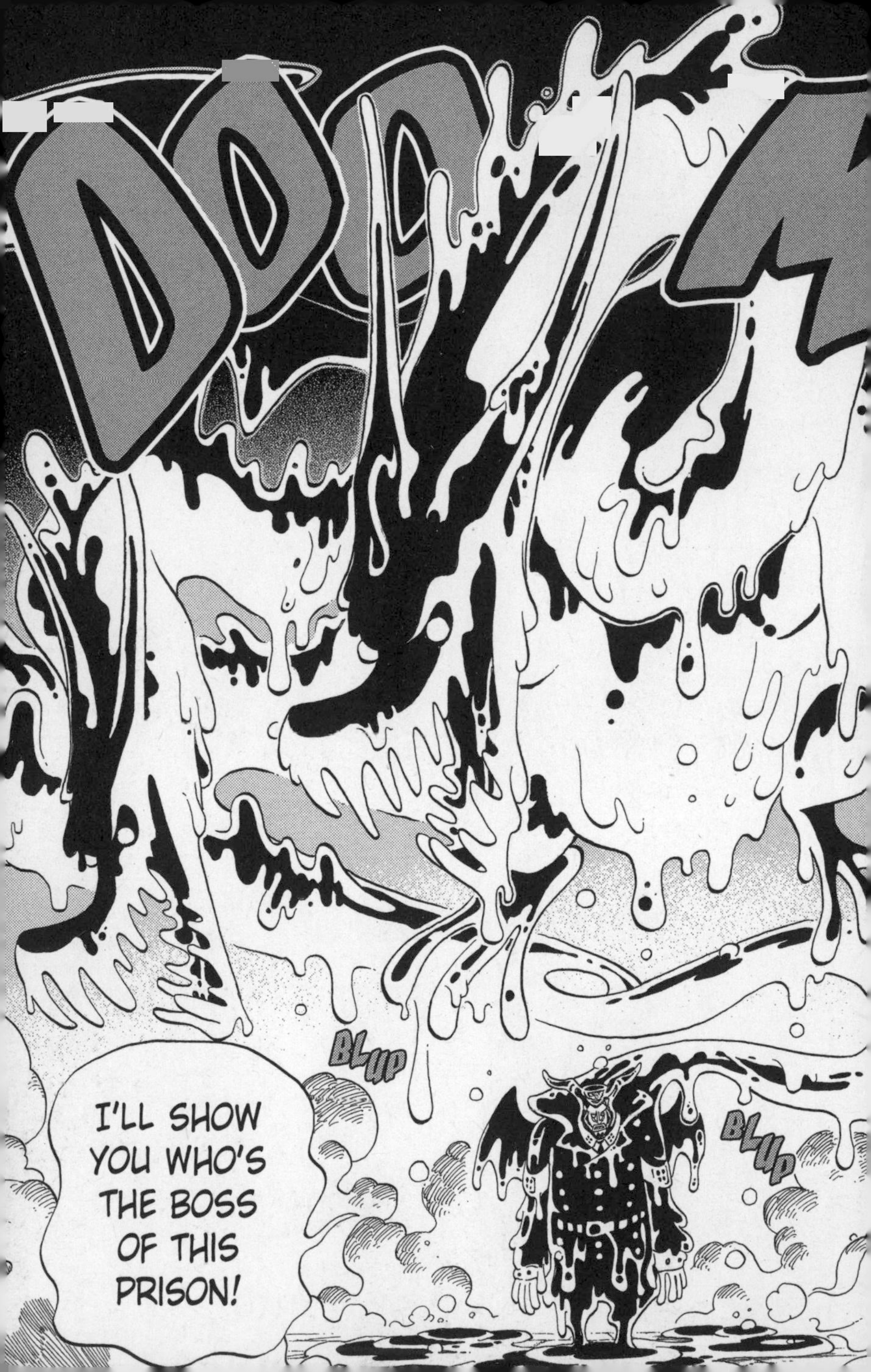
BLUP
I'LL SHOW YOU WHO'S THE BOSS OF THIS PRISON!
BLUP

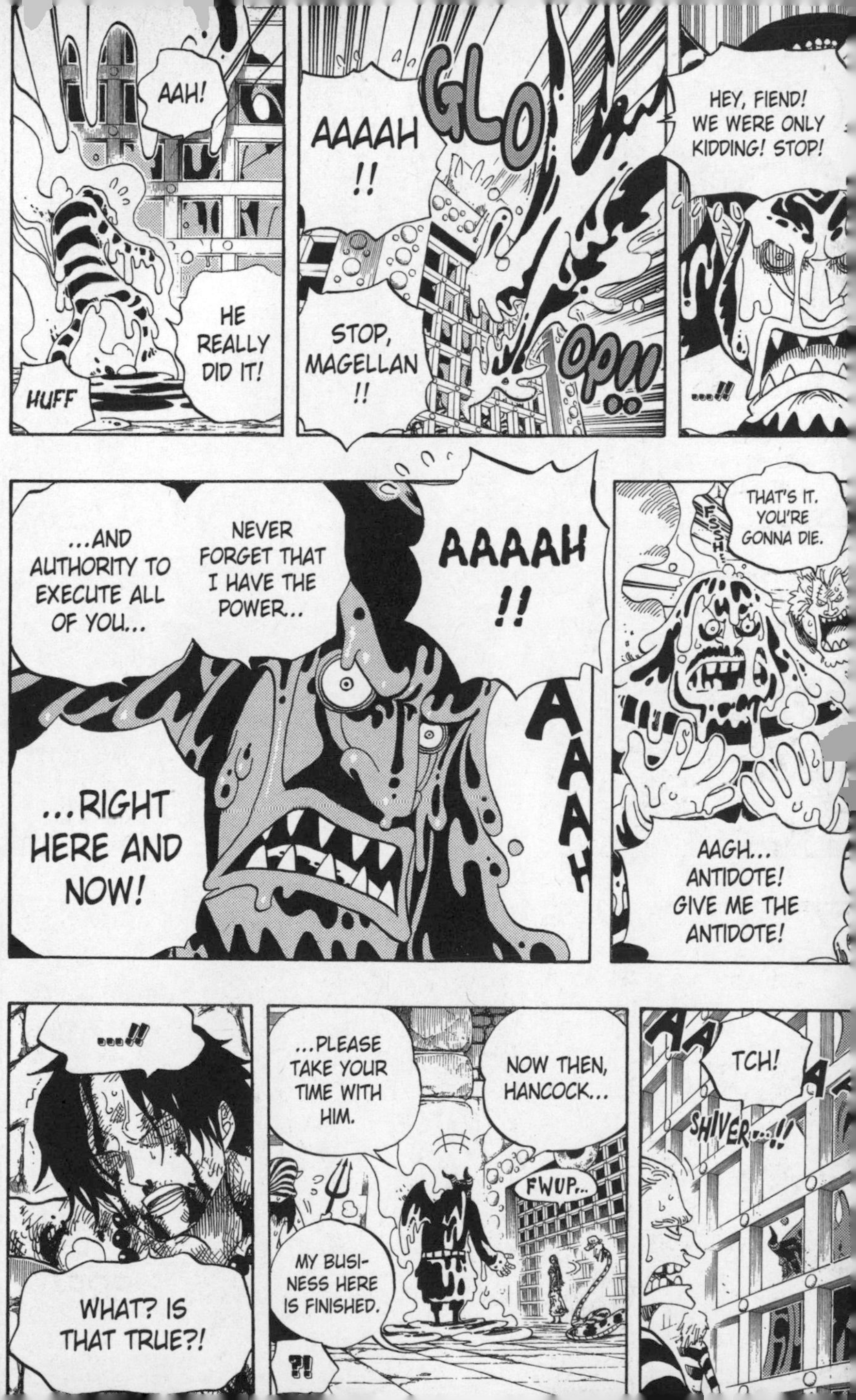
HEY, FIEND! WE WERE ONLY KIDDING! STOP!
...!!
GLO
OP!!
AAAAH !!
STOP, MAGELLAN !!
AAH!
HE REALLY DID IT!
HUFF
THAT'S IT. YOU'RE GONNA DIE.
FSSH
AAGH... ANTIDOTE! GIVE ME THE ANTIDOTE!
AAAAH !!
AAAAH
NEVER FORGET THAT I HAVE THE POWER...
...AND AUTHORITY TO EXECUTE ALL OF YOU...
...RIGHT HERE AND NOW!
AAA
TCH!
SHIVER...!!
NOW THEN, HANCOCK...
...PLEASE TAKE YOUR TIME WITH HIM.
FWUP...
MY BUSINESS HERE IS FINISHED.
?!
...!!
WHAT? IS THAT TRUE?!

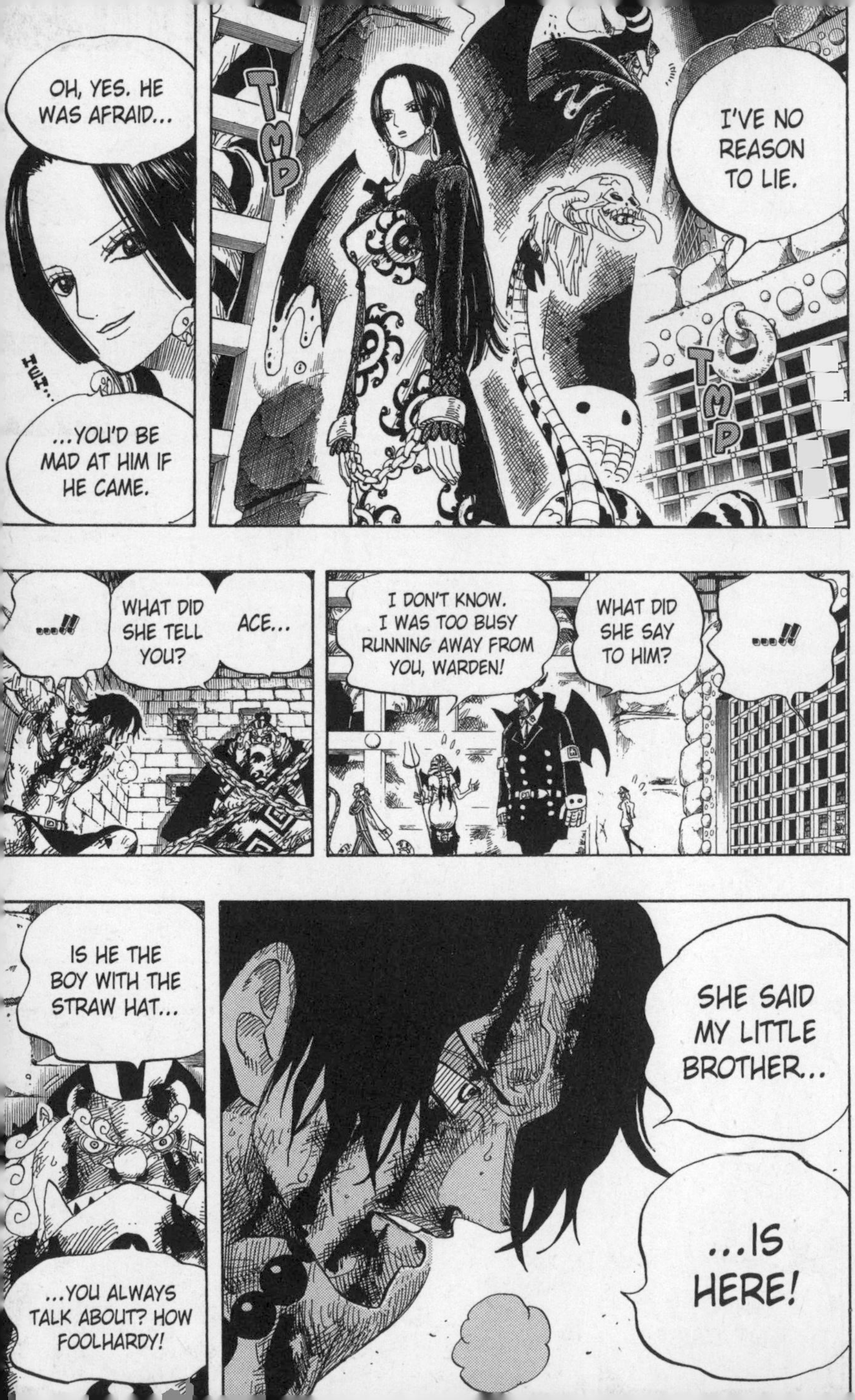
I'VE NO REASON TO LIE.
TMP
TMP
OH, YES. HE WAS AFRAID...
HEH...
...YOU'D BE MAD AT HIM IF HE CAME.
...!!
WHAT DID SHE SAY TO HIM?
I DON'T KNOW. I WAS TOO BUSY RUNNING AWAY FROM YOU, WARDEN!
ACE...
WHAT DID SHE TELL YOU?
...!!
SHE SAID MY LITTLE BROTHER...
...IS HERE!
IS HE THE BOY WITH THE STRAW HAT...
...YOU ALWAYS TALK ABOUT? HOW FOOLHARDY!

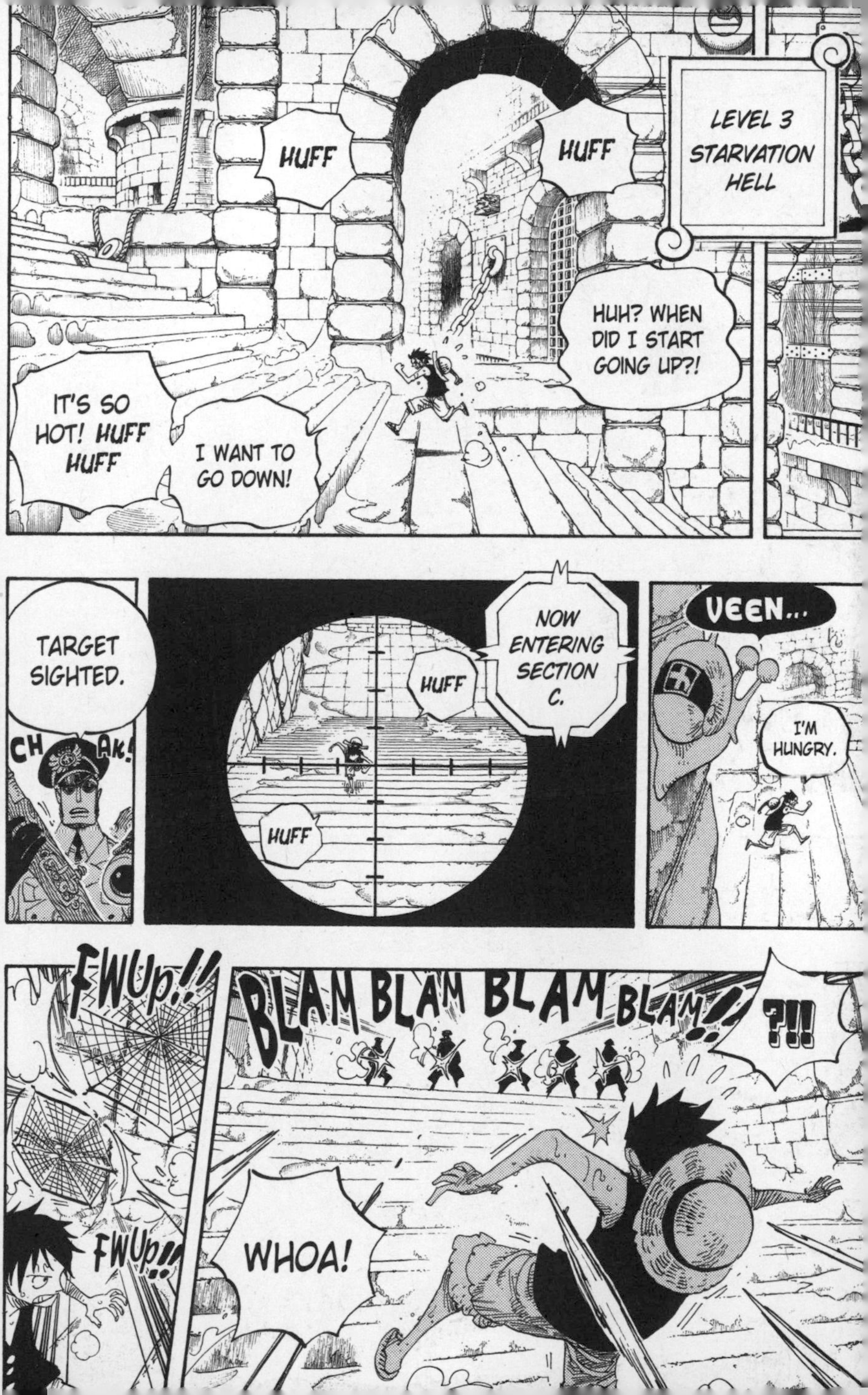
LEVEL 3 STARVATION HELL
HUFF
HUFF
HUH? WHEN DID I START GOING UP?!
I WANT TO GO DOWN!
IT'S SO HOT! HUFF HUFF
VEEN...
I'M HUNGRY.
NOW ENTERING SECTION C.
HUFF
HUFF
TARGET SIGHTED.
?!!
BLAM BLAM BLAM BLAM!!
WHOA!
FWUP!!
FWUP!!

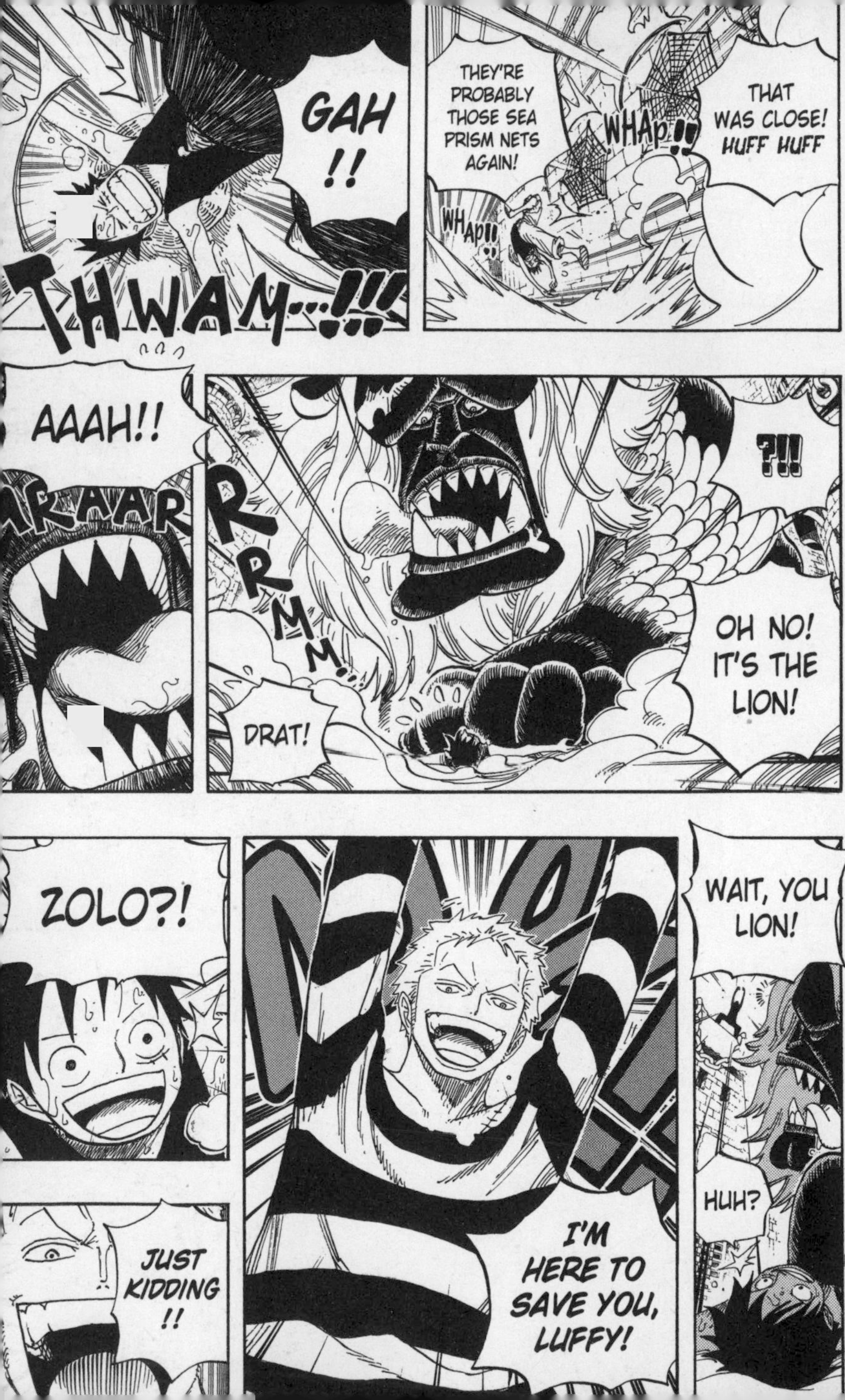
THAT WAS CLOSE! HUFF HUFF
WHAp!!
THEY'RE PROBABLY THOSE SEA PRISM NETS AGAIN!
WHAp!!
GAH !!
THWAM...!!!
?!!
OH NO! IT'S THE LION!
RRRMM...
DRAT!
AAAH!!
RAAAR
WAIT, YOU LION!
HUH?
I'M HERE TO SAVE YOU, LUFFY!
ZOLO?!
JUST KIDDING !!

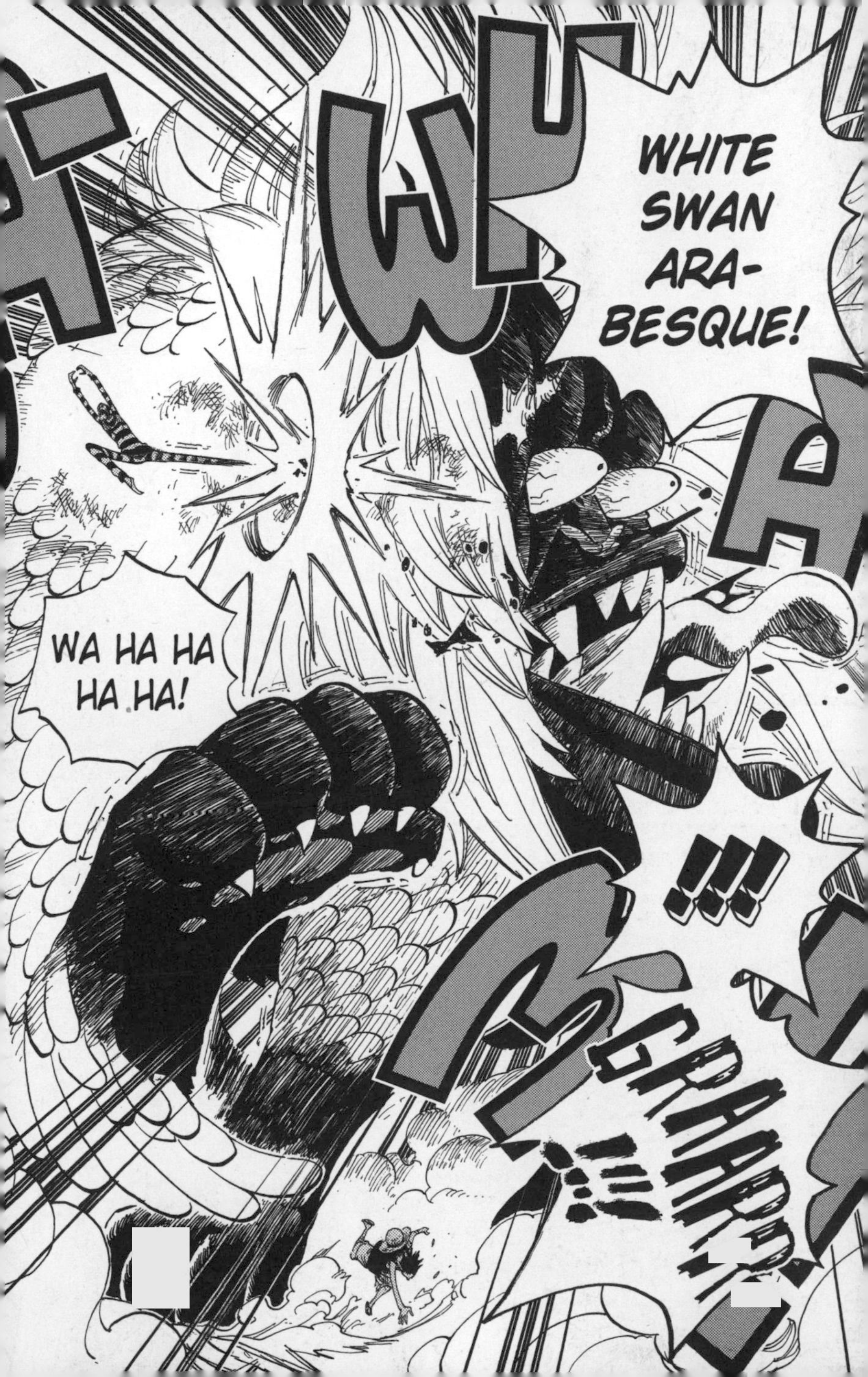
WHITE SWAN ARA- BESQUE!
!!!
WA HA HA HA HA!

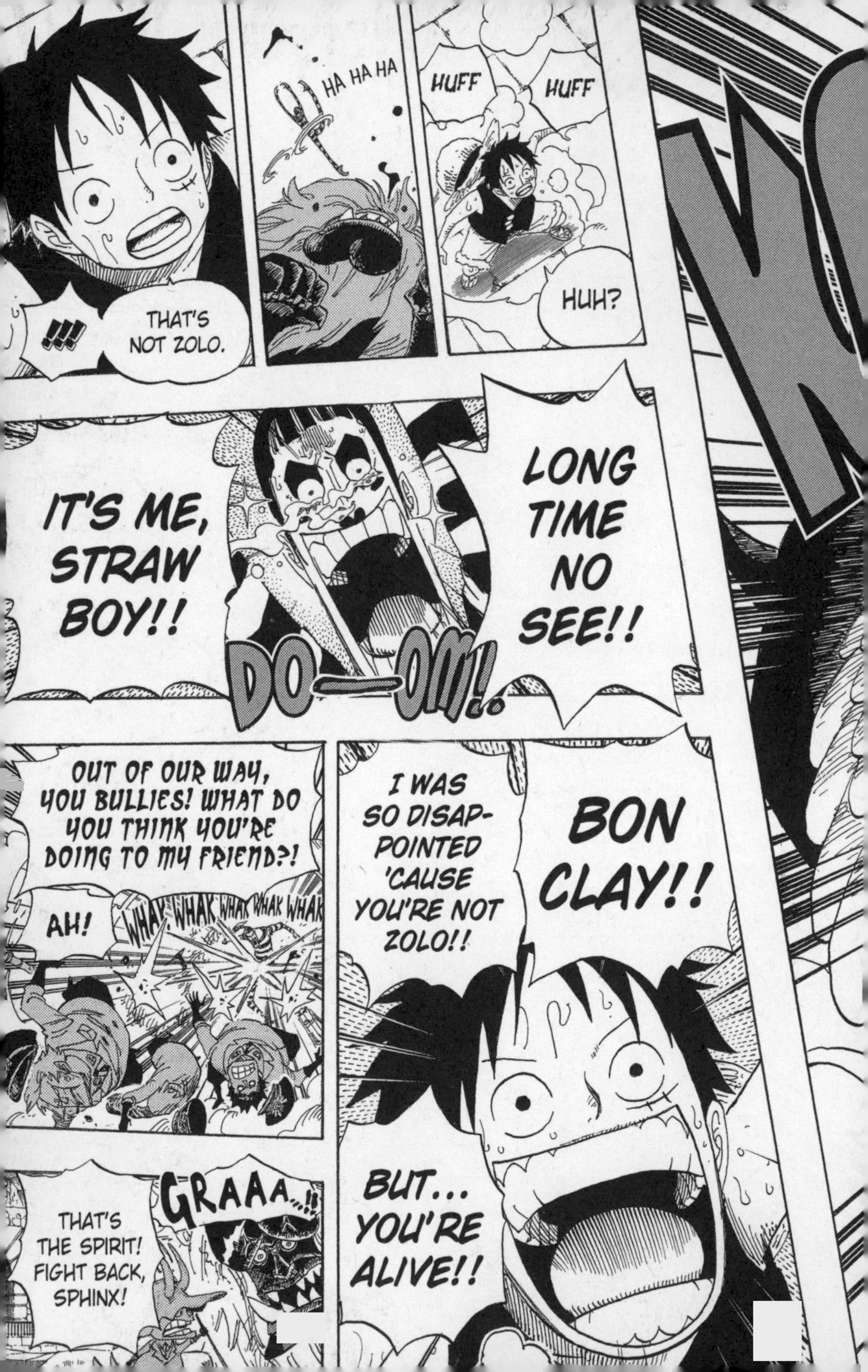

HUFF
HUFF
HUH?
HA HA HA
!!!
THAT'S NOT ZOLO.
LONG TIME NO SEE!!
DO—OM!..
IT'S ME, STRAW BOY!!
BON CLAY!!
I WAS SO DISAP-POINTED 'CAUSE YOU'RE NOT ZOLO!!
BUT... YOU'RE ALIVE!!
OUT OF OUR WAY, YOU BULLIES! WHAT DO YOU THINK YOU'RE DOING TO MY FRIEND?!
AH!
WHAK WHAK WHAK WHAK WHAK
GRAAA..!!
THAT'S THE SPIRIT! FIGHT BACK, SPHINX!

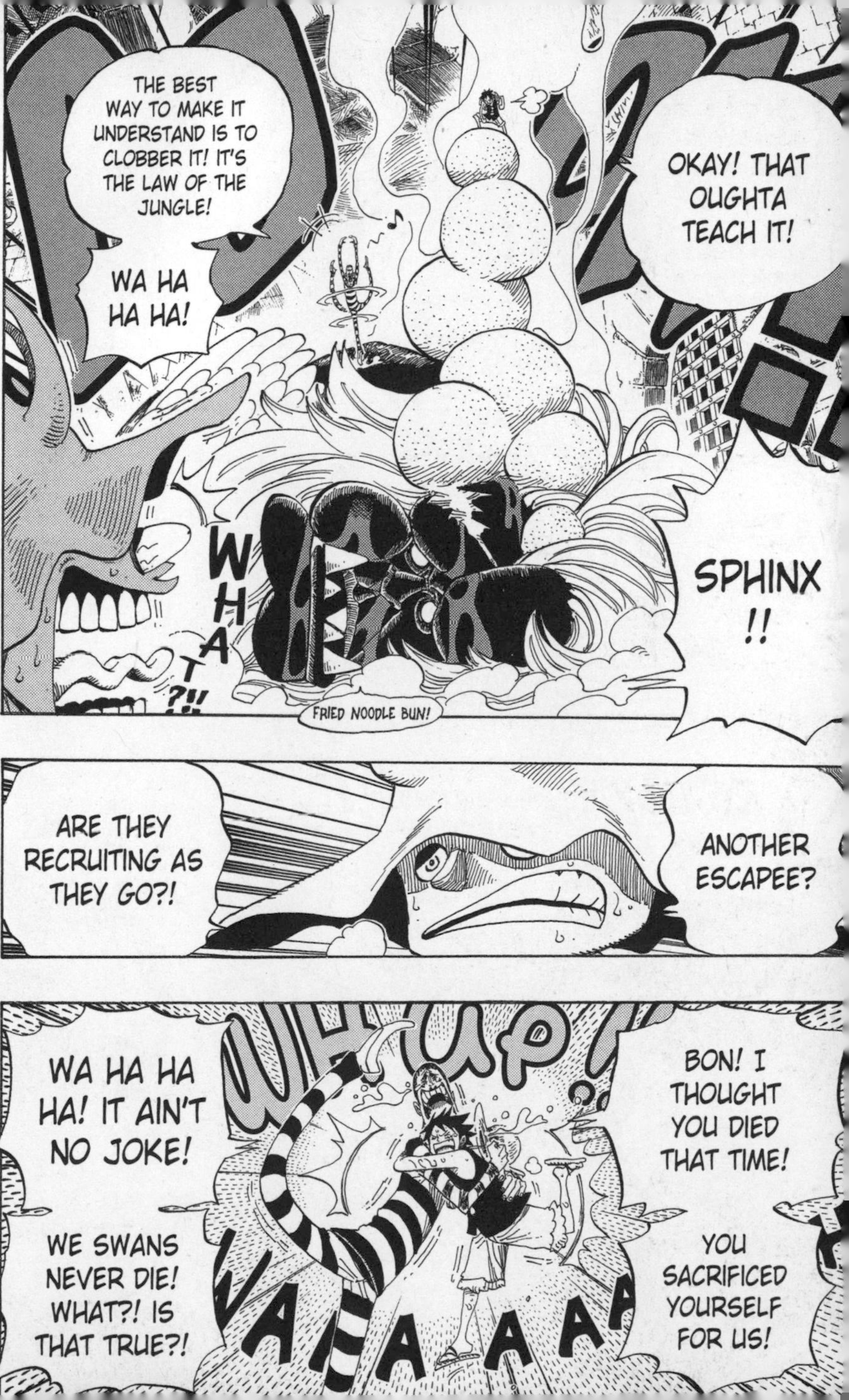
OKAY! THAT OUGHTA TEACH IT!
THE BEST WAY TO MAKE IT UNDERSTAND IS TO CLOBBER IT! IT'S THE LAW OF THE JUNGLE!
WA HA HA HA!
SPHINX!!
WHAT?!!
FRIED NOODLE BUN!
ANOTHER ESCAPEE?
ARE THEY RECRUITING AS THEY GO?!
BON! I THOUGHT YOU DIED THAT TIME!
WA HA HA HA! IT AIN'T NO JOKE!
YOU SACRIFICED YOURSELF FOR US!
WE SWANS NEVER DIE! WHAT?! IS THAT TRUE?!
WAAAAA

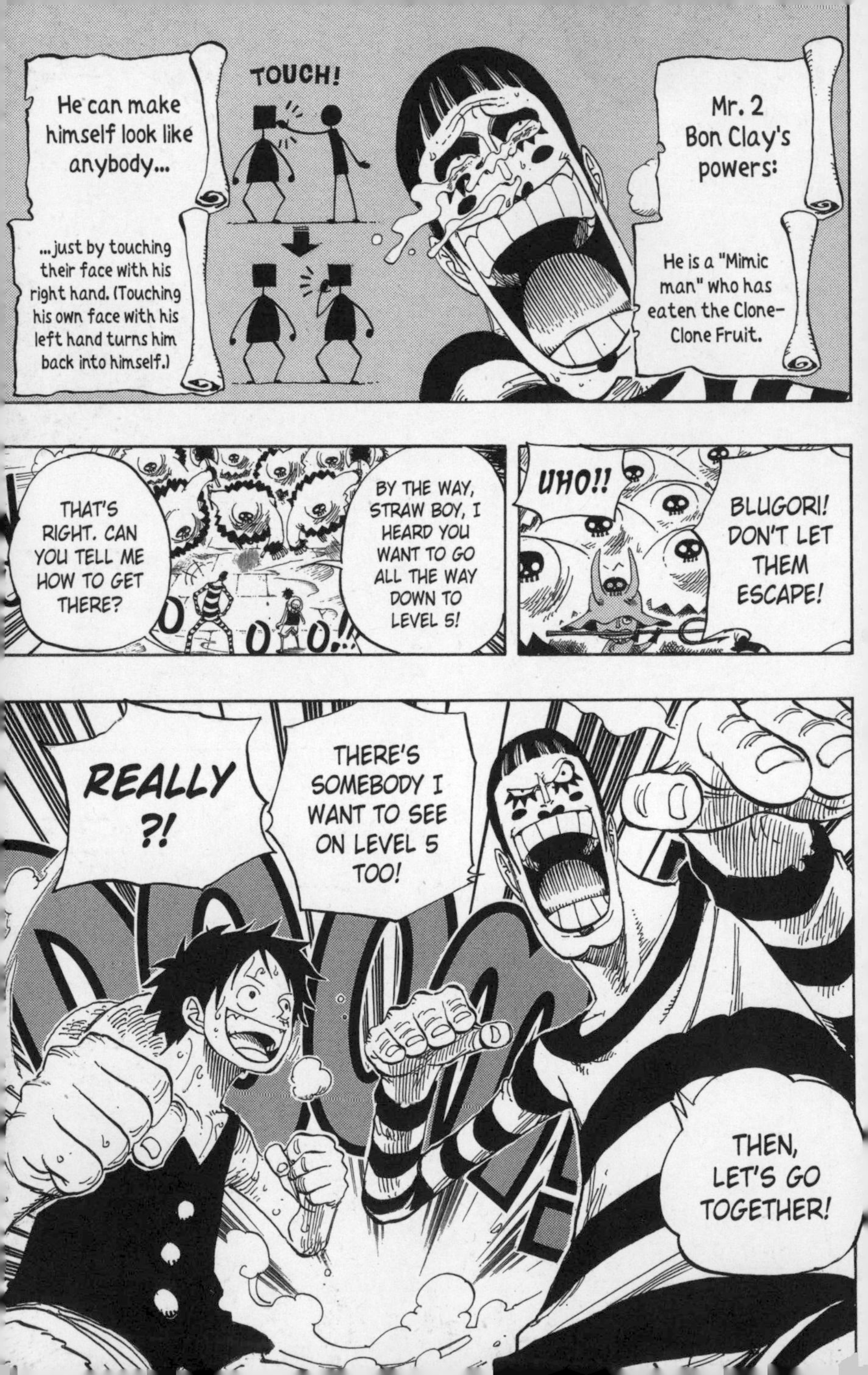

Mr. 2 Bon Clay's powers:
He is a "Mimic man" who has eaten the Clone-Clone Fruit.
He can make himself look like anybody...
TOUCH!
...just by touching their face with his right hand. (Touching his own face with his left hand turns him back into himself.)
BLUGORI! DON'T LET THEM ESCAPE!
UHO!!
BY THE WAY, STRAW BOY, I HEARD YOU WANT TO GO ALL THE WAY DOWN TO LEVEL 5!
THAT'S RIGHT. CAN YOU TELL ME HOW TO GET THERE?
THERE'S SOMEBODY I WANT TO SEE ON LEVEL 5 TOO!
THEN, LET'S GO TOGETHER!
REALLY ?!

JAILER BEAST MINOTAUR

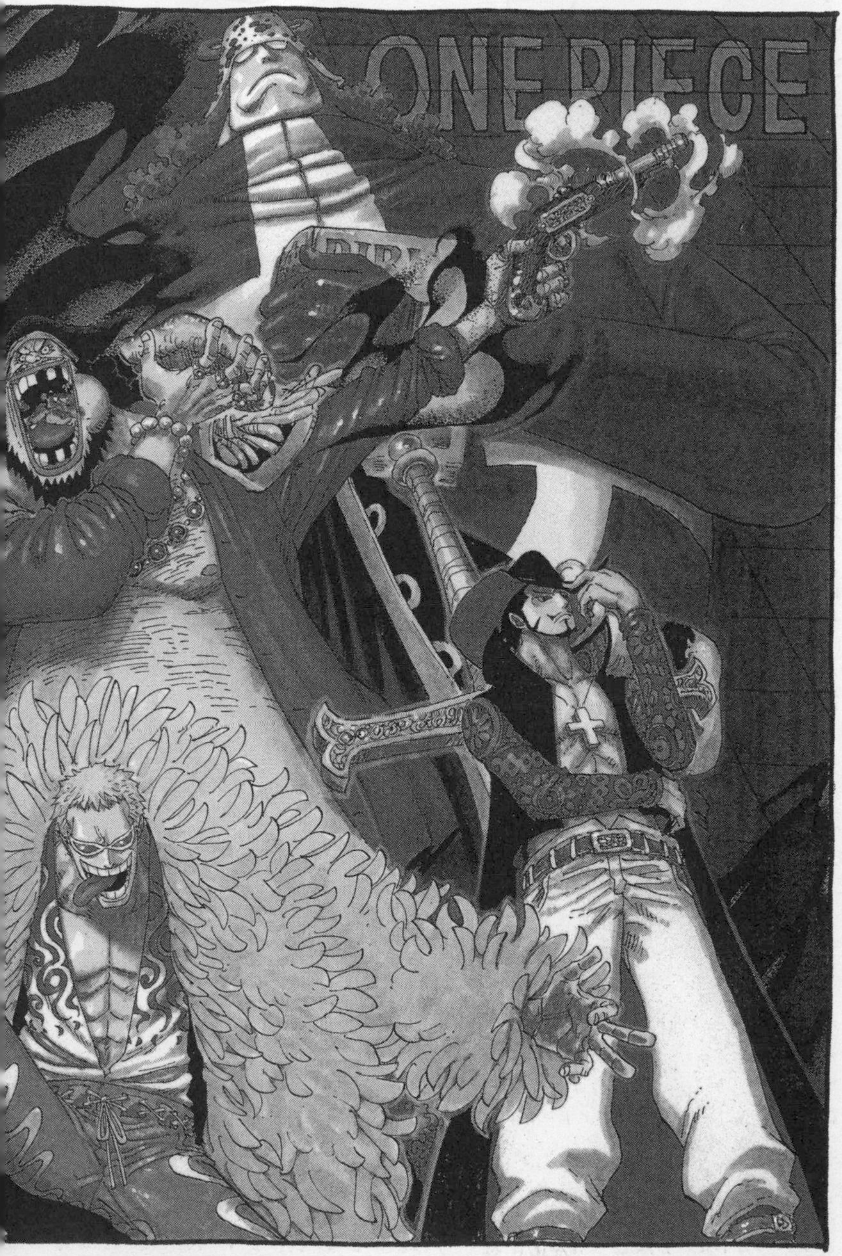
ONE PIECE

Chapter 532:

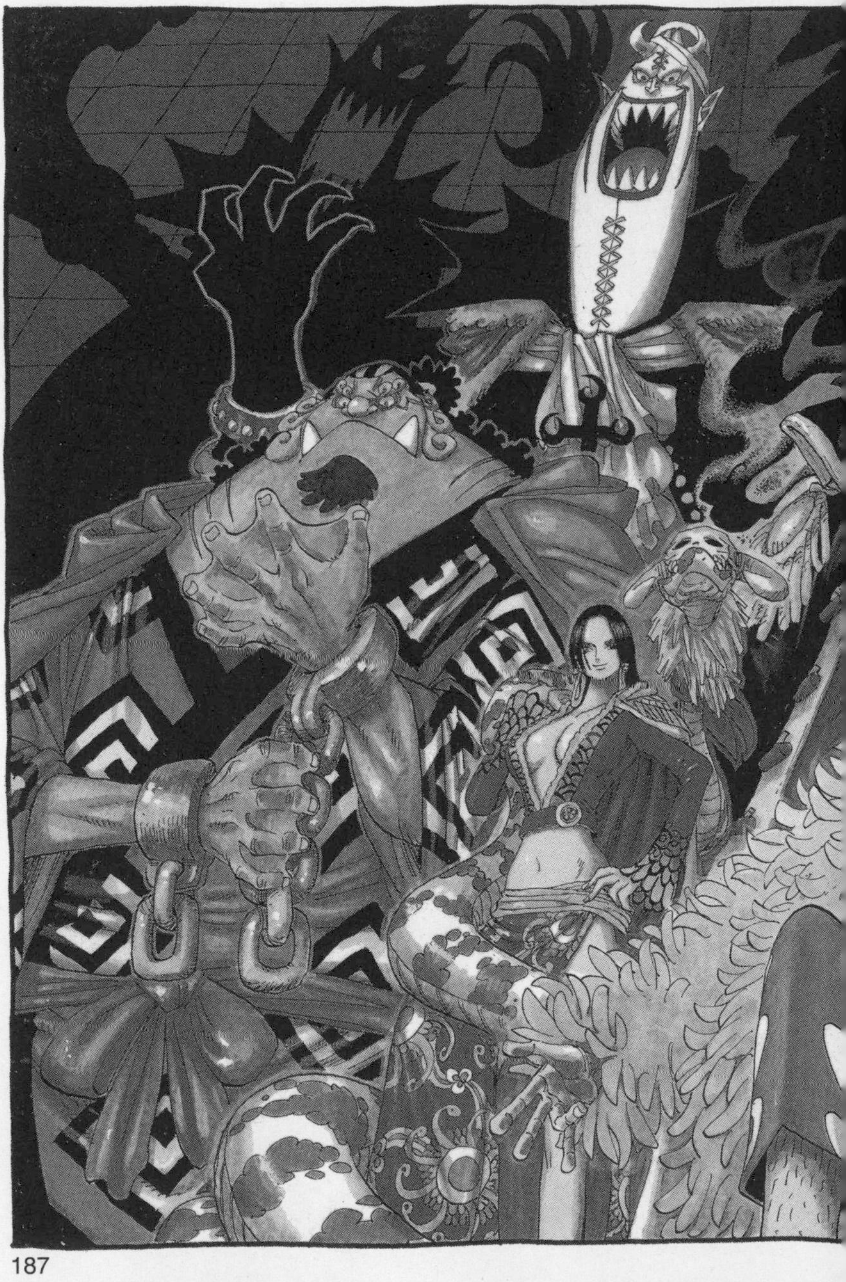

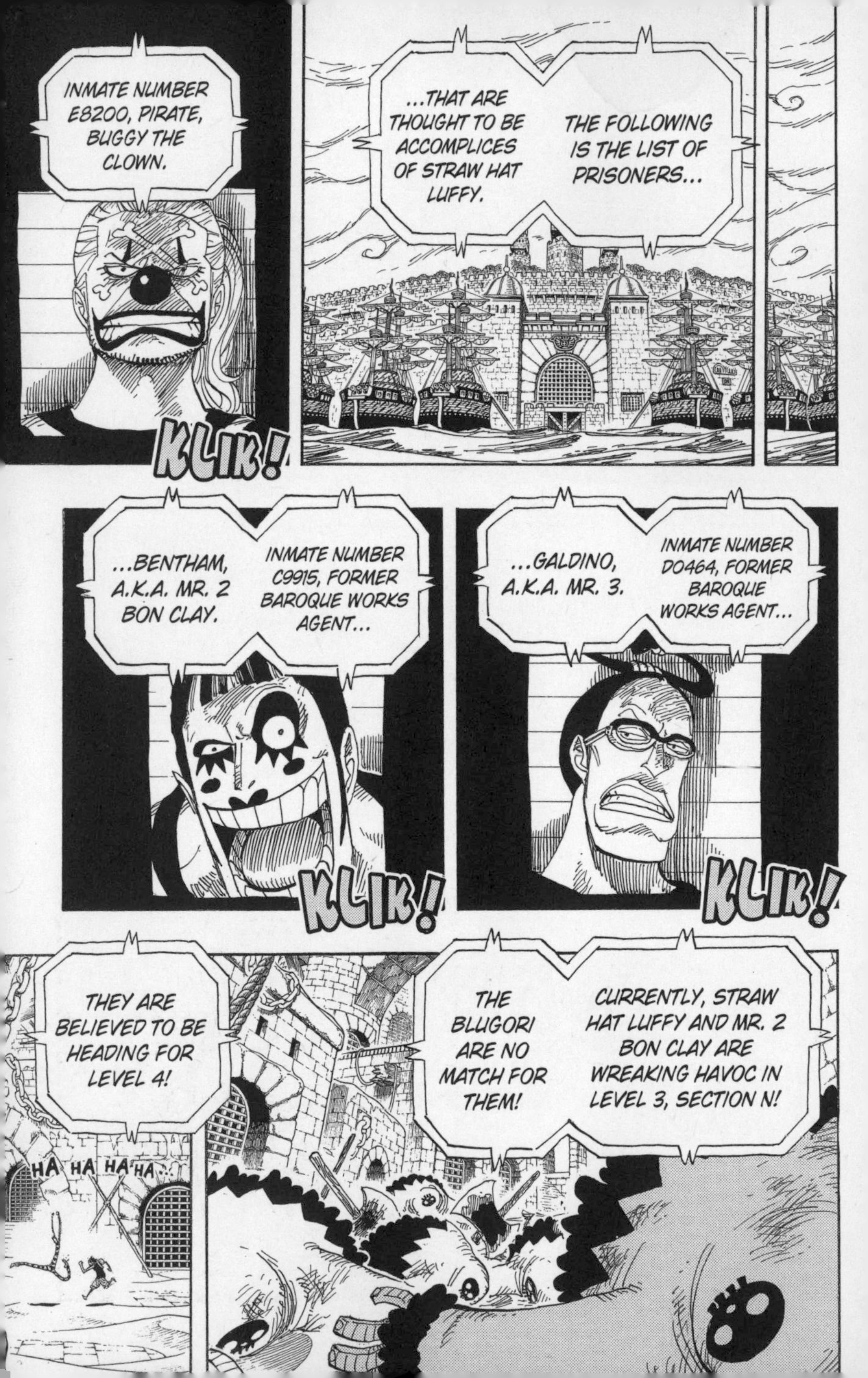
THE FOLLOWING IS THE LIST OF PRISONERS...
...THAT ARE THOUGHT TO BE ACCOMPLICES OF STRAW HAT LUFFY.
INMATE NUMBER E8200, PIRATE, BUGGY THE CLOWN.
KLIK!
INMATE NUMBER D0464, FORMER BAROQUE WORKS AGENT...
...GALDINO, A.K.A. MR. 3.
KLIK!
INMATE NUMBER C9915, FORMER BAROQUE WORKS AGENT...
...BENTHAM, A.K.A. MR. 2 BON CLAY.
KLIK!
CURRENTLY, STRAW HAT LUFFY AND MR. 2 BON CLAY ARE WREAKING HAVOC IN LEVEL 3, SECTION N!
THE BLUGORI ARE NO MATCH FOR THEM!
THEY ARE BELIEVED TO BE HEADING FOR LEVEL 4!
HA HA HA HA...

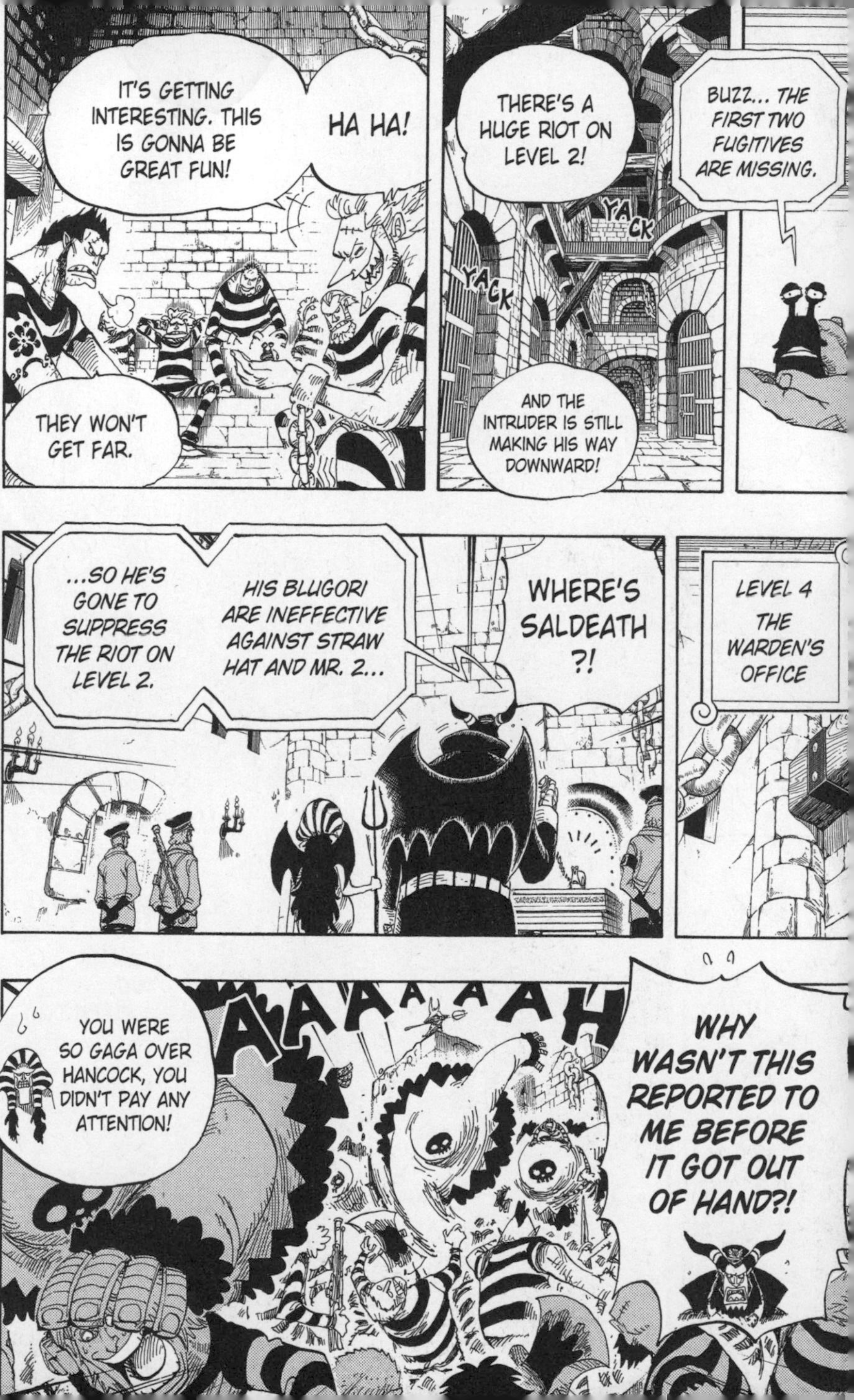
BUZZ... THE FIRST TWO FUGITIVES ARE MISSING.
THERE'S A HUGE RIOT ON LEVEL 2!
YACK
YACK
AND THE INTRUDER IS STILL MAKING HIS WAY DOWNWARD!
HA HA!
IT'S GETTING INTERESTING. THIS IS GONNA BE GREAT FUN!
THEY WON'T GET FAR.
LEVEL 4 THE WARDEN'S OFFICE
WHERE'S SALDEATH ?!
HIS BLUGORI ARE INEFFECTIVE AGAINST STRAW HAT AND MR. 2...
...SO HE'S GONE TO SUPPRESS THE RIOT ON LEVEL 2.
WHY WASN'T THIS REPORTED TO ME BEFORE IT GOT OUT OF HAND?!
AAAAAAAH
YOU WERE SO GAGA OVER HANCOCK, YOU DIDN'T PAY ANY ATTENTION!

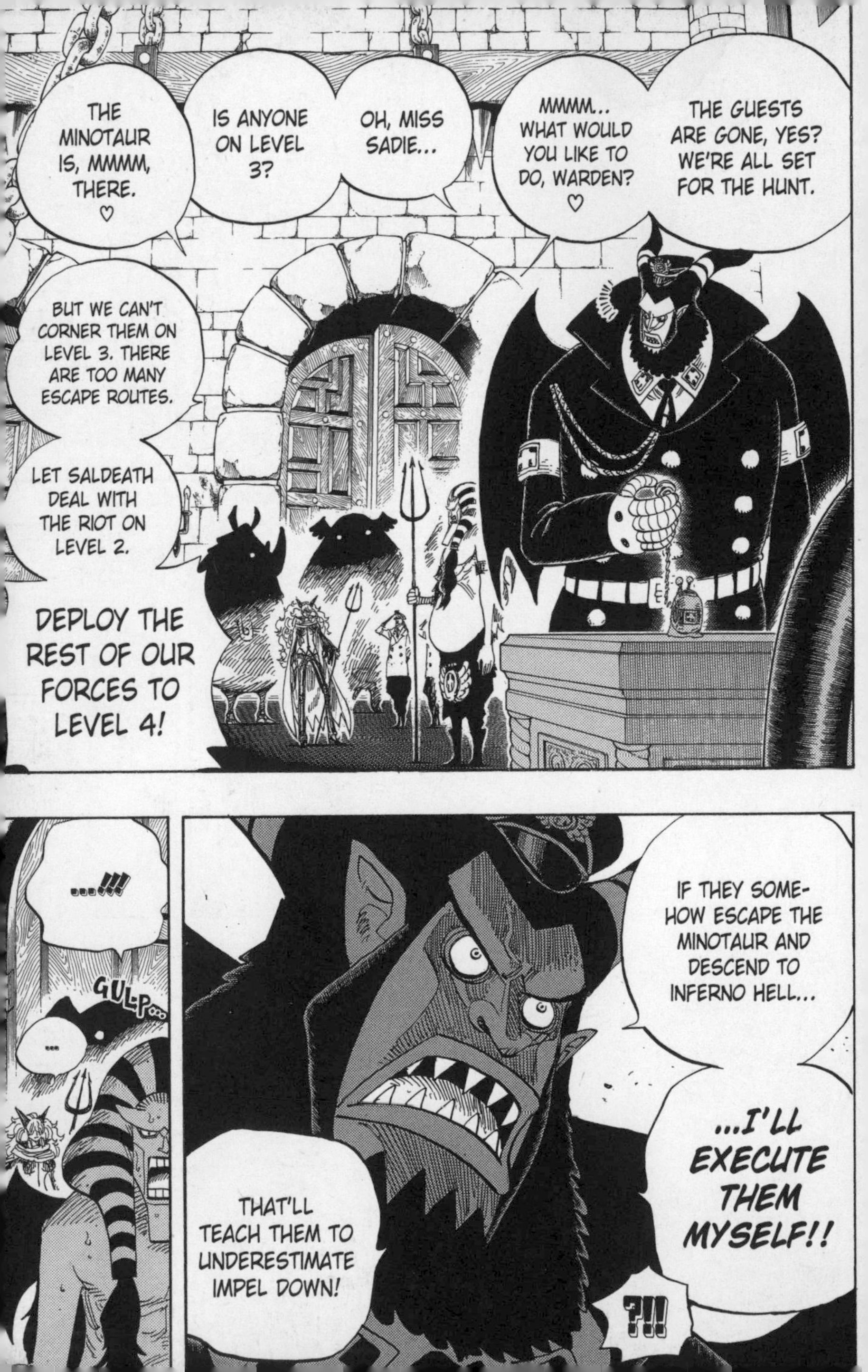
THE GUESTS ARE GONE, YES? WE'RE ALL SET FOR THE HUNT.
MMMM... WHAT WOULD YOU LIKE TO DO, WARDEN? ♡
OH, MISS SADIE...
IS ANYONE ON LEVEL 3?
THE MINOTAUR IS, MMMM, THERE. ♡
BUT WE CAN'T CORNER THEM ON LEVEL 3. THERE ARE TOO MANY ESCAPE ROUTES.
LET SALDEATH DEAL WITH THE RIOT ON LEVEL 2.
DEPLOY THE REST OF OUR FORCES TO LEVEL 4!
IF THEY SOME-HOW ESCAPE THE MINOTAUR AND DESCEND TO INFERNO HELL...
...I'LL EXECUTE THEM MYSELF!!
THAT'LL TEACH THEM TO UNDERESTIMATE IMPEL DOWN!
?!!
...!!!
GULP...
...

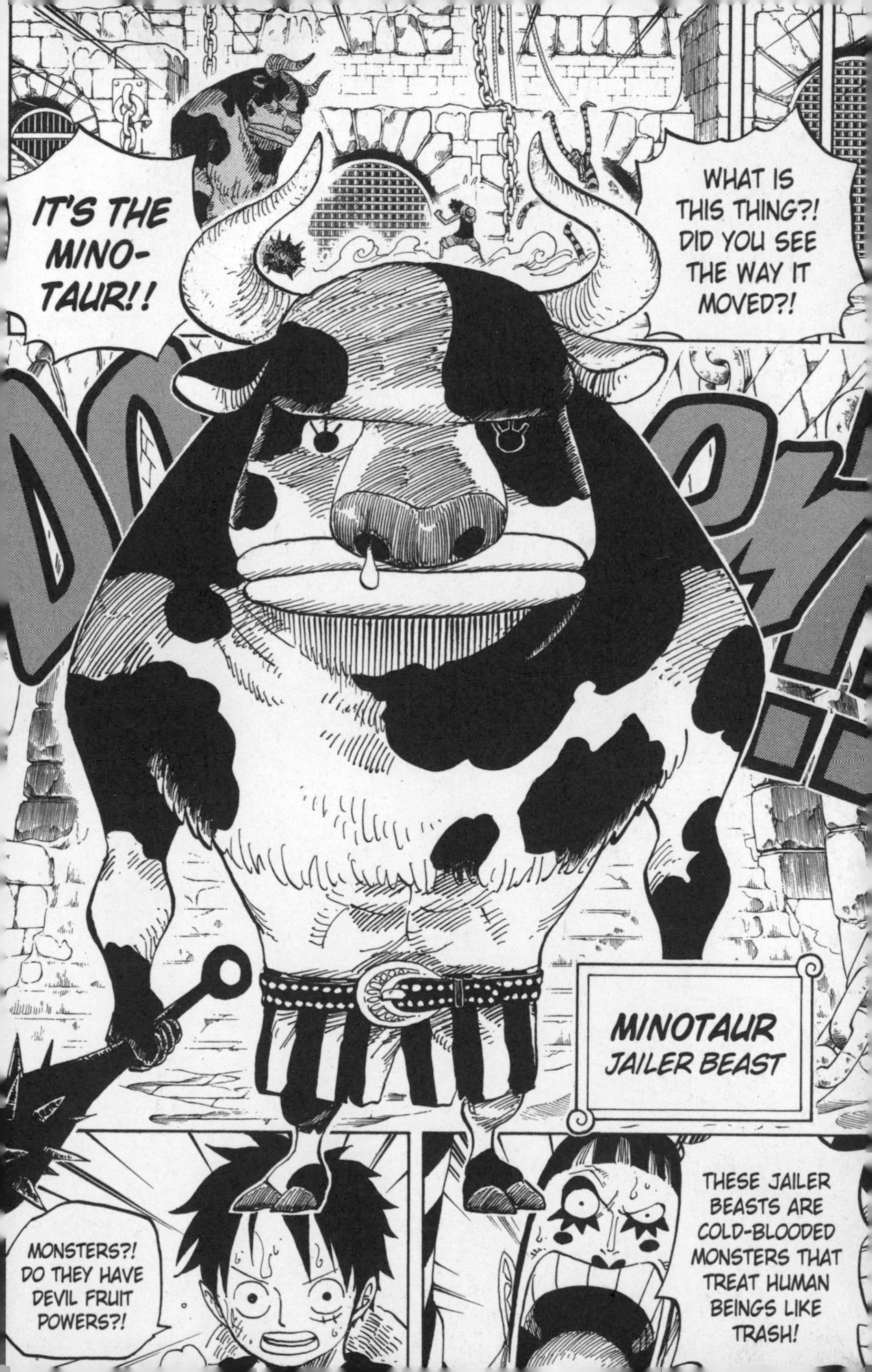
WHAT IS THIS THING?! DID YOU SEE THE WAY IT MOVED?!
IT'S THE MINO-TAUR!!
MINOTAUR
JAILER BEAST
THESE JAILER BEASTS ARE COLD-BLOODED MONSTERS THAT TREAT HUMAN BEINGS LIKE TRASH!
MONSTERS?! DO THEY HAVE DEVIL FRUIT POWERS?!

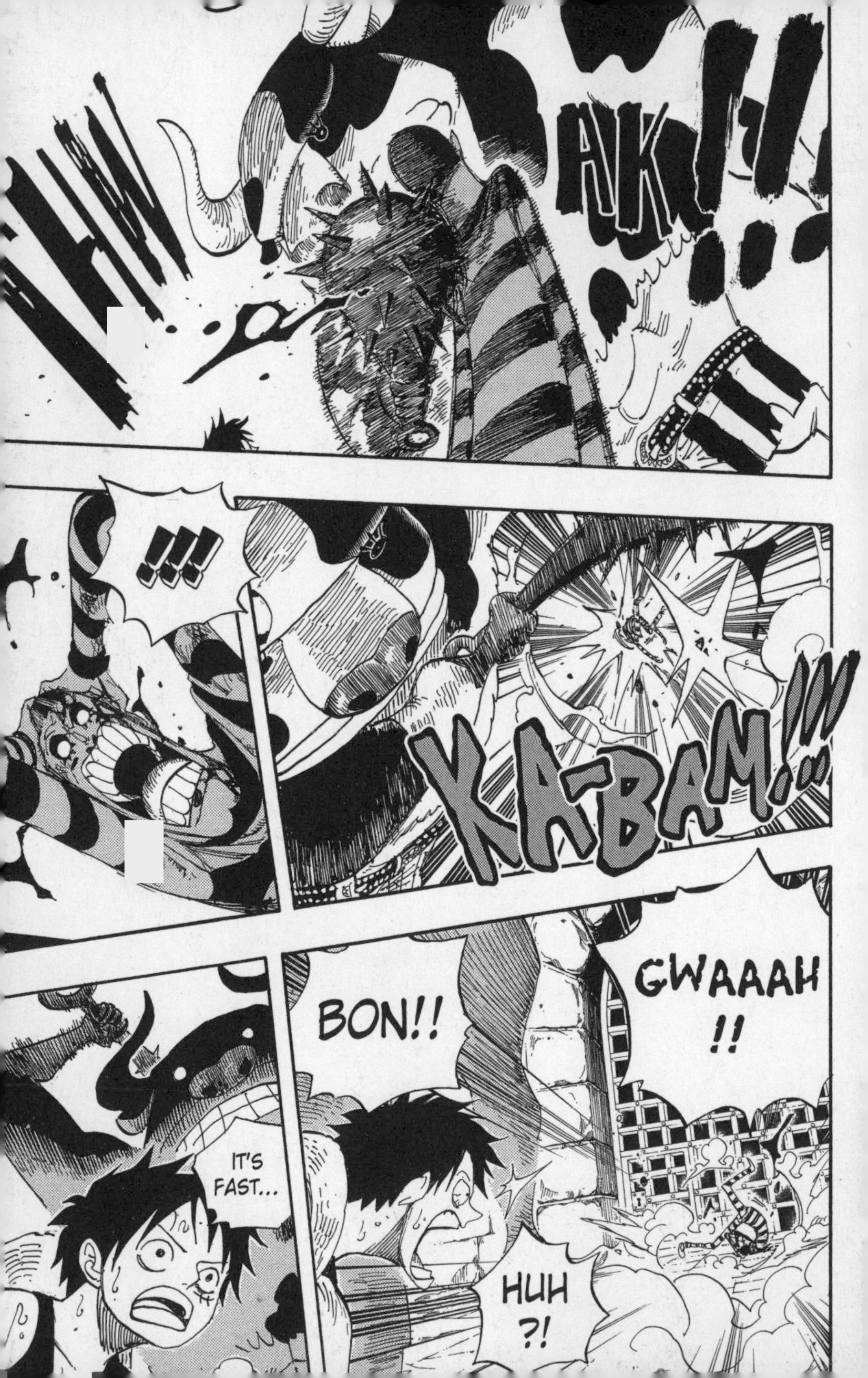
AK!!
KA-BAM!!!
!!!
GWAAAH !!
BON!!
HUH ?!
IT'S FAST...

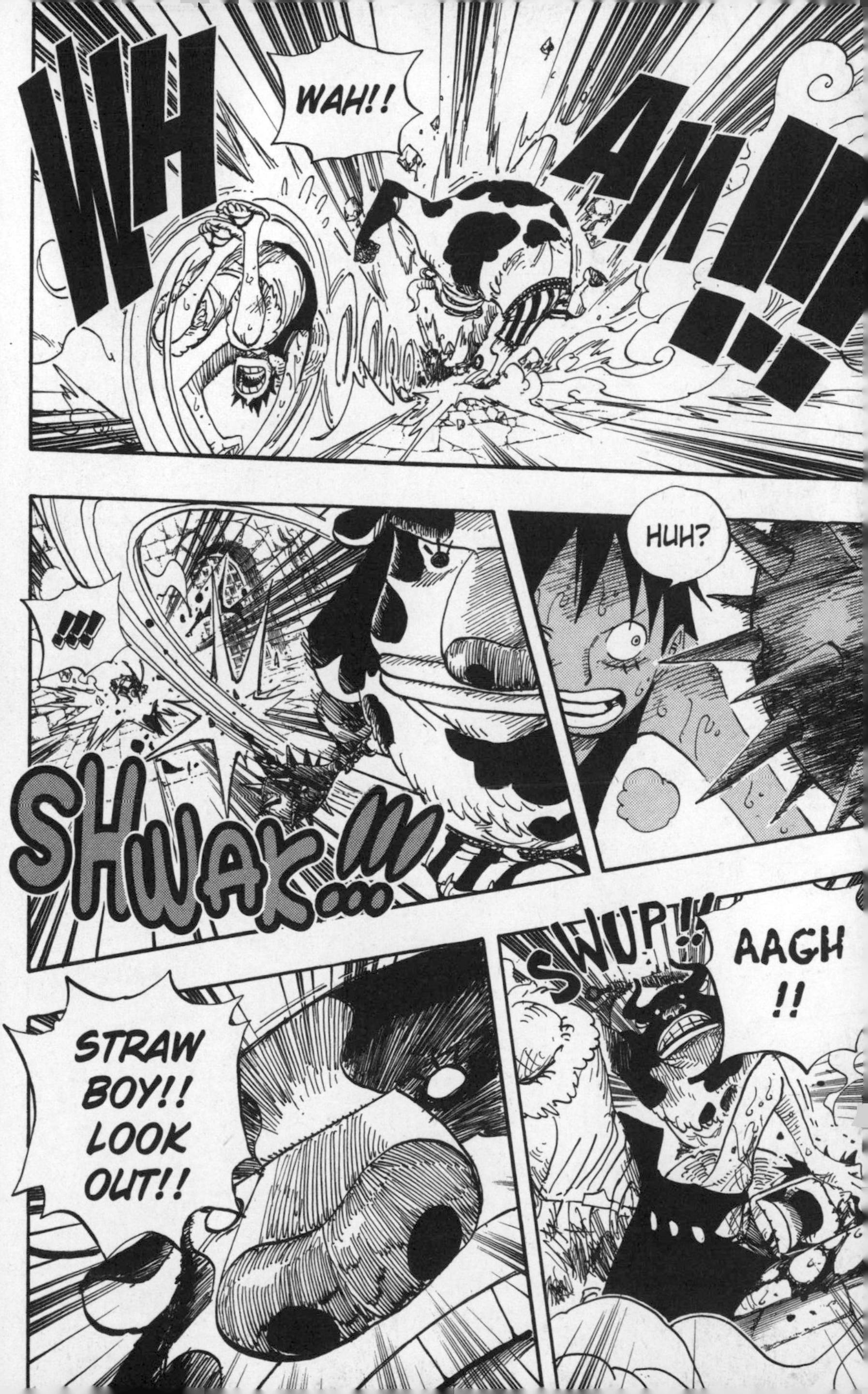
WHAM!!
WAH!!
HUH?
!!!
SHWAK...!!!
AAGH!!
SWUP!!
STRAW BOY!! LOOK OUT!!

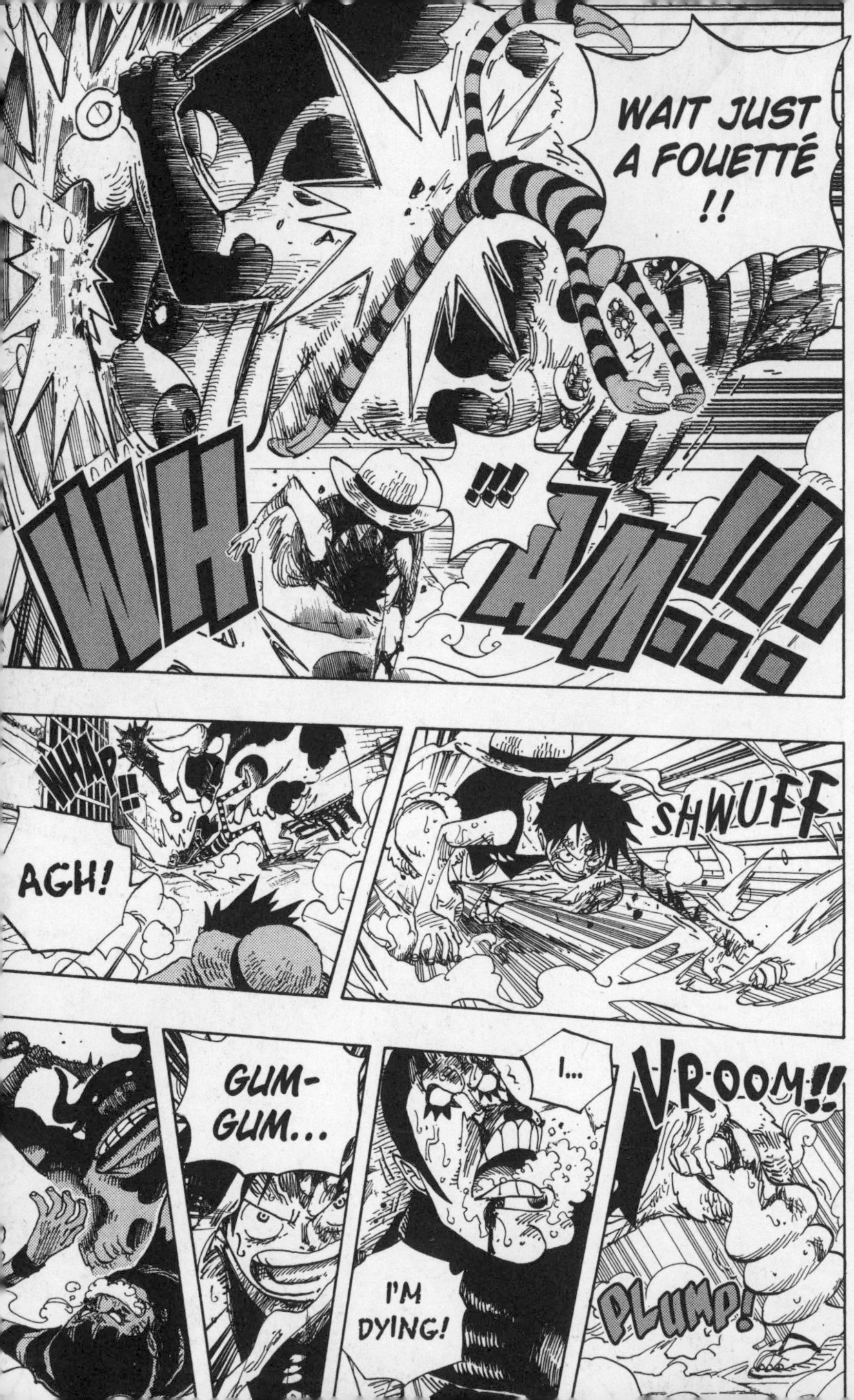
WAIT JUST A FOUETTÉ !!
!!!
WHAM...!!
SHWUFF
WHAP!!
AGH!
VROOM!!
PLUMP!
I...
I'M DYING!
GUM-GUM...

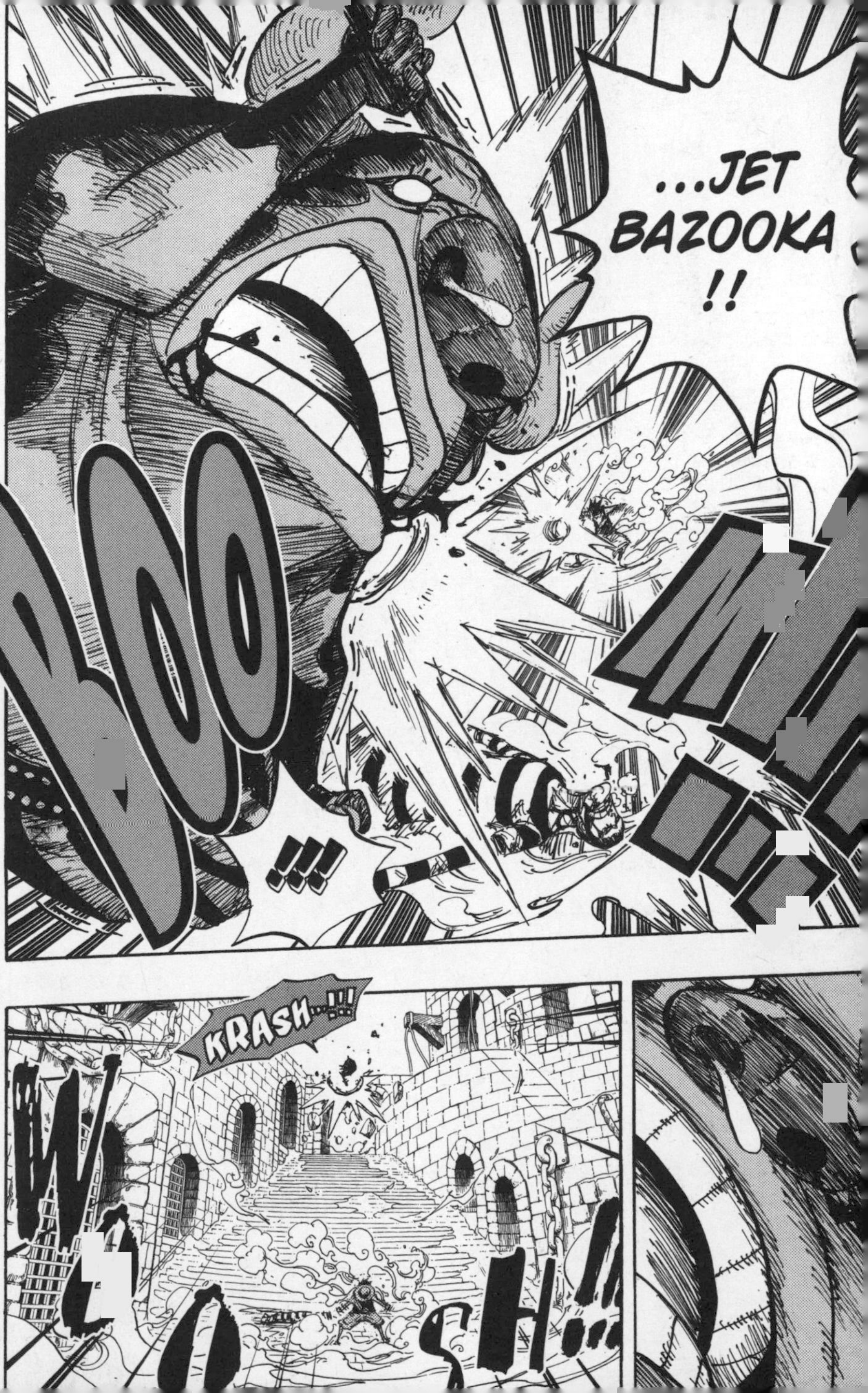
...JET BAZOOKA !!
KRASH...!!!

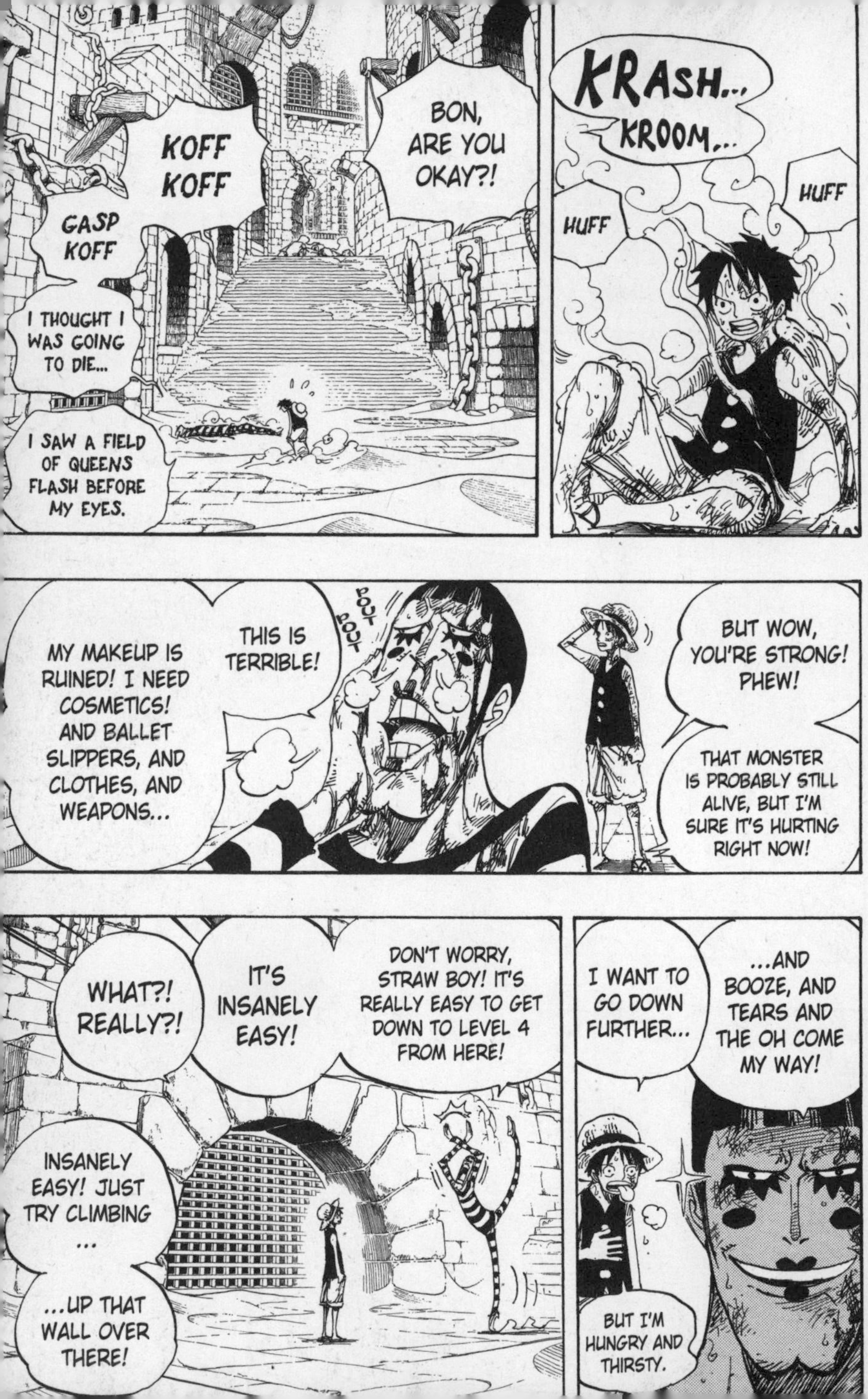
KRASH...
KROOM...
HUFF
HUFF
BON, ARE YOU OKAY?!
KOFF KOFF
GASP KOFF
I THOUGHT I WAS GOING TO DIE...
I SAW A FIELD OF QUEENS FLASH BEFORE MY EYES.
BUT WOW, YOU'RE STRONG! PHEW!
THAT MONSTER IS PROBABLY STILL ALIVE, BUT I'M SURE IT'S HURTING RIGHT NOW!
POUT POUT
THIS IS TERRIBLE!
MY MAKEUP IS RUINED! I NEED COSMETICS! AND BALLET SLIPPERS, AND CLOTHES, AND WEAPONS...
...AND BOOZE, AND TEARS AND THE OH COME MY WAY!
I WANT TO GO DOWN FURTHER...
BUT I'M HUNGRY AND THIRSTY.
DON'T WORRY, STRAW BOY! IT'S REALLY EASY TO GET DOWN TO LEVEL 4 FROM HERE!
IT'S INSANELY EASY!
WHAT?! REALLY?!
INSANELY EASY! JUST TRY CLIMBING ...
...UP THAT WALL OVER THERE!

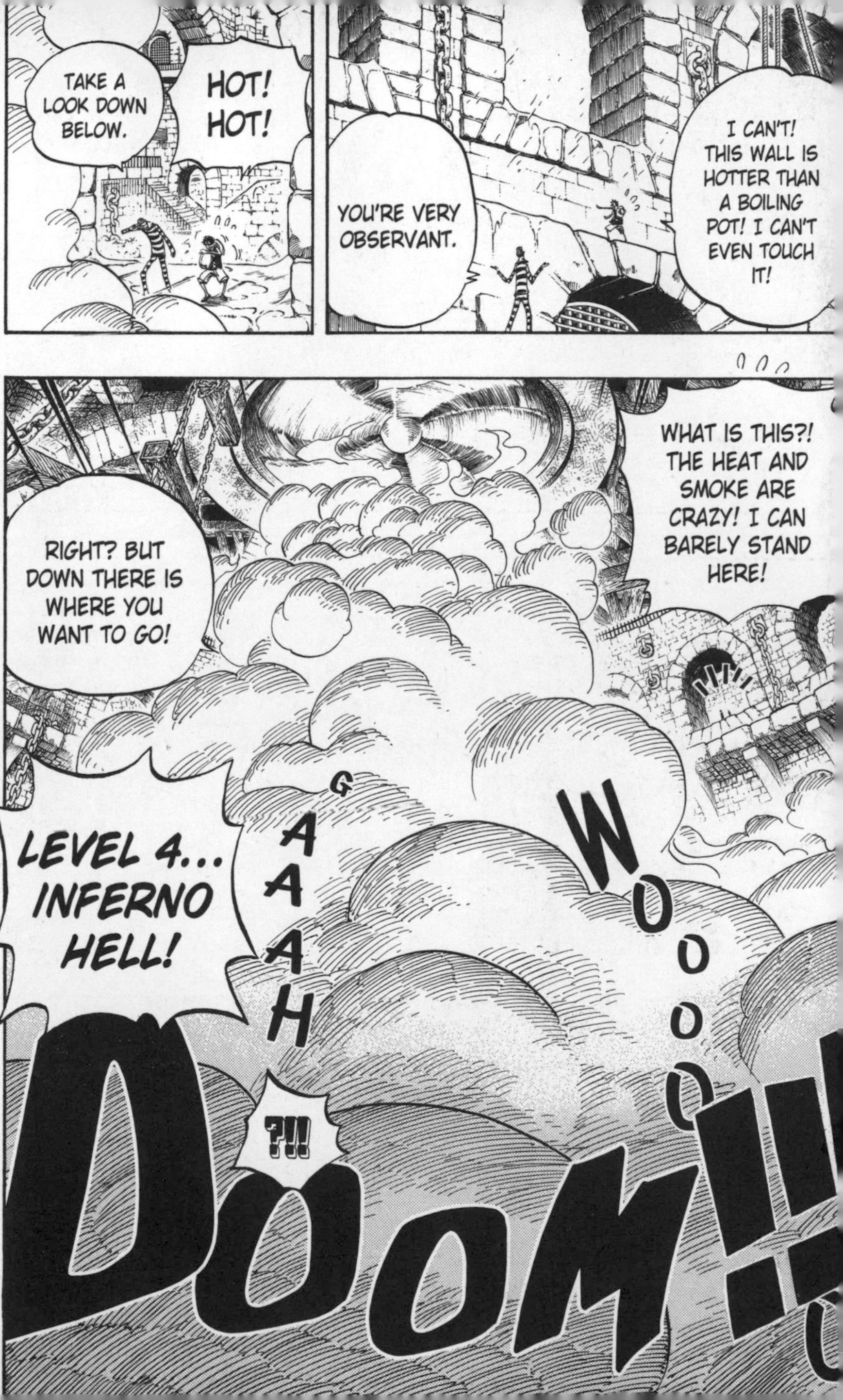
I CAN'T! THIS WALL IS HOTTER THAN A BOILING POT! I CAN'T EVEN TOUCH IT!
YOU'RE VERY OBSERVANT.
HOT! HOT!
TAKE A LOOK DOWN BELOW.
WHAT IS THIS?! THE HEAT AND SMOKE ARE CRAZY! I CAN BARELY STAND HERE!
RIGHT? BUT DOWN THERE IS WHERE YOU WANT TO GO!
LEVEL 4... INFERNO HELL!
WOOOO
GAAAH
?!!
DOOM!!!

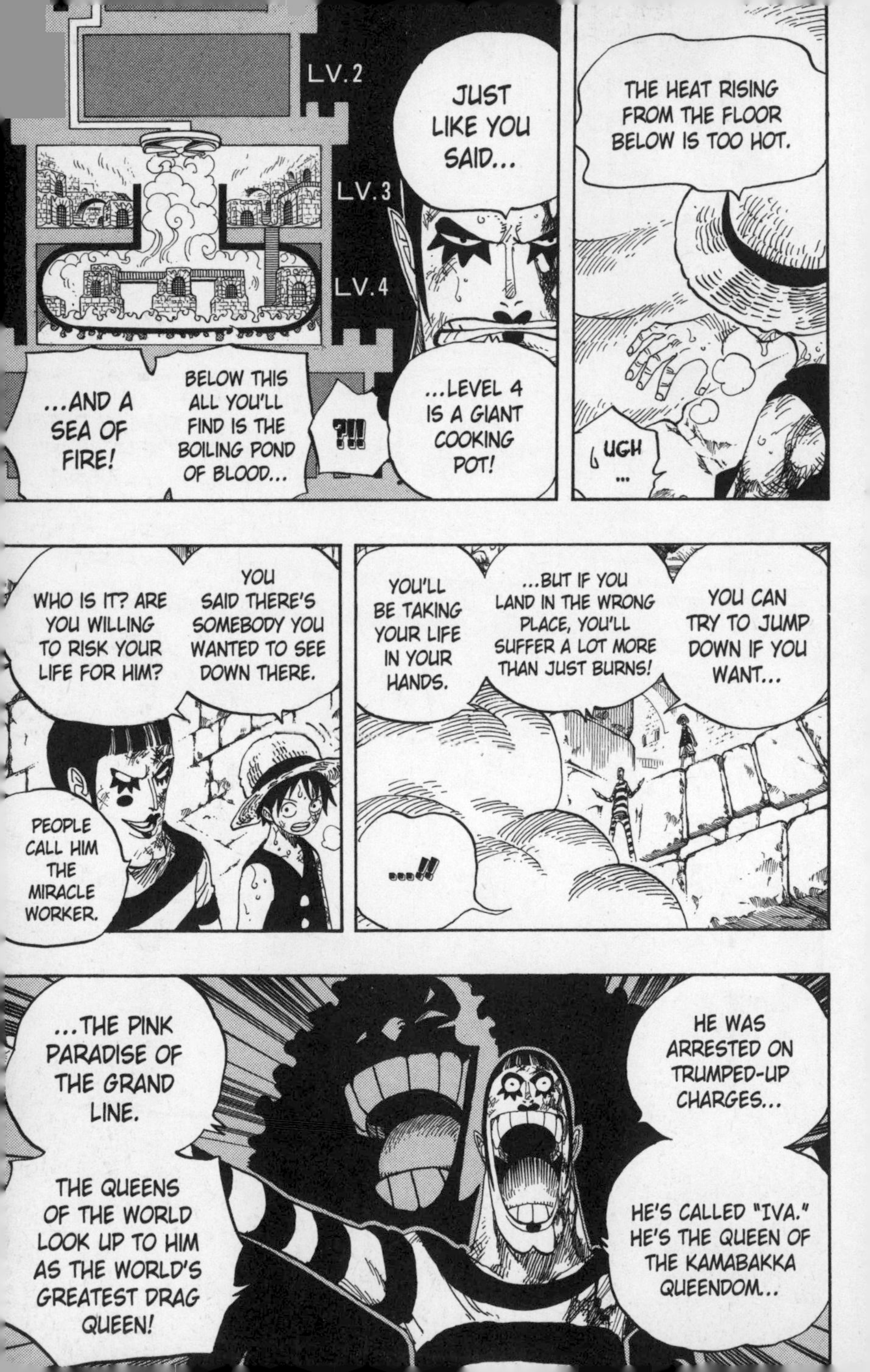
THE HEAT RISING FROM THE FLOOR BELOW IS TOO HOT.
UGH...
JUST LIKE YOU SAID...
...LEVEL 4 IS A GIANT COOKING POT!
LV. 2
LV. 3
LV. 4
?!!
BELOW THIS ALL YOU'LL FIND IS THE BOILING POND OF BLOOD...
...AND A SEA OF FIRE!
YOU CAN TRY TO JUMP DOWN IF YOU WANT...
...BUT IF YOU LAND IN THE WRONG PLACE, YOU'LL SUFFER A LOT MORE THAN JUST BURNS!
YOU'LL BE TAKING YOUR LIFE IN YOUR HANDS.
...!!
YOU SAID THERE'S SOMEBODY YOU WANTED TO SEE DOWN THERE.
WHO IS IT? ARE YOU WILLING TO RISK YOUR LIFE FOR HIM?
PEOPLE CALL HIM THE MIRACLE WORKER.
HE WAS ARRESTED ON TRUMPED-UP CHARGES...
...THE PINK PARADISE OF THE GRAND LINE.
HE'S CALLED "IVA." HE'S THE QUEEN OF THE KAMABAKKA QUEENDOM...
THE QUEENS OF THE WORLD LOOK UP TO HIM AS THE WORLD'S GREATEST DRAG QUEEN!

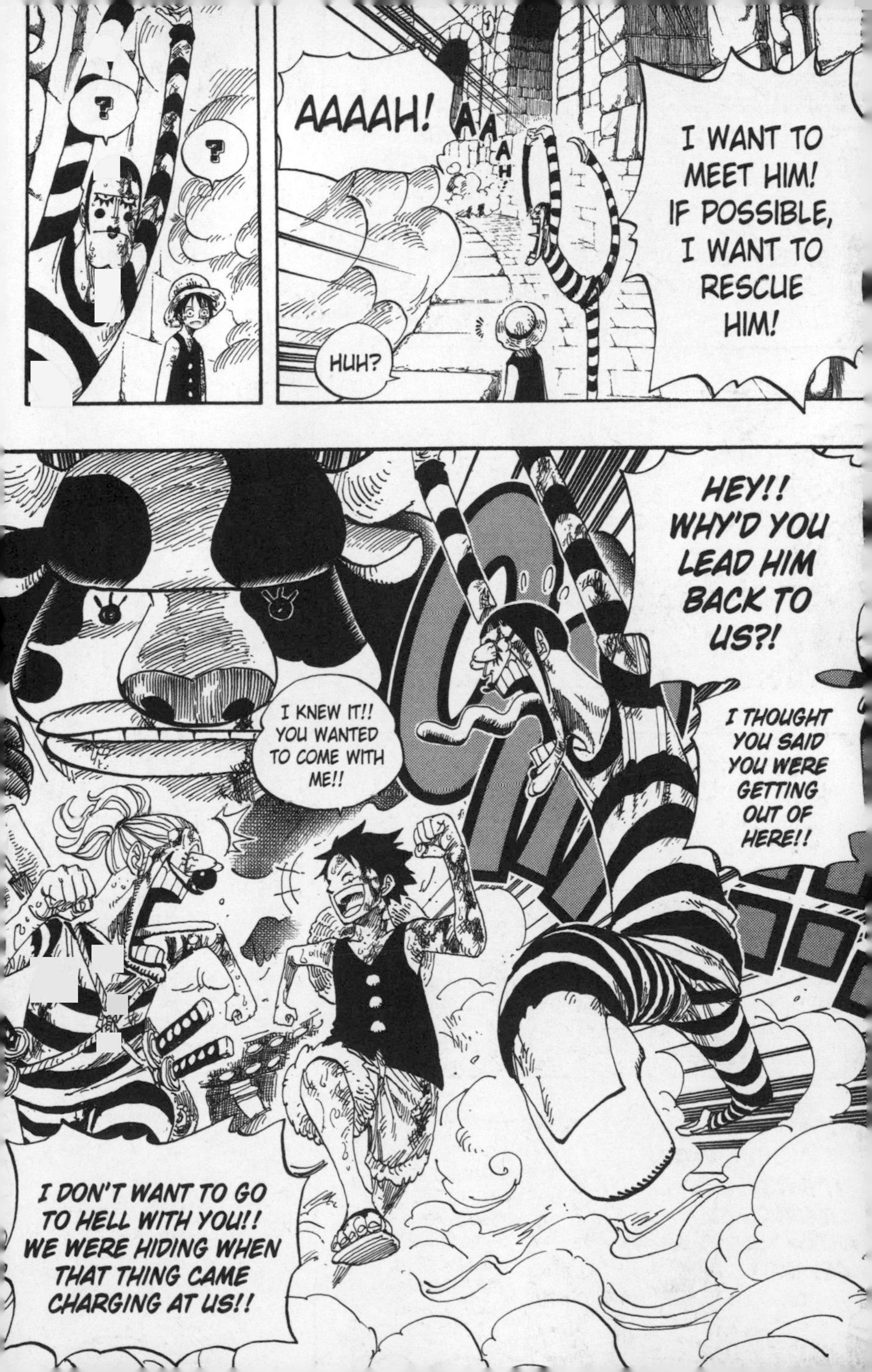
I WANT TO MEET HIM! IF POSSIBLE, I WANT TO RESCUE HIM!
AAAAH!
AAAH!
HUH?
?
?
HEY!! WHY'D YOU LEAD HIM BACK TO US?!
I THOUGHT YOU SAID YOU WERE GETTING OUT OF HERE!!
I KNEW IT!! YOU WANTED TO COME WITH ME!!
I DON'T WANT TO GO TO HELL WITH YOU!! WE WERE HIDING WHEN THAT THING CAME CHARGING AT US!!

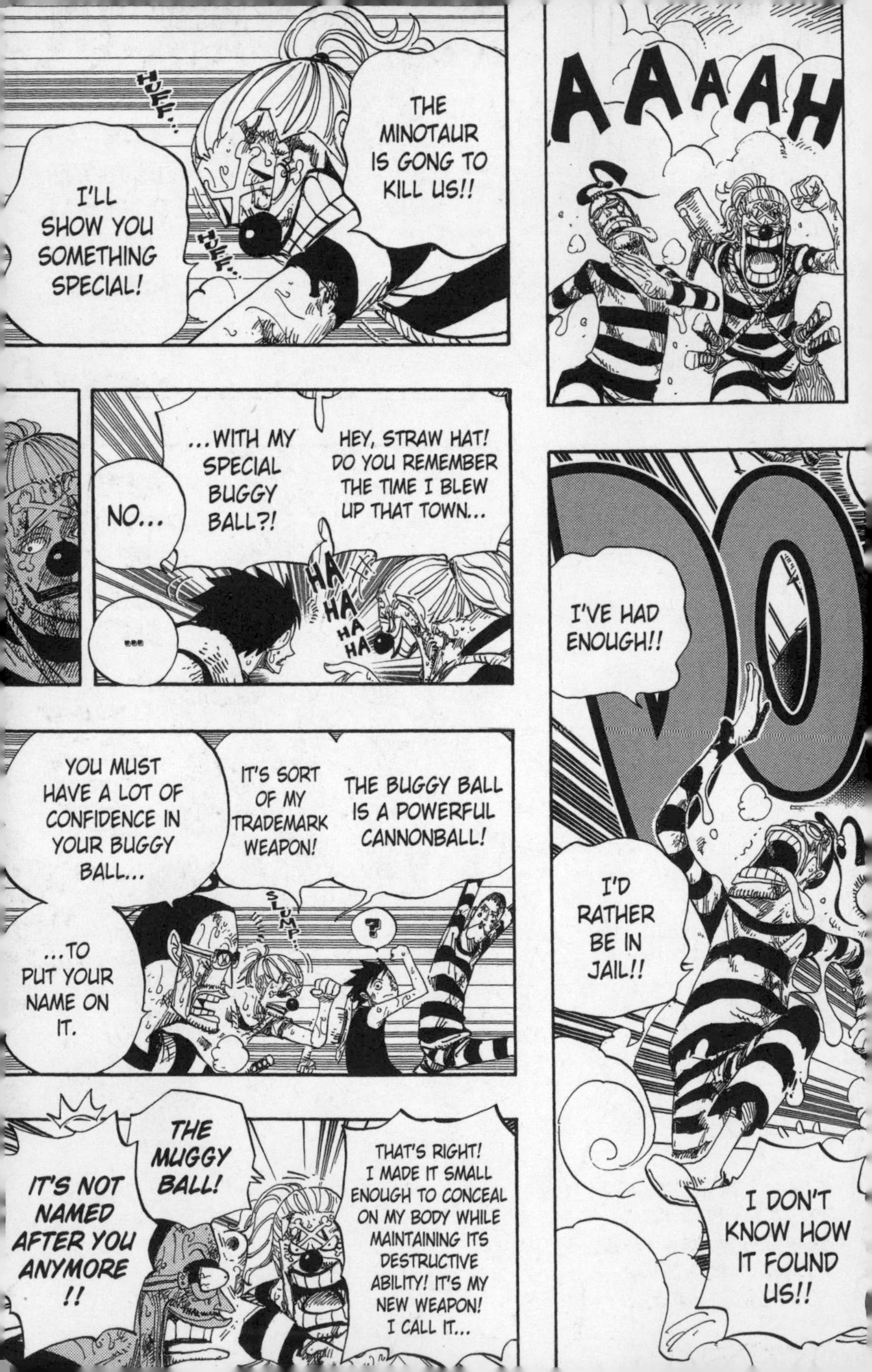
AAAAH
HUFF...
THE MINOTAUR IS GONG TO KILL US!!
I'LL SHOW YOU SOMETHING SPECIAL!
HUFF...
I'VE HAD ENOUGH!!
I'D RATHER BE IN JAIL!!
I DON'T KNOW HOW IT FOUND US!!
HEY, STRAW HAT! DO YOU REMEMBER THE TIME I BLEW UP THAT TOWN...
...WITH MY SPECIAL BUGGY BALL?!
HA HA HA HA
NO...
...
THE BUGGY BALL IS A POWERFUL CANNONBALL!
IT'S SORT OF MY TRADEMARK WEAPON!
YOU MUST HAVE A LOT OF CONFIDENCE IN YOUR BUGGY BALL...
?
SLUMP...
...TO PUT YOUR NAME ON IT.
THAT'S RIGHT! I MADE IT SMALL ENOUGH TO CONCEAL ON MY BODY WHILE MAINTAINING ITS DESTRUCTIVE ABILITY! IT'S MY NEW WEAPON! I CALL IT...
THE MUGGY BALL!
IT'S NOT NAMED AFTER YOU ANYMORE!!

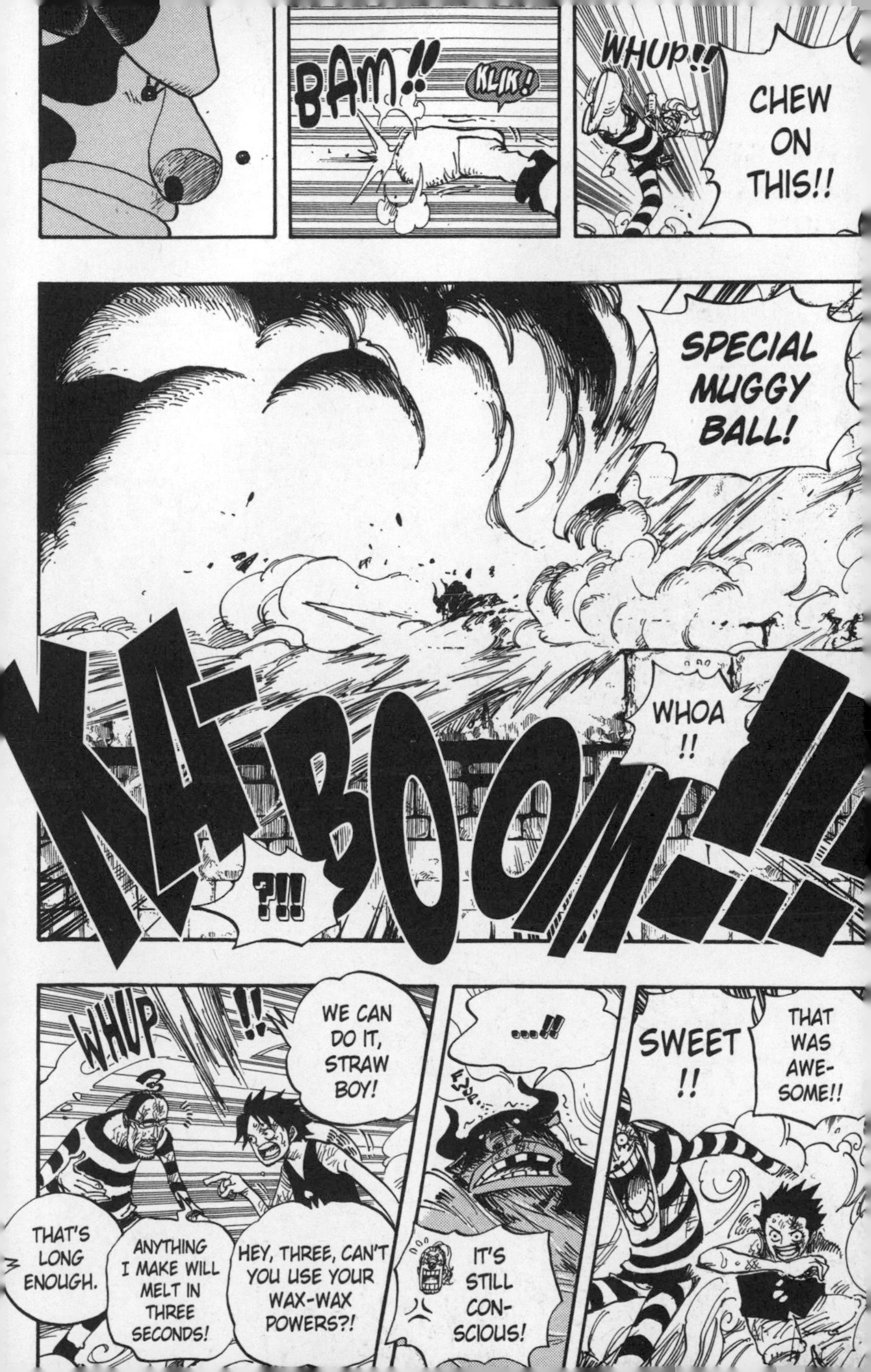
WHUP!!
CHEW ON THIS!!
BAM!!
KLIK!
SPECIAL MUGGY BALL!
WHOA !!
KA-BOOM!!!
?!!
THAT WAS AWE-SOME!!
SWEET !!
...!!
IT'S STILL CON-SCIOUS!
WHUP !!
WE CAN DO IT, STRAW BOY!
HEY, THREE, CAN'T YOU USE YOUR WAX-WAX POWERS?!
ANYTHING I MAKE WILL MELT IN THREE SECONDS!
THAT'S LONG ENOUGH.

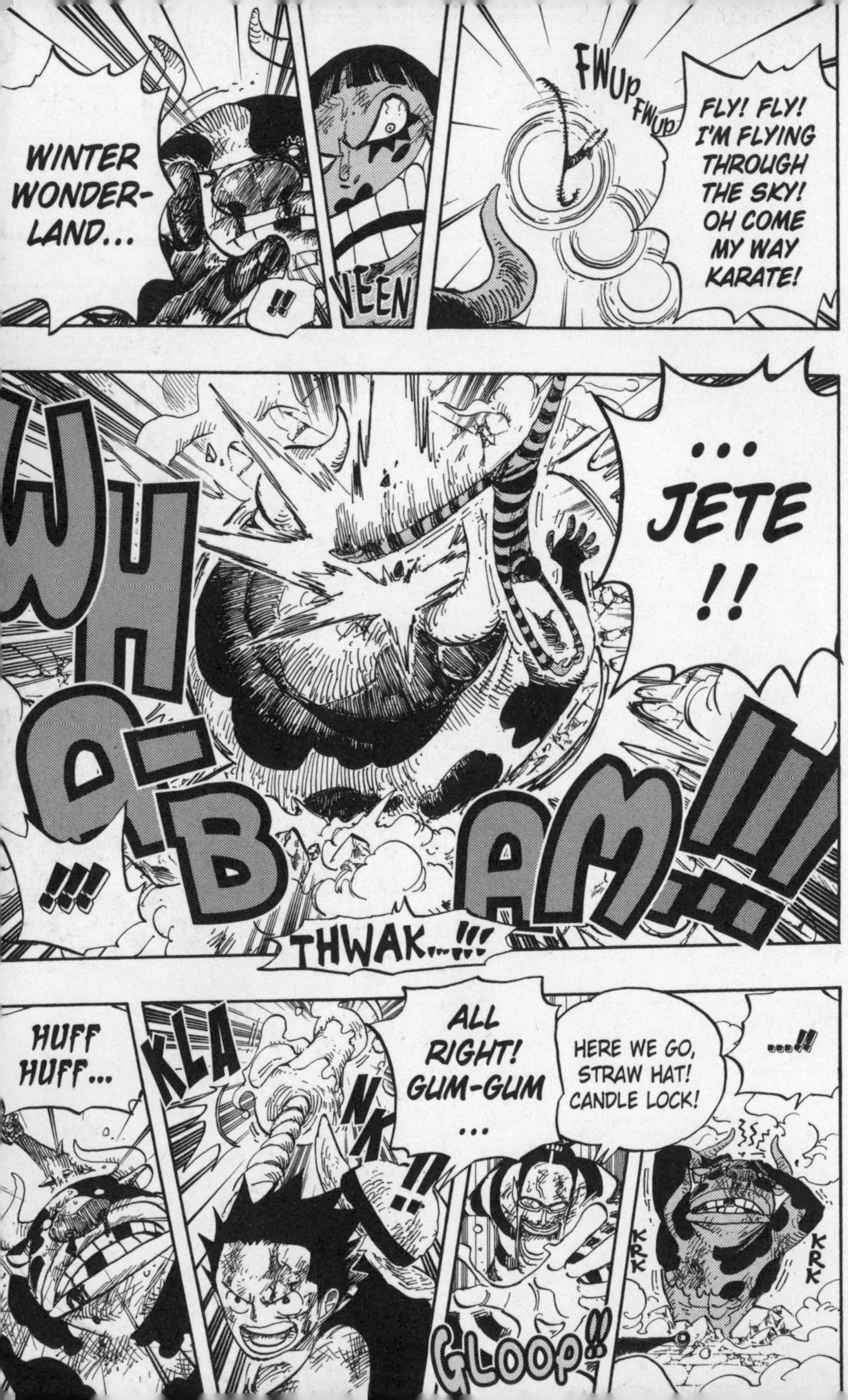
FWUP FWUP
FLY! FLY! I'M FLYING THROUGH THE SKY! OH COME MY WAY KARATE!
VEEN
!!
WINTER WONDER-LAND...
...JETE!!
WHA-BAM!!!
THWAK...!!!
...!!
KRK
KRK
HERE WE GO, STRAW HAT! CANDLE LOCK!
GLOOP!!
ALL RIGHT! GUM-GUM ...
KLA
NK!!
HUFF HUFF...

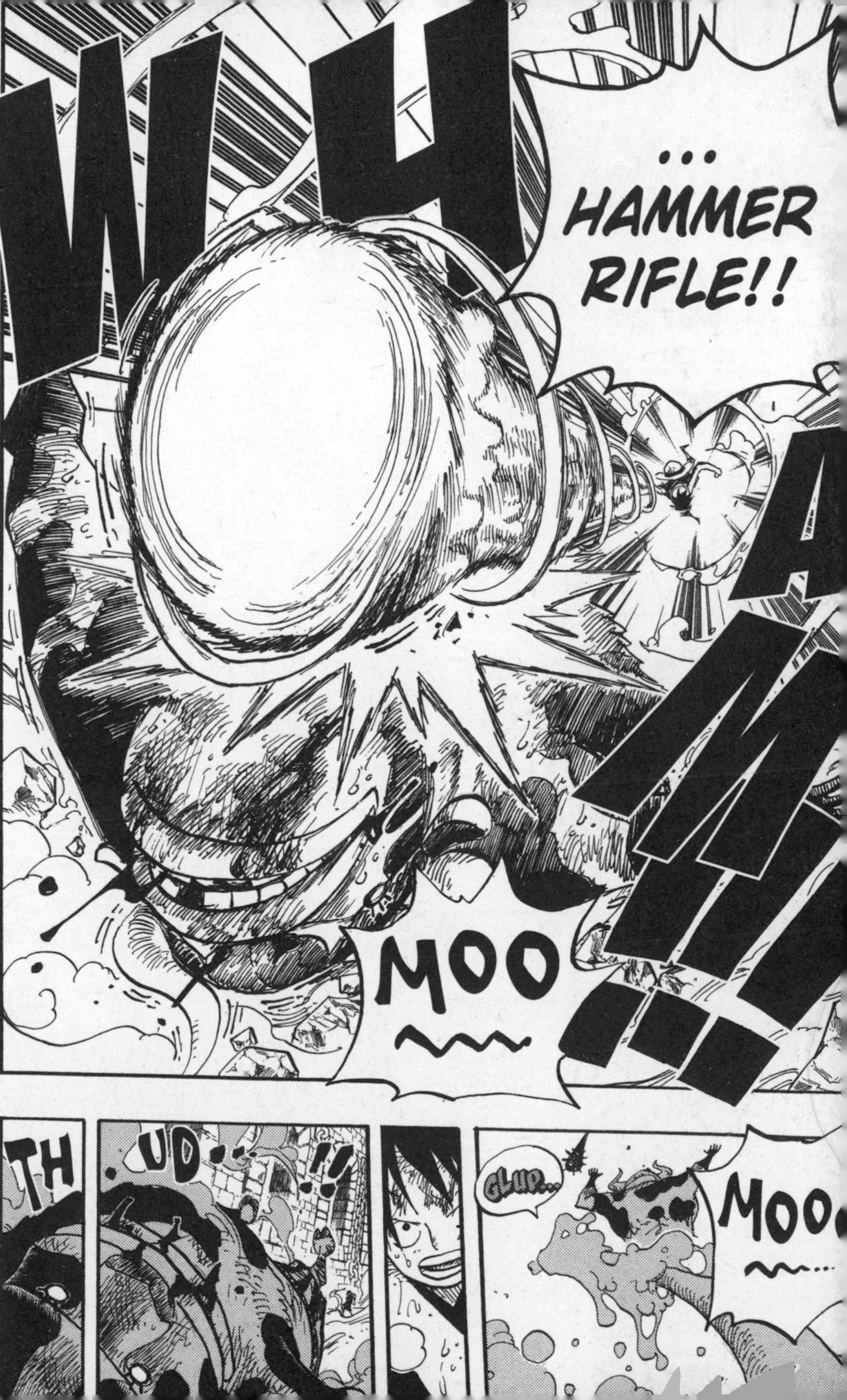
...HAMMER RIFLE!!
WH
AM!!
MOO ~~
MOO... ~~...
GLUP...
TH
UD...!!

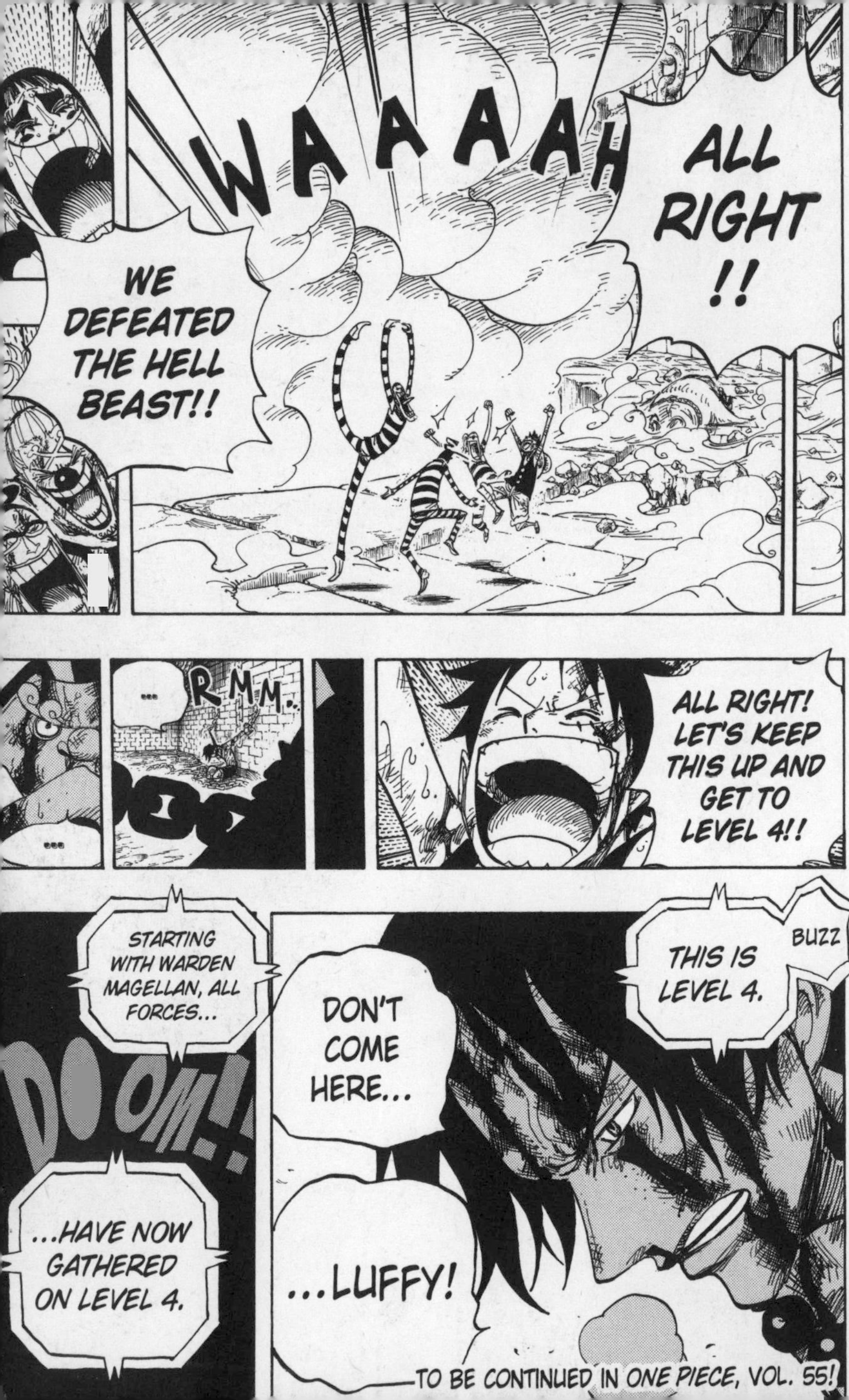
ALL RIGHT!!
WAAAAH
WE DEFEATED THE HELL BEAST!!
ALL RIGHT! LET'S KEEP THIS UP AND GET TO LEVEL 4!!
...
RMM..
...
BUZZ
THIS IS LEVEL 4.
DON'T COME HERE...
...LUFFY!
STARTING WITH WARDEN MAGELLAN, ALL FORCES...
DOOM!!
...HAVE NOW GATHERED ON LEVEL 4.
TO BE CONTINUED IN ONE PIECE, VOL. 55!

SBS Question Corner

OUR NAVIGATOR, AKEMI OKAMURA!

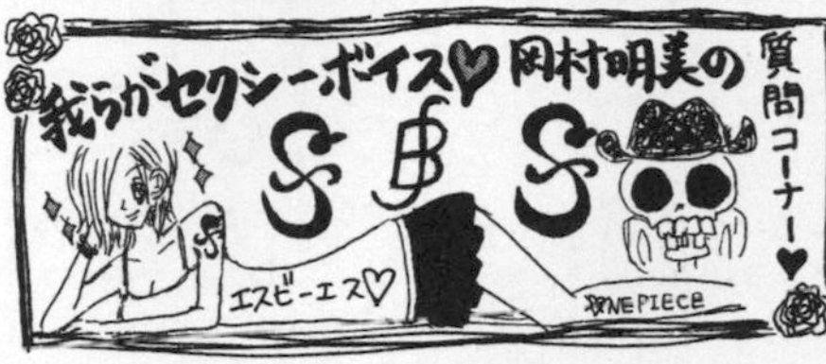
我らがセクシーボイス♥岡村明美の質問コーナー♥
SBS
エスビーエス♡
ONE PIECE

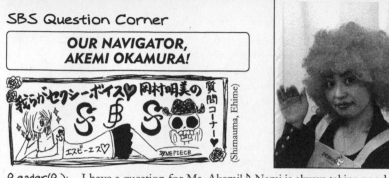

(Shimauma, Ehime)

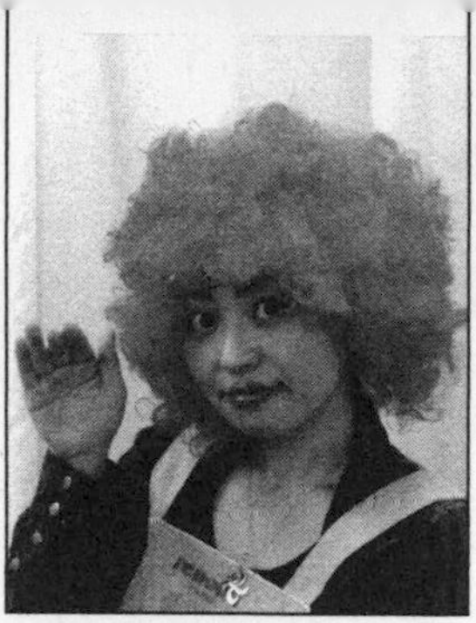

Reader(R): I have a question for Ms. Akemi! ♪ Nami is always taking good care of her tangerine trees, but do you like tangerines too?

--Kaorin

Akemi(A): I love them. ♡ I sit in my warm kotatsu table and eat them all winter.

R: I have a question! What's your type? Who would you like to go out with among the crew members of the Straw Hats?

--TMT

A: All of them combined. The thing called Gargon. ➡

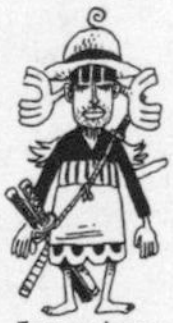

From volume 33, Gargon

R: Has there even been an…embarrassing line you had to say? If so, which one?

--Windy

A: In the script, the captain (Mayumi Tanaka) rewrote my line that says "Thunderbolt--Tempo." The "te" part in "Tempo" was rewritten with a "chi." That was so embarrassing when I screamed it out! [Note: replacing the "te" with the "chi" turns the word "tempo" into the word for male parts.]

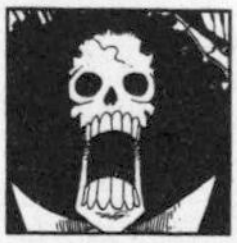

R: To Akemi Okamura on the Question Corner.

May I look at your underwear? --Corbuckle

A: No!

R: I always go on spending sprees. Can you give me some advice? In the voice of Nami, please.

--Hiromu

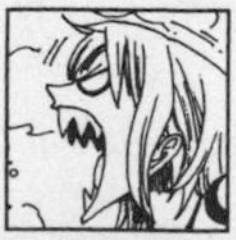

A: I'll lend you money. ♡ Only 30 percent interest! ♪

R: What does it mean to believe?

--Umeboshi Chazuke

A: Beats me!

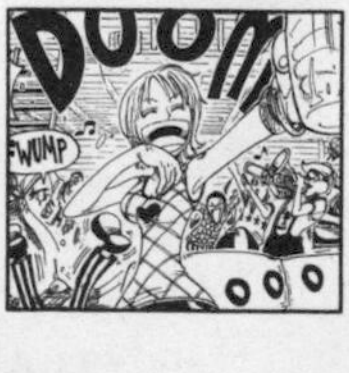
WUMP

R: Hello! My friend told me of the time he saw you on stage at Jump Festa. During that event, you said that you always go drinking after recording. If that's true, does that mean you hold your alcohol well? Like Nami?

--Aino

A: We often go out to party with the cast and staff of *One Piece*. We don't just go drinking. It's a party! ♥

R: Hello, Okamura! I have a question. In the previous Question Corner and the one before that, Tanaka and Nakai both said that they go for "realism" when they do their acts. Do you do the same? If you do, how did you go about doing it during the "Happiness Punch" part…? Ahem. Never mind. Forget I said that.

--Nami Fan Club Member No. 73

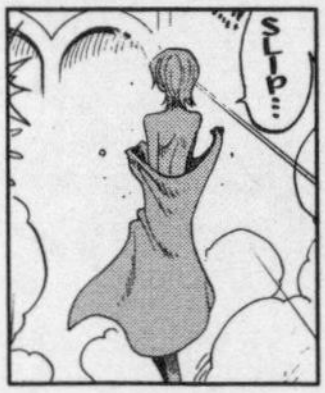
SLIP…

A: Of course I go for "realism," too! On that day, I didn't wear my underwea… What are you making me say?!

R: I have a question for Nami on the Question Corner. Nami often smacks the other crew members, but do you actually do it to the other voice actors? For realism? Also, why don't you smack Chopper too much? Because he's cute?

--Raccoon Dog

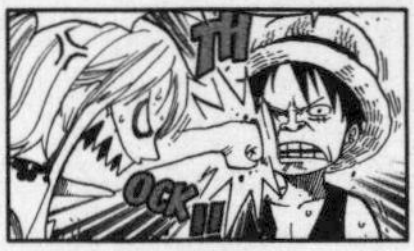

A: Of course I go for realism too! Chopper is played by someone who's a much higher senior member of the agency! (Behind-the-scenes circumstances♡)

R: Please draw a picture of your character! (Don't use any reference materials!☆)

--Tokoyan

A: ➡

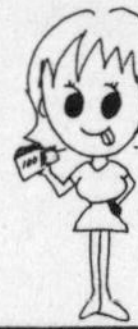

R: I have a question for Nami (Akemi Okamura). Nami always acts uninterested, but does she actually like gentlemen characters like Sanji?

--Blonde Winding Eyebrows Thick-Lips

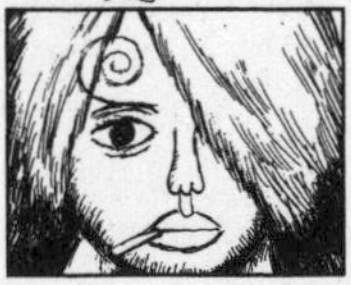

A: What? Sanji? A gentleman? I thought he was a cook.

R: During Thriller Bark, Nami was the only one who wasn't hit by the Negative Hollow. All right! Have the same be done to you like Nakai! "Take this! Negative Hollow!"

--Mayonnaise Black

A: Ugh… I'm sorry I'm so beautiful…

Oda: That's not negative! Okay. It's time, Okamura. The last question is a bit dangerous, so just brush it off.

R: Hello, Okamura. I often watch *One Piece* with my family members. So here's my question. If you were to take a trip, where would you want to go? (In Kuma's voice) Pop!

--Sou-kun

A: Noooo! (Somewhere warm, has a beach, has great food, has a pretty sky, has a hot spring, and a place where I can relax!)

Oda: You have way too many requests! Oh, there she goes. Goodbye, Okamura. And thank you! Now then! Look forward to the next Voice Actor Question Corner!

COMING NEX

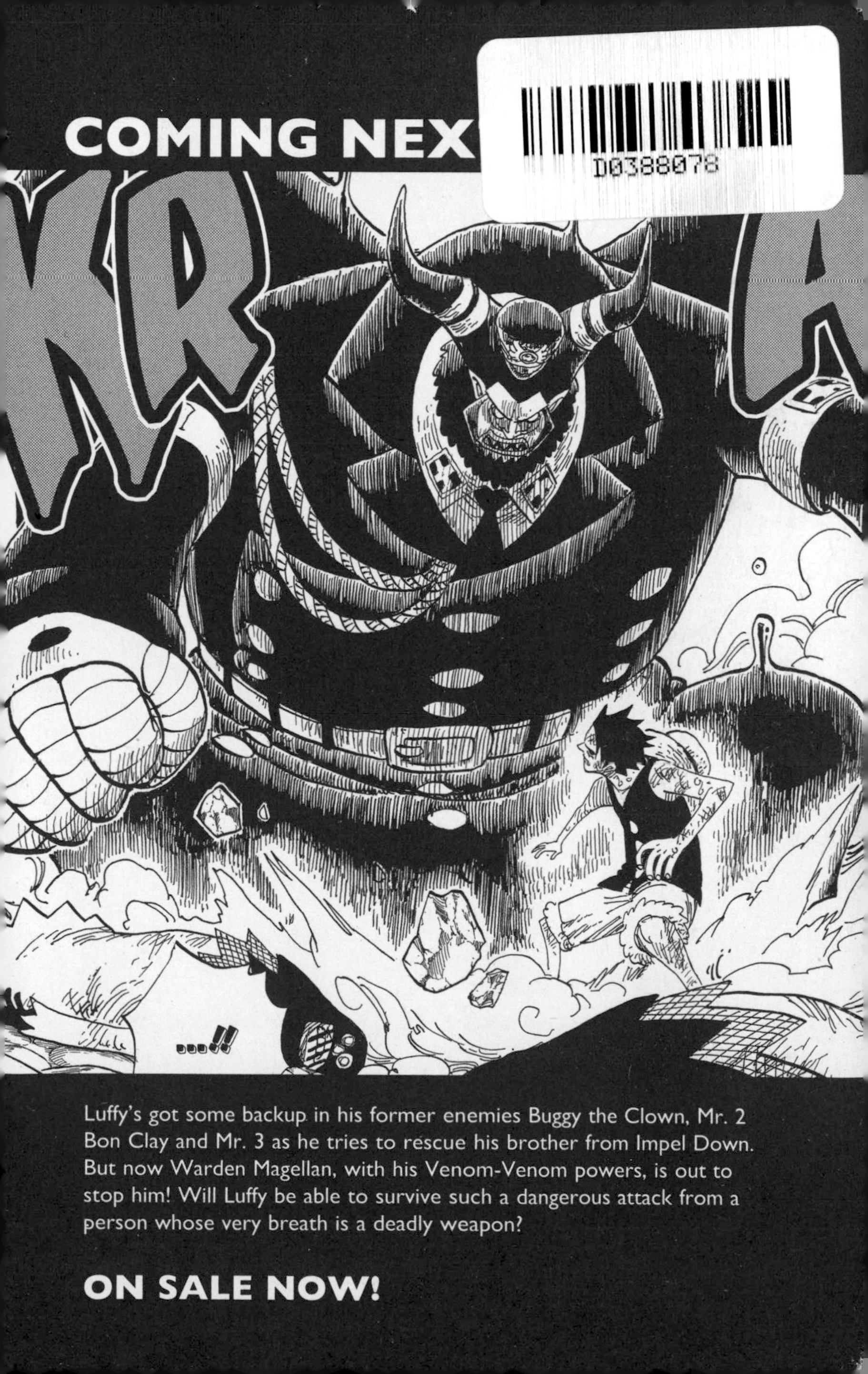
...!!

Luffy's got some backup in his former enemies Buggy the Clown, Mr. 2 Bon Clay and Mr. 3 as he tries to rescue his brother from Impel Down. But now Warden Magellan, with his Venom-Venom powers, is out to stop him! Will Luffy be able to survive such a dangerous attack from a person whose very breath is a deadly weapon?

ON SALE NOW!